Journal of Pentecostal Theology
Supplement Series
20

Editors
John Christopher Thomas
Rickie D. Moore
Steven J. Land

Sheffield Academic Press

Discerning

the Spirit(s)

A Pentecostal–Charismatic Contribution

to Christian Theology of Religions

Amos Yong

Sheffield
Academic Press

To Alma,
with love and gratitude

Copyright © 2000 Sheffield Academic Press

Published by
Sheffield Academic Press Ltd
Mansion House
19 Kingfield Road
Sheffield S11 9AS
England

Typeset by Sheffield Academic Press
and
Printed on acid-free paper in Great Britain
by Cromwell Press
Trowbridge, Wiltshire

British Library Cataloguing in Publication Data

A catalogue record for this book is available
from the British Library

ISBN 1-84127-133-0

CONTENTS

PREFACE

> Pentecostals must reflect on the work of the Holy Spirit in other religions and develop a theology of religions that better reflects their own understanding of the work of the Holy Spirit. The work of scholars in other Christian traditions has explored the role of the Spirit in other religions. Whether or not these scholarly explorations have a Christological or Spirit emphasis, it is here that a Pentecostal perspective on theologies of religion can make a fresh and useful contribution (Samuel 1999: 258).

I have been wrestling with the topic of this book since the winter of 1993 when I first began to study philosophy seriously. The occasion of this was my engaging the process philosophy of Whitehead, Hartshorne and their students, many of whom have been involved in the Christian-Buddhist dialogue. Because my parents are first generation converts from Buddhism to Pentecostal Christianity, my upbringing did not include an ecumenical world-view. As a PK ('pastor's kid') to Assemblies of God ministers, when I did ask questions about those in other faiths, I was given for the most part either the pat answer that they were demonically inspired to keep non-Christians in spiritual darkness or what I later learned to be the Barthian response as interpreted by Hendrik Kraemer: that the religions are failed human efforts to search for and relate to the divine. Having gone through a seminary education that included an introduction to Christian ecumenism, and having been exposed during the course of a second graduate degree at a secular university to the theological questions that derive from the experience of religious pluralism in our time, I realized that there was more to other religious traditions than had been communicated to me. At the same time, I was aware that my own ministerial affiliation with a Pentecostal denomination that placed a much higher premium on evangelism and world missions than on ecumenical involvement meant I would not find as many ecclesial colleagues on this path of inquiry as I would like.

This realization, however, did not deter me from pursuing this topic. In fact, I confess that I felt constrained to inquire into the question of whether or not and how the Holy Spirit, who has always been central to my own religious experience and theology, related to the masses in other faiths. When I read Harvey Cox's *Fire from Heaven* in 1995, my Pentecostal intuitions sensed that he was on to something even if I was wary—as many of my Pentecostal colleagues in the academy remain—of swallowing his argument lock, stock and barrel.

I have pursued this quest because of my conviction then, and now, that the questions posed by our contemporary awareness of religious pluralism have far reaching consequences for Christian theology in the twenty-first century. This relates not only to our understanding of and ability to get along with those in other faiths, but also to core theological issues related to Christian life and doctrine. If in fact Christians would embrace the Holy Spirit's prevenient presence and activity in the world in a serious way, I am persuaded that this would lead to a transformation of Christian theology and mission.

I am especially convinced that another dimension of fulfilling the Great Commission would be opened up to Pentecostals and charismatics willing to rethink seriously the question of the non-Christian faiths. My passion for this project derives, after all, from the depths of my own pentecostal experience of the Spirit which has, in turn, grounded my commitment to the Pentecostal–charismatic community of faith. Ours is a way of Christian life committed to mission, evangelism and the personal sharing of faith. I believe that it is not only possible but desirable for Pentecostals and charismatics to cultivate a sound biblical and theological ecumenism that will further motivate rather than weaken our living out the Great Commission. The wider ecumenism does not have to be understood as a threat to Christian mission. It does, however, challenge us with the fact that we are unable to live out more fully our Christian testimony apart from the power of the Holy Spirit. As was spoken through Zerubbabal, ' "Not by might, nor by power, but by my Spirit," says the Lord Almighty' (Zech. 4.6).

The work presented here can therefore be understood to be a labor of love for Pentecostals and charismatics around the world who are committed to the gospel of Jesus Christ. It is also, however, meant to be a humble contribution to the larger Christian conversation revolving around theology of religions. This conversation, going back as far as the World Missionary Conference at Edinburgh in 1910 and the Parliament of Religions at Chicago in 1893, is at least as old as the Pentecostal-charismatic movement itself. It is fair to ask what, if anything, a child can teach her parents. I take comfort in the fact that both child and parent are still learning the ways of the Spirit. It is my hope and prayer that the words that follow reflect in some way the inspiration of the Holy Spirit that has nurtured this child along the road toward maturity.

ACKNOWLEDGMENTS

This book is a slightly revised version of my doctoral dissertation, 'Discerning the Spirit(s): A Pentecostal–Charismatic Contribution to Christian Theology of Religions', defended at Boston University in the fall of 1998. Thanks are due to my *doktorvater*, Robert Cummings Neville, and first and second readers, Harvey Cox and Lucien Richard, for their guidance and for their providing me with space with which to develop my own theological ideas vis-à-vis their own. Their influence on my thinking can be seen throughout these pages.

The individuals—teachers, colleagues and friends—who have over the past six years helped me work through various stages of this project both in general and in the details are too numerous to list here. Many of you know who you are, and some of you will see your work quoted and your names referred to in what follows. To each and every one: Thank you!

I would be remiss, however, if I did not specifically mention two other groups of persons by name. The first is the group of Pentecostal and charismatic scholars and theologians who I have admired and challenged me in my own work. Frank Macchia, now at Vanguard University, has been a stimulating conversation partner over the years. The support I have received from this fellow classical Pentecostal theologian has been inestimable. The charismatic Baptist, Clark Pinnock, has encouraged me on from afar in innumerable ways. He has done his part in conveying to this classical Pentecostal the importance of a robust pneumatology to a fully trinitarian theology. Dr Harold Hunter of the International Pentecostal Holiness Church has, over the years, graciously made available to me bibliographic material, pointed me to resources, and let me into the network of Pentecostals and charismatics from around the world.

My thanks also are due to the editors of the *Journal of Pentecostal Theology* Supplement Series for their encouragement and work in seeing this manuscript through to publication. John Christopher Thomas read the manuscript over at least twice and offered numerous corrections and suggestions for improvement. Rickie Moore was my first contact with this Church of God Theological Seminary group when I sought to publish articles written during doctoral studies that have now been incorporated into this book in various places. These and the others mentioned above, however, are to be absolved from the errors of fact and interpretation which indubitably exist here.

Last but not least, my deepest gratitude extends to Alma, who has sacrificed more than should be asked of any wife so that her husband could be a perpetual student. She has been the steadfast and supportive force behind my life and work over the years. She has not only blessed me with three wonderful children—Aizaiah, Alyssa and Annalisa—but it is in large part because of her gifts and talents as wife, mother and life companion that I have had the time required to think and write. Her love and prayers are invaluable to me. Life with her has been a wonderful journey in the Spirit! It is to her that I dedicate this book.

ABBREVIATIONS

AJPS	*Asian Journal of Pentecostal Studies*
ANF	Ante-Nicene Fathers
BSac	*Bibliotheca Sacra*
CPCR	*Cyberjournal for Pentecostal-Charismatic Research*
CSR	*Christian Scholar's Review*
CurTM	*Currents in Theology and Mission*
EcRev	*The Ecumenical Review*
EvQ	*Evangelical Quarterly*
EvT	*Evangelische Theologie*
ExpTim	*Expository Times*
Greg	*Gregorianum*
HBT	*Horizons in Biblical Theology*
HeyJ	*Heythrop Journal*
HibJ	*Hibbert Journal*
HR	*History of Religions*
HTR	*Harvard Theological Review*
IBMR	*International Bulletin of Missionary Research*
Int	*Interpretation*
IRM	*International Review of Mission*
ITQ	*Irish Theological Quarterly*
JAAR	*Journal of the American Academy of Religion*
JBL	*Journal of Biblical Literature*
JBR	*Journal of Bible and Religion*
JEH	*Journal of Ecclesiastical History*
JEPTA	*EPTA Bulletin: Journal of the European Pentecostal Theological Association*
JES	*Journal of Ecumenical Studies*
JETS	*Journal of the Evangelical Theological Society*
JPT	*Journal of Pentecostal Theology*
JPTSup	*Journal of Pentecostal Theology*, Supplement Series
JR	*Journal of Religion*
JRelS	*Journal of Religious Studies*
JRT	*Journal of Religious Thought*
JTC	*Journal for Theology and the Church*
JTS	*Journal of Theological Studies*
KJV	King James Version

Missiology	*Missiology: An International Review*
MTZ	*Münchener theologische Zeitschrift*
NIV	New International Version
NPNF	Nicene and Post-Nicene Fathers
Paraclete	*Paraclete: A Journal Concerning the Person and Work of the Holy Spirit* (1967–1994) and *Paraclete: A Journal of Pentecostal Studies* (1994–1995)
Pneuma	*Pneuma: The Journal of the Society for Pentecostal Studies*
Rel	*Religion*
RelS	*Religious Studies*
RevExp	*Review and Expositor*
RTR	*Reformed Theological Review*
SJT	*Scottish Journal of Theology*
SPS	Society for Pentecostal Studies
SR	*Studies in Religion/Sciences religieuses*
TD	*Theology Digest*
TS	*Theological Studies*
TTod	*Theology Today*
TWOT	R. Laird Harris, Gleason L. Archer, Jr and Bruce K. Waltke (eds.), *Theological Wordbook of the Old Testament* (2 vols.; Chicago: Moody Press, 1980)
USQR	*Union Seminary Quarterly Review*
WesTJ	*Wesleyan Theological Journal*
WTJ	*Westminster Theological Journal*
ZKT	*Zeitschrift für katholische Theologie*

Chapter 1

INTRODUCTION

1. *Problem and Thesis*

In a recent, highly acclaimed book on Pentecostalism, *Fire from Heaven*,[1] Harvey Cox has suggested that the explosion of Pentecostal spirituality in this century may be part of the upsurge of a common human religiosity that is also the undercurrent to the efflorescence of ecstatic and indigenous faith traditions worldwide. He describes this global phenomenon as a configuration of three dimensions of religiousness: ecstatic speech (glossolalia, or related types of utterance), mystical piety (trance, visions, dreams, dancing, healing, and other kinds of religious experiences), and millennial fervor (apocalypticism and eschatological orientation). Together, these elements signify the restoration of what Cox calls *primal spirituality*, whereby individuals and communities all over the world who have been uprooted and marginalized by industrialization and modernization have tapped into and drawn energy from the wellsprings of *homo religiosus* in order to cope with personal and social changes. This spirituality has thus enabled its devotees to overcome the feelings of alienation and isolation characteristic of existence in the modern world and to reconnect with the forces of the cosmos and the realm of the sacred.

The success of modern Pentecostalism in Cox's analysis can be attributed in large part to the degree in which its restoration of primal spirituality within a Christian framework has allowed it to absorb and perhaps transform faith and practical elements of indigenous traditions and local cultures around the world. By so doing, Pentecostal spirituality has provided its adherents with the resources to re-engage their world. Cox suggests in his review of Pentecostalism worldwide that it has drawn from folk Catholicism and the various local traditions

1. Reading, MA: Addison-Wesley, 1995.

throughout Latin and South America, that it has incorporated elements of shamanism in Korea and other cultures along the Asian rim, and that it has advanced the emergence of a thoroughly 'Africanized' Christianity where the independent Churches of the sub-Saharan regions have fused Pentecostal and traditional African religious emphases on healing and ecstatic styles of worship. From this perspective, Cox is thereby not surprised that Pentecostalism is staging its most remarkable growth in the developing nations of the two-thirds world. The surge of Pentecostalism in these parts suggests that Pentecostal spirituality may be the most viable form of Christianity for a postmodern, post-Western and post-colonial world.

Two related complexes of questions arise from Cox's discussion. The first is whether or not his account of Pentecostalism as a species of primal spirituality is correct. Does Cox's survey of Pentecostal spirituality accurately reflect the empirical data? He has argued for at least phenomenological similarities between Pentecostal ritual and piety worldwide and that of various indigenous traditions. How far do such similarities extend, and to what degree does Cox take account of the differences? To what extent are his conclusions about Pentecostalism and primal spirituality pertinent to other indigenous traditions?

Cox's characterization of Pentecostal spirituality as similar to indigenous faiths and practices is one that has been resisted by Pentecostals and charismatics as a misunderstanding of their movement at best, and a distortion of the facts at worse. None of the three published North American responses to date endorse his assessment without reservation. Gary McGee (1996), an Assemblies of God historian, objects that indigenous groups could only be classified as Pentecostal by a tenuous stretching of the historical evidence. Meanwhile, on the Internet, Harold Hunter (n.d.) of the Pentecostal Holiness Church is unimpressed, and J. Rodman Williams (1998), a charismatic Presbyterian theologian, is concerned in spite of his overall appreciation of *Fire from Heaven* that what is distinctive about Pentecostalism, that is, its experience of the Holy Spirit, has been blurred by Cox's equating their spirituality with other indigenous traditions.

The only other published reviews from outside the North American context is by the dean of Pentecostal studies, Walter Hollenweger (1998), and the Swiss Pentecostal, Jean-Daniel Plüss (1996).[2] Coming

---

2. Those familiar with Hollenweger's commitment to forging a more ecumenical Pentecostalism would not be surprised at his positive appreciation of Cox's

from an ecumenical Reformed background, Plüss has less at stake than denominationally affiliated classical Pentecostals. He admits to having been moved to think deeply by Cox, especially about the theory of religion that links Pentecostal spirituality to that of other faith traditions. He twice states that *Fire from Heaven* is a 'dangerous book', especially 'for those who can read the writing on the wall' (1996: 104, 105). Plüss is less than clear about the portents of the inscription, but it is apparent that at least some of what bothers him, in both a positive and negative sense, has to do with Cox's suggestions regarding the relationship between Pentecostalism and indigenous traditions worldwide.

Assuredly at the ecclesial level and probably in many academic contexts, Pentecostals are very reluctant to accept Cox's proposal that they partake of the same or similar stream of spirituality as that of ancient and modern indigenous traditions. I think that this resistance can be attributed in large part to the attending theological implications of Cox's work, and only minimally to the argument that his phenomenological analyses are faulty. Yet because Cox is cautious in drawing theological conclusions from the data—and rightly so, given the nature of his book and the state of Christian theological understanding of non-Christian traditions to be discussed below—his descriptive analysis will remain suspicious to many Pentecostals. One of the objectives of this book is to further the theological exploration largely neglected by Cox via a self-critical Pentecostal response to his work.

The second complex of questions concerns Cox's theory of religion. The primary aim of *Fire from Heaven* is to catalog the development of Pentecostalism and to assess its spirituality. Yet implicit in this volume and even clearly enunciated in a number of places is a theory of religion which Cox argues to be applicable both to the varieties of indigenous traditions around the world and to what can perhaps be referred to as an emerging global religious consciousness. Is what is called primal spirituality the 'common human religiousness' that he assumes it is, and if

---

book. Hollenweger does not take issue with Cox's theory of religion. Instead, among other suggestions, he urges Cox to give Pentecostals more credit than he does for their developing theological sophistication. Implicitly, Hollenweger's review—as in much of his previous work over the past four decades—constitutes a challenge to Pentecostals to grapple more seriously from a theological perspective with the issues raised by Cox's thesis. It would be appropriate to see the following pages as a response to this plea.

so, are its three constitutive elements essential features of the emerging global religious consciousness? Is his thesis sustainable as a theory of religion for the twenty-first century?

These two related issues lead to the theological question that is at the heart of my investigation. If in fact Cox is at least partially correct about Pentecostal spirituality as a Christian confluence of elements of an original human religiosity, what are the attending theological implications? How does that affect Pentecostal theology in particular and Christian theology in general, and what does that say about the Spirit that Pentecostals claim is at the root of their own religious experiences? The answers proposed will also be suggestive for the ongoing formation of a Christian theological understanding of non-Christian faiths and religious traditions. If it is the case that there is a common spirituality between Pentecostalism and indigenous traditions, what can Christian theology learn from this about the systematic interconnections between human religiousness, salvation, the Church or divine Kingdom, eschatology, the Holy Spirit and the Christ? In short, is there something further that needs to be said about the God that Christians worship and about the Holy Spirit who is present and at work in the world?

My thesis is that a Pentecostal–charismatic perspective should be applied to the questions posed by Cox's book, and that when that is done, some unique insights can be gleaned about religious beliefs and practices which will further theological understanding about God's ways of being in the world and about human religiousness and spirituality. More specifically, I believe that the Pentecostal and charismatic experience of the Holy Spirit can provide an avenue by which a pneumatological approach to the non-Christian faiths can be constructed which will complement, and in some ways, perhaps advance the discussion of a Christian theology of religions.[3] Harvey Cox's categories, if sufficiently nuanced, in some cases revised, and in other cases given a more thorough pneumatological explication, can therefore play an important role in stimulating Pentecostal–charismatic reflection on this subject. The purpose of this book is therefore to contribute from one Pentecostal–charismatic perspective to the ongoing formation of a Christian *theologia religionum*.

---

3.   Cox realizes and suggests this himself in a more recent article (1997).

2. *Key Definitions and Limitations*

Most of the important terms and concepts will be introduced and defined at the appropriate places in the text. Before proceeding, however, I need briefly to spell out what is being developed: a *Pentecostal–charismatic theology of religions*. For the moment and until I elaborate in much greater detail in Chapter 5, I will follow the 'Introduction' to the *Dictionary of Pentecostal and Charismatic Movements* and define Pentecostalism and the charismatic movement as the 'two great renewal movements of the Spirit' (Burgess, McGee and Alexander 1988: 1) in the twentieth century, the former with roots in the Azusa Street revival in Los Angeles, California, from 1906–1908, and the latter emerging in later decades. References to 'Pentecostals and charismatics' will be generally to adherents and participants in both streams, even as I will occasionally only designate one without the other when I am referencing or commenting on what is distinctive to that group.

It is also essential to ask, What is a *theology of religions*? This is important because for many Pentecostals and charismatics, but especially the former, the idea of a theology of religions is an ambiguous one at best and a misguided one at worst, for at least two reasons. First, Pentecostals are especially insistent that *theology*, 'simply defined, is a study of God and His relationship to all that He has created...[and] must be derived from the revelation of God in the Bible, for in no other way could it be a reliable testimony for those who are searching after truth'; further, theological reflection must therefore be strictly delimited to 'what the Bible either explicitly or implicitly teaches' (Railey and Aker 1995: 46). Methodologically then, a theology of religions, particularly if by this is understood the contemporary world religions, is practically questionable in an a priori sense since the canonical Scriptures are silent with regard to the major religious traditions.

This leads to the second and related reason for the Pentecostal objection to the idea of a theology of religions. The Biblical data distinguishes between true and false gods, between the worship of the one, true God, and idolatry. Pentecostals have therefore generally followed the early Barthian (without always acknowledging Barth himself) distinction between divine revelation and the human religious quest (Railey and Aker 1995: 41). The latter apart from the former is bound to perennial failure and frustration. During their less charitable moments, and especially in the more popular literature, Pentecostals

have interpreted the Bible to depict human religions and religious systems as having Satanic or demonic origins (Williams 1953: I, 138-39).
A theological understanding of non-Christian religions is superfluous in
this framework.

Part of the purpose of this study is to argue for and encourage Pentecostals to re-examine the viability and the necessity of developing a
Pentecostal theology of religions. I agree that Pentecostal theology—
and Christian theology for that matter—begins with and is ultimately
bound to Scripture (correctly interpreted, it should go without saying).
At the same time, theology should be distinguished from *doctrine.*
Christian doctrine—for there are doctrines of other religious communities as well, as William Christian (1987) has reminded us—can be
understood as what has been universally believed, thought and confessed by the Church (Pelikan 1971: 1), or as 'religious truth based on
authority and officially formulated by some ecclesiastical assembly'
(Berkhof 1975: 16), or as the religious grammar by which the belief and
practices of communities of faith are guided (Lindbeck 1984), or even
as 'fundamental truths of the Bible arranged in systematic form' (Pearlman 1937: viii).[4] Central to these definitions, however, even if only
implicitly in the Pentecostal understanding, is the ecclesial reception of
articulated beliefs. Christian theology, on the other hand, should be
recognized as a provisional theoretical activity which attempts to correlate biblical revelation with our experience of the world and vice versa.
Strictly speaking, theology is nothing more than discourse about *theos,*
or God. Because such discourse can only be artificially circumscribed
(God-talk is by no means limited to Christians), few will disagree when

---

4.   Although Pearlman's theological text was one of the earliest attempts to
fashion a systematic Pentecostal theology, times have not brought about much of a
change in perspective in terms of the emphasis on Scripture that Pentecostal
Churches place on systematic theological reflection, almost to the complete neglect
of the interpretive process and contemporary concerns and applications. The back
cover of the most recent *Systematic Theology* textbook published by the Assemblies
of God identifies it as 'a complete look at God's Word' (Horton 1995). Even the
multi-volumed *Renewal Theology* which claims to be a systematic theology by J.
Rodman Williams, a charismatic theologian from the Reformed tradition, is really a
biblical theology in terms of genre (cf. Frank Macchia's lucid but critical review of
Renewal Theology on precisely this point [1994b]). In short, theology for
Pentecostals still tends to be monopolar—focused on what the Bible says—even as
it neglects the contemporary pole of interpretation. This book presents my contribution toward redressing this matter.

pre-eminent Christian thinkers like Wolfhart Pannenberg talk about the 'many-sidedness of the concept of theology as a comprehensive term for the quest for knowledge relating to Christian teaching' (1991: 6). As theological reflection is increasingly received by the larger Christian community as an accurate representation of Christian faith, specific ideas, concepts or propositions may attain the status of dogma or official Church doctrine. From another perspective, part of my objective is to retrieve some viable theological ideas from the history of Christianity and to press them into servicing the difficult issues raised by our contemporary experience of religious pluralism in the hope that these reflections may in time be deemed sufficiently valuable for Christian faith and practice so as to warrant their recognition not so much as mere speculations but as sound Christian teaching.

But why a theology of *religions* rather than a theology of *religion*? It has become almost axiomatic since the appearance of Wilfred Cantwell Smith's *The Meaning and End of Religion* (1962) that there is no such thing as 'religion' which we can essentially define. Rather, what we have are, in Cantwell Smith's terms, the subjective *faith* experiences of individuals within larger *cumulative traditions*, this latter including places of worship and social institutions, scriptures, theological, symbolic and doctrinal systems, liturgies, conventions, moral codes, myths, and so on, that can be observed historically and described empirically.[5] A theological understanding of the religious aspect of human experience should therefore be able to account for both the personal experiences of faith and the concrete manifestations of communities in pursuit of faithful living. In this sense then, it is more appropriate to search for a theology of *religions* as understood in all of their diversity, than to attempt what would be a futile search for a theological essence of religion.

---

5.   Ninian Smart (1996) has attempted to understand religious traditions as consisting of seven interrelated dimensions: ritual, myths or narratives, experiential or emotional, ethical or legal, social, material, and political. His third dimension would correspond most closely with Cantwell Smith's idea of faith although there are numerous overlaps between his other categories and the elements of Cantwell Smith's cumulative traditions. However, it is also probably the case that each dimension in Smart's typology could be understood in terms of Smith's twofold distinction since each dimension can and in most cases has been codified in some way, and it is up to the devotees to re-engage the various dimensions via communal or personal exercise of subjective faith.

Nevertheless, there have been a number of notable efforts in quest of the latter. Two of the boldest include Reat and Perry's (1991) hypothesis of a universal spirituality underlying the major religious traditions of the world, and an impressive who's who of scholars and thinkers that convened to discuss and develop universal categories of theological reflection which could 'be understood and embraced by persons of all religions or ideologies' (Swidler 1987: 19). Yet even the latter effort of attaining a 'universal theology', however, was criticized by one of the primary conference speakers both because the quest for universality has historically been a camouflage for the Western thirst for domination and because 'no theory is *universal* (rationality does not exhaustively define the human being)' (Panikkar 1987b: 122).[6]

A Pentecostal–charismatic theology of religions can therefore best be initially defined as the effort to understand both the immensely differentiated experiences of faith and the multifaceted phenomena of religious traditions and systems that is informed by experiences of the Spirit in the light of Scripture, and vice versa. It should offer both theological theory at a sufficient level of abstraction so as to be able to account for vastly contrasting phenomena, while at the same time remaining close enough to empirical reality so as to be able to engage the actual perception of God's presence and activity in the world and in the lives of faithful persons. The theology that emerges should therefore shed light on the personal and communal nature of faith, spirituality, religiousness and on faith traditions. Broadly conceived, these are all core constituents of the phenomenon of religion and will be used somewhat synonymously in this work.

This project is also motivated by a further conviction: that a theology of religions is intimately linked to the interreligious dialogue and that Pentecostals need to be involved in these conversations. The classical

---

6.   All italicized words or phrases in quotes throughout this study are original to their authors unless otherwise noted.

In trinitarian language, Panikkar objects to the 'total domination of the *logos* and a subordination of the Spirit' (1987b: 124), and prefers instead the piecemeal, dialogic quest for harmony that is based on an attitude that reality is fundamentally trustworthy; he calls this a 'cosmic confidence' (title of his paper and larger project; cf. Panikkar 1993). My own efforts to understand the non-Christian faiths attempt to redress the balance between the Word and the Spirit—what Irenaeus called the 'two hands of the Father'—and in that sense, is akin to Panikkar's concerns. I will return later to a discussion of Panikkar's trinitarian theology of religions.

Pentecostal understanding of other faiths calls for bold evangelistic witness leading to conversion. Proselytism, however, is currently a pejorative term in interreligious circles. This does not mean that Pentecostals should desist in their evangelistic activities. It simply means that proclamation should be held in tension with other modes of relating to those from other faiths. This would include service, organized debates, open forums, etc., which call for listening as well as speaking. Interreligious dialogue in the broadest sense covers this wide spectrum of activities. Whereas previous Pentecostal views of other traditions have not predisposed them to engaging in more than kerygmatic witness, cultivation of this more flexible attitude is now an urgent task. The pneumatological theology of religions to be developed here has this in mind as part of its objective. It will inform not only Pentecostal self-understanding but also provide the desperately needed theological argument for Pentecostal (and charismatic) participation in the interreligious dialogue.[7]

A preliminary word is needed regarding the limitations of this project. First, while I am of Asian ethnicity and was born and raised in part in Malaysia, and I will make an effort to draw from the global Pentecostal-charismatic experience, my interpretation of these experiences, however, are inevitably constrained by my North American Pentecostal framework and education. All that follows stands to be corrected by any interested party, but especially by my Pentecostal and charismatic friends, colleagues and partners in ministry. Second, because the approach taken here is pneumatological in orientation, I will not try to untangle the christological debates. I assume with minimal argumentation that there is—and to some degree always will be—a christological impasse. The problems that attend to a pneumatological theology of religions will not be avoided. I believe, however, that the two approaches are complementary and will sustain each other at their points of greatest weakness. Third, I am first and foremost a theologian by training, and only secondly either a philosopher or a historian of religions. My goal is to engage in a constructive Pentecostal–charismatic

---

7. Throughout this work, I will make the connection between theology of religions and the interreligious dialogue, sometimes even suggesting that they are equivalent. I recognize they are theoretically distinct; but I will argue that the cash value of the former is to be found in the latter. There will be a more extended discussion of this relatedness as I proceed.

theology. I am not therefore primarily interested in the history of Pentecostal or charismatic theological reflection or in why they have, as a general rule, tended to reject the interreligious dialogue or neglected serious consideration of other faiths, although these aspects of the tradition are surely important for what I hope to accomplish and will be touched upon. At the same time, I also hope to show that Pentecostals especially have been much more open to dialogue with people of other faiths than their rhetoric has let on. Further, the dialogue that is initiated in Chapter 8 with another, starkly contrasting, religious tradition (Umbanda) should be recognized within the context of the theological concerns which shape this study. I make no claims to be an expert on the Umbanda tradition, although I obviously hope that much of what I will say about it will accurately reflect an insider's perspective in order to minimize confusion and misinterpretation.

3. *Survey of Literature*

Other than two recent essays—one on a Pentecostal approach to interreligious dialogue (Solivan 1998) and another by a Pentecostal but focused on developing a theology of religions from the nineteenth century pietism of Christoph Blumhardt (Macchia, forthcoming)—to which I will return in Chapter 6, I am unaware of any theological reflection on the non-Christian faiths by Pentecostals to date. Systematic theology textbooks of the largest North American Pentecostal denominations do not even include the word 'religion' or any of its cognates in their indices.[8] The second essay of the Assemblies of God *Systematic Theology* devotes one section, a scant two pages, to 'The Concept of Religion' (Railey and Aker 1995: 40-41).

More astonishing is the fact that the Pentecostal openness to the person and work of the Holy Spirit has not led them to a more substantive theology of culture as a whole. In one place, we find an admission of the Spirit's presence and work in culture that is exceptional for Pentecostal theologizing. Raymond Pruitt, a Church of God of Prophecy minister, has acknowledged that the Holy Spirit 'inspires and qualifies

---

8. This is true of the three volume *Christian Doctrine: A Pentecostal Perspective* by French Arrington (1992–94) of the Church of God, Cleveland, TN, and also of *Foundations of Pentecostal Theology* co-authored by two theologians from the International Church of the Foursquare Gospel (Duffield and Van Cleave 1983).

men for their work in government, science, art, etc.' (1981: 287).[9] For the most part, however, Pentecostals have managed to ignore the repeated calls of the recognized expert on global Pentecostalism, Walter Hollenweger, for such reflection (1978, 1984, 1987, 1991, 1992, 1997 *passim*).

Things look a little better upon turning to the charismatic movement. This should be expected given the fact that many charismatics have either come from or remain within their respective denominations, including the Roman Catholic Church. Yet, there is a surprising dearth of material even from this stream. The term 'religion' is not even indexed in any of the three volumes of *Systematic Theology from a Charismatic Perspective* by J. Rodman Williams![10] Thankfully, one of the few exceptions comes from the hand of the Canadian charismatic Baptist, Clark Pinnock. Even though Pinnock began writing his own theology of religions with a North American evangelical audience in mind, he has more recently articulated a systematic theology organized around pneumatology through which he approaches other cultures and faiths (1996). He has also attempted to stimulate Pentecostals to 'develop a Spirit-oriented theology of mission and world religions, because of their openness to religious experience, their sensitivity to the oppressed of the Third World where they have experienced much of their growth, and their awareness of the ways of the Spirit as well as dogma' (1996: 274). I will comment further on Pinnock's theology of religions, and that of other charismatics who have given less extensive consideration to it and the interreligious dialogue, in Chapter 6. Needless to say, this book is in part a response to Pinnock's prompting and encouragement.

The larger Christian tradition has, of course, well-developed pneumatologies and theologies of culture. Again, however, while there have been those who have begun to chart a pneumatological approach to the religions, most have been provisionally submitted in essay form and none seem to have run this race to completion. I will take up this matter in a more detailed analysis of the work of Georges Khodr, Jacques Dupuis, Stanley Samartha and Paul Knitter in Chapter 3. I will also in that chapter examine insights drawn from Karl Rahner and Paul Tillich in the work of Joseph Wong and Lai Pan-Chiu respectively. It will be

9.   I am indebted to Mel Robeck for pointing this out to me in a personal letter, 27 December 1996.

10.   The subject of religion does not even appear in Williams's less-than-four-page discussion of general revelation and natural theology (1988: 33-36).

clear there that the problem opposing most of these tentative efforts is that which plagues all pneumatologies: the barrenness of abstract theological theory when confronted with the diversity of religious experiences and empirical faith traditions.

The one full-length book that has taken up a more concrete approach to a pneumatological theology of non-Christian faiths is Michael Lodahl's *Shekinah Spirit: Divine Presence in Jewish and Christian Religion* (1992). The concerns addressed, however, are, as the subtitle indicates, those central to the interreligious conversation between two sibling Abrahamic traditions. Yet because Lodahl does strive to develop a foundational pneumatology by drawing from the process metaphysics of Alfred North Whitehead, and because he does focus on a pneumatological hermeneutic that attempts to understand symbols of divine presence in both the traditions under his consideration, his is an important step toward a pneumatological theology of religions. I will re-engage Lodahl's book in Chapters 3 and 4 where I endeavor both to improve on his foundational pneumatology via an alternative metaphysical vision, and to enlarge the framework of plausibility of his pneumatological theology to include other faith traditions.

4. *Methodology and Outline*

The following chapter by chapter overview will identify the objectives to be pursued and outline the methods of investigation to be used. First, note the brief autobiographical vignettes that precede each chapter. These serve a dual purpose. First, any argument presented by a Pentecostal in part for Pentecostals needs to communicate in a tangible manner the emphasis on orality that is part and parcel of the narrative structure at the heart of Pentecostalism. The 'testimony' has always been the preferred form of discourse for Pentecostals and my use of such is meant as an invitation for them to take the 'pentecostal' nature of my arguments seriously. Further, however, I also wish to convey something of that genre to non-Pentecostals even as I endeavor to present an objective and dispassionate argument. Second, these reflections are rhetorical devices that present the problematic of each chapter even as they together cover themes the book engages as a whole. The issues taken up in this study are not simply abstract and idle questions. Rather they have emerged within the cultural, intellectual and religious context which has nurtured my second naïveté. A small part of my process of struggle will appear in these meditations. My argument will proceed as follows.

Chapter 2 will situate the larger framework of this study. There, I briefly sketch the history of Christian theological reflection on the non-Christian faiths, giving special attention to the issues and concerns raised by the heightened awareness of religious pluralism in the twentieth century. I highlight the tensions involved when, in an era of competing religious truth claims, Christian theological assertions are universally extended even as they are founded upon the particular historical personality of Jesus the Christ.

An alternative theological approach to non-Christian faiths through the third member of the Trinity as tentatively explored by more recent thinkers is summarized in Chapter 3. Recent developments in discussions about the *Filioque* as stimulated by Orthodox theologians will serve as the dogmatic point of entry into assessments of Orthodox, Catholic and Protestant efforts to rethink the question of the religions from a pneumatological perspective. The gain in this approach is that the recognition of the procession or mission of the Holy Spirit into the world as related to and yet distinct from that of the Son provides theological space that is greatly needed at the present time because while the person of Jesus Christ is a historical symbol of God's reality in the world, the Holy Spirit is *par excellence* the symbol of divine presence and activity in the cosmic realm. I argue, however, that what these pneumatological theologies of religions gain over christological approaches are in turn neutralized insofar as they have not developed adequate criteria by which to discern the presence and activity of the Holy Spirit over and against that of other spirits in the faith experiences and traditions of the world.

Chapter 4 presents the cornerstone to the argument of this book. I begin by suggesting that a pneumatological approach to the religions informed by the Pentecostal–charismatic perspective can best be advanced if what I call a 'pneumatological imagination' is cultivated. Such an imagination provides us with a fundamental orientation to God, ourselves and the world, and renders more plausible the idea of God as present and active in the world. Further, this imagination serves as the foundation—albeit, as I will explain later, a 'shifting' one—for our philosophical theology of the Holy Spirit. The central component of this foundational pneumatology will be a trinitarian metaphysics of creation and a theology of symbolism formulated in dialogue with

Charles S. Peirce, Robert Cummings Neville and Donald Gelpi. This reconstructed pneumatology also needs to relate, and yet retain a distinction between, the mission of the Holy Spirit and that of the Son in the divine economy of creation and redemption. It follows from the foundational pneumatology that the Spirit is present and active in some way in the non-Christian faiths as well. An overview of how this is or is not so will be presented by focusing on religious rituals. At the same time, however, because there are potentially as many, if not more, spirits operative in the world as there are religious traditions, the problem now becomes one of discerning where, when and how the Holy Spirit is present and at work in the non-Christian faiths. A theory of discernment that facilitates theological comparisons of religious symbols will therefore also be suggested.

At this point, I introduce the Pentecostal–charismatic movement not only as a resource for a pneumatological theology of religions, but also as the fount from which the pneumatological imagination operative in this study emerges. Because I draw from both the Pentecostal tradition and the charismatic movement in this venture, Chapter 5 will need to explicate the differences between the two (historically and sociologically) while arguing for their relatedness (theologically). Central to my argument is the nature and character of the Pentecostal–charismatic movement and the importance of experiences of the Spirit to its spirituality, religiosity and orientation to the world. In this chapter, some preliminary theological implications of the Pentecostal–charismatic experience for the pneumatology constructed in the previous chapter are sketched.

The idea of formulating a Pentecostal–charismatic theology of religions will sound ludicrous to the many Pentecostals who continue to adhere to the historical *extra ecclesiam nulla salus*—'no salvation outside the Church'—formula and who have been influenced, as most North American Pentecostals have been, by conservative evangelical theology. It will be beneficial to examine briefly the historical reasons behind this Pentecostal position, as well as to unearth some more optimistic attitudes from within the tradition about relating to adherents of other faiths. More important, however, is that Pentecostals and charismatics are at a crucial historical juncture, one with dire implications not only for them but for Christianity as well insofar as they represent her to the world. The need of formulating a critical theology of religions should be recognized and given priority. The urgency of this situation is ascertained from three standpoints: first, the global presence of the Pentecostal–charismatic movement; second, the Pentecostal–charismatic emphasis on witness and missions; and third, the Pentecostal passion for truth amidst the movement's continued quest for theological identity and theological maturity. These discussions comprise Chapter 6.

Poised now to return to our conversation with Harvey Cox, I complete the core of my argument in Chapter 7 by revising Cox's categories in light of the Pentecostal–charismatic experience of the Spirit. These categorial revisions both shed light on the empirical sources of the pneumatological imagination and fill in the vague foundational categories developed earlier. First, I lift up the importance of the *religious dimension of experience* as a comparative category and understand Cox's primal spirituality within this broader category. Second, I develop the category of *religious utility* which highlights the pragmatic orientation of Pentecostal spirituality and which includes elements of Cox's primal piety such as healing. Finally, the category of *religious cosmology* central to the orientation of both Pentecostals and charismatics is suggested as expanding on Cox's primal hope. By negotiating the dialectic both between divine presence and absence and that between the present and future, this expanded category provides some handles by which to grasp that most prevalent and yet elusive of notions: the demonic. It also forces the question of Pentecostal and charismatic discernment, thus preparing the way for evaluating and naming the spirits in the world and the non-Christian faiths.

Whereas others have remained contented with more or less general theological affirmations about the Spirit's presence and activity in the non-Christian world, I propose in Chapter 8 a detailed empirical investigation that tests the adequacy of the proposed categories and the explanatory power of the interpretive theology of symbols in an inter-religious dialogue between Pentecostalism and Umbanda. The choice of Umbanda is a risky one that needs to be defended. In elaborating on the tradition, I draw, as in Chapter 5, from the history and sociology of religion. In addition, however, Umbandist ritual is psychologically and phenomenologically detailed. The dialogue asks how the Umbandist experience can stimulate self-critical Pentecostal theological reflection even as it asks how the Pentecostal understanding of the Spirit can contribute to Umbandist theology. Tentative theological conclusions regarding the Spirit's presence and activity in Umbanda are drawn from this comparative exercise.

The final chapter includes ten theses for a Pentecostal–charismatic theology of religions derived from this study. It further deliberates on the implications for systematic theology posed by the turn to pneumatology in the formation of a Christian theology of religions. It also considers directions for further study prompted by this investigation.

The pattern of investigation which emerges in the following pages reflects the concreteness of the Pentecostal–charismatic experience of the Spirit. Insofar as the object of study is the Holy Spirit, this thesis can be appropriately considered a 'pneumatology of quest'. I want to be cognizant of approaches to the subject of theology 'from above', both in terms of the history of Christian dogmatics and also with regard to the central Christian conviction regarding the special revelation of God in Jesus Christ as central to Christian life and thought. At the same time, our contemporary global situation demands that theological truth claims be fully public, exposed to the scrutiny of all who would be interested in the subject being discussed. The following 'pneumatology of quest' is developed from the conviction that, at the very least, it should not be immune to empirical confirmation or falsification. May the quest proceed…

Chapter 2

THE CHRISTOLOGICAL IMPASSE IN
CHRISTIAN THEOLOGY OF RELIGIONS

Having been raised under a church pew as a Pentecostal preacher's kid, I know that I must have given my heart to Jesus many times over as a child. But my first and still vivid recollection of doing so dates back to when I was five years old. I remember watching a film on the prodigal son during a Sunday evening service. It may or may not have been my father who gave the altar call afterward, but whoever it was did not matter. I can still feel the tug on my heart and the tears streaming down my face; I can still hear the echoes of the call in my ear, the pitter-patter of my feet as I ran down the aisle into the open arms of the Father, as represented by Jesus, and the bawling out of my mouth as I accepted Jesus into my life. Is that not what being a Christian is all about—being a follower of Jesus, converted by his saving presence? Is there anything else more central than that? Does it also not follow that everything else is secondary in light of our relationship with Jesus, our best friend and yet our eternal savior? Or is it more the case that we are followers of the *Christ*? But is Jesus not the Christ, and is not Christ wholly the man Jesus? Is there a difference, or does it matter? But, how can it be that a carpenter from Nazareth can be my savior, and not only mine, but also that of the whole world?

Introduction

What is the current state of Christian thinking about theology of religions? What are the issues at stake, and what are the items most vigorously debated? In what ways would a pneumatological approach to a Christian theology of religions be able to advance the discussion? These questions situate the larger framework of this study. What I want to suggest is that a pneumatological approach to the religions provides some avenues by which Christian theology can free up some valuable space to reconsider the christological dilemmas that are at the center of the contemporary impasse.

In this chapter, then, I will highlight the tensions involved when Christian theological assertions are universally extended even as they are founded upon the particular historical personality of Jesus the Christ. I will proceed as follows. Section 1 will consist of a brief sketch of the history of Christian theological reflection on the non-Christian faiths. Developments in the twentieth century will take up Section 2 where I quickly trace the movement from theological exclusivism—the view that salvation is to be found only in hearing and responding to the Gospel via baptism into Christ's Church—to inclusivism—the view that other faiths may be paths to salvation but only because of the person and work of Christ—to theological pluralism—the view that the diverse religious traditions are divinely appointed paths to salvation in their own right.[1] This movement has not been uncontested. As will be evident, advocates have had to make their case around or through Christology, and detractors have countered that these attempts have been unsuccessful. In Section 3, I will systematically recapitulate the christological issues that remain to be resolved by looking at more recent efforts, especially on the part of evangelicals, to negotiate the christological dilemma.

It needs to be reiterated that my discussion throughout this chapter will be nothing more than an aerial overview focused on the problem posed by Christology to Christian theology of religions. Much more can and needs to be said about the theologies of religions surveyed in order to do justice to their authors. However, to do so would take us too far apace. My objective is to portray the breadth of the landscape of theology of religions without getting bogged down in the details except in one or two instances. This approach will do two things. On the one hand, it provides us with a broad background against which to appreciate the developments discussed in the following chapter as well as in the rest of the monograph regarding the problems and promises of a pneumatological theology of religions; on the other hand, it allows us to sort out those theological strategies that in all likelihood will not at

---

1.   This typology was first suggested by Race (1982). More recently, Ogden (1992) has proposed a fourth position: rather than all religious traditions being true as in the pluralist model, one or more *may be* true insofar as they respond to God's love (cf. Griffiths 1993). These and other variations to these positions have led many to question the value of these labels altogether. Nevertheless, keeping in mind the fact that these are not monolithic definitions, I will use them heuristically to illuminate the development of *theologia religionum* in this chapter.

present further the discussion of *theologia religionum* from those that may potentially contribute or lead to some resolution.

1. *Historical Survey of Christian Views of Other Religions*

The perennial problem for Christian theology of religions has been how the affirmation of divine presence in the universe of human religiousness can be compatible with the affirmation of salvation through the particular person of Jesus Christ. This derives from two strands in the Christian Testament which the biblical writers held in tension without attempting reconciliation. On the one hand, there is the clear declaration of God's universal love for the world. This love moved God to send 'his one and only Son' into the world (Jn 3.16) in order that 'the sins of the whole world' (1 Jn 2.2) would be atoned.[2] Universal love leads, as implied in the Pastoral Epistles, to universal salvation: for 'all men' (1 Tim. 4.10; Tit. 2.11).

On the other hand, it is also clear that this salvation is procured and effected only by the Son of God. True, Paul wrote, 'Everyone who calls on the name of the Lord will be saved'; but, he continues immediately, no one can call unless they believe, and they cannot believe unless they hear, and they cannot hear unless the gospel is preached to them (cf. Rom. 10.13-15). The kerygma is ultimately 'the name of Jesus Christ of Nazareth'; more important, Peter proclaimed, 'salvation is found in no one else, for there is no other name under heaven given to men by which we must be saved' (Acts 4.10, 12). In sum, God 'wants all men to be saved and to come to a knowledge of the truth. For there is one God and one mediator between God and men, the man Christ Jesus' (1 Tim. 2.4-5).[3]

For the past two millennia, Christians have wrestled with the tension posed by these two strands and made various attempts to reconcile them. One early effort was that of the second century apologist, Justin

---

2. All Scripture quotations throughout this book are from the New International Version unless otherwise noted.

3. This is just a sampling of the biblical references. For a more complete discussion of this twofold tension in Scripture, see Pinnock (1992: 17-80), where he attempts to do justice to the two poles of an optimistic soteriology based on God's universal salvific will and a high Christology founded upon the particular incarnation of the Son of God in Jesus of Nazareth. I will return to various aspects of Pinnock's work later.

Martyr (executed c. 165). He attempted to reconcile the two scriptural strands by appealing to the Johannine doctrine of the Logos. As the universal and eternal Word of God incarnate in Jesus of Nazareth, the Logos' presence in the world preceded that of Christ's and has been active in the lives of all persons at least in seed form (2 *Apology* 13).[4] This allowed Justin to assert not only that there are 'heathen analogies to Christian doctrine' (1 *Apology* 20) that is the result of general revelation, but also that Christ 'is the Word of whom every race of men were partakers; and those who lived reasonably are Christians, even though they have been thought atheists; as, among the Greeks, Socrates and Heraclitus, and men like them; and among the barbarians...' (1 *Apology* 46). At the same time, Justin by no means uncritically baptized all 'heathen' teachings and practices into the Christian fold. He relegated what was contrary to the truth of the Logos to the work of the Devil and his minions.[5] In short, while Justin was certain that the reach of God's salvific work was much more widespread even among those who did not profess or know Christ, he was equally sure that salvation was only available through the Logos and that all other beliefs and forms of worship were of demonic inspiration.[6]

Opinion during the Patristic era continued to waver between the two poles of God's universal love and the historical particularity of Christ and Christian revelation. Between thinkers like Origen (c. 185–254) who held to more optimistic views of final universal salvation, and others like Tertullian (c. 160–225) who were much less sanguine about their understanding of salvation and cautious against diluting the distinctiveness of Christian faith, were mediating positions like that of Irenaeus (c. 130–200) who granted the salvation of those who lived before the incarnation and responded in faith to the light that they had even as he restricted salvation in the Christian era to those who became

---

4.   Unless otherwise noted, all my quotations from the early Church Fathers will be from the American edition of the *Ante-Nicene Fathers* and *Nicene and Post-Nicene Fathers*, First and Second Series (repr., Peabody, MA: Hendrickson, 1994).

5.   I hope to be forgiven for not using gender-inclusive language in this case.

6.   This neat dualism has persisted throughout the entire history of Christian thought and has led some contemporary thinkers to misinterpret Justin as an 'exclusivist'—one who held to the belief that salvation was possible only through explicit confession of faith in Christ and Christian baptism (e.g. Keith 1992). This reading of Justin does not stand up, especially if the contemporary relevance of the category of the demonic is to be reassessed as I propose to do in Chapters 5 and 7.

members of the institutional Church. Irenaeus's position is far more complex in that, as has been pointed out by Tiessen (1993), there are some aspects of his theology of the unevangelized which can be taken in a more optimistic direction if extrapolated in the context of a much greater awareness of the non-Christian ignorance of Christ such as we have in our own day.[7] It should also be noted that the *Sitz im Leben* which shaped Irenaeus's thought was that of the prolonged second-century battle with gnostic heretics and their suspect christologies rather than the concerns with pluralism rampant in our own time.[8] His suggestion, however, was reinforced in the theology of Cyprian of Carthage (200–258) whose own ideas grew out of the mid-third century Decian persecution and the problem of the lapsed posed by the Donatists. For Cyprian and the faithful, the locus of salvation in Christ was to be found only in the Church and nowhere else: 'Whoever is separated from the Church and is joined to an adulteress, is separated from the promises of the Church; nor can he who forsakes the Church of Christ attain to the rewards of Christ' (*Treatise on the Unity of the Church* 6). In the thought of Cyprian, the universalistic element of the Gospel begins to be subordinated to a particularist Christology—and, more specifically, to ecclesiology.

Cyprian's doctrine was secured by the theology of Augustine and canonized later as the well-known *Extra Ecclesiam nulla salus* formula by the Council of Florence (1442).[9] With few exceptions, it has been

7.   This ignorance of other faiths, and especially of the world religious traditions, that Irenaeus labored under was one that hindered Christian thinkers from developing their own theologies of religions up until the last two centuries. One of the few exceptions is Clement of Alexandria's somewhat sympathetic reference to the Brahmins and the Buddha in his discussion of the origins of Greek philosophy. He must have received some information of more popular strands of the developing Buddhist tradition in which the Buddha had been exalted to a position of divinity (*Stromata* 1.15). For further discussion of the cosmic christologies of Clement, Irenaeus and Justin, see Dupuis (1966).

8.   In this context, it is unfortunate that Irenaeus did not develop his theology of the Word and Spirit as the 'two hands of the Father' (*Against Heresies* 4, Preface, 4). I will return to this in the next chapter.

9.   The explicit wording of the formula itself is derived from Fulgentius, Bishop of Ruspe (d. 533). Its emergence during the patristic period should be understood more so as a warning to schismatic or heretical Christians than to the unevangelized or adherents of other faith traditions; on this, see the informative study by Sullivan (1992).

the traditionally received position down to the present day. Gregory of Nazianzan, for example, was open to truths outside of Christianity, but was at the same time steadfast in his polemic against false gods (cf. Norris 1994). Others such as Nicholas of Cusa (1401–1464), Thomas Aquinas (1225–1274), the Jesuits, John Wesley (1703–1791), and Friedrich Schleiermacher (1768–1834) were perhaps on the whole more optimistic about the salvation of the unevangelized. These adopted a number of strategies to sustain their position such as holding to a variant of the cosmic Christology of the second century apologists, developing a more robust doctrine of natural revelation, appealing to prevenient grace, or accentuating the universalist element of divine love to the neglect of the particularist doctrine of incarnation and atonement.[10] Nicholas and Thomas had limited interactions with Turkish Muslims while the Jesuits were confronted with Chinese Buddhists and Confucians in the sixteenth and seventeenth centuries. These relationships undoubtedly influenced their own views of non-Christian faiths. Nevertheless, their relative optimism of salvation for the unevangelized never threatened to overturn the traditional *Extra Ecclesiam nulla salus* position. The classical connection between salvation, Christ and the Church was not seriously questioned for over a millennium.

This sketch of historical Christian understandings of the salvation of non-Christians has been necessarily brief.[11] Two points stand out from the foregoing. First, throughout most of the history of the Christian Church, questions regarding the unsaved revolved more around the unevangelized than the adherents of other faith traditions. This was in large part because Western Christians were exposed only to local faith practices or popular religious movements with less than lasting historical significance and not at all or only minimally to relationships with those in the major world religions who had well-developed world and life-views that stood out in sharp contrast to the Christian faith.[12]

10. On Nicholas of Cusa and Schleiermacher, see Pittman, Habito and Muck (1996: 77-84); on Thomas, see Riedl (1965); on the Jesuits, see Sullivan (1992: 82-102); on Wesley, see Thompson (1998: 98-100).

11. For a more complete discussion of the historical Christian responses, see Sullivan (1992) and Marshall (1993).

12. The Western monotheistic religions, of course, have common ancestry in Abraham. It is for this reason that up until the modern period, many Christians considered Judaism to be no more than a prelude to the revelation in Jesus Christ (some still do), and Islam to be a sectarian heresy of Christian faith.

Understandably, therefore, the question 'How can a Buddhist or a Hindu be saved?' rarely arose. Of more pressing import was the question regarding the salvation of those who had never heard the Gospel. Christians therefore gave more thought to a theology of the *unevangelized* than to a theology of *other religions* except that they condemned what they perceived to be the superstitions and idolatries of the neighbors with whom they interacted.

Second, the Christian doctrine of the salvation of the unevangelized emerged from the Logos-Christology of the second century and came to be dominated by an interconnected Christology–ecclesiology after Cyprian and especially Augustine. Christ as the savior of the world, clearly enunciated in the Christian Testament, was soon replaced by the Church as the vehicle of this salvation. As a result of this development, salvation was understood ecclesiocentrically: none could be saved apart from Christian membership, or, even more stringently, apart from hearing and receiving the Gospel followed subsequently by water baptism into the Church. This traditional position, also known as exclusivism, posited salvation within the boundaries of institutional Christianity (cf. Race 1982: 10-37; D'Costa 1986: 52-79; Sanders 1992: 37-80).

2. *Theology of Religions in the Twentieth Century*

This traditional exclusivist paradigm has lost its place of primacy in the face of two other competing models that have emerged over the course of the last two centuries: *inclusivism* initially and later on *pluralism*. Crudely put, inclusivism attempts to hold to the indispensability of Christ even while rejecting the ecclesiological definition of salvation, and pluralism understands all faith traditions as potentially equal paths to salvation. It is not surprising that the former view gathered momentum during the nineteenth century when the academic study of religion took shape.

From Exclusivism to Inclusivism

Max Müller (1823–1900), the great German philologist, has long been acknowledged as one of the founders of the discipline of comparative religion (Sharpe 1986: 35). His famous motto, 'he who knows one, knows none,' motivated his quest for comprehending the strangeness of other traditions. Sympathetic understanding inevitably dispels negative stereotypes, and more important, attitudes of superiority regarding one's own set of allegiances. This replacing of the old guard was nowhere more evident than at the 1893 Parliament of Religions when adherents from religious traditions across the globe convened in Chicago. In spite of the preponderance of Christians and the dominance of tenets of modernist theological liberalism as operating motifs during the Parliament, other voices were also heard. Delegates were impressed, for example, by the presentation of Swami Vivekananda, a disciple of Sri Ramakrishna, who extolled the virtues of a universal Hinduism able to promote an attitude of interreligious tolerance and account for the diversity of religions. The way for this announcement was both cultivated and furthered by thinkers such as Ernst Troeltsch who relativized the absolutistic claims of Christianity via a more historical conception of the religions.

Troeltsch's influence and significance even to the present day is unmistakable. He was one of the first to grapple seriously with the theological implications posed by the discipline of *Religionswissenschaft*. As a philosopher and theologian in Lutheran Germany, Troeltsch struggled to find a way between the traditional exclusivistic and absolutistic notions of Christianity and the thoroughgoing skeptical relativism suggested by modern historicism (cf. Drescher 1993: 159-69). What emerged for Troeltsch was the view of Christianity as relatively absolute—decisive for Western civilization in its 'breakthrough in principle to a religion of *personality*, opposed to all naturalistic and anti-personalistic understandings of God' (1991: 63), but only one among the many vital religious options available to the modern world. Similarly, Jesus as the foremost personal revelation of God did not vitiate other manifestations of the divine reality to be found in other traditions. In this way, Troeltsch was able both to grant some measure of autonomy and legitimacy to other religious faiths even while preserving the liberal Christian theological axioms of the universal Fatherhood and love of God and retaining some measure of conviction regarding the soteriological import of Jesus Christ.

Christian missions, which had blossomed during the nineteenth century, was thereby challenged not only by these theological developments but also by other political, social and ecclesial factors to expand its operations. Protestants pooled their resources to form the World Missionary Conference. Its first convention was held at Edinburgh in 1910 under the theme, 'Carrying the Gospel to All the Non-Christian World', followed by major conferences at Jerusalem (1928) and

Tambaram (1938). From the beginning, two distinct approaches to the non-Christian faiths can be seen: a more conservative theological and missiological thrust and a more open anthropological and history-of-religions attitude (see Friesen 1996). Their combination at Edinburgh resulted in a fair assessment of other traditions along with a re-affirmation of the Christian evangelistic obligation (Ariarajah 1991: 17-31). Whereas the latter attitude appeared to gain in acceptance at Jerusalem in the form of an openness toward the possibility of divine revelation being present at least incipiently in other traditions, the former was vigorously reasserted at Tambaram by the veteran missionary–theologian to Indonesia, Hendrik Kraemer (1938). Under the influence of the neo-Orthodox theology of Karl Barth and Emil Brunner, Kraemer argued for a discontinuity between Christian faith based on divine revelation and human religiosity erected on natural revelation. Kraemer, however, did not necessarily insist on defining salvation in ecclesiocentric terms: one did not have to be baptized or join the visible Church to be saved. Rather, the fate of the non-Christian was understood in christological categories. While Christianity as a concrete social and institutional phenomenon is fallible as a partly human construction and thus not absolutely true, Jesus Christ as the definitive and final revelation of God is of supreme soteriological significance. In this conception, Kraemer slid close toward inclusivism; yet for him and those influenced by his theology of religions, the Christian mission remained the urgent priority.

The Religions and Vatican II

This same movement from exclusive ecclesiocentrism to a more inclusive christocentrism took place in the Roman Catholic Church during the Second Vatican Council. Even prior to the Council, the Dominican theologian Yves Congar, drawing upon the distinction between Christ's visible and mystical bodies made initially by Pope Pius XII's 1943 encyclical letter, argued for stages of revelation, grace and faith such that the *Extra Ecclesiam nulla salus* was interpreted to mean not that the unevangelized and non-Christian adherents of other faiths were damned, but that 'the Church founded by Jesus Christ is in this world the only repository of the principle of salvation in its authenticity and fullness' (1961: 135). Other religions are not equally good, even though some may on occasion reflect aspects of the fullness of divine revelation exhibited in Christ and the Christian Church. This position was formally received by the bishops of Vatican II as seen in the decrees *Nostra aetate, Lumen Gentium, Ad gentes divinitus* and *Gaudium et spes*, as well as in numerous post-conciliar documents (cf. Stransky 1985; Ruokanen 1992; Sheard 1987). *Nostra aetate* §2 in particular spoke of the 'accurately defined insights of philosophy' among the Hindu sages and of the testimony 'to the essential inadequacy of this changing world' in Buddhism, and forthrightly declared the Catholic inclusivistic stance in an important paragraph:

> the Catholic Church rejects nothing of what is true and holy in these religions. She has a high regard for the manner of life and conduct, the precepts and doctrines which, although differing in many ways from her own teaching, nevertheless often reflect a ray of that truth which enlightens all men. Yet she proclaims and is in duty bound to proclaim without fail, Christ who is the way, the truth, and the life (John 1:6). In him, in whom God reconciled all things to himself (2 Cor. 5:18-19), men find the fulness of their religious life.

Catholic inclusivism found expression along these lines during and after the Council in the work of theologians such as Heinz Schlette (1963) and Joseph Neuner (1967, 1968), and in numerous publications by Hans Küng (1965, 1967: 313-19, 1973, 1976: 89-116).[13]

At the same time, however, the thesis of 'anonymous Christianity' advanced by Karl Rahner (1969, 1974, 1976, 1979b, 1982: 311-21, 1983a) has so far been the most productive not only in advancing Catholic thinking on theology of religions, but also in provoking counter-responses.[14] His theology of religions is set within the framework of both a transcendental anthropology featuring the category of *spirit* as the constituent part of our existence by which we are able to go

---

13. Given this move in Catholicism, a renaissance of the cosmic Christology of the early Church comes as no surprise; see especially the essays by Bayart and Fallon in *Indian Journal of Theology* 15 (1966).

14. For early responses, see Riesenhuber (1964), Hillman (1966) and Kruse (1967). D'Costa (1985) summarizes a good deal of the criticisms leveled against the 'anonymous Christian' idea even while he comes to Rahner's defense. Even though I cannot do justice to the breadth and depth of Rahner's theology of religions, I will spend a little more time reviewing his proposal because of the influence he has exerted in the ongoing development of theological inclusivism not only among Catholics but also on Protestants such as Clark Pinnock. Rahner is also important for the purposes of this thesis in that I will later attempt to develop a pneumatological approach to the religions along inclusivistic lines that retains certain elements of his thought.

beyond ourselves and are opened to contact with the infinite, and a revised neo-scholastic understanding of grace as the ontological and causal means by which we receive the self-communication of God. By the grace of God, therefore, we live as human beings in a situation which Rahner terms the 'supernatural existential'. In this situation, divine revelation is directly and existentially apprehensible by every person that grapples with personal issues in an ultimate way—in the very depths of his or her being—such that salvation is available even to those who have never heard the proclamation of the Gospel.[15]

Rahner therefore builds on Congar's 'mystical body of Christ' in his argument that there is or can be a state of being prior to the hearing of the Gospel or official ecclesiastical faith when a person can implicitly say 'Yes' to the grace of God. A person in this state fits into the Christian theological category of 'anonymous Christian' insofar as this acceptance of grace is 'present in an implicit form whereby [the] person undertakes and lives the duty of each day in the quiet sincerity of patience, in devotion to his material duties and the demands made upon him by the person under his care' (Rahner 1969: 394). At the heart of his thesis is the doctrine of God's universal salvific will. Because of this central axiom, Rahner is able to assert that 'the unlimited transcendence of man, itself directed of necessity toward God, is raised up consciously by grace, although possibly without explicit thematic reflection, in such a way that the possibility of faith in revelation is thereby made available' (1979b: 55). Rather than seeing the 'anonymous Christian' thesis as undermining the validity of the Church or the Church's mission, however, Rahner urges that the individual can (and should) be brought to explicit faith only by the Church faithfully carrying out its evangelistic mandate (1974).

The question remains of how it is that talk of the mediation of grace can avoid theological abstraction. Rahner suggests that one way in which grace is experienced is through the concrete practices and phenomena of other religious traditions. He asserts that other religions 'contain also supernatural elements arising out of the grace which is given to men as a gratuitous gift on account of Christ. For this reason, a non-Christian religion can be recognized as a *lawful* religion (although only in different degrees) without thereby denying the error and depravity

---

15. I am indebted here to Roger Haight's (1979: 119-42) lucid discussion of grace in Rahner's theology; see also Reno (1995) for Rahner's doctrine of transcendence.

contained in it' (1983a: 121). By 'lawful religion', Rahner means 'an institutional religion whose "use" by man at a certain period can be regarded on the whole as a positive means of gaining the right relationship with God and thus for the attaining of salvation, a means which is therefore positively included in God's plan of salvation' (1983a: 125; cf. 1981, 1983b). If one questions this, one questions that Christian faith itself is mediated through the social, ritual, institutional and even devotional practices shaped by the Christian tradition. Again, however, Rahner avoids the corollary whereby the Christian faith is completely relativized by distinguishing between Christ and the Church. Whereas in Jesus Christ the God-man, 'all the fullness of the Deity lives in bodily form' (Col. 2.9), Christianity and the Church as historical reality are still in the process of being transformed into Christlikeness (Rahner 1977: 40). Throughout, however, Rahner had always attempted to remain within the boundaries of theological reflection established by Vatican II. As such, the importance of the incarnation and Christology to Rahner's thought is clear, even if he has clearly broken away from the ecclesiocentrism of previous theology.[16]

From Inclusivism to Pluralism

The Catholic move toward christocentrism spurred further theological reflection about the adequacy of the christological paradigm to shoulder the weight of Christian theology of religions. This led to a further revision toward a pluralistic theology of religions.[17] Termed the 'Coper-

16. I will return to a more detailed discussion of Rahner's theology of religions in the next chapter.

17. *Pluralism* is a multivalent term. Mouw and Griffioen (1993: 17-18) have identified three of its most prominent types which they have termed (a) directional pluralism, (b) associational pluralism, and (c) contextual pluralism. (c) is more or less a quantitative designation for our contemporary consciousness of the manyness of things: we are aware of religious others; (b) refers more to the diversity of the political, social, economic and religious structures that govern modern, especially urban, life: we opt for different religious affiliations; (a) highlights the different ways that perspectives are directed or should be, the former being more descriptive, while the latter being normative and thus valuational. Their objection to the last type of pluralism, normative directional pluralism—that is, the demand for openness and tolerance of all members of society toward other positions even if such conflicts with their own values in the name of pluralism itself as a foundational social and axiological axiom—is due to the relativistic skepticism that ultimately follows. For the most part, advocates of a pluralistic theology of religions whom I

nican Revolution' in theology by one of its main Protestant advocates, John Hick (1980), pluralists have argued against exclusivists that the latter position blasphemes against the understanding of God as love since it arbitrarily excludes from salvation the many not privileged to be born within a Christian social context. They also urge, against inclusivists, that the christocentric solution is unsustainable due to its explicit Christian doctrinal connections and the resulting theological imperialism it foists upon religious others. By focusing away from Christ, a central symbol for Christians, toward the divine, a reality admitted by Jews, Muslims, Hindus, and some Buddhists, Confucians and Taoists, the hope is that a more adequate *theologia religionum* could be formulated to foster interreligious dialogue, understanding and relations. This is a theological strategy designed to give Christians equal rather than elevated seating in a public market swarming not only with a diversity of religions but also with an explicit awareness of such plurality (Hick 1984; cf. Coward 1985: 97-100; Cracknell 1986). Even this shift from christocentrism to theocentrism, however, has been insufficient since there are traditions such as Theravada and Zen Buddhism and philosophical Taoism that are essentially non-theistic. In his later work, then, Hick goes even further and suggests that all references to God or the divine be discarded so as not to prejudice dialogues with adherents of these traditions. Building instead on the Kantian distinction between noumena and phenomena, he proposes that religion is ultimately about the Real which is unknowable in itself and that all of our perceptions of the Real are penultimate or mediated experiences of its manifestations (Hick 1989a: 233-99). In the pluralist conception then, the great world faiths constitute 'different, but apparently more or less equally salvific, human responses to the Ultimate' (Hick 1995: 47).

What happens to Christ in Hick's 'Copernican Revolution'? In conjunction with his turn to pluralism in the early 1970s, Hick saw clearly that orthodox Christology had to be radically reinterpreted. His own contribution to *The Myth of God Incarnate* that he edited in 1977 signaled his jettisoning of traditional christological views, a position which

discuss here would agree with or at least pay lip service to Mouw and Griffioen's contention that there needs to be some norms by which to establish true from false or demonic religiosity. Yet just as many would also attempt to retain the argument that such can be accomplished even while holding to normative directional pluralism as defined by Mouw and Griffioen. As will be evident, I disagree along with the latter that such can be done.

he has in large part maintained up to the present. Jesus in Hick's theocentric theology of religions is not the incarnate Son of God, but rather a man anointed by the Spirit of God to a greater degree than other persons. The concept of incarnation is a mere metaphor that turns our attention to the presence of God in the man Jesus while highlighting his obedience to the divine will (1989b, 1989c, 1995: 57-59). What has happened in Hick's pluralistic theology of religions, of course, is that the universal aspect of the divine relationship with human beings has been emphasized to the neglect and the relativization of the christo-logical core of Christian faith.

Hick's work in this area has fueled an even greater response than has even Rahner's theory, including criticisms from those who argue that his 'demythologized' Christology is a remnant from the liberal theo-logical agenda of at least two generations ago, if not dating back to the turn of the twentieth century.[18] Yet his proposals have struck a chord with a number of other kindred thinkers, many of whom contributed to a volume edited by Hick and his colleague, Paul Knitter (1987), which argued for the truth of a pluralistic theology of religions. These have agreed with Hick that pluralism is not only a sociological datum descriptive of the diversity in the world of religions, but that each tra-dition also has something of lasting value to contribute to the religious experience of humankind, if not to the soteriological quest that we have all embarked on. While Hick has made his argument as a philosopher of religion, these others have supplemented his contentions by approach-ing the theology of religions via other starting points such as history (Wilfred Cantwell Smith), contemplative spirituality and an interdisci-plinary methodology (Raimundo Panikkar), and issues related to justice and the commitment to human liberation (Knitter and Aloysius Pieris).

18. This is the response of Carruthers (1990). The periodical response to Hick has been nothing short of voluminous. In addition to Carruthers's volume, there have also been a number of booklength responses, all of which contain extensive bibliographies of the secondary literature. The most recent, Gillis (1989) and Rose (1996), have been critical of Hick at some point—e.g. his less than nuanced under-standing of religious language in general and myth and metaphor specifically, and his flawed Kantian epistemology that fails to connect the Real with human expe-rience—even if they are sympathetic with the questions he has raised or with his overall position. My colleague Paul Eddy (1999) argues cogently that Hick's plural-istic proposal is finally incoherent, failing in part because his framework for the doctrine of the Real is covertly monotheistic—infected, as it is, by remnants of Hick's theistic Christian background.

In his article in the Hick and Knitter volume, for example, Cantwell Smith argues from a broad awareness of the unity and diversity of the history of religions that 'exclusive claims for one's own doctrine, or for any, is idolatry in the pejorative sense' (1987: 61).[19] His agreement with Hick's proposal to recognize the doctrine of incarnation as a myth is evident on this basis. Panikkar's proposal for genuine pluralism that recognizes and highlights the *sus generis* character of each tradition suffers from a similar christological defect. Bringing together contemplative strands in Hinduism, Buddhism and Christianity with an interdisciplinary background in science, philosophy and theology, Panikkar's suggestion is to move even beyond Hick's 'Copernican Revolution' toward a mystical intuition of the ultimate togetherness of God, humankind and the cosmos—what he calls the 'theoanthropocosmic' vision (1987a: 113).[20] Lost in this ethereal vision, however, is the particularity and concrete historicity of Jesus of Nazareth as the Christ (cf. MacPherson 1996).[21]

19. Smith's epoch-making *The Meaning and End of Religion* (1962) redefined for both religious and theological studies the concept of *religion* as faith—the personal, existential aspects of religious experiences—and historical traditions—the scriptures, institutions, rituals, doctrines, etc., that constitute the objective dimensions of religious life. As a historian, Smith has done as much as anyone to prepare the road for the pluralistic mentality in his efforts to heighten historical consciousness of the diversity within the world's religious traditions. (Cf. also Thompson [1976] for further discussion of how the arrival of modern historical consciousness has awakened us to the experience of diversity and plurality which did not accompany the awareness of religious otherness in previous times.) Yet, he has also made valuable theological contributions based on his ability to interpret the history of religions in terms of a unity within diversity and vice versa (cf. Smith 1981). For an excellent overview of Smith's contribution to theology of religions, see Hughes (1986). My own quibble with Smith's otherwise invaluable work follows Hugo Meynell (1985) who sees Smith overlooking the cognitive dimension of religion thereby smoothing over contradictory doctrinal assertions in the effort to place the human element of faith on a level playing field. It is unfortunate that a historian of Smith's caliber has not been able to acknowledge doctrinal distinctives without leveling them out in the end. More on this below.

20. Panikkar has thus been a vigorous spokesperson for a dialogically open comparative theology and philosophy of religion (1978, 1980).

21. More recently, Panikkar has called his mystical insight the 'cosmotheandric vision' (1993). For a recent assessment of Panikkar's contributions which date back over forty years, see Prabhu (1996). I am certainly not competent to render judgment on the lifelong reflection of someone with the background Panikkar has. Time

Christ, Liberation and the Religions

Do liberation theologians of religions such as Knitter and Pieris fare better? As one of the earliest American Catholic theologians to embrace pluralism, it is important for us to pay some attention to the developments of Knitter's thought. His first major publication was his Marburg doctoral dissertation (1974) in which he reflected as a Catholic on the religions in light of models proposed by Protestants such as Troeltsch, Barth and Paul Althaus. In his conclusion, he raised four sets of questions 'concerning Christology' (§86). First, does not the limitation of the reformational *solus christus* to the historical Jesus or to his mediation via the proclamation of the Church lead to a diluted understanding of revelation and to a kind of Barthian 'christomonism' even in terms of the doctrine of justification? Second and further, does not this limitation in effect render null and void any link between the orders of creation and redemption and cripple the soteriological effectiveness of the incarnation? Third, does not the mediation of salvation through the Word need to be supplemented by the internal work of the Spirit? And finally then, can theology of religions perhaps be more productive if developed along the lines of a cosmic Christology such that there is not just an intellectual but a real christocentrism in which the dynamism of salvation and the reality of the incarnation is propelled 'into the "*ta panta*" (Col. 1.15-20)' (1974: 229)? Clearly the issue Knitter is wrestling with even at this early stage in his career is the age-old problem of the tension between the universal and the particular.

The process of movement toward pluralism can be seen in Knitter's (1978) discussion of the work of Hans Küng, his Catholic colleague. Knitter complains that Küng's inclusivistic vision in *On Being a Christian* (1976) fails especially since such a position is not conducive to genuine dialogue with adherents of other traditions and also because incarnational Christology has to be reinterpreted along functionalist lines in the contemporary world where theology must answer not only

---

will tell if the Christian tradition is as pliable as Panikkar believes it to be, as well as whether or not it is perhaps more truthful to reality than Panikkar makes it out to be. However, I do think that there are adequate responses available to Panikkar if developed along the lines of a more robust pneumatology. This is a surprisingly untapped aspect of his thought given the explicitly trinitarian aspect of his theology of religions (e.g. 1973). While I will not presume to answer for Panikkar, my own work is sympathetic with the spirit of his quest, even if suspicious on many points of detail in the vision he sketches.

to its sources but also to its present public and to historical consciousness. In an article that appeared the following year, Knitter spoke of Christ in symbolic terms, claiming that 'the experience of salvation is not mediated through historical events in themselves but insofar as they are "mythified": symbols save; historical events (as events) do not' (1979: 651). This allowed him to encourage Christians to search for and acknowledge the divine salvific presence in symbols of other traditions such as that of the Buddha, Krishna and other Hindu avatars.

With the appearance of his landmark *No Other Name?* in 1985, Knitter's turn to pluralism was complete. In this book, he spoke approvingly of the theocentric model of Hick and Panikkar, and proposed in turn a non-normative 'theocentric Christology'. By this move, focus was placed on Jesus's own theocentric consciousness, on his proclamation not of himself but of the Kingdom of God, on the evolutionary and plurivocal forms of the Christian Testament christologies themselves, and on the confessional linguistic structure of early Christian exclusivistic christological claims. The particularity of Jesus necessarily requires that he be understood as a relative symbol of the divine mystery (1985: 202). The transcendental christologies of the early Church councils would be better off if reinterpreted along functionalist lines such that the doctrine of the incarnation can better serve as a vehicular symbol of God's self-communication and intention for humanity rather than as a literalistic picture of divine descent. Jesus is therefore unique, but not absolute or final in the manner claimed by classical theology. Such a non-normative theocentric Christology, Knitter says, would be a 'universally relevant manifestation (sacrament, incarnation) of divine revelation and salvation' (1985: 172) that would further advance the inter-religious dialogue.[22]

22. *No Other Name?* has generated a lively debate that continues to the present (cf. Swidler and Mojzes 1997). Earlier North American responses faulted Knitter's effort to define Christ theocentrically as wrong-headed since Christian conviction has always maintained that revelation proceeds in the reverse direction (we know something about God only because of the person of Jesus; cf. Heim 1987), and claimed that the theocentric vision was, in spite of its alleged openness and tolerance, really a disguised form of imperialism in that other traditions were somehow made to subsist within the pluralistic framework (somewhat in the same manner as Hindus have always claimed their system to be the most all-encompassing and hence also the most tolerant; cf. Braaten 1987). Knitter has, however, always not only taken his critics seriously (see 1987), but also attempted to learn from them, as his later books amply demonstrate (1995, 1996). Because my own

But does not the move to de-normativize Christ undermine our ability as Christians to render judgment on other faiths and ideologies—judgments that are sometimes urgently necessary?[23] This led Knitter down the path of a liberation theology of religions, briefly outlined in *No Other Name?* (1985: 192-97, 205-207), and more fully developed later in the volume he edited with Hick (1987) and elsewhere (1988, 1995). Theology is, after all, not just about orthodoxy but also about orthopraxis. Liberation theology's 'preferential option for the poor' not only provides an important element by which to discuss the constitutive elements of religious beliefs and practices, but also serves as a norm by which diverse faiths can be judged. Themes such as the Kingdom of God and the emancipation of a new humanity provide theological substance as well as common ground from which to launch interreligious discussion. In this manner, Knitter has moved the discussion in theology of religions from theocentrism to 'regnocentrism' and soteriocentrism (1989).

How is Christ's uniqueness understood in this framework? Knitter locates the uniqueness of Jesus in his message that insists that 'the reality of God cannot be truly experienced and known unless one is actively, historically, materially engaged in loving one's neighbors and working for their betterment in this world' (1994: 43). This is thus a 'relational uniqueness' which is inclusive rather than exclusive in acknowledging other salvific words, symbols and faith traditions. The Gospel and Christian missions thereby involve not only proclamation, but more importantly, service and dialogue. Christ is universal, decisive

pneumatological proposal is subject to similar criticisms as has been leveled against Knitter, I hope it will be evident that I have been able to learn from his thought and dialogic example.

23. Hick had raised this question back in 1981, and replied by insisting primarily on moral criteria to adjudicate soteriological claims: how well do religious doctrines, rituals, etc., 'promote or hinder the great religious aim of salvation/ liberation' (1981: 466). He quickly acknowledged, however, that the divergent conceptions of salvation or liberation in the religions make reaching a consensus on 'grading' them practically impossible anytime soon. Griffiths and Lewis (1983) respond that Hick seems to concede too swiftly on pluralist convictions that tolerance requires other claims to be accepted for what they are and integrated into a meta-perspective when what we should really be about is developing criteria by which to push, and render judgment on questions of truth. I am sympathetic with these critics' proposals (my work being one response to their call), but I think that they overlook Hick's own long and intense struggle with just such issues.

and indispensable, but not definitive and unsurpassable (1996).

Aloysius Pieris, a Sri Lankan Jesuit, has been instrumental in forging an Asian-Christian-pluralistic-liberation theology of religions. Any valid theology in Asia cannot be but pluralistic and liberationist simply because 'the Asian reality is an interplay of *Religiousness* and *Poverty*' (1986: 332). Central to this theology, then, has to be 'the building up of the "Kingdom communities" or "basic human communities" wherein Christian and non-Christian members strive together for the dawn of *Full Humanity*' (1986: 350). What is the place or role of Christ in such an Asian liberation theology of religions? It is imperative that the static/ontic and Western categories of Chalcedon be complemented by more holistic/dynamic and pluralistic models. Pieris therefore asks, Which Christ?, and proffers an Asian Christ assembled from the 'broken body' metaphor of Dalit theology, the 'Han-ridden body' of the Korean Minjung, and the 'breast-feeding Christa' of Asian women, among others (1996: 65-78). He tentatively suggests that 'an all-embracing Christology (call it universal if you like) is one that weaves together all three aspects of Christian discourse: Jesus as the *word* that interprets reality, the *medium* that transforms history, and the *way* that leads to the cessation of all discourse. Sophia?' (1996: 146). A *sophia* or wisdom–Christology leads us directly to a Spirit-Christology, or a christic–pneumatology. But before we launch into such a discussion, however, we need to complete our account of the contemporary dilemma by focusing on reactions to the pluralists, especially on those from the explicitly evangelical theologies of religions which have recently emerged.

3. *The Contemporary Dilemma*

The Reaction to Pluralism

Part of 'the problem with theological pluralism', Mark Horst has suggested, is that it is one thing to advocate tolerance as a virtue of personal character, but quite another to demand tolerance as a dogmatic principle (1986: 972; cf. Ogden 1988). John Wesley was one of the prime exemplars of the former, while contemporary pluralist thinkers are more of the latter stripe.[24] On both grounds, however, there has been more than an ongoing outcry against the pluralist argument.

---

24. Recall Mouw and Griffioen's fears about 'normative directional pluralism' mentioned in n. 17.

One of the strongest rebuttals to the pluralists has been those that have opposed their assumption of an essentialist theory of religion. The pluralist scheme, following Schleiermacher and especially Rudolph Otto, seems to require that the diverse traditions have all actually developed out of a primordial experience of the divine. This is in part what allows them to say that beneath the kernels of religious doctrines lies a core experience and that all faiths are thereby salvific in some similar sense.[25] By contrast, more recent theorists of religion such as George Lindbeck have argued that religious experiences are actually shaped by the cultural-linguistic matrix within which they occur, and that doctrines function in religious traditions analogously to the way grammars function in languages (1984). Along these same lines, even the soteriocentrism of Knitter and Pieris have come under fire from those who emphasize the utter incommensurability of conceptions of salvation especially in the world's religious traditions (Dinoia 1992; Heim 1995). It follows further that if in fact religious traditions originate not from a core experience but out of diverse cultural-linguistic frameworks, a pluralist theology of religions would be ultimately self-defeating in that religious differences are either ignored or trampled upon in being made to fit the pluralist paradigm. Even as pluralists demand toleration and respect for their interreligious dialogue partner and do not expect that the cherished convictions of the other tradition will be betrayed in the dialogic process, why then do these same pluralists attempt to dilute historic Christian truth claims and expect all Christians to do the same? Rather than making Christianity more palatable to others, our strategy may in fact terminate the dialogue prematurely if our partners feel that we have failed to represent our tradition faithfully. Interreligious dialogue should retain a place for apologetics even if that is not the only kind of exchange such conversations should consist of (cf. Griffiths 1991).

Part of the object of such apologetics is to get at the truth of religious beliefs. Hendrik Vroom (1990) has attempted to steer a middle way between pluralist essentialism and exclusivist discontinuity. To the question, Do all religious traditions worship the same God?, he responds that some do and some do not based on a comparative assess-

---

25. This is clearly the model of religion that Reat and Perry (1991) work with in their thesis that there is a single spiritual experience undergirding at least all of the major world religious traditions.

ment of the intended references of worship by religious devotees.[26] Opposing any a priori resolution, Vroom prefers instead the hard labor of comparative analysis. The import of the discipline of comparative theology for theology of religions is now clear. Previous theologies of religions erected solely on Christian scriptural and dogmatic data remain suspect inasmuch as they have neglected serious engagement and study of the actual religious phenomena that lie at the center of their subject matter.[27]

Yet truth is not only to be gotten via comparative or philosophic analysis; it is also supposed to be lived and proclaimed, being attested to by Scripture. Truth is not only a cognitive datum; it is also a relationship with Jesus Christ. It has been the evangelicals that have been the most insistent on these matters. Because many North American Pentecostals and charismatics have closely aligned themselves to evangelical theology, it is important to have some understanding of the recent development of evangelical thinking on theology of religions.

Enter the Evangelicals

Apart from the earlier work of Neal Punt (1980) and Norman Anderson (1984), evangelicals have been slow to rethink the traditional exclusivistic and ecclesiocentric position.[28] More recently, stirred by senior

26. A similar response is given by Donovan (1986) to the question of whether or not 'different religions share moral common ground': that interreligious dialogue may uncover common causes does not necessarily mean that there are universal common laws awaiting discovery after differences are set aside.

27. The discipline of comparative theology is still in its infancy even though there now exist some excellent samples on which to build such as Cragg (1986), Martinson (1987), Neville (1991b) and Carman (1994), as well as more specialized comparative projects like Ching (1977) and Yearley (1990) crossing over into Confucianism, Keenan (1989, 1995) into Buddhism, and Dunuwila (1985), Clooney (1993) and Thangaraj (1994) into Hinduism. I will return to the topic of comparative theology in Chapter 4.

28. I am less concerned about a precise definition of *evangelical*, doctrinal or otherwise, than I am in the broad tradition stemming from Luther. I would say that in North America, affiliates of the National Association of Evangelicals and members of the Evangelical Theological Society would be to the right of center on the evangelical spectrum, being more conservative theologically in upholding doctrines like biblical inerrancy and penal or substitutionary atonement. Neal Punt's argument, for example, for a 'biblical universalism' whereby all are saved and elect in Christ except those who the Bible clearly identifies as being lost is an optimistic Arminian position that few conservative evangelicals would publicly endorse

evangelicals like Anderson, a few other theologians such as Clark Pinnock (1988, 1990, 1992), John Sanders (1988, 1992) and Stanley Grenz
(1994) have attempted revisions of the classical position in the inclusivistic direction, and by doing so, have drawn the more conservative
defenders of the faith into the discussion. In order to understand the
conservative response, I will briefly outline Sanders's contribution.[29]

Sanders's book *No Other Name* (1992) focuses much more on the
question of the destiny of the unevangelized than on the historical
religions. Yet it is also an extended argument against the inadequacies
of exclusivism and universalism along with an equally sustained contention on behalf of inclusivism, bringing biblical, theological and historical data into a systematic whole. Appealing to stalwart evangelicals
like Wesley and C.S. Lewis, Sanders mounts a five-pronged argument
for inclusivism. First, salvation, being *sola fide* for all, is realized by
Christians through their awareness of the person of Christ and their
confession of his name; it is realized by other believers by their faithful
response to God in accordance with the light that they have. This
means, second, that general revelation may be salvific rather than solely
damning, as many evangelicals had previously held. Third, the triune
God effects salvation by the Holy Spirit even in the lives of those who
have not heard the Gospel. Fourth, a cosmic Christology ensures that

(1980). Yet it is important to note that on other issues, the evangelical spectrum is
just as vast as the liberal, if not even more so given evangelicalism's global forms.
For a good summary of the varieties of evangelicalism today, see Tidball (1994).

29. I will focus on Sanders here even though Pinnock has been more prolific
because I have discussed Pinnock elsewhere (Yong 1999b) and will do so further in
Chapter 6. Other expressions of inclusivist optimism can be found in the missionary
Evert Osburn (1989), the ecumenical-evangelical Gabriel Fackre (1995), the evangelical Anglican theologian Alistair McGrath (1995), the missiologist–historian
Ralph Covell (1986), and the evangelical philosopher Thomas Talbott (1997). Also
noteworthy is the World Evangelical Fellowship's not endorsing exclusivism at its
Manila consultation in 1992. The Manila Document called instead for further study
on the fate of the unevangelized because the delegates could not reach a consensus
on this issue (see 'The WEF Manila Declaration' in Nicholls 1994: 14-27, esp. the
discussion on 15-16); compare this with the more distinctly exclusivist position articulated by Harold Lindsell without much resistance from conference representatives at the International Congress on World Evangelization held at Lausanne in
1974 (Lindsell 1975: 1212-13).

while the incarnation is the supreme revelation of the Son of God, it was and is not the only manifestation of the Logos; all genuine engagement with the divine is an encounter with other disclosures of the Logos (1992: 239-40).

This leads to Sanders's fifth argument which draws from the reality of non-Christian faiths. From the three basic theological axioms of inclusivism—'a. Although God is best defined by the historical revelation in Jesus Christ, he is not confined to it... b. The biblical writers used indigenous names for God and made use of ideas, values, and practices compatible with the worship of the true God... c. In some clearly imperfect but nonetheless genuine sense, the Athenians did worship the true God' (1992: 241, 244, 246)—he concludes that God is at work redemptively in other faiths prior to missionary contact. Don Richardson's (1974, 1981) 'redemptive analogies' which find in small tribes around the world those who know God vaguely, those who are looking for special revelation lost to them, and those who have strange customs that prefigure the biblical message of redemption and forgiveness, is referred to approvingly. Yet some have insisted that more often than not, the result of general revelation is not the *praeparatio evangelica* that inclusivists envision but rather the pantheisms, polytheisms, demonisms, and the like, which have been documented by the history of religions. Even if Sanders is able to respond successfully to this query, in this context he merely instantiates Richardson's examples of God's gracious activity among those who are unevangelized and does not really probe Richardson's data for the purpose of formulating a comparative theological method. Interestingly, in his discussion of the local traditions, he asserts that 'the chief structural difference between these religions and Christianity is that they tend to be merely historical, whereas Christianity is both historical and eschatological. Moreover, they tend to be sociocentric (concerned with community) where Christianity is theocentric' (1992: 249). Sanders's concern, it is clear, is to mediate between the two poles of divine universality and christological particularity.

The conservative evangelical reaction to Sanders and moderate evangelical inclusivism has been sizable. The responses have been fairly predictable: that the inclusivist argument fails exegetically; that the authority of Scripture has been compromised; that the historic Christian stance of Augustine, Calvin and others in the Reformed tradition has been betrayed; that natural revelation is damning rather than salvific;

that the missionary mandate of the Church is jeopardized; that moderate evangelicals have conceded far too much to modernity.[30] Yet evangelical exclusivism has not been defended solely by those whose overall theologies have been conservative. Two trained in philosophy, Harold Netland (1987, 1991) in the analytic tradition and Stephen Franklin (1993) in the Whiteheadian, are overall theologically moderate even while they have retained an exclusivistic understanding of the religions. Netland's argument is essentially that of the logic of propositions: contradictory religious doctrines are by virtue of their assertions exclusivistic. What remains universal, however, are the canons of rationality which enable us to determine where contradictions and harmonies exist. Franklin argues via a process metaphysics for the historicity and factuality of the Christ event as the ontological and causal bedrock undergirding what he calls the 'existential-universal application of Christian themes' (1993: 51). In different ways, both retain the universal element of the tension in their theology.

Evangelicals, however, have also recognized the need to engage the pluralist position in debate. In a recent volume, Vinoth Ramachandra (1996), a Sri Lankan Anglican evangelical assessed the pluralist proposals of his South Asian colleagues (Panikkar, Pieris and Stanley Samartha). Ramachandra's dialogue with the pluralists are exemplary of an evangelical engagement with non-conservative Christian thinkers. However, his apologetics do not concern us as much at this stage as his constructive argument for an evangelical theology of religions and missiology. Following the neo-Barthian apologetics of the evangelical-ecumenical veteran missionary, Lesslie Newbigin, Ramachandra argues that the Gospel brings its own epistemology and rationality along with it. Further, because there is more continuity than discontinuity between the age of the Christian Testament, the early Church Fathers and our own socio-cultural situation, incarnational Christology can and should be retained with only a 'shift in emphasis' (1996: 239) rather than a complete abandonment of form. In short, Ramachandra insists not only that the Gospel of Jesus Christ is still able to speak to our times, but also that it is the only sure means by which the idols of modernity can be critiqued and exposed. The evangelical refusal to surrender the

---

30. E.g. Blue 1981; Glasser 1981; Fernando 1987; Nash 1994; Richard 1994; Geivett and Phillips 1995; Carson 1996; Erickson 1996. I discuss some of these responses in greater detail in Yong (1999b).

distinctiveness of the Gospel is the correct response given that the loss of distinctiveness and difference is what threatens the interreligious dialogue in the long run (cf. Hesselgrave 1990).

The Perennial Christological Questions
The debate continues unabated as evidenced by recent multi-perspective volumes involving representatives from multiple positions that have attempted to press the dialogue ahead (Ockholm and Phillips 1995; Sanders 1995; Swidler and Mojzes 1997; Heim (ed.) 1998). At the center of the controversy for all parties, however, is the person and work of Jesus Christ (cf. Anderson and Stransky 1981; Richard 1981; Nicholls 1994: 11-12; D'Costa 1990; Dupuis 1991; Knitter 1996; Dhavamony 1998). All of the christological questions posed with such force by Russell Aldwinckle (1982) almost two decades ago remain today. Who is Christ? Exclusive mediator? Constitutive mediator? Normative or perhaps even non-normative mediator (cf. Schineller 1976)? Is an absolute–relative Christology possible (cf. Thomas 1985)?

The situation is compounded when it is realized that any attempt to answer these questions may effect—and sometimes drastically so—other theological loci. Exclusivists, inclusivists and pluralists, ecclesiocentrists, christocentrists, theocentrists and soteriocentrists—each has to deal with the validity in applying christological norms to the extent of God's saving grace and love, the character and modality of the Kingdom of God, the presence and activity of the divine Spirit, the task and mode of Christian evangelism and missions, the depth of human depravity and sin, the quality of divine revelation, the means and reach of salvation, the relationship between creation and fall, and between the orders of creation and redemption. These are only some of the many interrelated issues that confront any Christian attempt to formulate a theology of religions. Further, the tensions between universal salvation and particular Christ, between prevenient grace and evangelism and missions, between biblical universalism and dogmatic election and predestination, continue to intensify (cf. Braaten 1987–88). All of these issues are important, Lesslie Newbigin reminds us, because they bear upon truth—theological and objective truth apart from our personal idiosyncrasies or 'values' (1989: 54). It is clear from the discussion in this chapter that Christology is central both to the construction of a Christian theology of religions and to its problematic. The christological dilemma confronts us with the crucial historical, existential and soteriological question, 'Who do people say the Son of Man is?' (Mt. 16.13).

None of these questions can be avoided, whether we are ecclesiocentrists, theocentrists or soteriocentrists, or even if we were to take an anthropological starting point (Surin 1983). As the preceding has shown, exclusivists or ecclesiocentrists surely have the historical and dogmatic tradition behind them in erring on the side of particularity and emphasizing the intrinsic connection between the Church and the person and work of Christ; yet they are also surely strained in having to answer questions about the destiny of those in non-Christian traditions or about the mode of salvation for the unevangelized. Inclusivists or christocentrists have been more successful in holding together both God's universal salvific will and the particularity of its expression in Jesus; yet not only does such a position still smack too much of theological imperialism, but questions of how such axioms are linked to the concrete religious traditions still have to be addressed. Pluralists or theocentrists opt first for the universality of the divine love and revelation; but most Christians are convinced that the cost paid in fundamental christological convictions is too steep. And just as God the ultimate mystery cannot be reduced to a set of abstract categories which are then filled out with conceptions of the ultimate in the different faiths, so is the category of salvation just as ambiguous and resistant to the proposals of its pluralistic advocates. The whole christological question is, after all, whether or not Christ is *the* savior or just *a* savior.

But what if we were to begin elsewhere, let's say, with the doctrine of Spirit? Surely, there is no doubt that the christological question would be merely postponed, not entirely dismissed. Eventually, Christology and pneumatology must be understood within a broader trinitarian framework (cf. D'Costa 1990: 16-29; Badcock 1997a: 267-73). Yet it would be intriguing to explore in that light how the Word and Spirit accomplish and mediate the salvific gift of the Father, both separately, if discernible, and in tandem. It is even the case that such may be a clue toward bringing together particularity and universality. But perhaps there is something that would be gained in postponing these discussions and focusing first on pneumatological issues and categories. Some theological space may be cleared in the meanwhile such that when the christological question reappears, there will be a different sort of playing field by which to pursue a resolution to some of these issues. Come Holy Spirit, shine your light upon our path…

Chapter 3

A PNEUMATOLOGICAL APPROACH TO THE RELIGIONS

My mother has never driven an automobile. There was one day when I was in either second or third grade when my father got caught up with some church business and forgot to pick me up after school. I waited out in the school parking lot for about three hours before he finally came by. I sat silently in the car on the way home, holding in my tears, while my father apologized for 'coming so late' (he's always been somewhat absent-minded). When I finally got home, I rushed up to mother and grabbed onto her and let it all out. Her holding me tight made me feel much better after a while. Somehow, this incident seemed to contribute to my understanding of God the Father as distant and of God the Spirit as our 'Comforter' (*parakletos*). But who was this 'Holy Spirit'? We had always been taught that the Holy Spirit was the Spirit of Jesus. The mode of spirituality I was raised in may have been pneumatic and charismatic, but its object was always clearly Jesus. I may have felt comforted by the Holy Spirit, but this consolation was always imaged by the arms of Jesus and symbolized by his presence. In many ways, ours was and is a Jesus-centered spirituality. There are many non-trinitarians within our tradition who call themselves 'Jesus-only' Pentecostals.[1] Our faith is thus central-ized on Jesus: the Spirit of God mediates the person and work of Jesus into our lives. So, the Spirit of God is also, or more accurately, is rather, the Spirit of Jesus—no more, no less! Or is that really the case?

Introduction

Albert Outler was surely both prophetic and short-sighted in an article anticipating the Seventh Assembly of the World Council of Churches titled 'Pneumatology as an Ecumenical Frontier' (1989). He was clearly insightful into the latent and untapped potentialities pneumatology held for the Church's ecumenical relations; he simply either overlooked or

---

1. Or better, 'Oneness' or 'Apostolic'. This latter is now the preferred label, especially among its academics and educated laity. I will briefly discuss this stream of Pentecostalism later.

just missed the fact that interreligious ecumenism had come to be as important as inter-church ecumenism, and that there has been a growing awareness that our understanding of the Holy Spirit plays a crucial role in these larger conversations. This is especially the case given the discussion in the preceding chapter. The Christian dialogue with other religious traditions has stalled at the christological impasse on more than one occasion, and theologians have struggled to resolve the christological dilemmas facing their proposals regarding how other faiths fit into the divine plan.

This chapter will focus on the emerging pneumatological paradigm in Christian theology of religions. I will trace in Section 1 its gradual development during the past three decades in the initial proposals by the Orthodox Metropolitan George Khodr and others, and focus on the related issue regarding the *filioque* that has been raised in the process. Section 2 will deal with more recent efforts to retrieve and refocus in a pneumatological direction the thought of two theological giants from a prior generation: Karl Rahner and Paul Tillich. Throughout this chapter, it will be argued that those who have made attempts toward a pneumatological understanding of the religions have stalled on one of two fronts: they have either returned to or been constrained by the christological dilemma, or they have failed to make a convincing case insofar as they have not been able to deal adequately with the issue of how the Spirit's presence and activity in other traditions is to be discerned. Much, however, can be learned from them, as can be learned from others who have contributed to the interreligious dialogue from a pneumatological perspective such as Michael Lodahl; the last section will focus on his efforts as a means by which to test the thesis argued in this chapter.

1. Promise and Problems in a Pneumatological Theology of Religions

Early Efforts: An Overview

The first person to suggest explicitly a pneumatological interpretation of the question posed by non-Christian faiths to Christian theology was George Khodr, Metropolitan of the Mount Lebanon Diocese of the Greek-Orthodox Patriarchate of Beirut, Lebanon.[2] This was the sub-

---

2. This entire sub-section summarizes material that I have covered elsewhere in greater detail (see Yong 1998b).

stance of his address to the Central Committee of the World Council of Churches (WCC) regarding the challenge of 'dialogue with people of living faiths' at Addis Ababa in 1971. His talk, titled 'Christianity in a Pluralistic World—The Economy of the Holy Spirit' (1971), was a direct inspiration to others—initially Samartha (1974), and later Knitter (1991)—to begin looking at pneumatology as a point of entry for an understanding of other faiths.[3] At the same time as Khodr but independently of him, Jacques Dupuis, was working in India and moving from the cosmic–Christ model brought to center stage by Vatican II toward a 'cosmic economy of the Holy Spirit' framework for understanding other faiths and for the interreligious dialogue (1977). Cumulatively, their efforts make evident both the promise of a pneumatological theology of religions and the problems associated with it.[4]

The entire objective of shifting to a pneumatological framework in order to understand non-Christian faiths is premised upon the recognition that there is a distinction between the economy of the Son and that of the Spirit relative to the redemption of the world. This is what Irenaeus called the 'two hands of the Father'. In its original context, the distinction was somewhat artificial in that the Bishop of Lyons was discussing the human composition of soul and flesh as deriving from 'the likeness of God, and moulded by His hands, that is, by the Son and the Holy Spirit, to whom also He said, "Let Us make man" ' (*Against Heresies* 4, Preface, 4). Irenaeus's intention, however, was to polemicize against the gnostic devaluation of the body. In defense of the incarnation of the Son, he thereby drew a valid and theologically significant distinction between the economy of the Son and that of the Spirit: it was the mission of the Son to be incarnate and to secure redemption through his life, death and resurrection; it was the mission of the Spirit

3.   Other theologians—considered below—who have explored a pneumatological approach to the religions also point to Khodr's address as that which launched this most recent movement (cf. Raiser 1989: 384). For an overview of Orthodox pneumatology, see the essay, 'The Holy Spirit in Orthodox Pneumatology' by the Lebanese Archbishop Aram Keshishian (in *idem*, 1992: 39-54).

4.   Khodr himself has unfortunately never developed his thesis any further, while the other three have written extensively on the topic of theology of religions even if not necessarily from a pneumatological perspective (e.g. Dupuis 1991, 1997, and Samartha 1990, 1991 [cf. the excellent summary of Samartha's work by Klootwijk 1992]; I discussed aspects of Knitter's *theologia religionum* in the previous chapter).

not to be incarnate, but to apply the redemption secured by the Son to the world. As it turned out, because Irenaeus elaborated at great length on the economy of the Son in *Against Heresies*—rightly so, given his concerns—and because later tradition has emphasized the conjunction and reciprocity between the Word and the Spirit, this distinction has been overlooked in the history of Christian thought, at least in the West.

Khodr's suggestion, echoed by Samartha, Dupuis and Knitter, is that a retrieval of Irenaeus's theological metaphor allows us to recognize the different economies of the Word and the Spirit. More important, it provides an altered theological landscape by which to understand the religions. No longer would they be strangers residing outside the chris-tological arena (Christ and the Church), but they can be legitimately recognized as dwelling within the province of the Spirit. While spatial imagery would be simplest to employ in understanding this distinction, I submit that such would be too simplistic and misleading. If reduced to spatial constructs, the economy of Christ can be conceived as demarcat-ing the boundaries of the Church and its mission, while all other institu-tions, social forces or religio-cultural realities not touched by the Church would be considered as being on the 'outside'. The economy of the Spirit in such a conception would then be considered to be 'larger' or 'broader' than that of the economy of the Word. Yet this threatens not only the reverse subordination of the Son to the Spirit, but perhaps also the dissolution of the economies from each other.

More appropriate would be to begin by recognizing the economies of the Word and the Spirit as overlapping dimensionally.[5] This allows for the interrelationship as well as distinction between both economies to be further defined as we gain theological, ontological and historical pre-cision. At the same time, non-Christian faiths can be understood as belonging to both economies, but in different respects. For starters then, it allows that they be conceived in pneumatological terms, related but not subordinated to or redefined by the economy of the Word. Within the Orthodox framework of Khodr's *theologia religionum*, the history of salvation is not defined ecclesiologically but rather in terms of the divine mystery of creation. In his words, 'the economy of Christ cannot be reduced to its historical manifestation but indicates the fact that we are made participants in the very life of God Himself. Hence the refer-

---

5.   I prefer to think in terms of dimensions in part, following Tillich (1963a: 15-17), because the notion of dimension does not spatialize or hierachicalize reality but rather recognizes its unity above the conflicts.

ence to eternity and to the work of the Holy Spirit. The very notion of economy is a notion of mystery' (1971: 123).

The theological advantages that flow from the pneumatological theology of religions suggested by Khodr can be briefly outlined. Whereas the failure to appreciate the distinction between the economies of the Word and Spirit may lead to an emphasis on the historicity of the incarnation relative to salvation and the non-Christian faiths, a pneumatological approach would accentuate the supra-historical event of the resurrection and underscore the eschatological relationship between salvation and the religions. Whereas not distinguishing between the divine missions may lead to defining the religions in ecclesiological terms, an explicit pneumatological framework would define both the Church and the religions within the common ground of the cosmos, or, theologically speaking, the Kingdom of God. Further, whereas an ecclesiological approach would see the religions as lying outside the history of salvation, a pneumatological approach would view the Church as a mediatorial instrument—and not the *only* instrument, it should be emphasized—of the Spirit's work of salvation. The view of the Church as being the first fruits of the company of the saved (1 Cor. 15.22) rather than the final contingent would then allow a redefinition of mission as well. Focus would not lie as much on conversion across religious lines—thus confirming the dualism between Church and world, culture and other faith traditions—as on transfiguration of the non-Christian faiths from within via the germination of the Gospel seed through the power of the Spirit. A pneumatological theology of religions may in fact assist in reducing feelings of religious or cultural superiority vis-à-vis those in other faiths and promote a more humble and Christ-like attitude, thereby allowing genuine interreligious communication and the sharing of the Gospel to proceed. For Khodr, 'the supreme task is to identify all the Christic values in other religions, to show them Christ as the bond which unites them and his love as their fulfilment… Our task is simply to follow the tracks of Christ perceptible in the shadows of other religions' (1971: 128).[6]

---

6.   I need to qualify what is said here in two ways. First, my summary of Khodr's address does not do justice to the nuances that permeate his own understanding of the relationship between the divine economies nor does it give enough space to the intricate ways that both missions relate to the religions. Second, I am purposefully accentuating the promise of a pneumatological approach to the religions in this synopsis even though I am aware that the christological dilemma

In short, failure to differentiate between the two economies inevitably risks the subordination of the mission of the Spirit to that of the Son and ultimately to an ecclesiological definition of soteriology. Acknowledging the distinction, on the other hand, enables a robust trinitarian and cosmological understanding of soteriology to emerge in the long run. While such a framework gives the implication that theological resolution has been found, this is deceiving. Much can be said about the religions if what is said remains within the realm of theological abstraction. A theology of religions that does not touch upon the historical traditions and concrete beliefs and practices of the faithful in the various traditions, however, will not really say much of substance in the long run. In short, to say that the Holy Spirit is both present and at work in the non-Christian faiths is one thing. It is quite another to say where and when the Spirit is present, and how or through what beliefs, practices, etc., the Spirit is at work.

The main issue related to a pneumatological theology of religions now comes to the fore: the problem of discernment.[7] It surely cannot be the case that everything that exists in other traditions is of the Holy Spirit. How then can we tell if and when the Holy Spirit is present and at work in other faiths? What are the criteria by which we can discern such presence and activity? More importantly, what safeguards exist against confusing the presence and activity of other spirits with that of the Holy Spirit, and, vice versa, confusing the presence and activity of the Spirit with that of other spirits (committing blasphemy against the Holy Spirit)? A Christian theology of *religions* needs to engage the actual religious realities about which it pontificates. The task of explaining where, when and how such realities are related to the divine plan therefore necessarily requires theological discernment.

It may be the case that the Christian criteria for discerning the Spirit's

---

confronting theology of religions today cannot be blamed solely on the failure to distinguish between the two economies. I am only trying to establish at this juncture that this failure is one, if not the dominant, source of the impasse, in order to render more plausible that a pneumatological approach is a promising way out.

7.   I have argued at greater length elsewhere (1998b, 1999b) that the issue of discernment is *the* key question confronting a pneumatological theology of religions. That discernment is the central question to pneumatology is also the driving motif behind Tim Gorringe's *Discerning Spirit* (1990). Gorringe, however, focuses not on the religions but on the Spirit's presence and activity in community, sexuality, politics and art.

presence and activity is and can only be christological, and that this is what aborted the pneumatological projects of Dupuis, Samartha and Knitter. All three reverted to books on Christology and the religions after preliminary explorations in the form of articles and essays in a pneumatological direction. Yet because none of them explicitly identify this problem as the driving rationale behind their return to Christology, I would suggest that they lacked the experiential and theological categories needed to sustain their efforts thereby bowing to the pressures exerted by christological issues almost by default.

On the other hand, the case of the charismatic Baptist theologian, Clark Pinnock, demonstrates a sustained move in the opposite direction: from a christological theology of religions towards a full-length systematic pneumatological theology. Pinnock himself does struggle just as mightily with the problem of discernment, and I will return to his work below in Chapter 6 when I am further along in developing that kind of pneumatologically discerning *theologia religionum* that is missing in the work of Samartha, Dupuis and Knitter. Yet it is important to mark here that the resources for a pneumatological theology of religions have yet to be explored in all their depths and that perhaps criteria can yet be discovered that are not overly constrained by christological issues. But is that, however, theologically feasible? This issue brings us to the heart of the trinitarian question. In order to begin formulating a response, it will be necessary to explore further the dogmatic significance of the distinction between the divine missions by focusing on the doctrine of the *filioque*.

Orthodox Theology and the Dogmatic Issue of the Filioque

Khodr himself does not explicitly mention the *filioque* in his address. He does, however, quote with approval the statement from the Orthodox theologian, Vladimir Lossky, that 'Pentecost is not a "continuation" of the Incarnation, it is its sequel, its consequence: ...creation has become capable of receiving the Holy Spirit'; Khodr concludes that 'the Spirit operates and applies His energies in accordance with His own economy and we could, from this angle, regard the non-Christian religions as points where His inspiration is at work' (1971: 126). Lossky, as is well known, had fervently argued that the doctrine of the *filioque* was what was most responsible for the subordination of the economy of the Spirit to that of the Son, resulting in the dominance of ecclesiocentrism in the theology of the Western Church. In contrast, he delineated the distinction between the divine missions which enabled Orthodox ecclesiology to be equally informed by Christology and pneumatology (see Lossky 1957).[8]

What, however, is at stake on this doctrine? *Filioque* applied to the doctrine of the procession of the Holy Spirit refers to an understanding of the twofold origins of the Spirit: from the Father 'and the Son'. Of utmost importance at this stage of the discussion is that a pneumatological theology of religions must address the question of whether or not the Holy Spirit proceeds from the Father alone, as the Eastern Church has argued in maintaining the priority of the Father, or from the Father *and the Son*, as the Western Church has traditionally countered in attempting to avoid what they consider to be an Arian strain in the tradition to demean the divinity of the Son. There are, of course, exegetical, dogmatic and historical issues that separate East from West regarding the doctrine of the *filioque* (Heron 1980: 66-73). The last, historical issue, should be considered separately from the other two, especially in light of the fact that there is a general theological consensus between East and West today that the *filioque* was inappropriately inserted into the Creed. Many theologians and even denominations have conceded on this basis that the *filioque* should be removed or at least not allowed to remain a hindrance in ecumenical relations between the two communions (cf. Vischer 1981; Stylianopoulos and Heim 1986).

Ralph Del Colle (1997), however, has reminded us that the exegetical and dogmatic questions bring to the fore two central theological issues: the monarchy of the Father and the intent of the *filioque* regarding the intra-trinitarian relations. To begin with, while the biblical data does assert both the hovering of the Spirit over creation as well as the speaking of the divine word in the creative act (Gen. 1.2-3), it is also clear

8. Catholic theologians such as the Dominican Yves Congar have acknowledged the validity of Lossky's criticisms to a large extent. Yet in defense of the Catholic reception of the *filioque* Congar has also warned against arguing on the basis of artificial constructions: 'we should not, surely, make a list of what we like and call it pneumatology and then of what we dislike and call it Roman Catholic juridicism!' (1986: 117). At the same time, however, historically, Orthodox trinitarianism has enabled a more open attitude toward other faiths than has Western theology. Khodr cites historical instances of such openness among the medieval Nestorians and Persians. A more contemporary example is the indigenous Kenyan Greek Orthodox Church; see, e.g., their Constitution and Rules in Githieya (1997: 238).

both that the Spirit is 'from the Father' and that the Spirit is also sent by the Son or sent by the Father in the name of the Son (John 14.16, 26; 15.26; 16.7). This has, over time, led to a host of proposed resolutions, including five alternative formulae submitted by the Faith and Order Commission of the WCC in a 1979 Memorandum:

- the Spirit proceeds from the Father of the Son
- the Spirit proceeds from the Father through the Son
- the Spirit proceeds from the Father and receives from the Son
- the Spirit proceeds from the Father and rests on the Son
- the Spirit proceeds from the Father and shines out through the Son.[9]

What is clearly agreed upon is the Father as the originating source of the Godhead. What is contested is the precise relationship between Father and Son relative to the procession of the Spirit, even if such a twofold relationship is undisputed.

Del Colle's solution is in part to resort to a Spirit-Christology by which to 'cognitively follow the inner logic of the Christian experience of grace, its deep trinitarian structure...relative to the procession of the Holy Spirit' (1997: 214).[10] He argues that 'knowledge of the Spirit is derivative, based on prior christological knowledge' (1997: 214), even though 'ontologically, the Holy Spirit is the ecstatic contact person between the Father's revelation of the Son and humanity' (1997: 215). On this basis, he addresses the *filioque* by proposing the following thesis on the trinitarian relations:

> The ecstasy of God's flowing forth (Spirit) from God as unoriginate source (Father) in relation to Godself (Son) and to the world of creatures (divine economy) presupposes in the inner life of God the expression of love bestowed and exchanged. The outpouring of that divine ecstasy toward the world in kenosis and plentitude is already the fruit of that which is a life-giving and neverending love (1997: 217).

9. For the text of the Memorandum, see Vischer (1981: 3-20).

10. My choice of Del Colle as a conversation partner follows from the fact both that he is not only an acute Roman Catholic theologian but also a practicing charismatic, and that his own 'deep trinitarianism' presents a formidable contrast against which I will need to articulate my own doctrine of the Trinity. Del Colle has also done some excellent work on relating his Spirit-Christology (1994) to the trinitarian structure of Pentecostal–charismatic experience (1992, 1993, 1996b) which I return to in later chapters.

I am very sympathetic to various aspects of Del Colle's proposal. At the same time, I want to register two protests. First, even while granting preliminarily to Del Colle that a deeper knowledge of the Holy Spirit presupposes a knowledge of Christ, I think it is undeniable that the possible experience of the divine apart from an explicit knowledge of Christ supports the contention that there is an experience of the Spirit that is not explicitly christological. The ancient Israelite experience of Yahweh was certainly mediated by the Holy Spirit, whom they recognized only as the 'divine breath'. Can we be so certain that present day Jewish and Muslim experience of the divine is not that of the Holy Spirit? I do not think Del Colle would insist on that; he would probably reply that any genuine experience of the Spirit ultimately retains a christological character. While such is much more acceptable, I would still push the prior question surfaced by the theology of religions: how does the Spirit work here and now in non-Christian faiths? It seems to me that defining our pneumatic experiences only christologically closes the door to any further development of a theology of religions since a dogmatic response simply vitiates the empirical encounter. I would want to withhold dogmatic judgment until we have had adequate opportunity to test this hypothesis regarding the pneumatic character of religious experience against the evidence.[11]

My second objection centers on a reluctance to distinguish between the immanent and economic Trinity. Following the Eastern Orthodox distinction between the unknowable divine essence and the perceptible divine energies, and those in the tradition of apophatic theology, I would argue not only that it is unprofitable to speculate on the intra-trinitarian relations, but that such relations are legitimately understood only within the framework of the divine economies of creation and redemption. This is not only sound biblically in terms of exegesis, but also theologically in taking divine revelation to be concerned with our salvation, and philosophically with regard to our understanding of the God–world, time–eternity, and one-and-many relations. The benefits of the *filioque* debate reside not in the light it sheds on the divine nature *ad intra*, but on the doctrines of creation and salvation. I would therefore want to radicalize Karl Rahner's axiom—'the Trinity of the economy of salvation *is* the immanent Trinity and vice versa' (1970)—in the

---

11. Of course, it is much easier for me, a classical Pentecostal raised in an environment inhospitable to creeds and the dogmatic tradition, to withhold such judgment than it is for Del Colle as a faithful Catholic!

direction of the divine economy while emphasizing that there is nothing further that can be known about God in Godself apart from what has been revealed in creation. In doing so, I would retain language about the 'immanent' Trinity only if by that we are talking about the mystery of creation, redemption and glorification as manifesting the essential nature of the divine reality, and not about internal or social communion among divine 'persons' abstracted from relations with the world or pushed behind the veil of a primordial eternity.[12]

My own reading of the present discussion regarding the *filioque*, then, is that there is sufficient ambiguity regarding the trinitarian relations as related to the divine missions such that not only should we resist dogmatism on this matter, but on the contrary, that necessary theological space is opened up for further reflection on the relationship between the Word and the Spirit precisely on this account. There is, on the one hand, a perichoretical relationality that is at the heart of the divine relation to the world: the economies of the Word and that of the Spirit are mutually related, and should not be subordinated either to the other. On the other hand, rather than being understood as being interdependent only upon each other and thus implying mutual definition, the divine missions should also be seen both as dimensionally affiliated and thus implying autonomy in relationality and vice versa, and as somehow commonly originating in the mystery of the Father. I am optimistic that a more thorough theological investigation of the distinction between the divine economies, perhaps against the background of theology of religions, may in fact pay off later in shedding some light on matters related to the trinitarian relations as I have interpreted them.

If pushed to state a formula, my preference would be the first alternative of the Faith and Order Memorandum.[13] Following Moltmann's

12. I have previously advanced aspects of this position (Yong 1997), and will elaborate further in the next chapter when I develop a foundational pneumatology.

13. My decision seems to be in line with Pentecostal intuitions as summarized in a fine discussion by Gerald Sheppard: 'pentecostals would find the Eastern Orthodox critique foreign in language but more familiar in content than that of the West' (1986: 413). I find further implicit support from the Latin American Pentecostal, Eldin Villafañe (1993: 183). The charismatic, J.R. Williams (1990: 153), opts for 'from the Father through the Son', *per filium*, the preferred formula of the Eastern Church. This is admissible so long as it is understood that there is no subordination of the mission of the Spirit to that of the Son. The Eastern starting point of the distinct trinitarian hypostases prevents them from this error.

repeated reminder that the Fatherhood of God is established only in the relationship between the first and second members of the Trinity (Molt-mann 1981a: 182-85, 1981b: 167, 1992: 306), I would thereby opt for an economic interpretation of this relationship and proceed from there to defend the Spirit's procession. This approach would support the quest for a pneumatological contribution to theology of religions. Recognition of the procession or mission of the Holy Spirit into the world relative to, yet distinct from that of the Son provides theological space that is greatly needed at the present time for reflection on the place of the religions in the economy of the Spirit.

Preliminarily then, a pneumatological theology of religions that validates the distinction between the economy of the Word and Spirit holds the christological problem in abeyance. For now, it is sufficient to grant that there is a relationship-in-autonomy between the two divine missions. For heuristic purposes, however, we will seek to investigate the religious dimensions of the Spirit's economy with the intention that christological issues will not be discarded forever. By so doing, I hope to avoid the mistake of Samartha, Dupuis and Knitter alike in returning too quickly to Christology. Again, it is not that Christology is unimportant or that the economy of the Spirit can be considered completely autonomously from that of the Son. It is just that the domination of the latter can be reasserted prematurely, before the pneumatological approach to the religions has been duly assessed and its value ascertained. At the same time, while this may mean that it would be legitimate for Christians to begin searching for the presence and activity of the Holy Spirit in non-Christian faiths, practices, beliefs, rituals and scriptures, the issue of discernment ensues again. Because there are potentially as many spirits operative in the world as there are religious traditions, if not more, how can a theologian of religions discern where, when and how the Holy Spirit is present and at work in the non-Christian faiths? It is at this juncture that the efforts of Dupuis, Samartha and Knitter in formulating a pneumatological theology of religions have faltered.[14] While they have asserted the ubiquity of the Spirit in the realm of human religiousness, they have failed to be sufficiently discriminating of actual faith traditions in order to support their theological assertions. More recently, the work of Rahner and Tillich has been proposed as being suggestive of a pneumatological theology

14. Pinnock, who I discuss later, also fails in this regard; Khodr does not even broach the question.

of religions. Can this situation be at least partially remedied by recourse to their work?

2. *Potential Resources from Mid-Twentieth Century Theology*

Karl Rahner and Paul Tillich are two of the most important theologians of this century. Rahner reflected extensively on a theology of religions while remaining faithful to the main lines demarcated by Vatican II, while Tillich was moved in the years after he concluded his *Systematic Theology* to consider rewriting it against the horizon of the history of religions. Of late, however, students of their thought have retrieved aspects of their theologies as suggestive of a pneumatological approach to the religions. In examining both of these recent efforts as well as the original material with which they worked, the two questions that emerged from the preceding discussion are posed: (1) Are there in the theologies of Rahner and Tillich resources by which to frame a more satisfactory understanding of the relationship between the 'two hands of the Father' vis-à-vis the religions? (2) Does either theologian, implicitly or explicitly, provide some criterion by which to discern the presence and activity of the Spirit in the other faiths?

Karl Rahner

The broad outline of Rahner's theology of religions was discussed in the previous chapter. Recently, however, Joseph Wong and Gary Badcock have built on this to make some intriguing suggestions regarding a pneumatological orientation in Rahner's *theologia religionum*. While Wong credits Rahner as inspiring a 'pneuma-christocentric' approach to the non-Christian faiths in view of the 'special role played by the Holy Spirit in mediating between the salvific design of God and the Christ event, as well as between this particular event and its universal saving significance' (1994: 619), Badcock emphasizes that Rahner's theology 'must be conceived to be primarily and decisively a theology of the Holy Spirit' (1997b: 149) in light of the fact that it is the Spirit that enables the human reception of divine grace and the self's experience of existential transcendence. While these are somewhat familiar themes, yet both Wong and Badcock also raise the previous question about the connection between Rahner's Christology and pneumatology as it relates to those in other faiths and to their religious traditions.

In his book *The Trinity* Rahner states his preference for the formula 'the Spirit proceeds from the Father through the Son' (1970: 66). He then opts to view Father, Son and Spirit as being 'relatively distinct' (1970: 68-73).[15] By this, on the one hand, Rahner means a logical rather than ontological relation in order to avoid tritheism. He thus follows the *filioque* in terms of understanding the distinction as deriving from the begatting of the Word and the proceeding of the Spirit: the relations consist in the communication of the divine essence from the Father 'to the Son and through the Son to the Spirit' (1970: 73). At the same time, on the other hand, he does clearly state that 'when treating of the economic Trinity, we are concerned with two distinct yet related ways (they determine each other, yet they constitute a *taxis*) of the free gratuitous self-communication of God to the spiritual creature in Jesus Christ and in the "Spirit" ' (1970: 83). By this, emphasis is placed on the freedom by which the Word was incarnate, and by which the Spirit descended at Pentecost—both of these free acts correlating with the freedom by which God has communicated Godself to us.[16]

While this is evidence of the close connection between Christology and pneumatology in Rahner's theology, yet this does not so far really tell us much about the Holy Spirit. Generally, Rahner speaks of the world being 'drawn to its spiritual fulfilment by the Spirit of God, who directs the whole history of the world in all its length and breadth towards its proper goal' (1979c: 204). More specifically, the Holy Spirit is the person which we engage in the depths of our existence and through whom we understand that 'God (hence the Father) *really* communicates *himself* as love and forgiveness, that he produces this self-communication in us and maintains it by himself. Hence the "Spirit" must be God himself' (1970: 67).[17] But did not the Holy Spirit mediate the gracious revelation of God to the ancient Israelites? If so, how does

15. Rahner favors the language of 'distinct manners of subsisting' to that of personhood for the Trinity (1970: 103-15), but nevertheless does use personal pronouns in his own theological writings. I will follow his usage in discussing his work, but will later submit my own preferences on this matter.

16. Badcock rightly notes that for all his insistence on the axiomatic equation of the economic and immanent trinities, Rahner refrains on speculating about the latter from the former (1997b: 150).

17. Rahner is here only speculatively elaborating on the dogmatic position of Vatican II: '...the Holy Spirit offers to all the possibility of being made partners, in a way known to God, in the paschal mystery' (*Gaudium et spes* 22).

the activity of the Spirit differ since the incarnation of the Word? Recognizing the full force of this question (cf. 1971b: 193-95), Rahner differentiates the hovering of the Spirit before Pentecost from the Spirit's descent at Pentecost, the latter the result of the release effected by the work of Christ (1971a: 189). Following his early theological theory of symbolism in which being actualizes or expresses itself as another, he suggests that 'the Church is nothing else than the visible manifestation of the Spirit in the world' (1971a: 187).[18] At Pentecost and in the creation of the Church, the bestowal of the Holy Spirit is then final, irrevocable and eschatological (1971b: 197). Ultimately, Pentecost releases the activity of the Spirit in the world which both clarifies definitively and incisively to individuals the obligation to accept responsibility for creaturely freedom and provides the grounds for absolute trust in the face of mystery (1971b: 198-201).

In the economy of salvation then, the Spirit 'brings about the acceptance by the world (as creation) in faith, hope and love of this self-communication' (1970: 86; cf. 1981: 41). Rahner characterizes these further as the ability provided by encounter with the Spirit to accept the claims upon human existence: the claim of the other for our absolute love, the claim of death for our exercise of faith in its face, and the claim of the future for our reaching forward in hope (cf. 1979c: 222-24). These experiences must necessarily be mediated at least in part through the religions. For Rahner, the

> institutions and theoretical objectifications [of] non-Christian religions can be categorial mediations of genuine salvific acts, both because they always retain some truth (at least the postulate of a transcendentality of man beyond the field of his immediate experience) and also because even false and debased religious objectivity can be a way of mediating a genuine and grace-given transcendentality of man (1983b: 294).

These elements of Rahner's theological anthropology and theology of religions thereby combine to allow Rahner to state not only that 'Christ is present and efficacious in the non-Christian believer (and therefore in the non-Christian religions) through his Spirit' (1981: 43; cf. 1982: 316-21), but also that 'anonymous Christians' are those who are 'justified by God's grace and *possess* the Holy Spirit' (1976: 291).

Can we recognize such states or processes in those of other faiths? Do, for example, experiences of religious *enthusiasm* imply the pres-

---

18. I will return to Rahner's 'The Theology of the Symbol' (1966) in the next chapter.

ence and activity of the Spirit?[19] Because this engagement with God is
an existential one that 'operates within human consciousness', this
means that enthusiastic experiences are expressions of 'natural, human
capacities which appear elsewhere in the history of religion taken as a
whole...to be found in a more or less pure, confused or distorted form
in every religion' (1979a: 39). Discernment of spirits is all the more
consequential. Yet Rahner is pessimistic about discernment focused on
the phenomenology of charismatic or enthusiastic experience since any
such encounter with the divine occurs within the depths of the human
soul even as mediated via both cognized and uncognized categorial
objects.

At the same time, Rahner does suggest that because expressions of
enthusiasm necessarily include a minimal experience of transcendence,
'in the totality of the phenomenon of religious enthusiasm there occurs
an experience of grace' (1979a: 44). This means that the 'critical
analysis of the categorial content of religious enthusiasm does not
necessarily place in question the basic experience of grace and of the
Spirit' (1979a: 48). Rather, the discerning of spirits in general and of
the Holy Spirit in particular is an ambiguous affair. It should begin with
the recognition that the experience of the Spirit is fundamentally the
experience of liberating grace. Rahner goes on to list in his essay
'Experience of the Holy Spirit' (1983d) some 'arbitrarily and unsys-
tematically selected examples' of how the presence and activity of the
Spirit can be identified. These include unrewarded acts of forgiveness
or unappreciated good deeds, the expression of basic and absolute trust
in the face of hopeless existence, the attempt to respond in love to God
in spite of the perception of divine silence or indifference, the hearken-
ing to one's innermost conscience, the renunciation of sin or evil, the
endurance of hopelessness, the faithful pursuit of responsibility, the
sincere cry toward God from one's inmost being, the faithful acceptance of death, and so on (1983d: 200-203). In all of these circumstances, our response is indicative of the Spirit's presence. However,
the 'criteria' outlined here are rightfully subjective in their existential-
ity: there is practically no means by which to objectify human attitudes
such as to be able to say conclusively, 'Here we have the Holy Spirit,

19. By *enthusiasm*, Rahner means to include all sorts of charismatic, mystical,
or other kinds of ecstatic phenomena; it is a general label by which he gathers a
number of different types of spiritual and religious experiences. I follow Rahner's
usage at this point.

and not another!' Pneumatology provides Rahner no true criteria, but only suggestive indicators of possible appearances of the Spirit's presence and activity. As Wong summarizes,

> wherever persons surrender themselves to God or the ultimate reality, under whatever name, and dedicate themselves to the cause of justice, peace, fraternity, and solidarity with other people, they have implicitly accepted Christ and, to some degree, entered into this Christic existence. Just as it was through the Spirit that Christ established this new sphere of existence, in the same way, anyone who enters into this Christic existence of love and freedom is acting under the guidance of the Spirit of Christ (1994: 630).

This provides a good general theological rule for discernment, but is such helpful theologically when confronted with empirical situations?

It is true that as a dogmatic theologian, Rahner is satisfied with general theological criteria to assist in the processes of discernment: 'conformity to the general message of the Gospel, to Scripture, to the faith and mind of the Church' (1979a: 49). Ultimately, however, Wong's labeling Rahner's theology 'pneuma-christocentric' rather than 'christo-pneumacentric' provides a key to understanding that Christ is the central criterion for discerning the Spirit's presence and work.[20] Following the logic of the *filioque* as identified by Orthodox critics such as Lossky and Khodr, pneumatology is ultimately put at the service of Christology even if the distinction between the two missions is articulated. The discernment of spirits both in the history of religions and in the interpretation of the human transcendental experience of God, is ultimately possible only as established by the criterion of Christ (1982: 57; 1983b: 295). As Rahner puts it,

> Jesus is the 'cause' of the Spirit, even if the reverse relationship is equally true, as is the case in unity and difference, and the mutually conditioning relationship of efficacious and final causes. Since the efficacious cause of incarnation and cross (i.e., the Spirit) has its goal within itself, as inner entelechy, and fulfils its own being (as communicated to the world) only in the incarnation and cross, the Spirit is from the outset the Spirit of Jesus Christ. Since this Spirit always and everywhere sustains justifying faith, this faith is from the outset, always and everywhere, a faith that

---

20. In other words, Rahner's system turns finally on Christology, not pneumatology. Note that neither the words 'Holy Spirit' or 'spirit' appear in the main text nor detailed table of contents to Rahner's magnum opus, *Foundations of Christian Faith* (1982)!

comes into being in the Spirit of Jesus Christ, who is present and efficacious in all faith, through this Spirit of his (1981: 46).[21]

Yet Rahner's failure to develop more adequate pneumatological criteria should not be held against him given the centrality of Christology
in his system. He did, after all, repeatedly reiterate that his intention
was not to provide a posteriori assessments of the religions (e.g. 1977:
32; 1979a: 35-36; 1982: 312-13; 1983a: 122). To say then that the main
problem with Rahner's theology of religions is his a priori approach as
a dogmatic theologian is to say that we are saddling him with our own
concerns. He has consistently suggested that others would need to work
extensively with the history of religions in order to test the fruitfulness
of his theological framework (e.g. 1981: 49-50; 1982: 321; 1983b: 294-
95).[22] Rahner should not therefore be expected to supply any more than
dogmatic criteria to judge the religions since such was not within the
horizon of his work as a theologian. Instead, it may be more appropriate
to place emphasis on his 'Christology of quest' as he himself labeled it
(1979c: 220-22). This quest is that in search of the *memoria* of faith
directed toward Jesus Christ as the absolute savior (1982: 318-21).

21. Since the cross did not, in Rahner's view, alter the dispositions of a previously wrathful God but rather only followed from the universal love and grace of
God, Badcock misreads Rahner as advocating Christ as only revealing the salvific
will of God rather than effecting it (1997b: 148-49). Wong (1994: 620-22) is closer
to the mark in seeing Rahner's Christology as both constitutive—being, in Rahner's
words, the 'final cause' of our salvation—and normative—in that the cross is not an
arbitrary but a 'real symbol' of God's saving grace (e.g. Rahner 1981: 46; cf.
Rahner 1966: 214-15). More specifically, Rahner prefers to think of the incarnation
in terms of 'sacramental sign causality' following Vatican II's naming Christ '*Ur-
sakrament*' and in line with the notion that in this life, the ambiguity of divine and
human freedom in history was overcome and salvation finally secured (1979c: 214).
I highlight this as an important distinction since there is in this framework of 'final'
or 'sacramental' causality much greater room to recognize the indispensability of
the economy of the Spirit in salvation history that is somehow accomplished and
yet not in the incarnation.

22. In a brief effort at comparative theology using Rahner's categories as a
springboard, Wong suggests both that the Tao as *Wu* giving birth to *Yu* corresponds
to the divine mystery and its gracious self-communication to the world, and that
Yin and Yang correspond to Logos and Pneuma as the two modes of the divine
self-communication (1994: 634). This is a good beginning, but far more work needs
to be done on the polyvalence of religious symbols than is undertaken by Wong in
order to even begin to articulate such conclusions. I propose to take up elements of
this task in the remainder of this study.

Thus, Rahner submitted both that 'saviour figures in the history of religion can certainly be viewed as signs that...[humankind] gazes in anticipation towards that event in which his absolute hope becomes historically irreversible and is manifested as such', and, that perhaps even an '*a posteriori* religious history of the presence of Jesus Christ in all religions would draw the dogmatic theologian's attention to implications in his own doctrine of that presence which he had hitherto overlooked' (1981: 50). The onus is thus placed on those of us who do not consider ourselves to be limited to dogmatics to pick up where Rahner left off. Yet, I want to pause before doing so to query others for further tools by which to accomplish our task.

Paul Tillich
During the last five years of his life, even while attempting to complete his *Systematic Theology* (the third volume appeared in 1963), Paul Tillich's joint seminars with Mircea Eliade at the University of Chicago convinced him of the need for a 'longer, more intensive period of interpenetration of systematic theological study and religious historical studies' in order that 'the structure of religious thought might develop in connection with another or different fragmentary manifestation of theonomy or of the Religion of the Concrete Spirit' (1966: 91). By the latter, Tillich meant the confluence of three types of experiences of the sacred: the sacramental where the Holy appears in the finite and the particular, the mystical which resists the 'demonization' of the sacramental (its objectification for manipulative purposes), and the prophetic that moves from the Holy to the 'ought to be' in quest for peace and justice (1966: 86-87). In these experiences of the Holy, a clearly dynamic understanding of religion is assumed whereby there is a movement from the engagement with the sacred to its objectification to a self-correcting mystical or prophetic criticism only to re-engage the Sacred again. Tillich thereby terms his a 'dynamic-typological' approach to religion but acknowledges that he is not satisfied even with such an account (1966: 86).

We catch a further glimpse of what Tillich was thinking about in his Bampton Lectures of 1961. Beginning with the definition of *religion* as 'the state of being grasped by an ultimate concern, a concern which qualifies all other concerns as preliminary and which itself contains the answer to the question of the meaning of our life' (1994: 3), he goes on to argue that such concerns take many forms: theistic, non-theistic,

global, local, secularistic, humanistic, as well as quasi- or pseudo-
forms of 'religiosity' (such as nationalisms, Fascism or Communism—
what Leonard Swidler more recently and appropriately terms 'ideologies'). In a further sub-category, however, there are 'religions of the
Spirit' like Protestantism and early Christianity insofar as such are 'free
from oppressive laws and, consequently, often without law altogether'
(1994: 7). 'Religions of the Spirit' are thus most conveniently contrasted with institutionalized traditions, legalistic faith expressions and
authoritarian forms of religious hierarchies. They are also frequently
dominated by mystical or prophetic types of experiences and expressions, thus capable of being judgmental of both other and of self. The
central criteria for such judgment for Christianity—and, Tillich would
not be hesitant to argue, for other traditions as well—is 'the way of
participation in the continuing spiritual power of...the appearance and
reception of Jesus of Nazareth as the Christ, a symbol which stands for
the decisive self-manifestation in human history of the source and aim
of all being' (1994: 51).[23]

Is the economy of the Spirit thereby subordinated to that of the Word
in Tillich's theology of religions? While we may think that such was
the extent of Tillich's ruminations about theology of religions, Pan-
Chiu Lai's recent book helps us see these Bampton Lectures as an
important background to the last installment of *Systematic Theology*.

---

23. This perhaps reflects remnants of the 'neo-Orthodox' strain in Tillich's
theology, being parallel in some respects to Barth's christomonistic view of revelation as the abolition of religion. To some degree, Tillich understood what Barth
was after in designating religion as human efforts at achieving salvation (cf. Tillich
1957: 80-86). However, the shift Tillich introduces removes the aspect of the 'abolition' emphasized by the early Barth and replaces it with a more Hegelian *auf-
gehoben* whereby Christ as the New Being 'takes in' that which is positive in other
traditions even while criticizing and 'removing' their negative elements. For
Tillich, 'in the depth of every living religion there is a point at which the religion
itself [in its institutionalized forms] loses its importance, and that to which it points
breaks through its particularity, elevating it to spiritual freedom and with it to a
vision of the spiritual presence in other expressions of the ultimate meaning of
man's existence' (1994: 62). The important difference between Tillich and Barth,
however, resides in their contrasting views of revelation. Barth emphasized Jesus as
the only genuine revelation while Tillich understood revelation in inclusive terms:
'the final revelation, the revelation in Jesus as the Christ, is universally valid,
because it includes the criterion of every revelation and is the *finis* or *telos* (intrinsic
aim) of all of them' (1951: 137); more on this below.

Lai suggests that not only is pneumatology the 'central theme for Til-lich's theology of the 60s' (1994: 115), but also that it is the key to Tillich's emerging theology of religions during this same period of time. In fact, Lai goes on to argue that Tillich's shift from a christocen-tric theology in volume two of *Systematic Theology* to a pneumato-centric theology in volume three was of such gigantic proportions that key elements of his Christology were called into question such that Til-lich could only lament, 'the system crumbles. What shall I do?' (quoted in Lai 1994: 116). Tillich did not live long enough to work out the details, even if he did grant in the preface to volume three that new organizing principles could shed light on neglected elements of a theo-logical system, perhaps resulting in a completely different method.[24] Lai's proposal, however, is suggestive for one of the two questions that we want to ask Tillich: how did Tillich see these two components of Christology and pneumatology fit into his overall system? If in fact there was a break in his thinking between volumes two and three of *Systematic Theology*, what was the shape of this rupture? To get at this question, it needs to be recognized that whereas in contrast to Rahner who proceeded from a transcendental anthropology, Tillich worked from an existential philosophy.

Tillich's system was initially erected on what he called a method of correlation (1951: 59-66). This approach allowed the questions to be posed by the current situation, informed primarily, given Tillich's understanding of religious matters as that which matters to us ultimately, by the depths of our existential concerns; theology in turn provided the answers to these questions. These answers come to us via divine revelation, by which Tillich meant both that such is beyond our own means of attainment and that such grasps us in the depths of our being. As Tillich understood it, revelation that meets us at such exis-tential depths is necessarily salvific (1951: 144-47), if we take such to be a gradual process of conversion and healing of our own self-aliena-tion, our estrangement from others and our reconciliation to God.

Against this background, Tillich understood the final, decisive and ultimate theological answer to be the revelation of Jesus the Christ as the New Being. Lai rightly points out that in the first two parts of *Systematic Theology*, Tillich labored to develop the universal implica-

---

24. This may mean, Tillich resignedly lamented, a 'new conception of the structure of the whole. This is the fate of every system' (1963a: 4). What follows should clarify Tillich's dilemma.

tions of a Logos-Christology. He recognized that the tension between 'the absolutely concrete and the absolutely universal' is central to Christian theology (1951: 16). Jesus as the Christ bridges the gap between particularity and universality precisely by disowning the particularity of his own being. By doing so, however, the New Being also bridges the tension 'between Christianity as a religion and Christianity as the negation of religion', accomplishing such by liberating himself

> from bondage both to a particular religion—the religion to which he belonged has thrown him out—and to the religious sphere as such; the principle of love in him embraces the cosmos, including both the religions and the secular spheres. With this image, particular yet free from particularity, religious yet free from religion, the criteria are given under which Christianity must judge itself and, by judging itself, judge also the other religions and the quasi-religions (1994: 52).

Tillich clearly felt confident that such an understanding of the Logos-Christology was able to secure the universal saving will of the divine mystery. The solution provided by the New Being had to be universal because the human predicament is universal (1957: 86). This universality, however, found more emphatic expression in Tillich's pneumatology elaborated in volume three. Here, a profound interpretation of life and its ambiguities forms the framework by which Tillich discusses the doctrine of the Spirit, what he calls the Spiritual Presence. Religion, as the depth dimension of life, is also fraught with ambiguities, demanding our discernment between the Holy and the secular, the divine and the demonic. Our historical existence permits only an ambiguous manifestation of the Spiritual Presence. As such then, all healing, possible only through the creation of the New Being in the individual, community, or world by the power of the Spiritual Presence, is also necessarily fragmentary (1963a: 280-82).

Discerning the Spiritual Presence is therefore a complex undertaking. Fundamentally, Tillich suggests that 'the Spiritual Presence is fully experienced only when...the mind is grasped in ecstasy' (1963a: 143).[25] This experience is at the root of the prophetic calling, allowing the

---

25. Tillich understands *ecstasy* to be synonymous with 'the state of being grasped by the Spiritual Presence' (1963a: 112); more specifically, it refers to any experience whereby the self is transcended, where 'reason is beyond itself, that is, beyond its subject–object structure' (1951: 112). This latter definition allows us to see at least in part why it is difficult to cognize or discern such experiences of the Spirit.

prophetic denunciation of institutionalized (read profaned or demonized) religion. For such ecstatic-turned-prophetic religion, 'the Spiritual Presence is the presence of the God of humanity and justice' (1963a: 143). Humanity and justice thereby emerge as distinctive criteria by which to discern the Spiritual Presence.[26] Other marks of the Spiritual Presence are to be found in the Spiritual Community, Tillich's preferred language for the Church. These include what have been traditionally conceived as the 'marks of the Church': love, faith, holiness, unity and universality (1963a: 155-57). Its universality flows out of the Pentecost event, 'expressed in the missionary drive of those who were grasped by the Spiritual Presence' (1963a: 151-52). From this, it also follows that 'there is no Spiritual Community without openness to all individuals, groups, and things and the drive to take them into itself' (1963a: 152).[27] This openness characterizes the essential trajectory of the New Being which determining features in human lives and communities include increasing awareness, freedom, relatedness and self-transcendence (1963a: 231-37).

At a more concrete level, Tillich did enumerate a number of other more 'conscious and noticeable manifestations of the Spiritual Presence' in his sermon, 'Spiritual Presence'. These include being led to prayer, relieved from anxiety, filled with courage to be, made to love, etc. In light of this, Tillich asks, 'who can say that he is in no way a

26. Justice is really the only normative principle that is articulated by Tillich in his second Bampton Lecture on 'Christian Principles of Judging Non-Christian Religions' (1994: 17-32).

27. In conceiving the Spiritual Community, Tillich has recourse to a distinction similar to Rahner's 'anonymous' and 'explicit' Christian in that the former speaks of 'latent' and 'manifest' stages of the Spiritual Community (1963a: 152-55). These parallel the traditional notions of invisible and visible Church. In an interesting twist, however, Tillich downplays any notion of linearity in his conception or any eschatological fulfillment of the latency of the Spiritual Community. Rather, the unstructured, uninstitutionalized and 'non-churchy' character of the 'latent' Spiritual Community is precisely that which enables its truly universal realization. Tillich does speak of 'ultimate salvation' and of 'ultimate revelation', and insists that such must overcome all the fragmentariness and ambiguity of life (cf. 1951: 147). Yet it would be a mistake to see him as advocating an historical realization of the Kingdom of God. Instead, his own understanding of the 'end of history being the elevation of the temporal into the eternal' provides a more consistent lens by which to understand Tillich's existentialism: the universality of the Spiritual Presence truly reveals the New Being and provides salvation to each person, community and moment of reality that is integrated into the divine life.

bearer of the Spirit? ...the Spirit is not bound to the Christian church or any one of them. The Spirit is free to work in the spirits of men in every human situation, and it urges men to let Him do so; God as Spirit is always present to the spirit of man' (1963b: 86-87).

Tillich seems to have had a rather well-developed criteriology for discerning the Spiritual Presence. Yet it is at the same time also fundamentally ambiguous given its existential categorial framework. What is unambiguous, however, is Tillich's insistence, finally, on the criterion of the New Being as manifest in Jesus the Christ. This is plainly articulated even in the third volume of *Systematic Theology* where Tillich develops his Spirit-Christology. True, Tillich does distinguish between the Jesus as the Christ, the Word of God and the biblical words, thereby insisting that 'the Spirit judges all commandments' (1963a: 268). Yet he insists at the same time on the biblical words as *the* criterion by which to identify 'the false elevation of human words to the dignity of the Word of God... Nothing is the Word of God if it contradicts the faith and love which are the work of the Spirit and which constitute the New Being as it is manifest in Jesus as the Christ' (1963a: 125). There is thereby a link established between the Spirit, the New Being in Jesus as the Christ and the biblical word of God. The Spirit has both preceded Jesus in the history of revelation and salvation as well as shaped the person of Jesus the Christ. Tillich thus clearly states that in Jesus as the Christ, 'the New Being appeared as the criterion of all Spiritual experiences in past and future' (1963a: 144). It is 'not the spirit of the man Jesus of Nazareth that makes him the Christ, but...the Spiritual Presence, God in him, that possesses and drives his individual spirit' (1963a: 146). Following the Apostle Paul then, 'the Lord is the Spirit' (2 Cor. 3.17), and as such, guides our own discernment of the Spirit's presence. In two revealing statements which deserve to be quoted in full, Tillich states

> In the divine economy, the Spirit follows the Son, but in essence, the Son *is* the Spirit. The Spirit does not himself originate what he reveals. Every new manifestation of the Spiritual Presence stands under the criterion of his manifestation in Jesus as the Christ. This is a criticism of the claim of old and new Spirit-theologies which teach that the revelatory work of the Spirit qualitatively transcends that of the Christ. The Montanists, the radical Franciscans, and the Anabaptists are examples of this attitude. The 'theologies of experience' in our time belong to the same line of thought. To them progressive religious experience, perhaps in terms of an amalgamation of the world religions, will go qualitatively beyond

Jesus as the Christ—and not only quantitatively, as the Fourth Gospel acknowledges. Obviously, such an expectation's realization would destroy the Christ-character of Jesus. More than one manifestation of the Spiritual Presence claiming ultimacy would deny the very concept of ultimacy; they would, instead, perpetuate the demonic split of consciousness (1963a: 148).

Then, declaring himself in the strongest of Christian terms, Tillich writes that

the only historical event in which the universal center of the history of revelation and salvation can be seen—not only for daring faith but also for a rational interpretation of this faith—is the event on which Christianity is based. This event is not only the center of the history of the manifestation of the Kingdom of God; it is also the only event in which the historical dimension is fully and universally affirmed. The appearance of Jesus as the Christ is the historical event in which history becomes aware of itself and its meaning (1963a: 368-69).[28]

This description of the relationship between the economies of the Word and the Spirit is consistent with that contained in the earlier volumes of Tillich's *Systematic Theology*.[29] Why then does Lai think that there is such a substantive transformation in Tillich's theology from the second to the third volume of the system? Lai notes correctly that while Jesus as the Christ is ontologically dependent on the Spirit, the reverse is the case epistemologically (1994: 129). More importantly, however, Lai recognizes that the move from a Logos-Christology to Spirit-Christology, if not synthesized, calls into question Tillich's method of correlation (1994: 144). The Logos doctrine was initially understood by Tillich as the principle of universality that correlated the

28. What is interesting is that this criterion of Jesus the Christ as the decisive manifestation of the New Being did not find its way into the only record of Tillich's actual engagement with another religious tradition. In the 'Christian-Buddhist conversation' found in the Bampton Lectures (1994: 33-48), he speaks of the convergence of the idea of the Kingdom of God with Nirvana and compares and contrasts Christianity's emphasis on participation and agape with Buddhism's focus on identity and compassion. Perhaps Tillich's mention of 'preliminary ends' to the dialogue simply means that eventually, even if not in this particular dialogue, such criterion should and will come to the fore.

29. Tillich developed the 'New Being in Jesus as the Christ' as the 'material norm of systematic theology' in volume one (1951: 50), and further elaborated on this in volume two (1957: 118-37). He further urged in volume two the fulfillment of Logos-Christology in Spirit-Christology ('adoptionist Christology' as he called it in 1957: 149).

manifestation of the New Being in Jesus the Christ with our existential dilemma (1951: 16-17). The shift to a Spirit-Christology rightly calls attention to the arbitrariness of just why Jesus of Nazareth is the decisive manifestation of the Spiritual Presence. Lai's solution is to develop the trinitarian principles inherent but never fully articulated in Tillich's system in order to accommodate both the Logos and the Spirit-Christologies and thereby found a theology of religions. His hope is that a pneumatocentric understanding of revelation and the religions allows for a much more dialectical reading of the relationship between Jesus as the Christ and other faiths. It would, he argues, allow

> the divine manifestations apart from the Christ event to play a more important role in theological construction, including re-interpreting the Christ event. As history and dialogue go on, the Christ event may receive different meanings, even though the Christ event might remain the same yesterday, today and forever. The Christ event as the criterion for Christian understanding of God is not static. A re-interpreted Christ event may serve as a norm to re-evaluate other divine manifestations in history (1994: 169).

While I am as a whole in sympathy with this suggestion, I am less optimistic than Lai about its plausibility even within a reconstructed Tillichian trinitarianism given Tillich's overall orientation to the trinitarian doctrine. In the first place, like Schleiermacher, Tillich considered dogmatic formulations of the doctrine problematic and thereby relegated its discussion to the end of this system (1963a: 285-94). Secondly, there is clearly an apophatic notion of the divine life *ad intra* in Tillich: God is best understood as the ground of Being. This is the only thing predicable about God which is not necessarily symbolic and that allows some measure of literal application. Thirdly, Tillich's trinitarianism can be best acknowledged only within the framework of the economy of salvation. He clearly states in his sermon 'Spiritual Presence' that the meaning of the Divine Spirit is 'God present to our spirit. Spirit is not a mysterious substance; it is not a part of God. It is God Himself; but not God as the creative Ground of all things and not God directing history and manifesting Himself in its central event, but God as present in communities and personalities, grasping them, inspiring them, and transforming them' (1963b: 84). (On a related note, it should be mentioned that Tillich rejected the *filioque* not on dogmatic grounds—he considered speculation of the divine life *ad intra* unprofitable—but precisely because it domesticates, institutionalizes, and indeed legalizes the Spirit [1963a: 149]). Yet it also cannot be denied, fourthly, that this economic trinitarianism is tempered by a distinct binitarian strain in Tillich's understanding of the divine life *ad extra*— the conjunction of the economies of the Word and Spirit in the world. For Tillich, the Spiritual Presence brings about the New Being in the world (1963a: 138-40); similarly, the Logos is the trans-historical character of the New Being (1957: 89). In short, the economies of the Word and Spirit are better understood, finally, in terms of the one movement of Spirit and Logos to actualize the New Being and to bring healing to a fragmented and ambiguous world.[30] All of these combine in the end to block Lai's efforts.

Whereas Rahner's pneumatology works in conjunction with his theological anthropology and is suggestive of the possibilities open to humankind to receive or resist the gracious self-communication of God *effected* (even if only finally so) in the economy of the Word, Tillich's pneumatology places more emphasis on the almost interchangeable confluence of the Spiritual Presence and the New Being as *manifested* in Jesus as the Christ. Therefore, while there is finally no subordination of either the Word to the Spirit or vice versa in Tillich's theology, this may be in part the result of an implicit fusion of the two economies in the history of revelation and salvation. At the same time, however, the economic trinitarianism—seen in part in Tillich's system—is pressed into service in an explicit manner by Michael Lodahl and may point one way forward.

3. *Shekhinah/Spirit:*
An Initial Attempt at a Pneumatological Approach

An excellent test case for a pneumatological approach to theology of religions is the groundbreaking *Shekhinah/Spirit: Divine Presence in Jewish and Christian Religion* by Michael Lodahl (1992). It is the only

---

30. For corroborative evidence on this point, cf. Cooper's (1997) argument that Tillich here followed the Apostle Paul who did not clearly hypostasize the Spirit but rather understood Spirit and Christ in almost synonymous terms. To some degree I follow this development. Yet I also find that Tillich's concern here, if correctly identified by Cooper, is misplaced in that an existentialist metaphysics is not as concerned as an Aristotelian one about hypostatic relations in the immanent Trinity. Be that as it may, any movement toward binitarianism not only has to fight against the broad sweep of the history of Christian doctrine and thought, but is also counterintuitive to the overall thrust of this project.

book of its kind I am aware of in which pneumatology provides the primary interpretative framework for an interreligious encounter. The fact that it engages Christian theology only with the Jewish tradition would still leave many unanswered questions about how such a pneumatology would fare against religious traditions that are not as closely connected. Yet because a Christian pneumatological perspective is potentially replete with insights for the interreligious dialogue, Lodahl's endeavor should not be neglected.[31]

To begin with, however, it would be instructive to focus on Lodahl's metaphysical presuppositions. Part of the uniqueness of this book is the author's basic commitment to a relational view of the world following the process metaphysics of Alfred North Whitehead. He finds in Whitehead's philosophy a means by which to understand how God relates to and acts in the world. In the language of process philosophy, God and the world are mutually and dynamically related. God provides 'initial aims' by which to lure the basic elements of reality toward greater harmony. These elements, 'actual occasions', respond to a greater or lesser degree thus allowing for the recognition of freedom at the fundamental level of reality and for the emergence of novelty in the world. God and the world are thereby conceived in a dipolar or panentheistic fashion as mutually influencing the other, and as co-creators of the eternal process of becoming.

In this framework, Lodahl understands the concept of 'Spirit' to refer not to a 'distinct hypostasis either beside God or within the Godhead, mediating between God and the world, but to *God's own personal presence and activity in the world*' (1992: 41). The Spirit is that by which God leads or lures the world. Lodahl grounds this argument on the biblical tradition of creation, covenant and redemption, especially as

---

31. I have been delighted to discover that Lodahl comes from the Wesleyan-Holiness background, the primary tradition which birthed modern Pentecostalism at the turn of the twentieth century. My dialogue with Lodahl is thus an important one that can be assessed from a number of different angles. Unfortunately, to my knowledge, neither Lodahl's Wesleyan-Holiness colleagues nor Pentecostals or charismatics have reviewed this book. This is not surprising, however, given the general orientations within both movements toward Judaism in particular and non-Christian faiths in general. I also surmise that Lodahl's commitments to process theology render him suspect at least to those in the Wesleyan-Holiness tradition. There has otherwise been a range of responses to Lodahl. Bramlett (1993) has a positive review while Bockmuehl (1996) a more critical one. Rogers (1994) provides a more in depth summary of *Shekinah/Spirit* than what I do here.

understood in and through the Hebrew Scriptures. The Hebrew *ruach*, the Greek *pneuma* and its corollary concept *sophia*, and the Rabbinic *shekhinah* are all seen within this context. The last is taken specifically to refer also to 'God's exilic suffering in relationship to, and together with, Israel' (1992: 53-54). Understood within the broader history of Jewish thought, Shekhinah points to both the constriction of divine breath so as to allow for the creation of the other—as in the myth of *tsimtsum* in the Kabbalah literature which Lodahl also draws on—and to the confinement or concentration of the divine presence in a particular place and activity, namely the Torah and in its reading, study and interpretation, as conducted by the rabbis. From the human perspective, there arises in the conjunction of process and Rabbinic thought the understanding of the intrinsic role that we play along with God in the cosmic drama of creation, fall and redemption. This is equally applicable to Christians as well as non-Christians. It is clear that Lodahl wants to counter exclusivistic Christian claims that would limit the Spirit's presence and activity to a select ecclesiastical group. Rather, as he suggests throughout (e.g. 1992: 16, 66, 70), a process theology of Spirit as divine presence would foreclose any such understanding and insist instead on the universal presence and activity of the Spirit in the lives of human beings in other religious traditions.

But does Lodahl do justice to the intimate connection between the Spirit and the Word posited by traditional Christian theology? It is clear that he is much more interested in obtaining as much distance as possible from the dominance Christology has exercised over pneumatology and theology of religions in the history of Christian thought. Yet even while Lodahl eschews any notion of an immanent Trinity, he argues that a Spirit-Christology can be approached 'from above' 'as long as Jesus is not cut off from the religio-historical context of the Spirit's work in Israel. For it is God's adoption of Israel, and the Shekhinah's faithful calling of the people Israel to godly sonship and daughterhood through Torah, which provide a context for Jesus as the Christ' (1992: 154). Within this framework, the 'pneumatic moments' of the Gospel witness to Jesus can be identified: 'the primary actor in the gospels is not Jesus, but the Spirit of the God of Israel' (1992: 190). Lodahl argues as an extension of a Shekhinah or Spirit-Christology both that these can be understood only within the broader doctrine of creation and Israel's covenant history with Yahweh, and that they demand our existential response in obedience and faithfulness to the demands made explicit in the covenantal and christological paradigms. This call is especially important given our experience of the depths of evil such as that encountered in the Holocaust.

It is here that Lodahl correctly sees many of the problems facing contemporary theology converging. Within his model, and even in traditional understandings of the doctrine of the Holy Spirit, the divine presence is universal. Where then was the Holy Spirit in the death camps of the Nazis? How can the Spirit's presence be comprehended against the murderous acts of the *Muselmanner*, and against the cries of helpless women and children, many of whom, Lodahl is careful to point out, had converted to the Christian faith? Can it be said the absence of the Spirit in this situation was what paralyzed an entire civilization, with a few minor exceptions, from taking any concrete acts of redemption or from voicing any protests in the name of God? Or, is it closer to the truth to ask, following Emil Fackenheim, whether the 'Christian silence concerning the Nazis so deaden[ed] the voice of the Spirit that the Spirit is now in virtual exile?' (1992: 126).

The question is that which should by now be familiar, but which is thrust upon us in a much more radical way: how can we speak of the Spirit's presence much less discern it at all? Is it not better to discuss the Spirit's absence? If so, how is such recognizable? Lodahl resorts to a dialogue with three post-Holocaust Jewish thinkers, Martin Buber, Emil Fackenheim and Arthur Cohen, in an effort to allow these questions to confront us in their starkest reality. From Buber and his attempted retrieval of Hasidism, Lodahl finds reinforcement for the view of the myth of the Shekhinah's exile as symbolic of 'God's presence in solidarity with those who suffer' (1992: 112). As such, God is also in exile, longing for healing and fulfillment, and in need of redemption just as we are. While this is God's fate, it is also a sign of our responsibility to respond to the challenge of loving God more in order to accelerate the healing process. Yet Lodahl does note that of the three Jewish thinkers, Buber, writing closer to the historical event of the Holocaust than the other two, had not yet been able to internalize that reality as *tremendum*.

Fackenheim and Cohen both take seriously the possibility that such healing of the world is impossible in our post-Holocaust situation. For Cohen especially, the Holocaust defies interpretation, meaning and rationality. Both thinkers, however, retain the notion of divine presence in the world in spite of the experience of the Shoah even if such is only 'fragmentary' (Fackenheim) or 'passive' under the constraints of history (Cohen). The Holocaust can only be a radical disruption of the divine presence. Out of this rupture, Fackenheim is led to interpret God's relationship to the world not so much in terms of saving presence but more so in terms of commanding voice as heard especially at Mt. Sinai. Such a 'commanding voice' understanding of God also necessarily assumes, if not requires or makes possible, our free response. The evidence thus far is that this voice has been ignored or disobeyed far more than not. Far too often, Fackenheim points out, we have 'quenched the Spirit' (cf. 1 Thess. 5.19). Cohen echoes these reflections, albeit drawing more specifically from the theological tradition of 'divine speech' read within a Kabbalist framework. Creation being a gestational or emanental flow of God into the void (*tsimtsum*) means that evil is a real and potent threat to God and the world. As such, intimately connected to the divine speech is the human response. Redemption, which Cohen does not speak much of, must then reside in our hands. In this way, Lodahl summarizes that 'God's speech creates the conditions for, but does not dictate the particulars of, human existence and activity' (1992: 130). The real problem is now relocated from theodicy to anthropodicy: 'it is finally and irrevocably up to human beings whether or not creation is experienced as God's ongoing speech' (1992: 131).

From this dialogue, a portrait of 'divine vulnerability' emerges. The Kabbalist cosmogony understands the creation of the world in mythic terms precisely as the emergence of a void left by the divine withdrawal (the first moment), and then the emanation of 'anotherness' from the forms or 'vessels' of potentiality invested by God into the void and then shattered by the impact of the divine light (the second moment). From this cosmogonic rupture, the potential to bring about restoration or healing is given to human beings (the third moment). For the Jews, such potential is intimately linked with the giving of the Torah and in the ongoing reading, studying and application of it in life. The divine presence and the divine vulnerability are therefore both evidenced in the commanding voice of the Torah and in the risk that entails whereby we are drawn into the process of mending the world.

For Lodahl then, divine presence is decipherable only via a 'hermeneutic of exile'. The hope of an unequivocal perception of the divine presence in the historical process will be forever disappointed because of the disjunction between our theological notions of such and our experience. There is therefore no possibility of 'an unambiguous appre-

hension of pure existence, of a divine site which circumvents the necessity of human interpretation' (1992: 140). Our prospects for 'discerning
the Spirit' are thus best mediated through texts, especially the sacred
Scriptures. But these only suggest images of the fleeting movement and
activity of the Spirit in the world. What is thus needed is an 'imaginative reinterpretation of our texts and traditions in order, perhaps, to
hear anew the address of the Spirit of God' (1992: 141). This reading is
always tentative. It is, Lodahl insists (1992: 97-102) in agreement with
contemporary Jewish literary theorists like Derrida and Harold Bloom,
nothing short of a meandering quest for elusive meanings now that the
divine presence is only fragmentary, and—ironically—perhaps even
most clearly perceived in the commanding voice that comes out of our
experience of the abyss, out of the void and darkness of the absence of
divinity. As Lodahl puts it, 'the image of groping and stumbling in the
darkness is a graphic reminder of the inescapably ambiguous nature of
the unavoidably necessary task of human interpretation of God's presence as Spirit' (1992: 143).

There is much to appreciate in Lodahl's bold revision of themes from
the center and periphery of the Jewish and Christian theological traditions for this post-Holocaust interreligious pneumatology. I think this is
a kairotic book. It is laden with rich insights on our (in)ability to per-
ceive and to conceive both the divine presence and the divine absence.
Yet it is clear that as an exploratory proposal, there remain many questions that need further analysis and critics that will need to be appeased.
Let me propose three clusters of issues that converge on the pneumatological theology of religions which is being developed here.

First, as attracted as I am to the viability of Spirit-Christology for
theology of religions and the interreligious dialogue, the question needs
to be asked about the satisfactoriness of the way such is developed in
Shekhinah/Spirit. One is struck by the obvious reverse subordinationism at work in this book. Whereas in previous eras pneumatology has
been subservient to Christology, in Lodahl's reconstruction, Jesus
Christ is explicated wholly within a pneumatological framework. There
seems to be little that pneumatology gains from Christology in these
pages. By so doing, Lodahl succeeds in accomplishing his primary
objective, namely, removing the offense of the particularity of Jesus as
the Christ. Is this, however, not a complete capitulation of what is distinctive of Christianity to its 'parent' tradition? Does not the interreligious dialogue involve genuine give-and-take in order to effect a mutual

transformation? How does the person and work of Jesus Christ not only relate to but effectively transform the Hebrew notion of *ruach* or the Rabbinic notion of the Shekhinah? How does the descent of the *pneuma* at Pentecost—an event about which Lodahl is completely silent—in the form of *ruach* further shape our understanding of divine presence? How does the Christian claim that the gift of the Holy Spirit has been promised to all 'whom the Lord our God will call' (Acts 2.39) affect a post-Holocaust Jewish–Christian pneumatology? Does the view of incarnation as the goal of creation fracture the Kabbalist cosmogony or does the idea of Jesus the Messiah as paradigmatic of divine grace and presence contribute anything to the Rabbinic understanding of divine presence as a commanding word? Perhaps these concerns are beyond the purview of *Shekhinah/Spirit*. But it would certainly be too simple to answer the question 'who do you say the Son of Man is?' by categories that appear to be derived from an adoptionist Christology.[32] *Shekhinah/Spirit* thus sends out a clear warning of the danger of neglecting or subordinating the mission of the Son in any Christian theology of religions utilizing a pneumatological framework.

Secondly, while Lodahl is on the right track to suggest, following postmodern deconstructionists, that all understanding is situated and that all quests for meaning involve an endless stream of interpretation, yet it is strange that within the pneumatological framework of his book, Lodahl assumes rather than argues that religious experiences are only or primarily textually mediated. Against this interpretation of religious experience are the many voices throughout history who have claimed a direct intuitive, perceptive, experience of the divine.[33] This is the classic controversy most recently and eloquently articulated by George Lindbeck (1984). The problem here is not that Lodahl agrees with

32. In this regard, one of the first efforts to construct a full-fledged degree-Christology, that of G.W.H. Lampe's 1976 Bampton Lectures, is still instructive. In *God as Spirit* (1977), Lampe reinterprets traditional categories like the pre- and post-existence of Christ, rather than simply discarding them. Undoubtedly, theological advance in the last twenty years necessarily demands that we do not hold to his conclusions. The point is that Lampe's method both confronts the difficult christological issues and provides us with a more fruitful approach to dealing with them than does Lodahl.

33. This mystical experience is, in fact, central to the argument of Blair Reynolds's *Toward a Process Pneumatology* (1990)! While it may seem odd that Lodahl makes no reference to Reynolds's book, this is explained by the fact that *Shekhinah/Spirit* was originally completed as a doctoral dissertation in 1988.

Lindbeck's cultural-linguistic theory of religion but rather that implied in this agreement is the notion that our interpretation circulates around the text and never gets at what it claims to engage—the Holy Spirit. This assumption seems unwarranted. Textual or other mediation of experience certainly says nothing conclusive about the objective reality of what is experienced. Lodahl is less than clear on this point. This is most evident in his approval of Fackenheim's notion of divine presence as 'commanding voice'. Is the Holy Spirit symbolic only of our obligation before the divine? The sweep of the Christian tradition would certainly resist such a move. But can the Holy Spirit amount to more than this in Lodahl's economic trinitarianism?

This leads to the third problematic issue driving Lodahl's proposal: his fundamental reliance upon process theological categories by which to explicate divine presence and activity. Space constraints prohibit me from any extensive analysis of the deficiencies that encumber process theism.[34] Two, however, can be briefly noted. First is the ontological implications attending the process doctrine of creation. Lodahl does not claim to address this issue, but the process insistence of the interdependence of God and the world clearly runs afoul of what Schleiermacher had previously identified as our 'feeling of absolute dependence'. In theological terms, this is our experience of grace. The suggestion of eternally evolving cosmic epochs does not merit serious consideration given the difficulties confronting the theory of the oscillating universe (cf. Davies 1992: 50-54). Lodahl claims to do theology partly within the framework of a doctrine of creation (and partly within the framework of the historical experience of Israel), yet his metaphysics is unable to articulate any meaningful theory of ontological, as opposed to cosmological, creation.[35] This is therefore fundamentally a

---

34. See Gruenler (1983) for an evangelical theological rebuttal of process theology. Neville's (1995a) 'challenge to process theology' (subtitle) is the more powerful critique in that it comes from one who has appropriated much of Whitehead's metaphysics and especially cosmology in his own systematic philosophy even while rejecting the concept of God elaborated by process thinkers. Various aspects of Neville's philosophical theology play important roles in my own constructive formation in Chapter 4.

35. This relates both to the why and how there is anything at all, as opposed to the why and how any particular thing is. Process metaphysics and theology can answer the latter question but dismisses the former—unjustifiably so, in my opinion—as a meaningless inquiry.

metaphysical issue which, as will be shown later, has reverberations for the doctrine of the Trinity.[36]

The second metaphysical problem that arises out of the process doctrine of divine presence as construed by Lodahl is that in the process scheme, God does not and cannot unilaterally act in the world. Rather, divine action is better understood in terms of co-creation: God provides a lure, what Whitehead calls an 'initial aim' to each subjective occasion that can be accepted wholly or in greater or lesser degree, resulting in a concrescent occasion. The Holy Spirit, cast in these categories, is and can only be a universal presence since there can be no actualities without an 'initial aim'. What then do we make of the suggestion that there is in the divine presence a divine absence? The latter in Lodahl's theology is at best a psychological illusion or at worst an anthropological dilemma. The radical evil thought to be accounted for in the myth of the Shekhinah in exile turns out to be nothing more than the ineffectiveness of deity to substantively influence free agents and random events in the world.[37] Are there other, more adequate metaphysical models by which to conceive divine presence other than that utilized by process theology?[38] Perhaps not, but the question is worth asking.[39]

36.   The trinitarian theology of process thinkers such as Joseph Bracken (1995) is on much more solid footing than that proposed by Lodahl. Bracken's problem, however, is an over-reliance on a social model in his process reconstruction of the doctrine of the Trinity. I will formulate an alternative trinitarian model in the next chapter.

37.   Process theologians such as David Griffin have noted the desperate need in process theology for a more robust doctrine of evil and the demonic (1991: 2).

38.   One area of doctrine in process theology has led me to look elsewhere for a metaphysical conception of God adequate to the Pentecostal–charismatic experience. This has to do with the anemic eschatology that accompanies process theology's conception of divine providence predicated in terms of God luring the world. The concept of 'God as future' being developed by the Catholic process theologian, Lewis Ford, seems to be on the right remedial path. The centrality of hope as a theological and existential category in the Pentecostal orientation toward the future necessitates a metaphysics that is able to underpin a more robust eschatology. Another unrelated, more technical matter that is even more of a cause for concern has to do with God's inability to experience us in the depth of our existential subjectivities, given the process metaphysical thesis that only past 'actual occasions' can be prehended, whether by God or otherwise. Neville has pointed out that such runs 'contrary to the widespread experience of God as the most real part of ourselves' (1995a: 20). It also runs against the reverse intuition deriving from ecstatic religious experiences (like that claimed at times by Pentecostals and

Let me gather up the threads of this argument and sum up the progress made so far. The hypothesis presented in Chapter 1 was that the Pentecostal–charismatic experience of the Spirit could provide insight into the Spirit's presence and activity in the world such as to further the formulation of a Christian theology of religions. The contemporary discussion of *theologia religionum*, Chapter 2 endeavored to show, had stumbled over the christological dilemma: the almost irreconcilable axioms of God's universal salvific will and the historical particularity of Jesus of Nazareth as Savior of all persons. The beginning of this chapter initially gave us reason to believe the Eastern Orthodox emphasis on the distinctions between the divine economies of the Word and Spirit would enable us to understand the non-Christian faiths within a pneumatological rather than a christological framework. As the discussion developed, however, we discovered that even such an approach had its problems and pitfalls. The former included that of the difficulty of discerning the Spirit's presence and activity in the world of religions apart from the christological criterion; the latter included the moves generated to deal with the problem of discernment, whether it be the tendency toward a binitarian theology (as in Tillich's Spirit-Christology) or one toward a purely immanent trinitarianism (as in Lodahl's adoptionist Christology). In short, three clusters of questions can be seen to have emerged so far: the first concerns the Spirit's presence and activity in the world; the second queries the Spirit's relationship to the Son; the last seeks to comprehend the doctrine of the Spirit within the framework of the Christian trinitarian faith.

What is therefore needed is a foundational pneumatology—an under-

charismatics) that there is a direct encounter with transcendence (divinity) beyond the split between object and subject. More on this later.

39. Unfortunately, Lodahl's second book, *The Story of God: Wesleyan Theology and Biblical Narrative* (1994), does not pick up substantively on the themes in *Shekhinah/Spirit*. Lodahl does devote one chapter each to Logos- and Spirit-Christology in this later book which does begin to remedy some of the concerns noted above. But he appears to be distancing himself from process categories, and hardly touches at all on the dialogue he had initiated earlier with the Kabbalist tradition. Regretfully for our purposes, the motif of *divine absence* is not taken up. It is only hinted at when Lodahl suggests considering Job's Leviathan as a symbol of the chaos risked by God in creation (1994: 56-59). It is difficult for me to say whether or not Lodahl's *The Story of God* is representative of his own theological development or of his being somewhat constrained by teaching in a Holiness institution.

standing of the Spirit that is able to address all of these concerns. I suggest that such can be best accomplished via the development of a trinitarian metaphysics. This explication of how (the Spirit of) God is present and active in the world should necessarily incorporate elements of Rahner's theological anthropology, Tillich's method of correlation and existentialism, and Lodahl's retrieval of Shekhinah/Spirit. It should also not be hesitant to make revisions to these proposals where required. The trinitarianism to be developed should relate the missions of the Word and Spirit without identifying them. It should also be sensitive to the classical Christian concerns regarding the doctrine of the Trinity as well as the contemporary methodological issues that confront transcendental theology. Rahner, Tillich and Lodahl are all suggestive in some respects for this venture, and less so in others. Out of this metaphysical vision, what I will call a 'discerning charismology' can be developed—especially within the framework of the Pentecostal–charismatic experience—by which to differentiate the presence and activity of the Holy Spirit from that of other spirits. This may finally be an ongoing process of interpretation (but not necessarily limited to that of textual hermeneutics) that is saddled with subjectivity (Rahner) and ambiguity (Tillich). To determine this, however, would be to take up Rahner's gauntlet and to engage theologically in an a posteriori manner with the history of religions. This will be the assignment in Chapter 8. In the meanwhile, the next chapter will put us in a better position to accomplish our task if we are able to move beyond Rahner, Tillich and Lodahl to tackle some of the unresolved issues their work has brought to our attention regarding a pneumatological theology of religions.

Chapter 4

DISCERNING THE SPIRIT(S): TOWARD A COMPARATIVE
SYMBOLOGY OF DIVINE PRESENCE

My upbringing was probably typical of many raised in the Pentecostal
tradition. I was socialized into the distinctives of Pentecostal beliefs and
practices. This included an early indoctrination into the expectation of
speaking in tongues as the 'initial evidence' of the personal experience
of the baptism with the Holy Spirit. This baptism was explained to me as
the prerequisite for powerful Christian witness (Acts 1.8). My questioning this doctrine probably began during my teens when I discovered
there were other Christians who were not tongues-speakers, and who
seemed to have just as vibrant a Christian witness. I recall writing a
paper on it during my undergraduate program at a Pentecostal Bible
college, but did not conclude at variance with what my denomination
taught. After graduation, I was granted a license to minister by the
denomination. I later enrolled in a Wesleyan-Holiness seminary for my
masters degree in historical theology. In this environment, at some
remove from the secure confines of Pentecostalism, I returned to do a
more thorough study of the exegetical foundations of the 'initial evidence' doctrine. My conclusions this time led to a rather tentative skepticism. I was torn apart internally because I did not feel like I could with
Christian integrity continue as a minister in my denomination, especially
since all ministers had to sign a yearly affidavit pledging allegiance to
this distinctive Pentecostal belief (among others). And yet, the very
thought of leaving the roots and wellsprings of my identity was unnerv-
ing. I called one of my former Bible college professors who had remained
at the college even after completing his PhD in theology at a major university. Our conversation convinced me that I did not need to act hastily.
I am glad I persevered through this since I eventually found the necessary resources to enable me to retain my denominational affiliation. Part
of the theological apparatus which came to my rescue was George Lindbeck's functional understanding of doctrine set within a cultural-linguistic theory of religion: doctrinal propositions are the grammar which
provide the rules for religious communities and shape the spiritual

aspirations, expectations and lives of devotees.[1] But the trade off in exploiting Lindbeck's theory is that tongues-speaking, while normative as a sign for Pentecostals, is no longer the *sine qua non* for other Christians' reception of the Holy Spirit. Other signs, evidences and markers would have to be allowed to point to or identify this experience. But which ones? Other ecstatic experiences? Less ecstatic but charismatic type experiences such as among those enumerated by Paul as the 'gifts of the Spirit' (1 Cor. 12.8-10)? Or, would Pentecostals apologists eventually have to concede that it is, after all, the 'fruit of the Spirit' which counts for more in terms of evidencing the presence and activity of the Spirit? Clearly, within the cultural-linguistic framework, the experience of Spirit-baptism is not necessarily heralded by tongues-speech; recognition of the experience may require an extensive process of interpreting a multitude of signs, symbols and other activities. Whereas a literalistic reading of the initial evidence doctrine would make discerning the Spirit fairly straightforward, it was clear to me that the critical turn for Pentecostalism confronts us with the complexity of such a task. Is such a trade-off worthwhile? Will it be convincing to classical Pentecostals? More importantly, is such a conception of religion able to account for the Pentecostal–charismatic experience even while it sustains our critical engagement with other religious traditions? On a more personal level, will I have the patience and the grace that was bestowed upon me in my earlier time of crisis for the many theological anxieties that now plague my engagement with the non-Christian faiths?

Introduction

Over 40 years ago, Henry Van Dusen asked the question that is before us: 'What is the relation of the Holy Spirit in Hebraic-Christian faith to the Divine Spirit in other religions? Is the relation primarily one of kinship or of contrast, of continuity or of radical discontinuity?' He recognized that the answer proposed was a bold and radical one for his time:

...the Holy Spirit is the fulcrum of all aspects of religious faith, and, therefore, the one best ground for consideration of the vast complex of

---

1.   I was also initially assisted by Donald Johns (1991), who recognized that a second naïveté would not be satisfied with the theological methods employed to defend the doctrine by previous generations of Pentecostals. Johns' recourse to newer tools such as redaction criticism, narrative theology and a hermeneutics of linguistics and semiotics undoubtedly paved the way for my own appropriation of Lindbeck's work. I have since come to question various aspects of Lindbeck's theory, but nevertheless still think it provides a viable approach to understanding the Pentecostal doctrine of initial evidence. I will return to this topic in Chapter 5.

issues just listed—natural religion, revelation, the relations of Christianity to other religions, and of the various divergent and sometimes
contradictory understanding of Christian Faith to one another. And that
this is so because the Holy Spirit concerns, above all, man's experience
of the Divine, or conversely, the Divine's impact upon the souls of men;
it is God-near and God-at-work; it is the meeting place of the Divine and
the human (Van Dusen 1958: 91-92).

Unfortunately, Van Dusen did not flesh out this proposal. I will attempt
to do so by developing a foundational pneumatology in this chapter. My
approach will be to take up the problem outlined at the end of the last
chapter in the reverse order since the question of how the Spirit is
present and at work generally in the world needs to be addressed before
we attempt to determine if and how the Spirit is present and at work
specifically in other faiths.

What is needed, I will argue here, is a metaphysical framework which
will ground not only a pneumatological interpretation of the religions,
but also a general understanding of divine presence and activity. I will
attempt to understand the symbolic significance of the Spirit against the
backdrop of the fundamental hiddenness of the Spirit in mediating the
continuous, creative, providential and salvific activity of the divine
reality.[2] From this, a theology of the Spirit will be sketched against the
christological and trinitarian moments of speculative theology. The goal
here is to develop a trinitarian theology by which to understand the
relationship between the divine missions without subordinating either
the Spirit to the Son or vice versa. In short, the objective in Section 1
will be, in the broadest of strokes, an outline of a trinitarian
pneumatology within the frameworks of a philosophical theology of
creation and of the God–world relationship.

2.   I will periodically use the masculine pronoun in referencing divinity. Pro-
nominal designations of the divine are a complex and, in some quarters of Christendom, divisive issue. I am aware of the important issues raised by the feminist
critique, as well as the cogent arguments advanced by others about the appropriate-
ness of utilizing the feminine pronoun (e.g. Gelpi 1984). It is also possible that
there are legitimate Pentecostal and charismatic reasons to pursue this transition.
However, in this work on non-Christian faiths I am already rushing head-on against
the Pentecostal stream, and I think it wiser not to complicate matters by addressing
this issue only partially. Suffice to say that there are both biblical precedent for the
use of the masculine relative to Spirit (the Greek noun, *parakletos*), and, as I shall
later argue, philosophical reasons to use the personal rather than impersonal pronouns when referring to deity.

Whereas Section 1 grounds the universal character of the Spirit's presence and work, Section 2 specifies how the Spirit can be present and at work in the realm of the religions. A pneumatological theology of religious symbolism will be developed that builds upon the foundational pneumatology. To get accurately at the religious symbols of other traditions will require a sophisticated comparative theology. This is in part what will enable a discernment of the Spirit's presence and activity in other religious traditions. The fundamental elements of this comparative theological method will therefore be briefly outlined in Section 3. The overall success of this monograph depends in large part on how well the argument in this chapter is developed. Whereas up to now I have been more or less content with a descriptive catalog of the labors of others, it is now time to advance the constructive argument central to this study.

1. *Divine Presence and Activity in the Christian Tradition: The Symbol of the Holy Spirit*

The objective in this chapter is to develop a foundational pneumatology, a theology of the Holy Spirit which is able to account for the presence and activity of God in the world.[3] This is an ambitious task since neither the notion of divine presence nor that of divine activity is unambiguous. This is especially the case in a world of religious pluralism since there are some traditions that lack a personalistic concept of God who acts in the world. A foundational pneumatology therefore presupposes the rethinking not only of theology proper but also of cosmology. It aspires to correlate the idea of God with that of the world: God should be the kind of reality that is able both to be present and to act, and the world should be the kind of thing that is able to be the locus of divine presence and activity. Before launching into the heart of the argument, however, a brief word needs to be said to clarify further the kind of *foundationalism* that is being attempted here.

Securing Shifting Foundations:
Toward a 'Pneumatological Imagination'
Mine is by no means the first attempt to construct a *foundational pneumatology*. Such was explicitly undertaken by the charismatic Jesuit

---

3. Elsewhere, I develop the argument for a foundational pneumatology in greater detail (see Yong 2000a).

theologian, Donald Gelpi, in *The Divine Mother: A Trinitarian Theology of the Holy Spirit* (1984). At this juncture, two things about Gelpi's book and work should be noted. The first is his commitment to a non-foundationalistic epistemology. This derives in part from his overall project of developing an inculturated theology in dialogue with the North American philosophic tradition stretching from Edwards and Emerson through Brownson, Abbott and Santayana, to Peirce, Royce, James and Dewey (cf. Gelpi 1988). Under the tutelage especially of the pragmatism of Peirce and his successors, Gelpi came to question the transcendentalism and a priori methodologies of neo-Thomists such as Rahner and Lonergan that he imbibed in his Jesuit training, and moved in the direction of a fallibilistic epistemology and empirical theology. Both moves are to be applauded. My own foundational pneumatology follows Gelpi in eschewing the strong Cartesian foundationalism that bases all beliefs ultimately on self-evident intuitions. It proceeds instead from what Peirce called a 'contrite fallibilism' wherein all knowledge is provisional, relative to the questions posed by the community of inquirers, and subject to the ongoing process of conversation and discovery.[4]

The *foundational* element in Gelpi's pneumatology then, is not primarily epistemological. Gelpi himself builds on the work of Lonergan

---

4.   In another place, I discuss at length the value of Peirce's method of inquiry for theology (Yong 2000b). I am aware that my appropriation of Peirce, Gelpi and others doing theology in conversation with the philosophic tradition may be a 'turn-off' to many Pentecostals and charismatics who would be inclined to take scriptural texts like Col. 2.9 literally. Even if they do not object on that basis, their complaint might also be that Gelpi 'employs such a wide range of philosophical approaches that he undercuts basic communication with most of those interested in a theology of the charismatic renewal' (Lederle 1988: 117). Yet Pentecostal–charismatic scholarship has grown in sophistication. There is a greater openness today than in the 1970s and 80s to seeing both the value and the need of rethinking not only theological but also philosophical categories for the experience of the Spirit. At any rate, foundational theologies, targeted as they are to the widest possible public, cannot escape the philosophical element which is concerned with methodological and presuppositional issues (cf. Tracy 1981: 3-98). I am taking the calculated risk that Pentecostals and charismatics are ready to enter into conversations with all parties interested in the subject matter. Further, as I suggest below, to argue for the truth of Pentecostal–charismatic beliefs and practices in this larger public would require an enlargement of their horizons of discourse.

who argued for foundations as one of eight functional specialties intrinsic to theological method (Lonergan 1979). The details of Lonergan's work need not detain us here; what is of import for him and Gelpi is the role of conversion in providing theology with foundations. Conversion, whether limited to intellectual, moral and religious dimensions (Lonergan), or taken to include affective and socio-political dimensions as well (Gelpi), both enlarges the horizons of one's ability to comprehend and integrate theological data and produces the needed transformation of soul such that one takes responsibility for one's theologizing relative to oneself and one's religious community. In this way, conversion supplies the foundation or indispensable pathway through which theology must eventually proceed. In its most basic form, for example, the idea of conversion suggests that one cannot theologize truthfully if one has never been disposed in any way to God to begin with.

Gelpi also has taken Lonergan's notion of foundation further in seeing conversion as a subset of the category of experience. His own appropriation of the North American philosophical tradition has allowed him to see the value of formulating a theory of experience which is potentially universal in scope, and applicable not only to human beings but also to God (1984: 82-102). The capability of such a theory to account for the experience of conversion generally and Christian conversion more specifically lies at the center of his theology of the Holy Spirit. 'Foundational' is thus employed in Gelpi's pneumatology as suggestive of the fundamental category of reality, including God, as descriptive of human experience, and as prescriptive or normative for the ways in which Christians (and others) should (eventually) experience God.

What is essayed here will be merely a sketch of a system when measured against Gelpi's accomplishments. While I incorporate some of his ideas, my own attempt to forge a foundational pneumatology differs from Gelpi's in two ways. First, whereas he has focused on the concept of experience and developed it primarily to account for the human experience of God, I employ the notion of foundation to emphasize the public nature of truth and to undergird the idea that the categories to be developed are potentially universal in scope and application. Such a rationality, however, would be tempered by an fallibilistic epistemology even while it emerges from the ongoing dialectical conversation between self-rationality and what David Krieger calls 'other rationality' (1991).[5] Such a revised (post-)foundationalism is required in order to ground a stronger theory of truth not relativized by cultural-linguistic worlds or perspectives. This is especially urgent given the claims and counterclaims of truth and the plenitude of falsity in the world of religions.

The second way in which the foundational pneumatology presented here differs from Gelpi is that of emphasis. Christian conversion is central to Gelpi's foundational pneumatology. What informs the foundationalism developed here, however, is not so much Christian conversion as it is a 'pneumatological imagination'—a way of seeing God, self and world that is inspired by the Pentecostal–charismatic experience of the Spirit.[6] It needs to be clearly acknowledged up front that the

5.   Krieger argues for the potential meaningfulness and truthfulness of theological truth claims across cultural-religious lines by means of a universal method of argumentation and a universal hermeneutics. He draws from Panikkar's diatopical hermeneutics, Karl-Otto Apel's ethics of discourse, Habermas's communicative action, Gadamer's philosophical hermeneutics and even Gandhi's pragmatics of non-violence, all in an effort to construct a theory of intercultural communication. The key for Krieger, however, is the later Wittgenstein's notion of finding our own reasonableness via the confluence of *other-rationality*—a notion embedded in the windows of language games open toward a universal horizon, thus allowing and in fact actually inviting correction in order to maintain rationality. Gelpi would want to insist that rationality and experience not be understood dualistically, and I concur. I do, however, think that Gelpi's own emphasis on a broad construct of experience at times overwhelms the process and activity of cognition. I hope to preserve both in what follows.

6.   The phrase 'pneumatological imagination' was coined by Professor Lucien Richard, who, upon reading the first draft of this chapter back in the summer of 1998, understood my project correctly as a parallel quest to that forged by David Tracy in his reflections on the 'analogical imagination' (1981). Professor Richard has graciously allowed me to claim the phrase as my own. I should, however, emphasize that I use the term 'imagination' in a slightly more technical sense than Tracy, in that I see it more as a synthetic process which bridges elemental perception and cognition in human experience (cf. Neville 1981: 139-76). The antifoundationalist critique therefore means only that classical foundationalism of the Cartesian type is dead; it does not mean that there are no foundations or that all knowledge sits on thin air. Where I part ways (emphatically, I might add) with Tracy is my insistence that theology cannot (and should not) be held captive by methodological issues or the lack of Cartesian certainty. I refuse to meander through the methodological maze without saying something of substance theologically both on the way and in the end. How the connection between the pneumatological imagination and the Pentecostal–charismatic experience of the Spirit

foundational categories presented here derive from the dialectical inter-play between the personal (including my own) Pentecostal–charismatic experience of the Holy Spirit and reflection on this experience from within the broader Pentecostal–charismatic community of faith. I therefore propose the metaphor of 'shifting foundations' to underscore the dialectic of Scripture and experience, of thought and praxis, of theology and doxology, of reason and narrative, of object and subject, of a priori rationality and a posteriori empiricism, of the self and com-munity, in all knowledge (cf. Proudfoot 1985; Charlesworth 1980). These are all elements which combine to inform the pneumatological imagination. As a methodological construct, however, the pneumato-logical imagination in turn both envisions the foundational categories and is shaped by them. I will therefore argue, on the one hand, that a theology of the Holy Spirit emerges out of our experience of God's presence and activity in the world even while I suggest, on the other hand, that it enables us to experience that presence and activity in more precise, intense and true ways. Further, the flexibility and cogency of the foundational categories developed here for identifying the pneu-matic and basic features of our world enables us to ground not only divine and human experience and reality but also that of the demonic and of nature.[7]

Having made these admissions, however, I will lay out the more abstract foundational pneumatology here before detailing the Pente-costal–charismatic sources of the pneumatological imagination in the next few chapters, for three reasons. First, because what is proposed is a foundational pneumatology, my claim is that the categories to be sug-gested are both vague enough and of sufficient explanatory power to warrant their being argued on their own terms. Sure, having a pneuma-tological imagination to begin with helps one to grasp more quickly the categories and see their specific applicability across the broad range of

---

enables this to occur is a by-product of this book and serves as my contribution, in germinal form, to the debate on theological method.

7.   The concept of the demonic is a corollary to a fully biblical pneumatology as well as central to the Pentecostal–charismatic *Weltanschauung*; it will be fully explicated later in this chapter and in Chapter 7. Equally important for Christian systematic theology is a pneumatological theology of nature; while a theology of ecology informed by the Pentecostal perspective is not the subject of this study, what is said here should provide the basic building blocks for such a project (see Daneel 1993).

human experience. As metaphysical categories, however, they should be self-illuminating to any who care to examine them. Second, the development of a Pentecostal–charismatic theology of religions in this monograph goes hand in hand with the provision of a viable model by which Pentecostals and charismatics can participate in the interreligious dialogue. My objective in this work is to engage not only my colleagues in Pentecostal–charismatic circles, but also a much wider public including those in other faith traditions. Such engagement requires the development of a more neutral language that translates what is meaningful for one religious tradition to all interested parties even while it preserves (or retains the capability of preserving) the deepest convictions of that tradition.

The third, more pragmatic, reason is aesthetic. While it would be legitimate for me to first sketch the Pentecostal–charismatic encounter of the Holy Spirit in order to present more concretely the formative experiences of the pneumatological imagination, it would move the lengthy, abstract argument in this chapter into the heart of my discussion of the movement and thereby cut into the flow of that narrative. What I propose to do instead is present the foundational pneumatology here and provide pointers along the way to later chapters where I will flesh out the empirical components to the theory. I therefore launch into the foundational pneumatology by developing a trinitarian metaphysics of creation in the next sub-section; proceed to elaborate on theological implications of the Word–Spirit relation in this framework; and conclude with a discussion of elements in a foundational pneumatology that is able to account for features of divine presence, activity and absence in the world. Throughout, it should be emphasized that this is but a provisional attempt to comprehend the universal presence and activity of the Spirit within the framework of the interreligious dialogue.[8]

8.   While this foundational pneumatology is informed by the work of biblical scholars (e.g. Montague 1994; Fee 1994) and historians of Christian doctrine and thought (e.g. Rusch 1978; Congar 1983; Burgess 1984, 1989, 1997), it assumes but does not directly engage exegetical and historical issues except insofar as they bear on the task at hand. What emerges, however, should be supported by the results from these other disciplines; at a minimum, nothing should contradict either sound scriptural interpretation or the received wisdom of the Councils and Christian thinkers throughout the ages. Note also that I rarely, if ever, refer to works by Pentecostal authors in this chapter. These will be reserved for Chapters 5 and 7

The Metaphysics of Creation in Trinitarian Perspective
In addition to the philosophical grounds noted in the preceding remarks, there are other, theological reasons, why it makes sense to begin work on a foundational pneumatology by focusing on the idea of creation. Most pertinent for our purposes is the perennial connection made between the Spirit and universality in the history of Christian thought. More recently, as shown in Chapter 3, the Christian encounter with the non-Christian religions in the twentieth century has led many to align the domain of the Spirit with that of the cosmos or creation at large even as that of Christ's has been more strictly delimited to the incarnation and the Church. What we have in common with everything and everyone else, regardless of nationality, ethnicity or gender, is our createdness—our dependence on something other than ourselves. While my affinity for such a demarcation was evidenced in the previous discussion, my reservations were also registered as well. To return to the problem outlined in Chapter 3, what now needs to be negotiated is how Word and Spirit can be related and yet remain sufficiently distinct so as to nurture a pneumatological approach to the religions. I think that Robert Neville's philosophical theology of creation *ex nihilo* provides an excellent point of entry towards a resolution of this dilemma.

For three decades now, Robert Neville, a philosophical theologian in the American pragmatist tradition, has given sustained reflection to the idea of creation *ex nihilo*.[9] He was initially set in this direction by his consideration of the problem of the relationship between the one and the many. (We confront this problem in the form of the relationship between universality and particularity.) From the standpoint of ontology, Neville asks how it is that the manyness of the world is held together in relative unity rather than being simply a welter of chaotic pluralities? A thing is what it is only by virtue of its being determinate relative to other things, and what relates any two things is itself a third. Neville sees that the one which holds together the many things of the world cannot then be any kind of thing itself, since if that were so, it would be determinate relative to other things and would have to find its relation to others via a third. But that would set in motion the quest for

when I fill out the theoretical argument developed here.

9.   Neville's imprint on my thinking will be evident at various points in this foundational pneumatology. In this sub-section, I draw primarily from part one of his philosophical theology, *God the Creator* (1992). There are extended discussions and elaborations of the idea of creation *ex nihilo* throughout the Nevillean corpus.

third terms ad infinitum, resulting in the dissolution of the one into the pluralities of the world. Rather, the one can only be a 'context of mutual relevance' wherein all things relate to each other. What is this 'context of mutual relevance'? Not any being nor even being itself if such be considered determinate in any respect, but rather the ground of being, or better, the *act* of creation. The many things of the world are found together by virtue of their being created as such.

Creation is thereby the transcendent act from which all things, even the categories such as space and time themselves, are determined. If time itself is created, creation cannot be *in* time. It is therefore necessarily eternal. Neville understands eternity to be the togetherness of all three modes of time—past, present and future—each in their own integrity and also in their relation to the other two (1993a). Creation is the establishing of this eternal context of mutual relevance for the modalities of time. Within this framework, two key implications of Neville's theory of creation need to be mentioned and discussed: the essential indeterminacy of the source of the creative act and the trinitarian character of the act.

The problem of the one and the many hence leads to the speculative metaphysical hypothesis of God as the indeterminate, or transcendent, creator of all things *ex nihilo*.[10] Classical Christian theology has therefore been correct in emphasizing the divine transcendence and the complete dependence of the world on such a transcendent source. This is the theological truth at the heart of the Christian doctrine of creation *ex nihilo*. At the same time, theologians have also perennially gone on to discuss the essential qualities and attributes of God *ad intra*. Creation *ex nihilo*, however, means that divine creating is free and, from our vantage point, arbitrary. God, in this view, is determinate only in relation to his creating the world. To be more specific, God gives Godself

---

10. There is a more extensive argument in favor of Neville's philosophical theology of creation in Yong (1997). There I defend the superiority of creation *ex nihilo* as a solution to the problem of the one and the many against other alternatives such as process theism, the doctrine of the finite God, ontological dualism and the Kabbalist *tsimtsum* cosmogony. Another theologian who arrives at the same solution as Neville to the problem of the one and the many, albeit from another direction, is Colin Gunton (1993). Gunton, however, would probably not be open to the view of God apart from creation as essentially indeterminate, given his own apparent inclinations toward a social doctrine of the Trinity. His emphasis is also much more on the fact of creation, in contrast to Neville's focus on the creative act.

the feature of creator only in the act of creating. To attempt to speak of divinity apart from creation is to attempt to predicate something of what is essentially indeterminate. Recall that determinateness is what it is only because of the creative act. Because of this, we cannot get behind the creative act to discern the reasons for creation. In this sense, the act of creation is entirely gratuitous. God as indeterminate in Godself is thus the creative act, the one that provides the unitive harmony for the manyness of the world. Our knowledge of God the creator, Neville proposes, 'must be knowledge of his determinate conditional features' (1992: 75), features which are relative to the created order. As he elsewhere insists, 'apart from creation, God is indistinguishable from nothing' (1991a: 40).[11]

Critics of Neville's theory would want to argue that in this framework, God is dependent on creation and his freedom to create is nullified. This is, however, in part to confuse epistemology with ontology. We know God to be creator only because of the creation, and have no noetic basis to speak of God as determinate in any meaningful sense of the term apart from creation.[12] Neville himself urges that it would be self-contradictory to understand God as having been necessitated to create since creation depends on God's creating rather than conditioning God's creating (1992: 113). God as mystery in Godself simply points to the fact that apart from creation, there is nothing to understand. The gulf between creation and the creator is most absolute at this point. This element of God's radical transcendence is tempered, however, by the feature of God's radical presence; I will elaborate further

---

11. Neville writes, 'to say that the creator is essentially indeterminate is only to say that nothing determinate can be attributed to the creator's essential nature. In fact, it is to say that there is no such thing as a determinate essential nature and that talk about the creator's essential nature is misleading; the determinate referent for knowledge of the creator's indeterminateness is part of the determinate but conditional feature of being creator' (1992: 76). Yet, we should not move too quickly from God being indistinguishable from nothing to God as nothing. As Neville says it, 'because the pure divine aseity would be unintelligible, we would have to say that God *could* not be Nothing. In fact, there is no reason to say God *is* Nothing, since God is determinate as creator of this determinate world' (1982: 51; italics Neville's).

12. It is appropriate here for me to register my agreement with the apophatic theology of Eastern Orthodoxy. I find their distinction between the revealed economic Trinity of divine energies and the obscure mystery of the essential Godhead to be helpful.

on this point below. But what, however, about the theological objection that the only way to protect the prerogative of God to create is to understand God in Godself as an eternal relatedness, an immanent trinity of persons, as suggested by the biblical revelation?

This leads to the second important implication of the idea of creation *ex nihilo*: the trinitarian character of the creative act. An analysis of the creative act itself reveals creator, created, and the power of creating that mediates between the two (Neville 1982: 69-73). On one level, what emerges is God as the transcendent and indeterminate source of all being, this determinate world as the terminus of the creative act, and the relationship between the two as the power of the creativity itself. Such a construct lends itself theologically to an economic doctrine of the Trinity, and I will elaborate on this later. On another level, however, further reflection on the creative act reveals trinitarian features immanent within the act itself. From what is created, we see that things are a harmonious configuration of pluralities bound together by norms of determinateness. Any thing is a harmony solely by being what it is. As such, it is normative in its unitive existence. In a secondary sense, of course, things can be and are measured against normative ideals: we imagine things can and should be better harmonized than they are. Normativity or formal norms in themselves, however, are entirely transcendent and indeterminate since they are both prior to all harmonies and instantiated in them. Neville distinguishes theologically between these formal uncreated norms and normative measures by designating the first the Word of God, or Logos, and the second the Word 'spoken' in creation (1982: 72). What we have, then, is God as the aboriginal source, the Logos as the norm, and the Spirit as the power of the eternal creative act, each relative to the created order. This is the meaning behind the patristic debate about the eternal generation of the Son and the eternal procession of the Spirit. In this sense, it is possible to speak of an 'immanent' trinity in the idea of creation *ex nihilo*.

Neville, however, would object to speaking about immanent trinitarian persons apart from or prior to the creative act. He would be very cautious about the 'vice versa' at the end of the axiom, 'the economic Trinity is the immanent Trinity,' heralded by Rahner. In this, Neville is not alone. I have already mentioned Lodahl's qualms about the doctrine of the immanent Trinity. Neville, however, is careful to locate the speculative problem at the right point, in the creative act, rather than at the wrong place, that of trinitarian persons apart from the world. At the same time, there are among Catholic, not to mention Protestant or Orthodox, theologians many who have voiced similar reservations (cf. Schoonenberg 1975, Congar 1983: III, 11-17, LaCugna 1991 and McDonnell [with LaCugna] 1988). These are all in agreement that since theology (God in Godself) derives from the second moment of reflection on *oikonomia* (God in relation to the world), we must be wary of proceeding too quickly from a conceptual distinction of immanent-economic to an ontological equivalence. As LaCugna has summarized, the two major problems that arise with an uncritical equation of the immanent and economic Trinity are the loss of divine ineffability, and, ironically, the implicit denial of the divine freedom given the symmetry asserted of God *ad intra* and *ad extra* (1991: 216-32). It has already been mentioned that Neville's interpretation of creation *ex nihilo* preserves both the divine mystery and freedom, precisely via the asymmetrical act of creation.

In anticipation of the formal introduction of Pentecostalism in the next chapter, it is noteworthy to mention here that there are important Pentecostal reasons for adhering to a trinitarian metaphysics of creation *ex nihilo*. To begin with, there is a general anti-intellectualist attitude inherent in Pentecostalism which eschews the speculative moment in the process of cognition. This disposition has not motivated many Pentecostals to extensive consideration of the trinitarian mystery. The result is that trinitarian Pentecostals have more or less adopted the classical Nicene and Reformation theological formulas without critical reflection. In spite of this acceptance, Pentecostals generally prefer to retain biblical terminology and metaphors in their theologizing. This results in much more of an emphasis among Pentecostals on 'God for us' than on God in Godself. The view of God as essentially indeterminate except as creator of all things *ex nihilo* is, I suggest, in line with the intuitive Pentecostal distrust of speculating on the divine life *ad intra*.[13]

What is ironic is that insofar as some Pentecostals have been given to 'speculation' on the person and nature of God in himself, they have vehemently denied the classical doctrine of the Trinity as verging on tritheism. This group of Pentecostals emphasizes the oneness of God in accordance to the biblical witness—thus their self-designated label as

---

13. Further clarification will be provided in Chapter 5 in my discussion of the Pentecostal–charismatic pneumatological imagination.

'Oneness' or Apostolic Pentecostals.[14] Yet their theological (read God in Godself) unitarianism translates into an economic trinitarianism. Jesus—savior—is the proper, revealed name of God. It belongs to the man from Nazareth since God was incarnate in this human being: 'the radiance of God's glory and the exact representation of his being' (Heb. 1.3); 'for in Christ all the fullness of the Deity lives in bodily form' (Col. 1.9). The Holy Spirit in this framework is the Spirit of Jesus, now present to the Church, not a separate member in a trinitarian God. A simplistic reading of the Oneness doctrine of God would be fairly equivalent to the modalist trinitarianism of the third century patristic fathers. This, as well as the Nestorian-like Christology of Oneness theology, require further dialogue between them and their trinitarian siblings. What is of import at this juncture, however, is that the metaphysics of creation *ex nihilo* alleviates the chief point of tension between the two groups. While Oneness Pentecostals deny that God is trinitarian in himself, trinitarian Pentecostals do not deny that God is (at least) one; both agree that God is revealed as Father, Son and Holy Spirit. The view of God defended here avoids the problem of deciding about what God is in eternity apart from creation, and enables both groups to focus on their common (trinitarian) experience of God. The theological and ecumenical gains made by this 'unitive' Pentecostal view of the Godhead should not be underestimated. Convergence at this theological level legitimates the claim that the theology of religions developed here is potentially able to represent both trinitarian and Oneness members across the Pentecostal spectrum.[15]

A metaphysical foundation has been laid for the pneumatology being developed in the above speculative hypothesis. How well it fares theologically, however, can only be decided *post facto*. In Neville's terms, the value of an abstract theory needs to be cashed out in more concrete specifications. Aside from an early essay (1982: 41-68), Neville has not reflected much on the pneumatological implications of his work. Yet

14. Because of their unorthodox doctrine of the Godhead, these Pentecostals have been rejected as heretical by trinitarian Pentecostals as well as more evangelical and conservative Protestant denominations. The most valuable introduction to Oneness Pentecostal history and theology remains the (unfortunately still unpublished) doctoral dissertation of David Reed (1978).

15. My article, 'Oneness and the Trinity' (1997), is devoted precisely to this problem, and contains a much more extended discussion of the philosophical, theological and ecumenical issues at stake.

even in that piece, he noted that the role of the Spirit in his philo-sophical theology—God as the activity of creating, and thereby being present to each thing—is almost a trivial one. To remedy this 'trivial-ity', he suggests that what is interesting about the Holy Spirit is its christological character (1982: 46). In a sense, Neville's pneumatology from this point forward goes the way of most other pneumatologies in the history of Christian thought in that the Holy Spirit becomes the 'silent member' of the Trinity and pneumatology is subordinated to Christology. To be fair, he does say at one point that 'the key to Christology is pneumatology' (1982: 88). Yet his own systematic theo-logy (1991a) moves much of the discussion of the Holy Spirit under the doctrine of sanctification even while a robust Logos-Christology takes center stage. I hope in what follows to help fill out, and thereby streng-then, the pneumatological component of Neville's abstract trinitarian theology of creation. Doing so will require that we give further attention to just how Word and Spirit are related and yet distinct, and how they are not only present but also active in the world. It will also lead us to consider how, where and when other spirits may be at work; this topic will go some way toward making an otherwise bland pneumatological discussion much more interesting!

Divine Presence and Activity in Word and Spirit

To build on Neville's ideas, I want to revert to the philosophy of C.S. Peirce, the founder of the American pragmatist philosophical tradition, by way of the work of Gelpi. Peirce's influence on Neville's thinking is considerable, as it has been on Gelpi's as well. Recall that one of Gelpi's books was devoted to the development of a foundational pneumatology (1984). In it, he attempted to understand the Holy Spirit both as the divine law that endowed created reality with continuity and as the divine interpretant that is God's experiencing, cognizing, evaluating and responding to the world. In an earlier book, Gelpi defined 'spirit' more generally as 'any legal, vectoral feeling' (1978: 168). The use of the notion of law conveys on the one hand the idea of mediation, and on the other the idea of normative assessment and judgment. The Holy Spirit in Neville's speculative hypothesis mediates the creator and creation, the Logos as an indeterminate norm and the 'spoken' Word of God. The congruence of his and Gelpi's thinking can be traced in part to the philosophy of Peirce.

There are two components of Peirce's pragmatism that I wish to retrieve for the purposes at hand: his reformulation of the categorial scheme, and his theory of signs.[16] Following a detailed phenomeno-logical investigation, Peirce came to understand reality in terms of three fundamental categories which he termed *firstness*, *secondness* and *thirdness*. *Firstness* is pure potentiality, the simple quality of a thing in itself. *Secondness* is brute struggle, the resistant factuality of a thing in relation to others. *Thirdness* is what mediates between the two, the uni-versals, laws and generalities that constitute the continuous process of reality. It is this last category that is most important for what I am try-ing to accomplish. Thirdness is Peirce's assertion of the reality of generals which nominalism denied. This nominalism, Peirce saw, was the error which had plagued all philosophical thinking since Ockham. On the ontological level, thirdness is relationality and process: it sig-nifies the becoming and the arrival of the future. This can be translated theologically into an understanding of the Spirit as the eschatological power relating past, present and future. On the metaphysical level, thirdness is rationality and legality: it points to a normative dimension of reality over and against irrationality and chaos, and calls attention to mind as fundamental to the world. This is the Spirit as the divine wisdom, or what Gelpi calls the 'the mind of God' (1984: 45). On the logical level, thirdness is generality and vagueness: it is suggestive of the continuity of reality and of the relationship between the one and the many, the universal and the particular. This is the Spirit as the universal–particular and the particular–universal, the perennial hidden member of the divine trinity, always pointing away from Spirit to the Father and the Son.[17] But each member needs the other two, and none

16. Discussions of Peirce's categories and theory of signs are both scattered throughout his *Collected Papers*. The categories are most conveniently treated as a whole under his phenomenology (1931: 141-80) and in his 1903 Lectures on Pragmatism at Harvard (1934: 29-76). Because of my own lack of training in the discipline of semiotics, I rely here on Michael Raposa's elaboration of the sig-nificance of the hermeneutics of nature in Peirce's philosophy of religion and theism, what Raposa calls Peirce's *theosemiotic* (1989: 142-54). Later in this chap-ter, I will have recourse to Neville's extension of Peircean semiotics to the inter-pretation of religious symbolism. This entire discussion sets the stage for the emphasis placed especially by Pentecostals on the sign function of their experience of the Holy Spirit which will be introduced in the next chapter.

17. Peirce himself, influenced by evolutionary theory, put it this way: 'The start-ing point of the universe, God the Creator, is the Absolute First; the terminus of the universe, God completely revealed, is the Absolute Second; every state of the

can be on its own. Father is related to Son only through the Spirit, and neither Father nor Son can be what they are apart from the Spirit.

As the divine wisdom or the mind of God, the Spirit can be said to interpret the Father and the Son. This leads to Peirce's semiotic theory. He has long been recognized, perhaps with Ferdinand de Saussure, as one of the modern founders of semiotics (e.g. Fisch 1983: 18). Central to his theory of signs is the definition of a sign as that which stands for something in some respect to someone. Signs are therefore thirds, mediating between knower and known. This points to the triadic structure, not only of knowledge but also of experience (cf. Gelpi 1978; 1984: 17-44). In Peirce's epistemology, perception is the mediation of signs of what is encountered in the world by way of their legal, habitual and general aspects. Human experience, which spans the spectrum from perception to cognition, involves the inferential sorting out of the general and vague elements of perception, forming hypotheses about them, predicting these results, and testing the predictions by re-engaging the world.[18] Peirce called these abduction, deduction and induction, and regarded them as the logic of reasoning at the heart of his own version of scientific method. This is potentially a never-ending process given that our interpretation of any sign can only be another sign, albeit (hopefully) more precise and true to its object. This means, however, that interpretation is an essential component of human life. What we experience is understood with greater and greater precision as we continuously interpret our experience. Our interpretations, of course, are structured with respect to our previously interpreted experiences. Thus Peirce emphasized the import of the community of inquirers which in effect allows us to approach any object of inquiry from diverse vantage points or respects. This process terminates, whether for us individually or together as a community, when the inquiry regarding any particular

universe at a measurable point in time is the third' (1931: 187). While this is obviously too simplistic, there is some truth to it which needs to be rendered with more theological precision. This is what is being attempted with the help of Peircean interpreters such as Neville and Gelpi.

18. Peirce distinguished between *generality* and *vagueness* by saying that the law of the excluded middle did not apply to the former while that of contradiction did not apply to the latter (1934: 300). This is because both demand further specification. Our perception of a table is vague in terms of its color, hardness, coarseness, etc.; the table could be smooth. It is general regarding the kind of color or degree of coarseness.

object yields satisfactory habits for engaging the world, and doubts about the object are minimized. Inquiry may be reopened any time experience surprises us with an unexpected result.[19]

In should now be clearer that while on the theological level the Spirit is the divine person who mediates Father and Son—in Augustine's terms, the Spirit is the love that binds together Lover and the Beloved (*De Trinitate* 15.17.29)—in Peirce's semiotic framework, the Spirit interprets the creator to creation (and vice versa). In other words, our experience of the world and the emerging interpretations thereof point to the creator. This Peirce suggested in his essay, 'A Neglected Argument for the Existence of God' (1935: 311-39). Michael Raposa summarizes Peirce's vision as *theosemiotic*:

> The universe is God's great poem, a living inferential metaboly of symbols. Fragments of its meaning are accessible to the human intellect, most especially to a genuine community of inquirers devoted to discovering that meaning and governed by the principles of a valid scientific method. These will be the basic principles of logic of abductive conjecture, deductive explication, and inductive testing. So Peirce's theory of inquiry supplies the rubric for what is, in essence, a complex theological method. That method commences with an act of interpretation, a reading of the signs that are presented in human experience, proceeds with the exploration and clarification of that interpretation, and then with its utilization as a rule for living, a habit of action (1989: 144).

In this scheme of things, the Spirit is the supreme relation between us as knowers and the self-revealing God. As supreme relation, the Spirit is also non-objectifiable and therefore only accessible symbolically.

The world is therefore symbolic of the divine which we experience and interpret, always partially, by the presence and activity of (what we symbolize as) the Holy Spirit. Peirce's cosmology and epistemology are both suggestive for understanding Tillich's and Rahner's theology of symbolism. I have already noted in the previous chapter that for Tillich, all theological language is necessarily symbolic. In light of the triadic structure of experience proffered by Peirce, we cannot but shy away from claims regarding direct, unmediated experiences of the divine. All religious experience is symbolically structured. Our experience of God takes place through an inferential perception of the Spirit's legal and

---

19. This is the legacy of pragmatism which Peirce left behind. I will argue in Chapter 7 that Pentecostals are qualified Peirceans with strong pragmatist tendencies.

habitual endowment of the world which enables human understanding. Our cognition is the verbal, ritual or other symbolic expression of our experience of the world made possible by the Spirit. As Killian McDonnell says, 'to speak of pneumatology is to raise hermeneutical questions' (1982: 144).[20]

There was also occasion to mention briefly in our earlier discussion of Rahner his theology of the symbol. For him, as for Tillich, religious symbols retain their revelatory power because they participate in a more intense and recognizable manner in the very reality they symbolize. Yet 'participate' perhaps fails to capture the concreteness of Rahner's theology of symbolism. Rahner insists on an ontological understanding of symbols as the necessary expression and self-realization of being. Within the framework of his neo-Thomistic view of the relationship between nature and grace, the physical is symbolic of spiritual reality. The human body, for example, is the symbolic self-expression and realization of the human soul, even as the Logos is that of the Father (Rahner 1966).

Peirce's categorial scheme is able to account for all that Rahner proffers, and perhaps more. For Peirce, firstness is pure potentiality that acquires self-determination only over and against another (secondness). Such mutual determination is thirdness, apart from which neither of the two are accountable. In short, relationality is at the heart of reality, and Peirce's triadic construct is suggestive of how nature and grace can each retain the integrity of their essential character even while being mutually related. So Peirce would have been able to say that being expresses and realizes itself in an other. But he is better equipped to say how this necessarily occurs within his triadic notion of reality over and against the dipolarity in Rahner's neo-Thomistic theology. Further, Peirce was also able to give consideration to the symbolic character of the human being (1934: 185-89). This followed from his equating experience and interpretation within a triadic framework.

Peirce did not otherwise give much thought to the theological interpretation of his categorial scheme, but Neville and Gelpi have. I wish at

20. Elsewhere, McDonnell illuminates this point theologically by saying that we cannot really reflect about reflection since that would be 'using thinking in attempting to discover what the "object" of thinking is. In much the same way we must use the Spirit to understand the Spirit...because the Spirit is the universal comprehensive horizon within which any and all theological reflection is possible' (1985: 216); on this point, cf. 1 Cor. 2.10-16.

this point to bring together elements of Neville's doctrine of the Logos and Gelpi's pneumatology to get at the question of how the Word and Spirit are related and yet distinct. My argument proceeds from the theological notion that Word and Spirit are the 'two hands of the Father'.[21] As such, they are *both* present universally and particularly in creation, and, in the words of Congar, they 'do God's work together' (1986: 21-41). By so doing, I not only second what has been generally affirmed about the historical particularity of the incarnation of the Logos and the cosmic universality of the Spirit, but also lift up the contrasting term somewhat neglected by each of the traditions. There is a universal dimension to the Logos; thus the fecundity of the doctrine of the cosmic Christ. But there is also the particular dimension of the Spirit, as has more recently been emphasized by Colin Gunton (1993: 180-209). As will be seen, however, the dimensions of universality and particularity differ for each. The dimension of the Word is the thisness and whatness of things—what Scotus called their *haecceities*; that of the Spirit is the howness and relatedness of things—their continuity and significance. Both Word and Spirit are universally present and active because they are at the heart of every particular determination of being, albeit in different ways.

How is this the case? The speculative hypothesis being developed here suggests that things are what they are because they are created by the Father, through the Word, by the power of the Spirit.[22] Nothing can be apart from being instantiated according to the norms of the Logos by the working of the Spirit. Neville has developed an elaborate theory of the Logos following Plato in *Philebus*. According to Plato, determinateness consists of four elements: form, components to be formed, the mixture of the two, and the resulting value or harmony. Neville goes on to say that 'the Logos is thus the character of God expressed in each determinate thing by virtue of its determinateness, and it consists in the

---

21. The scriptural underpinning for the distinction is most clearly articulated in the Gospel of John: 7.37-39; 14.26; 15.26; 20.21-22. It is also implicit in Paul: Rom. 8.16-17 and Gal. 4.4-6.

22. This explains the Eastern Orthodox emphasis on the Father as the aboriginal source of the divine missions. Apart from the economic sending of Word and Spirit, the Father is the mystery of the world—the indeterminateness of being (Neville), the Nothingness of the Godhead beyond the Trinity (Eckhart), the 'eternal, immortal, invisible, the only God…who lives in unapproachable light' (1 Tim. 1.17, 6.16).

implications of form, components, actuality, and value. To say that Jesus was the incarnation of the Logos is thus to say that he epitomized or realized these four in some perfect way' (1991a: 45). The details of Neville's doctrine of the Logos need not detain us. What is important to note at this point is that anything that *is* is by virtue of its determinateness a symbol of the real presence and activity of the Word.

The same can be said about the Spirit. There are two functional elements central to Gelpi's doctrine of the Spirit: that of law and that of illumination or interpretation. Both are drawn from Peirce, and reflect the category of thirdness. From this Peircean starting point, Gelpi proceeds to engage Whitehead's theory of prehension. The Jesuit theologian argues that Peirce's triadic construct of experience strengthens Whitehead's case for construing reality as an experiential process. He goes on to suggest that what is found in human experience—qualities, facts and laws—is applicable to the divine experience as well (1984: 83-102).[23] The Holy Spirit, in Gelpi's pneumatological appropriation of Peirce's categories, is the divine interpretant, the ruling law of the divine experience, the measure of divine activity, the guarantee of continuity in the divine plan of salvation, the legal guardian of the divine intentions, the mediator of the Logos to the world, and the presentational reality of God to the human inferential perception, illuminating especially to those who have faith. Against Peirce's tendency to understand law mechanistically at times, Gelpi is careful to emphasize that

> laws are dynamic forces. And the laws which shape personal growth are living laws. For real persons live. When predicated of the divine Breath [Gelpi's preferred name for the Spirit], the term "law" connotes, therefore, supreme vitality. As a legal entity, a self, the divine Breath is experienced by believers as a *life force*. And as -co-creator [sic], co-redeemer, and co-sanctifier with the Father and Son, She is also perceived in faith as a *life source* (1984: 87).

The movement in terminology from law to life force is a natural one. The confluence of notions of legality, vitality and power means that Gelpi's 'vectoral feeling' is probably too mild. More accurate would be to speak of the Spirit as a field of force (cf. Pannenberg 1991: 382-84;

---

23. Gelpi's category of *experience* is analogous to Neville's use of *thing*. This is probably due to the former's focus on the human dimension of reality and the latter's broader cosmological emphasis. Both, however, agree with Whitehead that events are what is fundamentally real. My own inclination is to follow Neville except when I refer specifically to the human dimension.

Moltmann 1992: 195-97; Welker 1989; 1994: 235-48; Snook 1999). Each determination of being is what it is by virtue of the presence and activity of the Logos within the force fields set in motion by the Spirit, the supreme field of force. The Logos is the concrete form or pattern of each thing even as the Spirit is the power of its actualization and instantiation.[24]

This twofold presence and activity of Word and Spirit is operative in creation, incarnation and glorification. The doctrine of God as creator *ex nihilo* therefore means that 'by the *word* of the Lord were the heavens made, their starry host by the *breath* of his mouth' (Ps. 33.6, my emphases).[25] The juxtapositioning of these metaphors capture the congruence of Word and Spirit in the creative act. This is the case not only with regard to the ontological constitution of things but also with regard to our knowledge of them. The Spirit illuminates the symbolic structure of reality that enables us to know. Every determination of being therefore reveals the divine through the Word and by the Spirit, at least partially. The more intense the concentration of the form of the Logos in any field of the Spirit, the more harmonious the determination of being.

Christian faith holds that God is fully revealed in Jesus Christ, the supreme incarnation of the Word by the power of the Spirit. According to the theory being developed, either a Logos- or a Spirit-Christology can be employed, depending on the respects of interpretation. The former has been dominant in the history of Christian thought, focused as it

---

24. Pannenberg also uses the language of *information* and *energy* (1994: 109-15).

25. The Hebrew word for breath is *ruach*, also translated 'spirit' throughout the Hebrew Bible. Cf. also other references to the creative power of the Spirit: Gen. 2.7; Job 33.4; Ps. 104.30; Prov. 3.19-20, 8.30. These references are not uncontroversial. Divine 'wisdom' in Proverbs, for example, has been interpreted christologically rather than pneumatologically. Marie Isaacs, however, argues for the pneumatological connection without denying some christological implications (1976: 145; cf. Schwarz 1983: 1460-61; Suurmond 1995: 37-41). Michael Green, however, is convinced that these should be taken to convey the Spirit as animating and energizing force rather than a creating power (1975: 28-29). Yet taken together, what Isaacs and Green have to say strengthens rather than weakens my own argument which sees creation as a thoroughly trinitarian act, including that of the Spirit as power of creation; on this point, see the rich exegesis of the creation narratives by Michael Welker who lifts up the interrelationship of divine action and creaturely response within networks of power relations (1991; 1997a).

has been on the concept of incarnation. Its reinterpretation would suggest that the indeterminate norms, ideals and values of the Logos were supremely structured—enfleshed (Jn 1.14)—in the person of Jesus. In this way, it is appropriate to speak of Jesus as *homoousios* with the Father, to use the patristic term, in that the configuration of the Logos in him is the exact self-communication of the Father in revealing and saving power. Jesus as an historical figure therefore also anticipates the eschatological revelation of the very being and reality of God. For this reason, in things that ultimately matter (i.e. of soteriological significance), the Spirit is of Jesus the Christ (Jn 14.26, 16.14-15; Rom. 8.9; Gal. 4.6; Phil. 1.19; 1 Pet. 1.11) and points eschatologically to him. In short, the Logos as concretely manifest in Jesus is revealed to us by the Spirit as the face of the divine. Apart from the Logos, the Spirit is impotent and empty.

Whereas Logos-Christology accounts for the what of the incarnation, Spirit-Christology answers the question of how. As Irenaeus noted, 'without the Spirit of God we cannot be saved' (*Against Heresies* 5.9.3). This highlights the scriptural witness to the Spirit's role in the birth, anointing, deeds, passion and resurrection of Jesus (e.g. Lk. 1.35; Mt. 3.16; Acts 10.38; Heb. 9.14; Rom. 1.4). The advantages of this move, as Rosato has pointed out, are its biblical rather than speculative nature, its eschatological rather than historical perspective, and its soteriological rather than ontological orientation (1977: 435-38). I would emphasize, however, that a fully trinitarian Spirit-Christology is able to adjudicate all of these positions in their proper place.[26] The logic of

26. Del Colle (1994: 157-69) notes that Spirit-Christology takes one of two forms: either a 'reduced' binitarian model or a thoroughly trinitarian one ('pre-' or 'post-Chalcedonian', to use his classification). The former reflects the inchoate idea of the Trinity and is essentially adoptionistic (Jesus being merely a man anointed by the Spirit), while the latter is incarnational and trinitarian. An example of what he calls a modern post-Chalcedonian revisionist Spirit-Christology is Lampe's *God as Spirit* (1977). Del Colle prefers to follow his fellow Roman Catholic, David Coffey (1979), in speaking of trinitarian hypostases. I think the trinitarian Spirit-Christology suggested here is able to account for all that is biblically necessary as well as much of what is insightful in Del Colle's and Coffey's conciliar models, while avoiding some of the difficulties which inevitably arise in moving from medieval to modern and even postmodern philosophical presuppositions. My proposal is, however, revisionary insofar as it proposes a chastened speculative theology and emphasizes the preservation of the apophatic moment both in doxology and in ontology. I am optimistic that Killian McDonnell is right in saying 'as long as

trinitarianism defended here derives both from the theory of creation as well as the biblical testimonies. As such, it claims to be able to explicate the redeeming work of God within the broader canvas of the divine act. Whether or not this succeeds will need to be judged at the conclusion after the vague theory has been specified with respect to Pentecostal–charismatic theology and spirituality and the interreligious dialogue.

For now, it needs only to be said that our position avoids adoptionism since there was never a moment that Jesus was not the supreme exemplification of the Logos. It avoids docetism since it need not be tempted to deny the full human character of the incarnation of the Word. It avoids subordinationism since the person of Jesus is the product of the Father through the Word by the Spirit and neither Word nor Spirit act in isolation in Jesus. And finally, as additional support, our theory also avoids modalism in that it denies any succession in the revelation or manifestation of the two hands of the Father. Every determination of being exhibits the presence and activity of the divine being: Father creating something through the Logos by the Spirit. The person of Jesus is simply the most complete instance of this. It should therefore be clear that even as pneumatology needs Christology, so is the reverse true. Apart from the Spirit, the Word remains indeterminate.[27]

pneumatology is truly Trinitarian, the controls are built in' (1985: 212), even if my own inclinations are to reinterpret the divine reality away from the classical model of interpersonal relations toward one that is able to account for both the naturalistic and personalistic dimensions of reality.

27. A word needs to be said about the charge that our Spirit-Christology is unable to establish either the ontological uniqueness of Jesus or explain why it is that the Word was incarnate in Jesus rather than anyone else. On one level, the last question has a simple answer analogous to why this world and not any other: because of the gratuitous act of creation. On another level, our metaphysics acknowledges the uniqueness of each determination of being simply insofar as it is and serves its purpose for being. Yet it also needs to be considered that posing the question of uniqueness outside of a substance metaphysics perhaps renders that issue moot. Gabriel Moran's insightful analysis of the word 'uniqueness' suggests a twofold and thereby dialectical explication of the term, both of which capture movement as part of its essence (1992). On the one hand, 'uniqueness' refers to definition by abstraction and possession by exclusion; paradigmatic here is the boundaried individual. On the other hand, 'uniqueness' refers to inclusive relationality, the depth dimension or cosmic transcendentalism which makes each thing more and more unique insofar as it is open to the whole; paradigmatic here is the movement toward totality. Moran tests his thesis by a variety of ways. As

Finally, the eschaton will bring about the full manifestation of the Logos in the absolute power of the Spirit. The character of the Logos as explicitly revealed in Jesus and partially discernible in all other determinations of being will be finally unveiled through the illuminating power of the Spirit. This unveiling, however, will not only be epistemic but also ontic as well: we will not be interpreting the person of Jesus (doing Christology) or tracing symbols of the Logos via the movements of the Spirit in the world. Rather we will come to participate in the fullness of the divine life by the Word through the Spirit. Put in mystical terms, this work of the Spirit is to illuminate the beatific vision; in anthropological or soteriological terms, it is to deify human beings into the image of Christ; in ecclesial terms, it is to perfect the Church, the body of Christ; in cosmic terms, it is to usher in the Kingdom of God; in theological terms, it is to glorify God. The Spirit is the divine member who ultimately transforms the determinations of being so that they are conformed to the image of God as revealed in Jesus Christ. When this is done, 'then the Son himself will be made subject to him who put everything under him, so that God may be all in all' (1 Cor. 15.28).[28]

The preceding claims go some way toward achieving an understanding of how Word and Spirit are clearly distinct and yet related in the divine scheme of things.[29] Yet they are also vague with respect to what is being referenced. This is as the case should be, given that human knowledge gets at its object by way of generals and that we are also saddled by our finitude. One of the characteristics of vagueness, however, is that it allows for greater specification by what may be otherwise categorically contradictory. The next step is to flesh out how

---

applied to the human being, the movement to selfhood as individualistically or atomistically conceived brings out the first meaning of 'uniqueness'. Human being as being-toward-death and as movement toward communal, social and environmental solidarity—what Moran interprets the Jewish-Christian idea of resurrection to be—highlights the second aspect of human 'uniqueness'. Jesus, a particular individual empowered by the Spirit as well as the eschatological savior to be ushered in by the same Spirit, is unique on both counts.

28. I will return to a discussion of the import of eschatology to the Pentecostal–charismatic pneumatological imagination in Chapter 7.

29. Not coincidentally, the togetherness of Word and Spirit is a deep conviction of Pentecostals and charismatics. I will touch in the next chapter on how our experience of the Spirit differs from that of our experience of the Word, what Del Colle calls the distinction between the *Spiritus praesens* and the *Christus praesens*.

the abstract features of the foundational pneumatology are illuminated by concrete experience.

Elements of a Contemporary Foundational Pneumatology
The argument thus far is that Word and Spirit are distinct—as form and meaning, concretion and continuity, norm and legality, etc.—and yet related dimensions of being. The significance for pneumatology is that this metaphysical hypothesis allows us to speak of the presence and activity of the Spirit in a way that is not strictly christological. Yet, as Lodahl has reminded us, a true theological account should also find some way to speak of the absence of divinity. The following exposition will therefore take its cues from our experience of divine presence, activity and absence. First, a further word about 'experience'.

Following Peirce and Gelpi, all experience can be understood as mediatedness and is, theologically, essentially of the Spirit.[30] Our experience of God is not qualitatively different from our experience of anything else (see Proudfoot 1985). All come through via perception and suggests to us, in a series of intuitions, that there is something there, not ourselves, that demands our understanding. We go about a process of inquiry to appease our curiosity (or surprise, or anger, as the case may be). What is different about our experience of God is that it relates us to a dimension of being that includes but is not exhausted by normal experience. This is a dimension in which there is a heightened sense of truth, beauty, excellence, goodness and reality as it was and is meant to be. I therefore prefer to speak of a *religious dimension of experience* rather than of 'religious experience' itself (cf. Smith 1995: 39-40).[31]

In this dimension, we experience first the Spirit's *presence*. Because experience does begin with our senses, our first engagement with the Spirit is with the concrete determinations of being. This is the bodily, or incarnate aspect of the Logos. Yet, in and through this engagement, we

---

30. Gelpi notes that experience is a 'weasel word' with a variety of meanings. These include common wisdom, that which is revealed by the five external sensations, conscious cognition, the entire spectrum of human evaluative activity, and a broad definition that includes both the what and how of knowing (1994: 1-3). My use of the term throughout will be consistent with Peirce's as explicated above.

31. As will be clear from my discussion both in Chapters 5 and 7, the Pentecostal-charismatic experience of the Spirit both informs and confirms the abstract categories proposed here.

come into relationship with an other. This leads us eventually to an experience of the 'more' that we intuit in our engagement with the world.[32] There is an unfathomable depth dimension to our experience which calls continuously for a re-engagement with the other. Ralph Del Colle perceptively suggests that

> God who is triune relation is present in nature as the very source of the interrelation of all things. The interpersonal divine love that is Trinity makes space for the world, and energizes it by creating the cosmos to exist with all things in relation to one another. The more we discover our relation to other humans, to the non-human creation, and recognize the interconnectedness of all things, we experience the One who transcends all things and yet is in all things as the source of their dynamic interrelation (1992: 293-94).

It only needs be said that our experience of relationality, and through this, of God, is mediated by the presence of the divine Spirit. The theological tradition has termed this our experience of prevenient grace. If discussion is terminated here, Neville correctly notes that our experience of the Spirit's presence would be rather inconsequential.

Things do get a little more interesting when we consider the complexity of interpersonal relationships we experience, for example, as members of the body of Christ. The life of Jesus released, and continues to release by virtue of the resurrection power of the Spirit, a powerful field of force whose influence continues in the Church. The Church is the continued incarnation of the norms, ideals and values most completely revealed in the man Jesus. The difference between the two is their unsurpassable blend in Jesus, whereas the Church remains tainted by imperfection. In both, however, the actualization of the Logos occurs by the workings of the Spirit. We experience a heightened sense of the Spirit's presence via our participation in the body of Christ.

This is the case in part because what we experience as members of the body of Christ is not only the Spirit's presence, but his *activity* as well.[33] The sending of the Spirit at Pentecost actualized the force field

32. David Tracy calls this 'the uncanny' (1981: 355-70); cf. Frankenberry (1987: 93-98).

33. It is because the Spirit acts on and engages us as personal beings that I think it appropriate to use the personal rather than impersonal pronoun for the Spirit. Further, as Peirce saw, thirdness as relationality is also richly suggestive of divinity as personality. But I think we are hard pressed to defend, with Gelpi, the idea of a tri-personal God (1984: 103-24; 1988: 115-21), especially on biblical grounds alone

which was initiated by the configuration of the forms, ideals and values centered in Jesus. Prior to the sending in Christ and at Pentecost, the Spirit was sent to and through the Hebrew prophets, among other forms. The purpose of these specific outpourings of the Spirit differs from that of his inaugural mission in the creative act. Whereas the latter determines the orders of nature within which all things are related, the former intensifies the personal dimension of the webs of relationships within which human beings find themselves constituted. More to the point, the mission of the Spirit in the prophets, in Jesus and in the Church created force fields of faith, hope and love. Entrance into and participation in these fields enable human beings to move from estranged, wounded, broken and destructive relationships into reconciling, edifying, healing and saving ones.[34] Whereas our experience of divine presence is more so an aesthetic quality, that of divine activity moves us into the realm of ethics.[35]

Eschatological salvation is of God, through Christ, by the Spirit. The supreme norms, ideals and values instantiated in Jesus are what all things will be judged against in that context. Historically, however, things should be judged by their norms of existence and by how well they fulfill their purpose for being. With regard to the former, the question is whether a greater degree of aesthetic harmony is possible for a thing measured against its ideal norms. With regard to the latter, the question is whether a greater degree of environmental harmony is possible for a thing measured against the norms of its relationships to other things. The application of these norms are read against the thing itself and the things in relationship to other things, e.g., how well it serves itself and the purposes of others. What counts are the values of a thing when measured according to its ideal norms and when seen

(cf. Yong 1997). Gelpi does acknowledge the divine element of mystery which I want to emphasize. Yet God revealed in Jesus is our savior, and is supremely personal in this event. The question of the personhood of God is in some sense an empirical matter to be gauged by our perception of divine presence and activity in the world relative to ourselves. In another sense, it is a matter of faith to say how such presence and activity is articulated. Yet, of course both moments inform each other. *Doing* theology is what helps, at least in part, with sorting out the important differences of when and how we can speak of God in personal terms.

34. How this works in Pentecostal–charismatic life and practice will be discussed in Chapter 7.

35. These are the feeling and evaluative or active dimensions of experience in Gelpi's explication of Peirce's categories.

against its purposes. The activity of the Spirit in this is to integrate a thing into its environment in a way such that it can be authentic to itself and of service in its relationships with others. Things so constituted are thus said to declare the glory of God (e.g. Ps. 19.1). People also are capable of glorifying God, the difference being that we can choose not to do so, i.e., decide not to be what we were created to be, or not to fulfill our purposes for being relative to others. Pneumatological norms are satisfied to the extent that determinations of being brought about by the Spirit are authentic to themselves (i.e. not perverted) and do fulfill their created purpose (i.e. serving others rather than being destructive). To the extent that the world is being transformed from a place with lesser degrees of harmony to one in which the harmonies of things are heightened and intensified in their interrelatedness, to that extent we can say that the Spirit is at work in the world.[36]

There are thus degrees to which we can experience divine presence and activity in the world. Negatively speaking, there are also degrees to our experience of the lack of divine presence. This is what Samuel Terrien calls the 'elusive presence', the *Deus absconditus atque praesens* (1978). In our finitude, our experience of the Spirit gives us only fleeting glimpses of God being with us and at work. More often than not, we have a much stronger sense of divine absence. Is this just a psychological issue? To some degree, yes; but not completely. Our failure to grasp the divine presence must, at least in some instances, point to *ichabod*—the departure of the divine glory (1 Sam. 4.21). This was certainly the experience of Jesus in his cry of dereliction on the cross, and Christians have no reason to believe that he was play-acting. But how can this be given the theory of creation within which we understand the God–world relationship to consist? More specifically, if Word and Spirit are the two hands by which the Father creates, is present to, and acts in the world, how is it metaphysically possible that

---

36. The strength of this theoretical account of divine action in the world through Word and Spirit is that it supplies the metaphysical underpinnings for the discussion of more specific features of God's activity in the world, whether in terms of primary or secondary causality, the lure of the future, uniform or personal action. Because each of these models, analogies, or sub-theories account for different aspects of divine action, I would extend Owen Thomas's suggestion about 'two perspectives and languages' to ascribe such (1983: 232-33) to multiple perspectives and languages respecting different things, events, etc. I suggest that the theory sketched here is vague and flexible enough to do just that.

God is 'absent' from the world? To get at this apparent paradox is to get at a problem which has no doubt been percolating throughout this chapter: whether or not there is any such thing as freedom in a world in which all determinations of being are created by God, and if so, how.

Neville himself has given extensive consideration to this issue.[37] He suggests, in effect, a three-tiered argument. In the first place, he distinguishes between ontological and cosmological causation. Recall that creation is eternal, and what is created is temporal, including time itself. As the transcendent creator of all determinations of being, God is indeterminate except as God gives Godself the feature of being creator via the act of creating. In this sense, it is important to note that 'God's causation is not a relation but an immediate production' (Neville 1978: 115). Secondly, the kind of world God has created is such that freedom is one of the constitutive features of certain determinations of being. This is what is meant by cosmological causation. Things are created to have effects. Certain things, persons, are conscious agents with conscious effects. God is the author of the 'ontological context of mutual relevance' by creative fiat who sustains the temporal relations of determinate causes and effects across space and time. Cosmology is able to account for these causes and effects apart from God. The world is the kind of place that accommodates the integrity of freedom, whether as intentions, actions or choices.

The way God produces each thing while preserving the integrity of freedom in them is by creating the subjective or spontaneous element at the heart of every thing. This is the third tier of Neville's argument for creaturely freedom. Recall that things are what they are by virtue of the relationship between their pure possibility or quality of feeling in themselves and other things. The quality of pure possibility is created by God and arises out of the subjective process. There is no antecedent

---

37. Recognizing that freedom was the first and foremost problem confronting his speculative hypothesis, Neville turned immediately from *God the Creator* to a prolonged period of reflection and writing on this topic in the late 1960s and early 1970s. The results were published in two volumes. *The Cosmology of Freedom* (1974) generally articulated a metaphysical theory of levels of personal and social freedom within the framework of a Whiteheadian cosmology, and *Soldier, Sage, Saint* (1978) developed the personal aspects of freedom in spiritual formation and religious life. The following cursory summary is drawn primarily from two sections in the latter volume where Neville treats the metaphysical issues at stake in his philosophical theology (1978: 104-16).

causal reason for their being. Their spontaneity serves only the purpose of integrating for the moment the previous causal (cosmological) determinants of being into a new whole. God is creator of the feeling of spontaneity, but the decisions which are made in the process of becoming are 'the self-constituting of the temporal event or agent' (Neville 1982: 108). On one level, it is appropriate to say that God determines everything in the sense that God provides the spontaneity for their self-determination; this is metaphysical causation. On another level, events or persons are both determined by prior effects as well as spontaneously determine their subsequent effects; this is cosmological causation. Resolving the alleged incompatibility between divine creation and creaturely freedom in this way allows us to see not only how the Holy Spirit can be both present and 'impotent' or absent, but also gives us grounds to argue for the presence and activity of other 'spirits' in any event or thing.

The experience of divine *absence* therefore remains essentially spiritual. In its negative forms, it is properly termed 'demonic'.[38] Extremely radical evil is symbolized across religious lines by the Satanic.[39] Rather

---

38. It is arguable that no viable pneumatology can avoid dealing with the demonic—the contrast term to the Holy Spirit. Parthenios, Patriarch of Alexandria and of all Africa, recognized this in his speech at the 1991 Assembly of the World Council of Churches (1991: 33). It is for this reason that I cannot go all the way with Ashok Gangadean's attempt to develop a 'comparative ontology' to adjudicate universality and particularity across religio-cultural-linguistic worlds (1995). Gangadean's 'worlds' are too tame; as such, they would cooperate nicely with his suggestion of developing a trans-categorial rationality combining elements from Advaita nondualism and a silence-oriented praxis. I would suggest that this is not because Gangadean does not have an experience of the demonic—what I later call 'divine absence'—but because he lacks a pneumatological imagination that actively engages that reality rather than relegating it to the margins. For myself, the central, and indeed palpable reality of the demonic demands prophetic response, rejection and action. More on this in Chapter 7.

39. Don Cupitt (1990) misinterprets the awareness of *divine absence* as a signifier that all that remains is our own endless interpretive activity. As I will argue, however, the experience of divine absence is not only our *feeling* of the nihil, but a positive and horrific encounter with it. Thus, while creation *ex nihilo* in Cupitt's deconstructive *a*-theology points to no more than our own creative activity in diverse socio-linguistic worlds, he can pull this off only by denying the full implications of the historicity he wishes to embrace: that there is a 'more' signified even in the infinitude of language; that there is an objective world which gives rise to interpretation and experience; and, that the nihil or the demonic cannot be simply

than taking up space with prolegomena to justify our attention on this matter, I will simply delve into the discussion and ask that judgment on the method employed and the value of what is presented be withheld until the hypothesis sketched here is later tested against the empirical evidence. My chief dialogue partner for this theoretical sketch will be Walter Wink, longtime Professor of Biblical Interpretation at Auburn Theological Seminary, New York, and author of the trilogy, *The Powers* (1984, 1986, 1992).[40]

Wink's basic thesis is that the biblical language for the powers names and identifies our experience of and engagement with a reality that has both inner and outer aspects.[41] 'As the inner aspect they [the powers] are the spiritualities of institutions, the "within" of corporate structures and systems, the inner essence of outer organizations of power. As the outer aspect they are political systems, appointed officials, the "chair" of an organization, laws—in short, all the tangible manifestations which power takes' (1984: 5). Both aspects go together and neither can be in isolation from the other. The powers are thus heavenly and earthly,

---

wished away but has to be wrestled against and overcome. In the end, Cupitt's vision appears to be but a radical extension of the nominalism opposed by Peirce.

40. As is well known, of course, Tillich was one of those most responsible for restoring the reality of the demonic into theological discourse. His work, along with cultural events in the 1960s and 1970s, have fueled interdisciplinary research on Satan, demonology and radical evil, resulting in a plethora of publications during the past few decades. Bolt's (1994) is a valuable bibliographic essay. Aside from Pentecostal sources which I will mention later, part of what has informed my own understanding include Olson (1975), Binyon (1977), Green (1981), Hollenweger (1988), Garrett (1989), D. Williams (1990), McAlpine (1991) and Lane (1996). Approaches from other disciplines have also been helpful. The history of the idea of the evil and its prime symbol, the devil, is canvassed by Russell (1988). Kelsey (1978) utilizes a Jungian approach, while Peck (1983) and Shuster (1987) present psycho-pathological analyses. How rhetoric of the demonic serves social functions and structures power relations is discussed by Pagels (1995). A fairly comprehensive biblical treatment of angels and demons is given in Caldwell (1983). Yet as Helmut Thielicke admonishes in reflecting on the demonic from within his experience of Nazi Germany, the quantity of scriptural proof texts—and, as a corollary, the extensive literature—does not even begin to bring us face to face with the *reality* of the demonic (1963: 163); his chapter on the demonic is profoundly insightful.

41. Wink devotes detailed attention to the language of power in the Christian Testament: *arche* and *archon, exousia, dynamis, thronos, kyriotes* and *onoma* (1984: 13-38). Aside from Nigel Wright (1990: 43-50; 1996: 161-62), I am unaware of whether other Pentecostals and charismatics have seriously engaged Wink's work.

spiritual and material, divine and human, invisible and structural. But they are also good as well as potentially evil. Wink notes that the biblical *mythos* clearly identifies the powers—including Satan himself, at least in his origins if not also at the end—as servants of God (1986: 9-22). The emergence of evil is best related in the myth of the primeval fall. Historically, however, human choices play a decisive role in the perpetuation of demonic powers (1986: 30-39). Once unleashed, these powers seem to have a life of their own. Yet they are without influence apart from being 'incarnate' in forms, structures, institutions, organizations, nations, and even in persons and church movements. For Wink, then, there are clearly powers at work in the world, some of which are demonic in character; yet none of these operate apart from the oversight and ultimate control of God.

What Wink has to say is important, and its adaptation, with some minor adjustments, to the foundational pneumatology being developed here can be mutually enriching. Now because Wink's objective is to reinterpret the biblical language of powers for our time, he devotes only scant attention to metaphysical issues. Yet his own theology of the powers is clearly congruent with the philosophical theology elaborated here. There are clear affinities between the inner aspects of the powers as understood by Wink and our category of thirdness, and between the outer aspects and that of secondness. Returning to Gelpi's basic definition of spirit as any legal or vectoral feeling, we can venture the hypothesis that the demonic is a law or nexus of laws that attempts to pervert the determinate forms of being and establish force fields of destruction—what the Bible calls the 'law of sin and death' (Rom. 8.2). Its origins derive from the existential spontaneity of each event or thing as endowed by the divine creative act. This is the category of firstness missing from Wink's dipolar demonology. (His assumption of a panentheistic model of God derived from process theology fails him at the same places as it does Lodahl.) As firstness, the existential spontaneity of things points to the mystery of evil—that a decision can be made in freedom against the norms, ideals and values revealed in Jesus Christ. To the extent that the spontaneous self is constituted away from God and its divinely ordained purpose for being, to that extent it unleashes, at some point if not at the moment of its initial conception, force fields of the demonic and is inexplicable.[42]

42. This is the truth behind the theory of evil as privation or negation. As such, evil is nothingness, the mystery of non-being, and in some senses, of God as well;

Once unleashed, however, the demonic takes on terrifying features through space and time. Whereas the Holy Spirit works to constitute each thing in its own normative integrity within the broader harmony of relations, the demonic strives toward maximizing inauthenticity and estrangement in the world. It does so through force fields that tempt each thing to overestimate its significance and purpose, and to over-reach its sphere of influence (see Shuster 1987). This results in a distortion of a thing's identity and a disruption of its network of relations. Relationships infected by the demonic are no longer mutually supporting and reinforcing but rather self-seeking and destructive. This is especially the case when the demonic is incarnated in persons. The reality of this aspect of human experience—what theologians and psychologists have called demonic oppression or possession—legitimates our consideration of demons as personal beings. They pervert our self-understanding such that our God-given identity and purpose are misplaced and eventually destroyed. We are driven to compensate for this by the reckless absorption and misuse of others instead of repenting and returning to God. Continued exposure to and collaboration with the demonic produces massive structures of destructive power. As Lodahl has reminded us, the Holocaust is a horrifying example of how genocidal acts can be inspired through institutions established by human actions.[43] The unchecked growth of the demonic results in estrangement from others and, ultimately, separation from God—what has traditionally been called hell.[44]

I need to be theologically precise at this point since the biblical principalities and powers are multivalent. Henry Lederle, for example, has insisted that biblically speaking, it is more appropriate to speak of the

in the words of Deutero-Isaiah: 'I am the Lord, and there is no other. I form the light and create darkness...' (Isa. 45.6-7).

43. Thus Erazim Kohák correctly notes that 'while there is misfortune, even tragic misfortune in nature, radical evil comes into the world through human will' (1975: 54); this is also M. Scott Peck's argument (1983). I would add that demons in this scheme can be understood as real thirdness which influence secondness; the stronger the influence or habituation, the more vivid our experience of the embodiment of evil.

44. Again, however, hell is the ultimate mystery of non-being and also of God as well. Wink (1986: 39-40) calls attention to the symbolic situatedness of eternal torment 'in the presence of the holy angels and of the Lamb' (Rev. 14.10). Hell is what it is by virtue of its alienation *and* yet relatedness to the creator. This may also be behind Luther's idea of the demonic as the wrath of God (cf. Lindberg 1975).

demonic relative to individuals rather than to social structures (1987).[45] Lederle wants to preserve human responsibility both in the moral and the socio-political sphere. Better, however, to distinguish between at least three distinct but related biblical understandings of the principalities and powers. First, the powers are 'spiritual forces of evil in the heavenly realms' (Eph. 6.12). Second, the powers are the human authorities established by God that operate social or political institutions (Rom. 13.1-8). These persons can do God's bidding or degenerate into sinful rebellion. Thirdly, and by no means lastly, the powers may be understood to refer to actual social and political structures or institutions (according to Rev. 13.1-7). Now whereas Lederle reads this last passage metaphorically rather than ontologically, I see no need to do so once we specify the respects of these references. As thirdness, the powers are spiritual forces described in the Ephesian epistle. Yet their influence can only be measured in concrete realities—secondness—such as those referred to in the Apocalypse. The human referent to the powers simply points to our freedom and complicity in the perpetration of sin and evil in this world. Demonic strongholds are established via human agency and intensify with our persistent rebellion against God. Social structures take on a demonic character when the corporate actions of human beings ensue in destruction and grow beyond human control. To look at the demonic in this way, however, is not to deny their ontological reality as spiritual force fields bent on destruction.

As spiritual realities, then, it is also possible to understand the demonic as a contrast symbol to that of the Holy Spirit. The Holy Spirit, as suggested above, points to the idea of law or legality, rationality, relationality and processive continuity culminating in the eschaton. The Spirit's reality is experienced as a field of force within which all things find their true identity in relationship. The Spirit's work is to constitute each thing authentically in accordance with its own norms and purposes even while bringing all things together ultimately under the normative measure of all other norms: Jesus the Christ. In this light, the demonic sets in motion force fields or habits of chaos, irrationality, isolation or alienation, and stagnation. The demonic resists the transformative and eschatological work of the Holy Spirit—

---

45. Lederle is a South African theologian, at least formerly a participant–observer in the Pentecostal movement even if he is presently better considered an outsider. I will return to other aspects of his work later.

what Moltmann calls 'the coming of God' (1996a). Our experience of the demonic reveals our inauthenticity, our failure to live in accordance with our divinely instituted purpose for being, and our refusal to contribute in harmony with others to their good, preferring instead to use them for our selfish ends.[46] Its objectives are contrary to the divine norms, ideals and values as revealed in Jesus Christ; thus, the demonic opposes the eschatological invasion of the Kingdom of God (Mt. 11.12).[47]

In sum, our foundational pneumatology has led to an understanding of the Spirit as the divine power who constitutes the manyness of world, each in its own authenticity and integrity, and who unites the manyness of the world in harmony. Insofar as the Spirit is present and at work, the norms, ideals and values of each thing will be fulfilled. In this sense, it is possible to understand the mission of the Spirit as distinct from that of the Word. Eschatologically, of course, there will be a convergence of Spirit and Word in the full revelation of the divine mystery.

46. Some of what I am suggesting has already been articulated by Tillich in his *Systematic Theology*. His classic definition of the demonic was the elevation of whatever was conditioned or finite to absoluteness or ultimacy. This self-elevation results from denying one's autonomous or rationally normed purpose for being, being inauthentic to one's integrity, and exceeding one's sphere of influence. All of these are rectifiable only in and by the Spiritual Presence. The demonic, by contrast, is that which is irrational (1951: 114), that which divides or 'splits' (1963a: 103), and that which is unwilling to accept the temporality of existence (1957: 69). On the human level, 'a demonic structure drives man to confuse natural self-affirmation with destructive self-elevation' (1957: 51). Demons thus 'participate in a distorted way in the power and holiness of the divine' (1963a: 102). They do what even Jesus refused to do, in acknowledging his self, place and purpose as a man: claim the ultimacy that belongs only to God (1951: 148; cf. Jn 12.44).

47. Angelic beings can be understood in this model also as spiritual realities that have inner and outer aspects. Their legal tendencies are force fields within the divine field of the Spirit that counter the work of the demonic and enable each person (or church, institution, etc.) to exist in accordance with his or her (its) purpose for being. Eschatologically, of course, angels long for the final revelation and glorification of the Logos in all things, and work to create each of us in the image of Jesus. In biblical parlance, angels are 'ministering servants, sent to serve those who will inherit salvation' (Heb. 1.14). For an intriguing suggestion as to how the Holy Spirit or the angelic and the demonic are engaged by humans at the psychological level as conscience and as adversary, see Ulanov (1975).

2. *Religious Symbolism: A Pneumatological Understanding*

What drives this foundational pneumatology is both a vision and a problem. The vision is the pneumatological imagination inspired by the Pentecostal–charismatic experience of the Holy Spirit. The problem is how Word and Spirit are related and yet sufficiently distinct so as to enable a theology of religions to develop within a pneumatological framework. The preceding theology of the Holy Spirit presents both a vision and a framework by which to understand divinity's relation to the diverse realms of human undertaking, including that of politics, economics, art, morality and, our arena of immediate interest, religion. I propose, therefore, to apply the categories of presence, activity and absence developed in our foundational pneumatology in an effort to interpret human religiosity.

The hypothesis of *divine presence* poses several implications for a theological understanding of religion. To reiterate, each thing is constituted according to its own norms and is an expression of some ideal or value, by the power of the Spirit. The Spirit's presence should thus be assessed on at least two levels. On the first, ontological level, all objective elements in the world of religions, including sacred texts, founding myths, institutions and organizations, temples, rituals, conventions and moral systems, etc., are what they are by virtue of being created as such. The Spirit is the mediator of the pure possibilities open to each thing. On the second, concrete level, where things constitute themselves in their own existential spontaneity, the extent to which each thing succeeds in representing itself authentically to and situating itself harmoniously in its environment would mark, to a greater or lesser degree, the Spirit's presence. This is why Tillich is correct to say that every religious tradition is, on the one hand, 'the creation and the distortion of revelation,' and on the other hand, 'based on revelation' (1963a: 104).

There are two important consequences that follow from this consideration of divine presence in the world of religions. The first is that even if Cantwell Smith's distinction between subjective faith and objective religious traditions is a valuable one for the historian of religions, it does not follow that the Spirit is only present in one and not in the other. On the contrary, every determination of being bears the Spirit's presence at some level. This allows us to focus on the 'enfleshment' of the Logos in religion by the power of the Spirit, whether in its texts, traditions, rituals, etc. On the one hand, it enables us to understand the movements of the Spirit better than if we followed Lodahl's suggestion of the Spirit as textually mediated since there is now the entire range of what constitutes religion which demands our critical interpretation. On the other hand, of course, our task is intensely complicated precisely because it is not just texts that require interpretation but the broad sweep of human religiosity. The results, however, of such an investigation of the phenomena of religion is more conducive to a holistic comprehension of this dimension of human experience. This is also more congenial to an accurate understanding of the Pentecostal–charismatic experience which demands interpretation of the experiential dimension of spirituality over and against an emphasis on textuality in religious life. This is to move beyond verbal and imagistic symbols to that of prayers, dances, gestures and many other richly textured human ways of being which claim to represent the divine presence and activity.

The second consequence that follows from our explication of divine presence in religion raises the question of what Tillich referred to as the religious distortion of revelation. I propose that this is best understood under the category of *divine activity*. The issue here is whether, over the course of time, what is created comes to constitute itself within a field of force that enables it to represent itself authentically to and situate itself harmoniously in its environment. Is the thing true to its created nature, and by extension, to its purposes relative to other things, or does it overreach itself, become inauthentic, and develop either in isolation or parasitically in relation to others? Movement in the direction of the former marks the Spirit's activity. Applied to the phenomena of religion, we are led to ask how the life span of any theological idea, system of doctrine, devotional ritual, sacred text, dance pattern, meditative exercise, or any other religious datum, functions relative to religious life in particular and to human life as a whole. The work of the Spirit is to create through such phenomena authentic human life and relations. Let us take, as an example, a more detailed look at the Spirit's activity as symbolized in religious ritual.

What would a pneumatological interpretation of ritual look like? Following Peirce's insistence that all human activity are signs that point to something else, religious rituals can be profitably understood as actions that stand for something (e.g. the divine in theistic traditions) to someone (the practitioner) in some respect (the objective aimed at in performing the ritual). It is clear that rituals can be understood from many angles. Anthropologically and sociologically, ritual has been analyzed as an instrument of human socialization (Durkheim 1915) or routinization (Smith 1982: 53-65); as the creation of liminal spaces in which socio-structural hierarchies are leveled into egalitarian communities (Turner 1977); as an activity to remake the world of human community, whether because it suffers from social upheaval (Geertz 1973: 142-69), emotional or aesthetic turmoil (Lewis 1980), or even the rule of patriarchy (Caron 1993). From a socio-psychological perspective, ritual activity mediates cathartic healing (Scheff 1979). Mircea Eliade's life work as a historian of religions has been devoted to an explication of ritual as the means by which humans recreate primordial space and time, and participate in the divine life (e.g. 1987). Harvey Cox points to the element of fantasy in ritual which serves to stimulate human creativity (1972: 83-89; cf. Dupré 1998: 77-91). Or, ritual could combine any or all of these elements in the liberative transformation of human persons and communities (Driver 1991).

This is by no means an exhaustive listing of theories of ritual. Particular rituals may or may not be accurately understood in any of the proposed theoretical frameworks, much less all of them. They do, however, help us to begin asking the right kinds of theological questions regarding the Spirit's activity. Do religious rituals embody the norms, ideals and values that they claim, and, more importantly, are such mediated to practitioners of ritual activity? Do rituals promote social cohesion? Do they enable religious devotees to negotiate social change? Are they emotionally and aesthetically transformative? Do practitioners experience healing and liberation in or through the ritual process? Do they intensify human creativity?

Theologically, then, the 'spirit' of any ritual is the force fields of laws, feelings and habits it instantiates in its practitioners. For Christians, the Holy Spirit is present and at work in the Eucharist, for example, when the Christian is transformed both to be a more authentic human being as measured by the norm of Jesus, and to lead a life of service in relation to others. Applied to non-Christian rituals, the issue is whether the ritual in question actually results in the reception of divine revelation, the experience of divine presence, the regeneration of divine salvation, etc., as appropriate to the claims alleged by its practitioners. To the degree that the objectives, norms and values of particular ritual acts can be identified, and to the degree that such are achieved in the devotee, to such degree we can speak of how religious rituals symbolize and mark the Spirit's activity.

The value of a pneumatological theology of religions can now be seen in clearer light. I have argued that insofar as Word and Spirit are related but yet distinct as the two hands of the Father, we should be able to identify dimensions of the Spirit's presence and activity which are not constrained by that of the Word. These, I have proposed, are marked by experiential realities such as relationality, legality, rationality, and processive and harmonious continuity. These are signs of the Spirit's presence and activity in the world generally and in the religious dimension specifically. Of course, the work of the Spirit is to constitute each thing in its integrity within its environment, and determining a thing's integrity or authenticity is to ask questions about its norms, ideals and values; this is the presence, whether intense or attenuated, of the Logos. There is thus no final escape from Christology, and this is the truth about the relation between Word and Spirit. But the question at hand is whether or not to impose christological norms up front or perhaps later in the dialogue. A pneumatological approach to the religions gives us sound theological reasons to take up the former as a strategy for the interreligious conversation.

There is, of course, a serious complicating factor. It may be that certain rituals have developed into fields of force directed toward objectives that either deny or overreach the forms, ideals and values which constitute their beings and purposes, and it may be that participation in such rituals do accomplish such objectives in their practitioners. This is the problem of *divine absence*, the terror of the demonic. Demonic rituals are those whose inner 'spirits' are intent on destroying human integrity, disrupting social relations, producing alienation and estrangement, obstructing personal healing and communal reconciliation, inhibiting human creativity, and so on. Daniel Williams proposes a theological understanding of ritual as the means by which we name, exorcise and overcome the demonic (1990: 21-23). What we thus need are new christic and pneumatic rituals both to discern the perverted forms of the Logos and force fields of destruction, and to triumph over them. We have come full circle back to the problem of discernment again.

3. *Discernment and Comparative Theology*

Our discussion has, however, advanced since leaving the topic of discernment in Chapter 3 in that we have developed some more strictly, even if provisional, pneumatological guidelines by which to distinguish the presence, activity and absence of the Holy Spirit in the world of religions. By doing so, we are now also in a position to identify what Christopher Morse calls 'faithful disbeliefs' about the Holy Spirit (1994). Taking his cue from the admonition in the first Johannine epistle, 'do not believe every spirit, but test the spirits to see whether they are from God' (1 Jn 4.1), Morse rightly says that the call to belief is not a call to believe everything and that there are in fact many things that contradict what we in fact should hold fast as Christians. Such is all the more urgent when dealing with the diversity of spirits in the religious dimension because of their symbolic significance regarding things of ultimate concern. The transition from abstract philosophico-theological theory to a concrete pneumatology of religions thus calls for an interpretive scheme for religious symbols. This may be called a theology of discernment.

Aspects of Christian Discernment
The criterion for testing the Spirits urged upon the Johannine community is fundamentally christological.[48] This is undoubtedly formulated to address the pressing problem of docetic gnosticism confronting that Church (1 Jn 4.2-3). Would different contexts draw forth other criteria? The answer would seem to be both 'yes' and 'no,' with a decided

---

48. There are a good number of passages dealing with true and false prophecy (and prophets). Other Christian texts that discuss discernment more specifically are Heb. 5.14 and 1 Thess. 5.21-22 regarding good and evil, and 1 Cor. 12.10 regarding the charismatic gifts. Elsewhere, I provide exegetical warrant for my views on spiritual discernment by engaging the biblical materials from the standpoint of foundational pneumatology (see Yong, forthcoming). With regard to the theology of discernment, there is an enormous amount of extant literature. Aside from biblical commentaries on the relevant scriptural texts, the following can also be consulted: Kelsey 1978; Boros 1978; Bouchet 1979; Price 1980; Hiebert 1985a; Küng 1987; Ukpong 1989; Schweizer 1989; and Gorringe 1990. I will discuss Pentecostal and especially charismatic theologies of discernment more specifically in Chapter 7.

emphasis on the latter, as borne out by reflections on the topic in the eighteenth century and in our contemporary era.

In the midst of the First Great Awakening in New England during the years 1740–42, Jonathan Edwards wrote *The Distinguishing Marks of a Work of the Spirit of God.*[49] One of the notable features of this treatise is his discerning of spirits from two directions: a negative and a positive approach. The latter was what Edwards called 'scriptural evidences'. The marks of the Spirit's presence and activity among a people included the exaltation of Christ in their lives, the hindering of the progress of Satan's work, the growth in commitment to the Scriptures and confidence in its truth and divine character, the increase of love for God and neighbor, and the overall redirection away from error toward the truth. Edwards's negative approach was delineated to identify that which did not count in an a priori fashion as a sign of the Spirit. Among these he included unusual or extraordinary works, bodily effects such as tears, trembling, groans, shrieks, or other contortions, mental effects such as those causing agitation or commotion in crowds, impressive flights of the imagination, and the fact that people seem to be imitating the words or deeds of others. Edwards argued that all of these were by themselves potentially compatible with the work of the Holy Spirit. There was also no a priori reason to deny a genuine work of God even if imprudent and irregular conduct, errors of judgment, delusions of Satan, and gross and scandalous practices were judged present. That individuals persist in these things would only prove that they themselves have not persevered in the work of the Spirit; the entire revival could still be the result of the visitation of the Spirit.[50] For

49. This treatise can be found, among other places, in the Hickman edition to Edwards's *Works* (1988: 257-77). It is a useful place for us to begin discussion on the discernment of spirits for a number of reasons. First, Edwards's was motivated to write this tract by concrete and pressing circumstances of enthusiasm which accompanied the revival. This means, second, that the guidelines suggested by Edwards can still be meaningfully applied to Christian revivalism, of which the modern Pentecostal–charismatic movement is one species. Finally, this is not only vintage Edwards, but also a theological classic, along with those portions of the Ignatian *Exercises*, on the subject of spiritual discernment. It is exemplary of discussions on this topic, both in the import of its insights and in the limitations of its scope.

50. There are, undoubtedly, apologetic elements at work in this treatise. Edwards was one of the central figures in the revival. I should also note Edwards's final 'negative sign': the fact that hellfire and brimstone were essential components

Edwards, 'that there are some counterfeits, is no argument that nothing is true' (1988: 265).

Two things are clear in Edwards's discourse: that Christ and the Scripture are central to any positive evaluation of the Spirit's presence and activity, and that the phenomenology of religious experience is not a sure guide to discerning the Spirit. In an essay on discerning the spirits written in the context of an increasing intercultural awareness of religious pluralism, veteran missiologist Paul Hiebert confirms Edwards's intuitions. Hiebert is aware that the discoveries in the history of religions no longer allow proclamation of the superiority of the Christian message based on miracles, religious experiences, spiritualities, religious-moral codes, or even resurrections. There are, he insists, 'no simple phenomenological criteria by which we can test the presence of the Holy Spirit' (1985a: 151). Under these circumstances, Hiebert humbly proposes a few exploratory suggestions. The Spirit is present and at work when God is glorified through Christ; when Christ's lordship is magnified in life, worship and thought; when spiritual practices are consistent with that in Scripture; when the fruit of the Spirit are borne; when spiritual maturity is evidenced; when the entire gospel is presented in a manner that avoids any imbalance; when the body of Christ is united rather than divided; and when recognition is given to God being at work even in the mundane experiences of life.[51] While Hiebert does conclude with a reminder that 'we need to keep a sense of divine mystery' (1985a: 161) in these matters, the biblically inspired and christologically centered cast of the criteria he suggests are unmistakable.[52]

of the proclamation of the Gospel. This conviction is in line with the overall orientation of the author of 'Sinners in the Hand of an Angry God'.

51. This last criterion Hiebert calls 'wholism,' the idea that there is no dualism between God and nature. As a criterion, it focuses away from 'supernatural' acts of God, traditionally defined as miracles, toward the divine presence and activity at all levels and in all realms of life.

52. This is the case also with Thomas Michel's (1983) criteria for discerning the Spirit in Islam: the words of Christ, the rule of love for one's neighbor, and the values of the Kingdom of God. Using these criteria may tell us if there is anything in Islam of import to Christians; such would probably be trivial to Muslims. Just as needed for the interreligious dialogue is to allow Muslims to speak on their own terms—i.e. from the Qur'an and the Sufi tradition—about *rūh*, or the Spirit (e.g. Kritzeck 1975; Khoury 1983).

There is no problem with Edwards's approach given the context of the Great Awakening. There are basically two spiritual domains that Edwards's guidelines identify: that of the Holy Spirit and that of Satan and his legions. His readers and parishioners would have agreed with him that the revival could be assigned to either source. Hiebert's criteria would not be problematic if it were an in-house activity indulged by Christians. They would, in fact, be helpful for Christians attempting to distinguish between the Holy Spirit and other spirits among themselves for themselves. But Hiebert specifically identifies his context as that of a religiously plural world. How legitimate is it for Christians to discern the spirits in non-Christian traditions? Are there only two kinds of spirits—the Holy Spirit and demonic spirits? Would this be simply saying, 'No, the Holy Spirit is not there' or would such also involve pronouncing what other spirits are present? Would Christians be in any kind of position to determine what kind of other spirits are present and active in a non-Christian tradition? How appropriate would it be for Christians to name spirits in other traditions? Or, to reverse this line of questioning, how would Christians feel if non-Christians were to 'discern' or name the spirit(s) involved in Christian life, thought and activity? Would non-Christians be in any kind of position to determine the spirit(s) present and at work in the Christian tradition? Would not Christians simply dismiss the assessments of non-Christians whose classifications for spiritual reality may not include either the categories or labels of 'holy' or 'demonic'?[53] In short, discerning the spirits in other traditions is not only a theological matter; it also has far reaching, religious, social and political ramifications.

It is here that the distinctions made by Hans Küng in an article on 'an ecumenical criteriology' may be useful (1987). To be fair, it should be noted that Küng's interest is more so in discerning true from false religiosity than it is in the discernment of spirits. Yet what is of value is the overall framework of his proposals. Küng distinguishes three general

53. That all 'discerning' in the interreligious arena may be no more than our imposing our own names and categories upon others and vice versa leads Zwi Werblowsky to comment that 'after reading about the "unknown Christ of Hinduism" all one can do is to wait for a Mahayana Buddhist to write on the unknown Buddha of Christianity. Sooner or later the point is reached where even theologians have to ask themselves whether they wish to be taken seriously or whether they are engaged in inventing new variations of the old Humpty Dumpty game' (1975: 153-54). In what follows, I hope to take this concern seriously.

categories of criteria which correspond to three spheres of ecumenical dialogue. At the outermost level, a general ethical criterion is applied to all human endeavors, institutions, and indeed, religious traditions. That which is humanitarian is genuinely religious; that which is not is false or bad religion. At the middle level, the criterion of faithfulness to canonical origins is applied to each tradition. A religious tradition is true to the extent that it remains faithful to its authentic essence as scripturally defined. (Note: Küng does not tell us what to do with non-textual traditions.) At the innermost level, the specifically Christian criterion of Christ is directly applicable only to Christians. It is by faith that we live our life in commitment to Jesus Christ. As Christians, however, we cannot but share our convictions with others. This specifically Christian criterion is, then, applicable in an indirect sense to non-Christians, but only insofar as Christians faithfully apply this criterion to themselves first.[54]

There is, clearly, a tension for the Christian discernment of spirits in non-Christian traditions. On the one hand, we cannot avoid Christian criteria; on the other hand, to be fair to others in the interreligious dialogue, their own internal criteria have to be invoked at some level. Yet none of the levels identified by Küng can be kept in isolation from the other two. From the Christian perspective, faithfulness to Christ necessarily entails faithfulness to the Christian canon, and commitment to a humanitarian ethic, and vice versa. In other words, the discernment of spirits cannot be solely an in-house Christian affair. In order that what is discerned not be distorted beyond recognition, discernment has to be a dialectical process through each level. Where one begins is not as important as the process itself. I take comfort in the face of this complex task from Eduard Schweizer's reminder that distinguishing 'between the Spirit of God and other spirits is itself a gift of the Spirit of God' (1989: 406; cf. 1 Cor. 12.10).

The Interpretation of Religious Symbols

The Christian discernment of spirits in other traditions is thus an indissoluble two-part process of interpretation and comparison. First, the other tradition needs to be able to speak for itself, to identify its own symbols, and to define their references. Second, categories of comparison and contrast need to be identified to facilitate understanding and

---

54. At this level, it is correct to say with Jean-René Bouchet that 'fundamentally discernment is a particular kind of proclamation of the gospel' (1979: 105).

adjudicate contrary theological claims.[55] What this does is provide us with a mechanism by which we can not only distinguish (Greek *dia-krisis*) between different conceptions of spirit(s), but make some preliminary decisions about truth or falsity. Discerning the spirits is, in this sense, an exercise in *comparative theology*. Let me elaborate by focusing first on the adjective, and then on the noun.[56]

Comparative theology involves the hermeneutical process of identifying, classifying and interpreting the similarities and differences between religious symbols.[57] This means, first, that the phenomena of the other tradition has to be defined by them on their own terms (cf. Paden 1988: 51-68). This step is absolutely crucial since insiders to a tradition will see things differently than outsiders, and identify things of *importance* that outsiders fail to see.[58] Allowing insiders to register what is important about their tradition is central to the foundational pneumatology in place here. Recall that part of the pneumatological criteria developed earlier involved a thing's authentic representation of its being and accomplishment of its purpose relative to others. To reflect further on religious ritual, this first step would allow practitioners to

55. James Dunn tells us that discerning the Holy Spirit requires in part our 'interpreting' or 'comparing' (Greek *sunkrino*) spiritual things spiritually (1998: 314, his rendition of 1 Cor. 2.13). Note also that Peirce's contemporary, Royce, who was very much influenced by the former's theory of signs, wrote: 'the method of interpretation is always the comparative method. To compare and to interpret are two names for the same fundamental cognitive process' (1968: II, 280). This quote is taken from Royce's Lowell Lectures (1913), wherein he developed Peirce's idea of interpretation as a communal process of inquiry.

56. Clooney makes very similar distinctions but discusses them in reverse from myself (1993: 4-7).

57. J.Z. Smith has called our attention to *differences* in any comparative project (1982: 19-35). Similarities should always be similarities-in-difference; otherwise, we would be talking about identical things and wasting our time.

58. *Importance* is a technical term in Neville's theory of theory which points to a thing's value (1995b: 48-57). He distinguishes six sites of importance: *theoretical*, relating to formal commitments deriving from the categorial classification of a thing; *singular*, related to a thing's infinite density and value by virtue of its being what it is; *intrinsic*, related to a thing's achievements relative to others; *extrinsic*, related to a thing's causal conditioning of other fields; *relational*, a subclass of extrinsic, related to the interconnectedness of things; and *perspectival*, related to how a thing rates the value of other things from its location in the environment. These are valuable distinctions in themselves. I use the term in its broad, inclusive sense.

classify properly those things which are important in any ritual with regard both to its aesthetic value in itself, and to its purpose or utility relative to its practitioners. At this fundamental level, we can tentatively acknowledge the Spirit's presence and activity insofar as the practice of any ritual by devotees do not deviate essentially from its controlling norms, and the devotees get out of the ritual what it is supposed to impart.

To complete the task of discernment, however, requires taking the second step of developing comparative categories.[59] This is imperative since the task of discerning the Spirit involves the comparison and contrasts of phenomena in diverse religio-cultural traditions. Not only is the concept of 'spirit' defined very differently in different traditions, but there are also traditions which lack such a concept altogether. Given the Christian presupposition that the Holy Spirit is at work universally to a greater or lesser extent in the non-Christian faiths, what is required is that the religious symbols of other traditions be accurately classified in more vague categories in order to open up avenues for comparison. The categories themselves should arise out of the insider's classification of the data, even while the formation of the categories will enable a more precise identification by them of what is important. Whether or not the vague categories preserve the importance of the things compared will need to be hashed out in an a posteriori fashion in the interreligious dialogue by participants on both sides.[60] The goal in a pneumatological approach to the religions is to find sufficient analogues in other traditions to the Christian doctrine of Holy Spirit such that we are put in a position to pursue the comparative task and affirm or deny the Spirit's presence or activity. A basic question at this level, for example, would be whether or not a non-Christian religious ritual accomplishes in its practitioners values or relations similar to what the Holy Spirit works

59. On this, see Mountcastle (1978: 21-42). Neville himself has developed a theory of comparison from Peirce's logic of reasoning (see Neville 1995b: 74-54).

60. This a posteriori hashing out in the interfaith conversation also serves another important purpose not directly related to discerning the spirits in the other, but quite directly related to that of discerning the self and the home tradition. This is because dialogue with the other provides a mirror that allows critical perspective to emerge on the latent world-view presuppositions that may otherwise not be accessible (cf. Yong 1999c: 316-26). Interreligious dialogue, therefore, is as much a journey of critical self-discovery as it is a faithful Christian discernment of the other.

through Christian rituals. In sum, what is important about a ritual in itself, and relative to the religious ends of its practitioners, both as determined by them, become yardsticks by which we can discern the Spirit to a greater or lesser degree.[61]

How might the interreligious dialogue develop in light of the comparative theology of discernment sketched so far? Among the few efforts to pursue a similar project that I have been able to identify, Peter Lee's essay, 'Dancing, *Ch'i* and the Holy Spirit' (1994), is exemplary. Lee begins by describing various folk and religious dances among the Chinese. Out of this, the Chinese philosophical concept of *ch'i* was seen to suggest itself as a category by which to capture the important elements expressed in these dances. Explicating the content of *ch'i* as understood by select individuals in the history of Chinese thought allowed other vague categories to emerge. Lee was eventually led to attempt some provisional comparisons and contrasts between *ch'i* and the Holy Spirit in spiritual categories such as energy, discipline, service and gracefulness.[62]

While Lee's effort is to be applauded, we must also be warned against subsuming the differences of the 'other' within our own conceptual framework. Theological imperialism is imperialism whether it

61. This is a variation of Küng's middle-level religious criteria based on faithfulness to canonical origins. The weakness in his model is that he assumes, without justification in my opinion, that the primordial event in question is truly revelatory of the divine and not skewed by the demonic. I will return to this in more detail later.

62. There have been a number of other efforts to work in this direction, with a greater or lesser degree of success. England and Torrance (1991) have collected a number of illuminative essays attempting to discern the Spirit's movement in the religious stories, histories, movements and rites of Asian peoples. Of the two essays devoted to discerning the Spirit in the religions in the second volume of *Credo in Spiritum Sanctum*, Khoury (1983) attempts to understand 'spirit' within the framework of the Qur'an, while Dhavamony (1983) allows the *Trimurti* and *Sacchidananda* to speak on their own terms before undertaking a comparative Hindu-Christian analysis. Martinson attempts to define the category of spirit under more or less universal functions of vitality, (self-) transcendence, and personhood, and goes on to understand similar Taoist, Confucian and Buddhist notions as evidence of the Holy Spirit (1987: 182-99). I think he is on the right track, even if there is much more of a dialectical interchange between universal and local perspectives in the act of comparative theology than his own effort lets on. All of these are exploratory pieces which lack the integrative depth and reconstructive breadth that I am attempting here.

occurs up front in aggressive apologetics or toward the end in the subtleties of the interreligious dialogue.[63] The question that needs to be asked is whether or not, in continuing with Lee's project, there is a truth to the Chinese symbol of *ch'i* on its own, before imposing our own pneumatological criteria or paradigm on it. This moves the discussion from the meaning of *ch'i* to its truth.[64] Now, as aforementioned, Peirce himself admitted all interpretants of symbols to be other symbols. The meaning of any symbol could be explicated by other symbols within the system, and articulated in terms of its effects. Any symbol can satisfy the coherence theory of truth simply by virtue of its strategic nesting within the larger religio-cultural-linguistic system. Yet Peirce did not thereby discard the view of truth as a dyadic correspondence between a sign or symbol and its intended object. This is one of the superior features of Peirce's epistemology and theory of truth when compared to the presuppositions of most anthropologists and historians of religion.[65]

In one of his most recent books, Neville (1996) has developed a theory of religious symbolism by fusing elements of Peirce's semiotic theory and Tillich's theology of symbol. That truth is a dyadic relation,

63. On the surface of things, it is impossible for anyone undertaking the kind of project attempted here to avoid the charge of what Gangadean calls 'semantic imperialism'—the effort toward theological universalization through a particular religious language (1995: 227). What would need to be established up front, however, is the right of insiders to define their tradition and to reject labels or categories offered by their partners if such do not get the phenomena correctly. Of course, it is also important for Christians to defer to their dialogue partner and to be vulnerable to correction. Again, Krieger's suggestion of deriving a universal rationality by means of other-rationality (see n. 5), while certainly ambitious, is the kind of objective that any attempt at systematic theology worth its name should aspire to.

64. This is, ultimately, the difference between comparative theology and comparative religion. The latter succeeds whether or not the truth questions are asked; its focus is simply on understanding (Sharpe 1986). Eliade was a masterful religious comparativist (cf. 1974). But, realistically, the serious study of religion requires that historians of religion grapple with religious truth claims, even as any theology worth the paper it is written on has to engage seriously the history of religions. W.C. Smith made these points long ago (1959) and has devoted a lifetime to bridging the gap between theology and religious studies (e.g. 1962, 1981, 1993). In doing so, he has proven to be a noble representative of the tradition of Schleiermacher, Otto and Van Der Leew.

65. This is the point made by Geerts (1990) in his comparative analysis of the contributions of Peirce and Victor Turner for interpreting religious symbols. Again, I refer the reader to my paper on Peirce (Yong 2000b).

even if interpretation is a triadic one, is central to Neville's theory. Neville acknowledges with Peirce that meanings are normally generated by or codified within the religio-cultural-linguistic framework they subsist in. At some level, however, devotees claim that their symbols engage them with the divine (or the transcendent).[66] Neville distinguishes these levels both in terms of meaning and reference. At the religio-cultural-linguistic level, symbols have *networks* of meaning in which reference can be found by *extensional* means to other symbols in the system. At this level, there may be layers and layers of symbolism, all interconnected within smaller or larger networks of meaning. At the transcendent level, however, symbols have *content* meaning in which reference is determined by the *intentionality* of the devotee with regard to the divine. Now whereas *comparative* theology focuses on religious symbols and their extensional references, comparative *theology* asks about their intentional references. This scheme makes it possible not only for us to take the claims of religious practitioners seriously, but also perhaps to identify analogous references to the divine Spirit.

We are able to do this, Neville argues, by way of the faculty of imagination which is religious in character. This is the case, he suggests, because of the 'world-constructing' function of the imagination, whereby it images 'boundary conditions orienting the experiential world' and separates that off from the infinite (1996: 58). Religious symbols, Neville therefore maintains, are thus *finite/infinite contrasts* (from Tillich 1951: 237-41) which unveil to the imagination realities or structures of reality that shape our world.[67]

Neville's theory has the further advantage of detailing how it is that symbols function to transform souls in devotional and cultic contexts. Symbols are transformative to the extent that they truly engage devotees with the divine. This takes place by means of a carryover of value

66. I will use 'divine' and 'transcendent' interchangeably; the latter is a broader category which would include references to ultimate reality in non-theistic traditions such as Theravada Buddhism, Taoism and Jainism.

67. Besides drawing directly from the work of Tillich, Neville credits his understanding of the religious character of the imagination to his colleague, Ray Hart (1985). Those aware of the work of the early Rahner can also see similarities between Neville's functionalist theory of imagination and Rahner's notion of the imagination as enabling access to the transcendent (see the discussion of the imagination in part three of Rahner 1968).

of the object symbolized into the life of the devotee and of the cultic community. Because true symbols participate in the reality they symbolize, they are able to convey or impart the value of this reality to the interpreter's experience. At the same time, true symbols merely point to the divine and then negate themselves by pointing the devotee (or the cultic community, if the symbol is engaged in a communal context) toward religious praxis.[68] In short, religious symbols have both representational and performative aspects by which they refer to the divine and provide a guide to life.[69] It may be possible with the help of Neville's theory to push the question of how and when the Spirit is active in the lives of persons in non-Christian traditions.

There is, of course, much more that can and needs to be said about Christian discernment than can be appropriately covered under phenomenology, semiotic theory and comparative theology. I will argue in Chapter 7, for example, that discerning the spirits requires cultivating the pneumatological imagination. At this point, however, a word of caution needs to be emphasized from the preceding discussion. If Schweizer is right, as I believe he is, that discernment is ultimately the work of the Spirit of God, then any theological agenda I may have will need to be confessed and abandoned. True openness to the Spirit, what Justin Ukpong calls true spiritual *kenosis* on the part of the theologian, involves a 'self-emptying and complete self-surrender to the power of the Holy Spirit' (1989: 421). I cannot be truly discerning if I am 'out to prove something'. In that case, I will find only what I am looking for. Truly discerning the spirits requires me to be open to that which the Holy Spirit wishes to reveal in any situation.

We are now poised to examine my overall argument that the Pentecostal–charismatic experience has been a heretofore untapped resource for a pneumatological theology of religions. Whereas this chapter has presented the theory behind the pneumatological imagination, the next chapter will furnish the experiential, practical and

68. Here is the paradox: 'living symbols' for Tillich were true only to the extent that they were self-negating. The truth of any symbol depends on the principle that 'the Unconditioned is clearly grasped in its unconditionedness. A symbol that does not meet this requirement and that elevates a conditioned thing to the dignity of the Unconditioned, even if it should not be false, is demonic' (1960: 91-92).

69. I have provided a much more extended summary of Neville's theory of symbolism elsewhere (Yong 1998a: 43-49).

confessional stance from which this imagination emerges.[70] At the same time, the Pentecostal–charismatic experience to be delineated next should also confirm the central elements and intuitions of the foundational pneumatology sketched here as well as shed further light on the relationship between the two economies, the nature of the religious dimension of experience, and the Spirit's presence and activity in the world.[71] Come Holy Spirit, like a mighty rushing wind, and give us cloven tongues by which we may articulate your ways and your deeds...

70. The public nature of my argument needs to be emphasized. While the pneumatological imagination developed here derives from the Pentecostal–charismatic experience, it is by no means the property of or accessible only by those with this experience. I would suggest that individuals like Hollenweger (1988), Moltmann (1992), Welker (1994) and others have proposed non-Pentecostal–charismatic versions of this imagination. Their categories differ from mine, but that all derive from a fundamental pneumatological orientation can be confirmed by those who assess the evidence impartially.

71. As with any sketch of a theological system, however, what is proposed here has to be assessed both within the broader Pentecostal–charismatic framework that follows, and then, further, in a thorough, and yet still provisional, full-length systematic reconstruction that is yet to be written. This book is a seed sown toward this larger project.

Chapter 5

THE PENTECOSTAL–CHARISMATIC MOVEMENT: A FRAMEWORK FOR UNDERSTANDING

Paul's question to the Ephesian disciples, 'Have ye received the Holy Ghost since ye believed?', is one that most Pentecostals are at least somewhat familiar with.[1] The point is to move, as the Ephesians did, to a recognition that believing in Jesus is only the beginning, and that there is more to the Christian life, viz., receiving, or, in Pentecostal terms, 'being baptized', in the Holy Spirit. My own baptism in the Spirit was an unforgettable event. I was twelve when it occurred during the annual family summer camp held by our denomination in 1978. It was an altar experience above all altar experiences that stretched over six or seven hours over three nights after the evening sermons. I recall tarrying with a small circle of my friends during that first evening. We did not have to wait long before the Spirit descended. My friends and I were moved deeply and powerfully as we prayed together. There were extended outbursts of tears, cries, prayer and praise, all interspersed with prolonged periods of glossolalic utterance. We encouraged and exhorted each other, adding to our circle other friends who could see that something dynamic and very real was taking place in our midst. There were other prayer groups scattered across the altar space. We were more or less oblivious to them (and to the world around us), except when we were, on occasion, baptized with new waves of the Spirit received from the effects of the encounters of others with God. We did not want this to end. We gradually dispersed, although not without each of us gathering our thoughts on our own and reflecting on the experience while basking in the presence of the divine

1. Acts 19.2, from the KJV. This is, of course, a debated translation/interpretation of the Greek text, εἰ πνεῦμα ἅγιον ἐλάβετε πιστεύσαντες, which appears in the NIV as, 'Did you receive the Holy Spirit *when* you believed?' (italics mine). The issue is whether or not Luke intended to communicate the reception of the Holy Spirit as subsequent to that of believing. Pentecostal clergy and laity generally do not question the subsequence doctrine. Pentecostal academics are divided on the issue. My use of the KJV provides one window into an important point of debate in Pentecostal–charismatic theology and spirituality.

Spirit. It happened again over the next two nights, although the density
of the encounter was not as thick as at the first. I have since experienced
the Spirit on numerous occasions, but never so completely immersed in
his presence as when it happened here. I do not recall now whether or
not I consciously identified this overwhelming experience of the Spirit as
an experience of Jesus. That it was an intense and lasting experience,
there can be no doubt.

Introduction

This chapter serves to contextualize the 'pneumatological imagination'
developed in the previous chapter by introducing the Pentecostal–
charismatic movement and the dominant themes and emphases in its
developing theological understanding. The fundamental questions
addressed here are: what is the Pentecostal–charismatic movement?
How should it be defined historically, sociologically, religiously, spiritually and theologically? What are the distinctives which set it apart
from other Christian groups and movements? What is it about the
Christian experience of Pentecostals and charismatics which shapes
their view of God, the world, and their relationship to both? Attempts to
answer these questions will serve to secure the empirical foundations
for the theology of the Holy Spirit developed here. Further, because I
draw not only from the Pentecostal tradition in this monograph but also
from the charismatic movement as well, one of the central questions to
be dealt with is why these movements should be taken together rather
than separately. I am therefore not only assuming there is a distinction,
but also that there is both a legitimate relationship between the two and
that their contribution to the discussion at hand can be strengthened if
jointly conducted.

I will proceed as follows. Section 1 will survey the historical development of the modern Pentecostal–charismatic movement from its
beginnings in the United States in the early 1900s to its present configuration worldwide. The phenomenology of Pentecostal–charismatic
experience at the heart of this tradition will be the subject of the second
section. This being the wellspring of the 'pneumatological imagination', I will argue that the variegated experience of the Holy Spirit is
central both to the expression of Pentecostal–charismatic religiosity and
to their being-in-the-world. The final section will be a brief sketch of a
Pentecostal–charismatic theology of the Spirit. This will demonstrate
how the foundational categories developed in Chapter 4 are empirically

grounded in the Pentecostal–charismatic experience and derive, in part, from the 'pneumatological imagination'. Taken as a whole, this chapter will provide us with a reservoir of theological ideas and resources to articulate a Pentecostal–charismatic theology of religions and participate in the interreligious dialogue.

1. *Historical Overview*

Labels for religious movements are often as misleading as they are informative. We are unable, however, to do without them. I will therefore organize the following historical survey by way of the two labels, 'Pentecostal' and 'charismatic'. I will supplement this with a brief comment about the global nature of the movement that draws from both the Pentecostal and charismatic streams.

Classical Pentecostalism
The designation 'classical' for what was originally known simply as 'the Pentecostal movement' derives from the early 1970s in response to the impact of the charismatic movement in the mainline denominations and the Roman Catholic Church. It generally denotes the 'modern' or twentieth century Pentecostal churches and denominations which have their origins in the United States during the 1910s and 20s.[2] There is a loose scholarly consensus that the movement's beginnings can be traced to the lives and work of two men: Charles Fox Parham and William Joseph Seymour.

Charles Parham (1873–1929) was a Holiness preacher whose ministry led him to found the Bethel Healing Home in Topeka, Kansas, in

---

2. Time and space preclude comment on pre-twentieth century 'pentecostal' movements. The name, of course, comes from the biblical account of the outpouring of the Holy Spirit on the Day of Pentecost (Acts 2). Early twentieth century Pentecostals were convinced that they were reliving this primitive Christian experience in 'the last days' after two millennia of the Spirit's absence from a backslidden Church (Wacker 1984). More recently, however, Pentecostals have come to acknowledge both that their roots lie in the Keswick Reformation and Holiness movements of the nineteenth century (e.g. Synan 1975 and Strachan 1975), and that there have been other charismatic movements throughout the history of the Church (e.g. Robeck 1985; Bernard, *et al.* 1989: 19-31; Bernard 1984: 282-303; 1996). Other valuable histories of early Pentecostalism include an initial work by Kendrick (1961), a more sophisticated account by Synan (1971), and a sociological evaluation by R. Anderson (1992).

1898.[3] Being very much a part both of the nineteenth century Holiness quest for signs of the second work of grace as well as the emerging dispensationalist movement, Parham came to the conclusion that xenolalic tongues were proof of Spirit-baptism, and that such would also be an incontrovertible sign equipping the saints for the final evangelistic harvest before the second coming of Christ (cf. Acts 1.8 and Mt. 24.14).[4] Bethel Healing Home was transformed into Bethel Bible College in the fall of 1900, and Parham led his first batch of students in the study of the 'Bible evidence' for the baptism in the Holy Spirit while following the biblical model of 'waiting for the outpouring of the Spirit in the upper room' (Acts 1.13, 2.1).[5] On January first of the new year, Agnes Ozman (1870–1937) was the first of many Parham students to speak in unknown tongues. Over the years, these students were commissioned to evangelism and the mission field, being zealous for the work of the Lord, and full of the Holy Ghost and power.[6]

William Seymour (1870–1922), born to former slaves Simon and Phillis Seymour, joined Parham's Bible school when it was moved to Houston, Texas, in December of 1905.[7] Through a series of circumstances, by April of the next year Seymour found himself pastoring a

3.   We are indebted to James R. Goff, Jr's invaluable scholarly biography of Parham for a deeper understanding of Pentecostal origins (1988).

4.   *Xenolalia* is tongues-speech in an actual foreign language unknown to the speaker but recognizable by those who know it; the emphasis here is on the content of utterance. Another variation is *akolalia*, where hearers identify an actual language even when such is not actually vocalized; the emphasis here is on hearing (cf. Acts 2.6). Both xenolalia and akolalia come under the broader rubric of *glossolalia*, a catch-all term for all kinds of ecstatic tongues-speaking. I will return to a discussion of tongues-speech in the next section.

5.   Bethel Bible College closed almost as quickly as it was opened, lasting only a few months into the spring of 1901 (see R. Anderson 1992: 51-58; my thanks to David Bundy for this reference).

6.   Needless to say, not very many returned from the mission field with success stories about 'glossolalic evangelism'. Faupel has assessed this aspect of early Pentecostalism in detail (1996b).

7.   Seymour never really became a member of Parham's school, given the racial climate in the South during this time. He was, however, allowed to sit just outside the door in the hallway and absorb Parham's teachings. Seymour's life-story is available in D.J. Nelson's 1981 dissertation. Other sources which deal with the substantive contributions of blacks to the origins and shape of Pentecostalism include Paris (1982), MacRobert (1988), Sanders (1996) and Hollenweger (1997: 18-141).

small but growing congregation in an old building at 312 Azusa Street in downtown Los Angeles. Convinced by Parham of the 'Bible evidence', Seymour's preaching led to an outbreak of glossolalia which was the central feature of the Azusa Street revival from 1906–1908 (see Robeck 1991). Parham himself came to visit in October 1906, but was aghast at the intermingling of races in Seymour's services. Although this led to a break between the two Pentecostal pioneers, the global revival was effectively launched through them. It is perhaps no coincidence that a white and a black man were jointly appointed to spearhead this movement which has since crossed numerous racial barriers. In the words of Frank Bartleman, a lay preacher and reporter-participant at Azusa Street, this was where 'the "color line" was washed away in the blood' (1980: 54; see Irvin 1995).[8]

The innumerable itinerant and self- (or should we say, 'Spirit-') appointed preachers who streamed forth from Azusa Street eventually saw the need to organize themselves. They recognized that much more could be done for the united witness of the gospel, the funding of world mission and evangelism, ministerial training, and the production and printing of curriculum and other materials if their resources were pooled together. Out of these considerations, a number of denominations were formed, the largest of which include the General Council of the Assemblies of God and the International Church of the Foursquare Gospel. Along with other denominations such as the Church of God, Cleveland, Tennessee, and the Church of God in Christ which had already been incorporated but whose leaders were influenced by the Azusa Street revival and quickly led their groups into the emerging Pentecostal movement, classical Pentecostalism took shape.

All was not well, however, in the youthful Pentecostal movement. The emphasis on individual reception of the Holy Spirit fostered an experientialism and subjectivism which did not incline many Pentecostals to external authorities. Schisms were almost the rule as evidenced even in the relationship between Parham and Seymour. The single most decisive issue in terms of overall long-term impact was the split over the 'New Issue' concerning the doctrine of the Godhead

8. As always happens, however, what God has brought together, human beings have found ways to put asunder. White and black drifted apart from each other after Azusa Street, and formed their own denominations and coalitions. Only very recently, however, have the two groups been reconciled; for this historic event to which I will return in another context, see Macchia (1995b).

between the trinitarians and the Oneness groups in 1916 (Menzies 1971: 106-22; Reed 1975). From this, the Pentecostal Assemblies of the World, the United Pentecostal Church International, and numerous other denominations bearing the name 'Apostolic' were formed (Clanton 1970). Besides their denial of the doctrine of the Trinity, other distinctive Oneness practices include a strict code of external holiness, water baptism 'in Jesus' name' exclusively, and the less widespread teaching that salvation is incomplete until the individual has repented, is water-baptized, and filled with the Holy Spirit.[9] At the turn of the twenty-first century, it is estimated that Oneness adherents number over one-fourth of all Pentecostals in the United States (cf. Barrett 1988: 824, and Barrett and Johnson 1998).[10]

In any case, early Pentecostals, whether Oneness or trinitarian, Holiness or Keswick, white or black, were generally those whose social location played at least some part in predisposing them towards Pentecostalism. These were, generally speaking, a socially marginalized, politically voiceless, economically deprived and ecclesially slighted group (R. Anderson 1992). They were also culturally and intellectually despised. Yet it is clear that their experience of the Spirit provided them with the voice, status, power and means by which their place in the world and, more importantly, the Kingdom of God, was legitimated.

The Charismatic Movement
We will pick up on our outline of classical Pentecostalism and the Pentecostal experience of the Spirit in due time. In America, however, Pentecostals were awakened from their dogmatic slumber by the appearance of the experience of the Holy Spirit in the mainline and Roman Catholic churches. Even more recently, a 'third wave' has emerged, contributing further diversity to an already variegated global movement. Let us briefly look at these in turn.

'Neo-Pentecostalism' signaled the appearance of tongues and other charisms in the mainline churches.[11] It had its stirrings in the 1950s in

---

9.   The baptismal formula and soteriological doctrine are nicely summarized, for Oneness adherents, in Acts 2.38.

10.   David Reed (1997: 74) follows Gregory Boyd's estimate of five million Oneness Pentecostals worldwide; I think this is a gross underestimation given the feeling I get that Oneness churches are even more vigorous outside the United States. I do not, however, have any hard data to back up this claim.

11.   *Charisms* is from the Greek term, χάρις, meaning grace. It points theolog-

part because of the ecumenical witness of the South African Pentecostal, David Du Plessis. His willingness to take the Pentecostal message to any and all listeners earned him broad audiences among those
yearning for spiritual renewal in the older denominations.[12] The drizzle
of the 1950s became a downpour in the 1960s when Episcopalians,
Lutherans, Presbyterians, Methodists, Baptists, among others, received
the Holy Spirit and spoke in other tongues (Quebedeaux 1983). Neo-
Pentecostal presence in the mainline churches led in many instances to
an increase in personal piety, commitment to evangelical witness,
deeper Bible study, and openness to more intense forms of spirituality
which inevitably accompanied the manifestation of the charismata.
Although there was initial, and in many cases, strong resistance against
this movement by denominational hierarchies, these have been more or
less resolved over time allowing many 'neo-Pentecostals' to remain in,
and in some cases, return to their churches. The 1970s saw the
establishment of official charismatic renewal agencies within all of the
larger mainline denominations, the Orthodox Church, and even in some
of the smaller groups, both in North America and elsewhere.

The charismatic movement in the Roman Catholic Church got off to
a little later start, and was even more of a jolt to classical Pentecostals
than the renewal movement in the Protestant denominations.[13] The
more open climate following the Second Vatican Council allowed for
Catholics to pursue and experience charismatic phenomena beginning
during the spring of 1967 at Duquesne University and the University of

ically to the Spirit's activity in the world through human beings and covers a broad
range of phenomena including but not limited to the charismata and office-gifts outlined in various places in the Christian Testament (e.g. Rom. 12.6-8; 1 Cor. 12.7-
11, 28-30; Eph. 4.8-12). I will discuss these further in Chapter 7.

12. Du Plessis's ecumenical engagements earned him the title 'Mr. Pentecost'
even as it cost him his Assemblies of God ministerial status and affiliation. He was
eventually restored to communion by the denomination. An autobiographical
account of aspects of Du Plessis's ecumenical ventures can be found in his *The
Spirit Bade Me Go* (1970).

13. Until the Catholic charismatic renewal, of course, both sides vilified the
other. Many early Pentecostals were especially influenced by fundamentalist anti-
Catholic rhetoric which still remains in some classical Pentecostal circles. Synan's
(1984: 97-118) is a sober and succinct overview from a classical Pentecostal perspective. Early Catholic historical accounts of and theological perspectives on the
renewal include O'Connor (1971), Gelpi (1972), Montague (1974) and Laurentin
(1977).

Notre Dame. The renewal in the Catholic Church has since taken a variety of forms, whether in retreat settings or in the formation of covenant communities at diocesan, regional, national or even international levels. In addition to the phenomena and experiences accompanying the neo-Pentecostal movement, however, Catholic renewal has also featured a deepened Marian devotion among the laity and a heightened sense of sacramentality in practice and theology among the Church's leaders and thinkers. Classical Pentecostals often have a hard time understanding Marian piety among Catholic charismatics. Other divisive issues include that of proselytism and Catholic conversions, especially in the two-thirds world, to classical Pentecostal denominations. These tensions remain at all levels of Catholic-Pentecostal relations. What is usually less well known among Pentecostal laity and even ministers is that the formal Roman Catholic–Pentecostal dialogue begun in 1972 has provided a forum for mutual understanding and been a resource for the resolution of some of these matters.[14]

Since the 1970s, the charismatic movement in America has, to a certain extent, taken on a life of its own apart from classical and neo-Pentecostalism, or the Catholic Church. Central to this latest surge are the growth and expansion of healing and prophetic ministries, many of them reaching back to the 1940s and 1950s, the founding and establishment of independent and megachurches, the soaring market of televangelism, and the emergence of wholly new churches and denominations (Hummel 1993). Many of these phenomena have converged in what C. Peter Wagner, world renowned missiologist at Fuller Theological Seminary, has called 'the third wave of the Holy Spirit' (1988). In addition to these elements, however, Third Wave charismatics emphasize signs and wonders, power confrontations in evangelism and healing, and a reinterpretation of what St Paul alluded to as 'spiritual warfare' (2 Cor. 10.4). For Third Wavers, the realm of the demonic is very much a reality, but so is the victory wrought by Christ over these

14. Classical Pentecostal participants of these dialogues have generally been the more ecumenically minded academics and ecclesiastics in the mold of Du Plessis. They have not, however, represented their denominations in any formal sense since classical Pentecostals are, on the whole, still suspicious of organized ecumenism. The fall 1990 issue of *Pneuma: The Journal of the Society for Pentecostal Studies* contains the final reports of the first three quinquennium of dialogue covering 1972–1989. The report for the latest session, 1990–1997, is in the spring 1999 issue of the same journal.

principalities and powers; believers simply need to exercise faith in order to participate in this victory. While it is clear that not all healing ministries, megachurches, televangelists, or newer denominational structures would count themselves as part of the Third Wave, a large number of these organizations and key individual leaders have embraced aspects of Third Wave theology and practice. The fact that the Third Wave *Weltanschauung* is replete with spirits and demons and corresponds to that of many non-Western cultures has led some analysts to attribute the recent success of the Pentecostal–charismatic missionary endeavor to this correlation (e.g. Brouwer, Gifford and Rose 1996). Pentecostals and charismatics, however, are quick to insist on the distinctive Christian response of exorcising these demonic spirits 'in the name of Jesus' in contrast to the attempts to placate the spirits that are widespread practices among folk and indigenous religious traditions.

It is arguable that the Third Wave, if taken as a whole to include its theological and practical emphases rather than limited to its official individual and organizational sponsors, does indeed partake in the same stream which has fed the neo-Pentecostal and charismatic movements. I have thus included them under the broader 'charismatic' label.[15] For now, however, the major differences between charismatics of all stripes and the older classical Pentecostal movement should be noted. Charismatics come from much more diverse social and ecclesial backgrounds than do classical Pentecostals. They almost always deny the classical Pentecostal doctrine of initial evidence even if they accept tongues and charismatic phenomena as part and parcel of the 'Spirit-filled' life. For these and other reasons, they have either remained in their original denominations when possible, or joined newer, local independent churches. All of them, however, have contributed especially during this past quarter century to the emergence of a global Pentecostal–charismatic culture (cf. Poewe 1994; Hocken, *et al.* 1994).

15. All three, and more, are discussed by Peter Hocken in his article, 'Charismatic Movement', in the *Dictionary of Pentecostal and Charismatic Movements* (Burgess, McGee and Alexander 1988). The *Dictionary* also contains an extensive article on the 'Catholic Charismatic Renewal' by Francis Sullivan. I will later comment on how classical Pentecostals have both resisted and received what the Third Wave has washed to shore.

Global Pentecostalism

The year was 1958 when Henry Pitt Van Dusen first referred to the Pentecostal movement as the 'third force in Christendom', besides the Roman Catholic and Protestant Churches.[16] Van Dusen's designation was far more prophetic than descriptive, given the advance of Pentecostal missions up to that time compared to its explosion since. In the past forty years, however, Pentecostal forms of Christianity have literally flourished across the globe, not least because of the emergence of the charismatic movement. The following can be no more than a terse report on these phenomena in Asia, Africa, and Latin and South America.[17]

There is, as yet, no overview of Pentecostalism in the continent of Asia as a whole. Regional and national studies, however, are growing by the number. Most prominent on a national scale is the Pentecostal Church in Korea with Paul Yonggi Cho's 700,000-member Yoido Full Gospel Church, the largest congregation in the world, in the vanguard. Also impressive is the fact that up to one-third, if not more, of Taiwan's 300,000 Protestants are of Pentecostal–charismatic stripe. Numbers are more difficult to gauge in China, with estimates ranging widely from four or five million upwards to sixty(!) million Protestants in house churches across the mainland. Yet even if we were to stay with the

16. This is the same Van Dusen who I quoted from at the beginning of my foundational pneumatology in the previous chapter. I get this citation from Pomerville (1985: 20; it originally appeared in Van Dusen's 'The Third Force in Christendom', *Life* [9 June 1958: 113-24]). It should be noted, however, that the following discussion of 'global Pentecostalism' includes churches and movements whose members resist identification especially with classical forms of Pentecostalism. Defining 'global Pentecostalism' is itself a complex task, raising issues like who gets to do the defining and for what purposes. My own account relies more on the phenomenology of religion and the sense that most within these movements would endorse what I call the pneumatological imagination as their way of being-in-the-world. It also serves to make a theological point regarding the centrality of experiencing the Spirit in the Pentecostal–charismatic movement.

17. One should not forget its expansion in Europe as well, as Harvey Cox reminds us (1995: 185-212); I will not say much about European Pentecostalism, however, except later insofar as it contributes to our overall discussion of *theologia religionum*. But as far as Pentecostalism around the world is concerned, part three of Cox's *Fire From Heaven* gives a kaleidoscopic view. Walter Hollenweger, the dean of scholarship on Pentecostalism, also provides global coverage of the diffusion of the movement (1972, 1997), as does section II of a recent collection of papers (Dempster, Klaus and Petersen 1999).

more conservative figures, what is more certain is that part and parcel of the growth inland is the emphasis on the charismatic gift of divine healing. This testimony to the vibrancy of the Pentecostal–charismatic movement in China can be found in many other parts of Asia, stretching west as far as India and south to Singapore and Indonesia. In almost every place where the Pentecostal message and the charismatic impulse has penetrated, both churches modeled after classical American Pentecostalism and more indigenous type movements wherein acculturation of the Christian gospel has gone far deeper are evidenced. At the same time, signs that the Asian Pentecostal–charismatic churches are coming of age can be seen in their active mobilization of missionary projects directed outward to other nations.[18]

Assessment of the Pentecostal–charismatic movement in Africa is complicated by the upsurge of countless indigenous or independent Pentecostal–type churches which cover the continent. While this has led at least to terminological confusion, it is best to distinguish three broad categories of churches: Pentecostal churches of Western origin, newer independent Pentecostal churches perhaps the result of an 'African charismatic movement' over the past quarter of a century, and older independent Spirit-type churches founded by Africans for Africans driven in part by a reaction against white colonialism and in part by a concern for retaining more of a continuity between their Christian thought and practice and traditional African religiosity (A. Anderson 1991: 3; 1992). The most famous churches in the last category are the Kimbanguist Church in The Congo, the Zionist churches of Southern Africa, and the Church of the Lord (Aladura) in Nigeria. There are, however, solid classical Pentecostal establishments both in southern and western Africa, even if the most profound impact of global charismatic Christianity seems to be taking place in the latter region, particularly in Nigeria and Ghana. That Pentecostals and charismatics together

18. Yoo's (1988) is the most complete history of Pentecostalism in Korea while Adams's (1991) focus is on Cho's ministry. Synan (1994) mentions over 350,000 Roman Catholic charismatics in Korea as well as the fact that there are four other Pentecostal–charismatic type churches in Seoul alone which rank among the largest in the world! For Taiwan, see Rubinstein (1988). For the Chinese Church, see Martinson (1988) and Deng (1993). Hummel (1993: 291) quotes David Barrett (World Christian Encyclopedia, Lausanne: Statistical Task Force, 1992) regarding 60 million Chinese Pentecostals. For India, see Pulikottil (1998). For Asian Pentecostal-charismatic missions, see Mullins (1994) and Hackett (1996).

comprise one of the largest Christian groups in Africa should caution us against underestimating the extent and popularity of this joint movement.[19]

Unlike Asia and Africa, we are fortunate to have the solid sociological study of Pentecostalism in Latin America as a whole from David Martin (1990). He and many others have pointed to the socioeconomic, cultural and political factors at work in Latin American modernization, urbanization and secularization that have contributed to igniting the Pentecostal revolution (e.g. Glazier (ed.) 1980; Stoll 1990; Westmeier 1993; Sepúlveda 1994). Yet as weighty as these factors are to the development of Pentecostalism in Central and South America, it would be simplistic and reductionistic to stop there. In almost every Latin American nation, without exception, the blistering growth in the ranks of the Pentecostals, who Latinos usually identify under the broader label of *evangelicos*, has come at the expense of networks of base-communities connected to a movement intent on revitalizing the Roman Catholic Church as well as in the face of surging folk and indigenous religious traditions. Compared to the African scene, however, Pentecostal–type churches in Latin America have, more often than not, resisted the temptation to adopt indigenous features or expressions. The point is that people are not only making social, economic and political decisions, but also religious ones, and these latter need to be factored into any analysis of Pentecostal growth in Latin America. If the estimates are right that one in four Latin Americans will be *evangelicos* and one in six Pentecostals by the turn of the twenty-first century, David Martin's talk about a 'Protestant explosion' would seem to be rather mild in hindsight.[20]

19. A valuable bibliographic essay on African Pentecostalism is Corten (1997). Daneel (1987) provides a good introduction to the broad landscape of African independent Spirit-type churches. For Kimbanguism, see Martin (1975); for the Bantus, see Sundkler (1961); for the Aladura, see Turner (1967). For South Africa Pentecostalism, especially its classical strands, see Oosthuizen (1975), A. Anderson (1992), Anderson and Otwang (1993) and Pillay (1994). Ojo (1988 and 1995) is a solid guide to the charismatic movement in Nigeria while Gifford (1994) and ter Haar (1994) do the same for Ghana.

20. The statistics come from Oneness Pentecostal leader and academic, Manuel Gaxiola-Gaxiola (1991: 107). Corten's (1997) bibliographic essay also covers Pentecostalism in the Caribbean and Latin America, and mentions most of the important publications following the movement's eruption since the mid-1960s. One noteworthy item not mentioned by Corten is Kenneth Gill's dissertation on the

All in all, it is clear that the turn-of-the-century Pentecostal revival in North America among the socially bereft has been replicated during the past few decades around the world among people in similar social circumstances. Yet it is also clear that what people are experiencing is genuinely religious and that these need to be understood as such. While I do not pretend to resolve the complex post-Weberian debate regarding the relationship between religiosity and social, political and economic movement, I do think that there is a theological point to be made even if it is one which Pentecostals and charismatics have been slow to understand, articulate and act on. This is the connection between the Spirit's presence and activity on the one hand, and between the Spirit's activity and our own participation in such on the other. The remainder of this chapter will therefore focus on this central experience of the Pentecostal and charismatic movement, first on a phenomenological level, and then toward a more theological interpretation.

2. *The Pentecostal–Charismatic Experience of the Spirit*

While the preceding survey gives us some flavor of what the worldwide Pentecostal–charismatic movement is like, the question of what it is that binds together this diverse scattering of peoples and churches remains. I will argue here that it is the experiences of the Holy Spirit— what is often referred as, but not limited to, the charismata—that links Pentecostals and charismatics together (cf. Pomerville 1985: 80-92). It is this mutual experience of the Spirit that inspires what I have called the 'pneumatological imagination'. This mutually informing experience and imagination not only justifies the connection between the two groups, but in doing so, also provides the basis for a collaborative approach to the non-Christian faiths. To demonstrate this argument, I will focus my discussion on the phenomenology of Pentecostal and charismatic ritual as the framework within which the Holy Spirit is encountered.

Rituals of the Spirit
Years of participation in and research and reflection on the origins and global variations of the Pentecostal–charismatic movement has led

widespread development of Apostolic (Oneness) Pentecostalism in Mexico (1989). I will discuss further the literature on Latin American Pentecostalism in general, and Brazilian Pentecostalism more specifically, in Chapter 8.

Walter Hollenweger to a normative definition of the essential features of its spirituality. These include:

1. an emphasis on the oral aspect of liturgy;
2. theology and witness cast in narrative form;
3. maximum participation at the levels of reflection, prayer and decision-making, and therefore a form of community which is reconciling;
4. inclusion of dreams and visions into personal and public forms of spirituality, so that the dreams function as kinds of icons of the individual and the collective movement;
5. an understanding of the body and the mind which emphasizes the experiences of correspondence and relationship between the two (1986: 551-52).

These features can be understood as being at the center of the Pentecostal-charismatic experience of the Spirit. The fact that Hollenweger does not mention glossolalia specifically should not be misleading. He does not mention the dance, the clap, or the shout either. The vague features he does mention, however, are sufficiently broad so as to apply to Pentecostal or charismatic expressions in diverse cultural environments. Glossolalic prayer may be emphasized more in Korean contexts; rousing song-singing is a feature of Latin American Pentecostalism; the dance may be more prominent in certain independent or Spirit-type African churches; the shout may be especially noticeable in African-American Pentecostal circles, and so on. What can be expected in any Pentecostal or charismatic manifestation is democratic (read oral) participation in ritual, a merging of public and private domains, and a holistic expression of spirituality in mind, body and the affections. These, then, are elements of the pneumatological imagination which emerge out of Pentecostal–charismatic experience of the Spirit, enabling both their engagement with the world on the one hand, and their pursuit of the Spirit on the other.[21] In short, there is a hermeneutical spiral present

21. Positively stated, Hollenweger's normative features capture in large part the 'constants' of the pneumatological imagination of Pentecostals and charismatics which can be identified under the more abstract categories of divine presence and activity. The negative 'constants' include those subsumed under the category of divine absence, which I will elaborate on in Chapter 7. I prefer the categoreal constructs since they are vaguer and thereby potentially more productive for the inter-religious dialogue.

in the Pentecostal–charismatic encounter with the Spirit.

In order to see further how this spiral is played out, a closer look at Pentecostal–charismatic ritual is in order. In an illuminating article, Daniel Albrecht has given us a lens by which to examine Pentecostal–charismatic spirituality at work (1992). First, *rituals* and *rites* are distinguished. The former are the large-scale constructs within which Pentecostal spirituality is communally enacted, as in worship services, prayer meetings, camp retreats, etc. The latter are specific phases of these services, whether they be during praise and worship, the sermon, the altar session, etc. Albrecht then goes on to consider the ritual *field*, ritual *modes of sensibility* and ritual *consequences*. Briefly, the ritual field is the context created to facilitate the divine–human encounter. Central to this field are the auditory (music, song-singing, testimonies), visual (other engaged worshippers), and kinesthetic and tactile dimensions of Pentecostal–charismatic worship. This combination which emphasizes the kinesthetic is probably what is distinctive about the Pentecostal–charismatic experience. Participants believe that their motions in the worship of God (as well as affections, words and thoughts) are an icon of the divine being itself: 'they move even as God moves' and 'they experience and express the actions of God, the movements, upon and through the worshippers' (Albrecht 1992: 113). The goal of Pentecostal–charismatic worship, as Albrecht notes, is the experience of the presence and activity of God, and this is felt, thought and psycho-physiologically engaged.[22]

Ritual modes of sensibility discussed by Albrecht are the attitudes which shape each worshipper's engagement with the various rites. Such may be moods of celebration or contemplation, what Albrecht describes as the active expression of praise and thanksgiving or the active waiting upon the divine word. Or, the congregation could also move into a mode of 'transcendental efficacy', by which is meant the 'ritual work' phase of the service where believers expect pragmatic consequences such as healings, miracles, Spirit-baptism, visions giving personal or congregational direction, and so on, to flow from their encounter with the divine. Finally, ritual consequences are the unintended benefits (at

22. Cf. Lawless's insightful application of Peirce's semiotic to Pentecostal glossolalia (1980). She correctly notes, however, that Peirce's focus on the cognitive dimension of signs is unable to explicate fully the emotive and even somatic dimensions of the glossolalia in Pentecostal–charismatic experience.

least not consciously so) which accrue from ritual participation. Drawing from Victor Turner's idea of *liminality*, Albrecht sees such by prod-
ucts as *communitas* (communal reconciliation and social solidarity),
self-conscious reflexivity (deliberation on the implications of encounter
with divine presence usually issuing forth in creative expressions of
faith), and transformation (whether at individual, filial, ecclesial, or less
frequently, even social levels) fostered in believers as a result of
consistent ritual participation.

The value of Albrecht's essay for our purposes lies in the fact that his
discussion derives from extensive fieldwork in three Californian con-
gregations, each representing one of the trajectories—classical Pentecostalism, neo-Pentecostalism, and Third Wave—which combine to
inform the contemporary North American Pentecostal–charismatic
landscape.[23] It goes without saying that his discussion of the character
and functions of Pentecostal ritual takes us at least part of the way
toward making good the claim regarding a global Pentecostal–charismatic culture even if the order of the rites in this or that Pentecostal or
charismatic service at any one place is different from that of any other.
The issue in Pentecostal–charismatic ritual is not adherence to a specific
order of rites—that would be anathema to the emphasis on spontaneity
and freedom valued by Pentecostals and charismatics—but the congregation's holistic involvement and engagement with the divine presence
in anticipation of receiving something transformative from a new work
of the Holy Spirit in the ritual process.

How the pneumatological imagination informs this aspect of Pentecostal-charismatic ritual needs to be emphasized. It is clear from
Albrecht's analysis that while charismatics and especially Pentecostals
dislike the term 'ritual' and its connotations, and even while they prize
the freedom and liberty to respond spontaneously to God, worship services are designed in such a way so as to cultivate Pentecostal–charis-

---

23. In addition, the import of this piece is that Albrecht has translated his
observations into an elaborate theory of ritual even while retaining the empirical
cast of his work. The validity of the theory will show itself at significant points
when I test it against Brazilian forms of Pentecostalism in Chapter 8. Note that
Albrecht, a classical Pentecostal, completed his doctoral work on Pentecostal ritual
at the Graduate Theological Union in Berkeley, California, in part under the supervision of Gelpi. The publication of his dissertation (Albrecht 1999) appeared too
late for me to make use of in this work. He is the 'former Bible college professor' I
refer to in my introductory testimony in Chapter 4.

matic values and expressions even while ensuring that all things are 'done in a fitting and orderly way' (1 Cor. 14.40). What is 'fitting', however, is that which brings the symbols to life in such a way that the Spirit's presence and activity is truly mediated to the ritual participant. This means that the Pentecostal or charismatic is actively and wholly engaged in worship, that he or she experiences personal liberation perhaps leading to transformation in other contexts, that there is room for novelty and creative expression even within a pre-established ritual format. Glossolalia, healings, dances, etc., are charismatically endowed manifestations which are iconoclastic to the degree that the freedom of God to do the unexpected and, in many cases, the impossible, is embraced. In short, Pentecostals and charismatics exclaim, 'We've had Church!' because of a transformative encounter with divinity.[24]

Encountering the Spirit

The presence and activity of the Holy Spirit is thus central to Pentecostal-charismatic spirituality and *Weltanschauung*. I want to focus the argument next on the experience of Spirit-baptism not so much because there is a homogeneous understanding of what it denotes among members worldwide but because it probably best symbolizes the distinctive orientation of the Pentecostal–charismatic imagination, and also because of its theological import for the global movement. I will show that classical Pentecostals, neo-Pentecostals, charismatics and Third Wavers all agree that no matter how 'Spirit-baptism' is actually defined, it is *sus generis* to their Christian experience. There is thus a general consensus about its phenomenology, and its function and purpose for Christian life. In short, the doctrinal symbol of Spirit-baptism brings us closest to what, if anything, can be termed the 'essence' of the Pentecostal–charismatic experience (cf. McDonnell 1979: 96), even if that should be critically qualified, as will be done here.

As the South African theologian, Henry Lederle, has shown, there is no end to theological distinctions that Pentecostals and charismatics

---

24. This reflects St. Paul's statement that 'where the Spirit of the Lord is, there is freedom' (2 Cor. 3.17), as well as the literalness with which Pentecostals and charismatics take the repeated promises of Yahweh through the Hebrew prophets to accomplish something new among the people of God (e.g. Isa. 42.9, 43.19, 62.2; Jer. 31.31; Ezek. 36.26-27). It also supports what Tom Driver says about the need for liberating Christian rites that are transformative for both individuals and whole communities (1991: especially 212-23); more on this in Chapter 7.

have been driven to in attempting to render precisely what Spirit-baptism is (1988). There are a diversity of interpretations of Spirit-baptism among classical and neo-Pentecostals in which the experience is understood to denote the initial infilling of the believer by the Holy Spirit at salvation and regeneration, or where it identifies an intense encounter with the Spirit at some point in time subsequent to regeneration. Catholic sacramental interpretations of Spirit-baptism talk about it as the experience of 'the release of the Spirit', of 'the flowering of baptismal grace', or other such terminology. Integrative interpretations attempt to combine both sacramental and non-sacramental views in some way.

These intra-Pentecostal–charismatic disputes cannot be resolved here. My own suggestion, which I will develop in greater detail below, is to understand the Pentecostal–charismatic experience of the Spirit as a 'sacramental sign' without the traditional Catholic 'sacramental baggage' such as the doctrine of *ex opera operato*. At this point, however, I want to lift up some of Lederle's conclusions. He says, for example, that Spirit-baptism is not so much about stages or sacramental 'releases'. Rather, it is about the 'essential insight that the Christian life should have an experiential dimension to it. In openness to the Spirit and in the acceptance of the full range of spiritual gifts or charisms lies the genius of the Pentecostal and charismatic movements' (1988: 215-16). Lederle's terminological confusion should not detract from the value of his findings. Of course, all Christian life has an 'experiential' dimension to it, in the broad sense in which this notion is used in this work (see Chapter 4). What Lederle is calling attention to is clarified in the second sentence quoted: the experience of the full range of the charismatic *activity* of the Spirit. These include, Lederle goes on to say,

> charisms such as prophecy, healings, miracles, discernment, and speaking in tongues. Perhaps these were accompanied by a new depth in one's relationship to Christ, or doxological praise, fresh power to serve, new enthusiasm to pray, a deeper sense of God's presence and involvement in our lives, a new openness to being led and being guided by the Spirit, etc. (1988: 216).

I would concur with Lederle in that I also see 'Spirit-baptism' as a construct which emphasizes this dynamic orientation toward the Spirit's activity in Pentecostal–charismatic spirituality and life.[25] But I would

25. This was, in essence, also the suggestion of the Dominican charismatic

also want to emphasize the 'present-ness of the Spirit' that American Assemblies of God theologian, Frank Macchia, has pointed out. Macchia has put forth a suggestive theology of glossolalia which sees tongues in part as both an eschatological theophany and as language *coram Deo* (1992). Drawing upon Otto's language of *mysterium tremendum et fascinosum*, Macchia highlights the experience of the awesome, overwhelming and mysterious presence of the Spirit in the Pentecostal–charismatic encounter with the divine. These are crucial moments in the formation of the pneumatological imagination. The merit of Macchia's treatment is that it brings to prominence our more or less passive reception and acknowledgment of the Spirit's *presence* in the community of saints. The experience of Spirit-baptism is an experience of the divine self-disclosure. This is the gracious gift of God; our response is absolute self-surrender, symbolized in part by our speaking in other tongues *as enabled by* the Spirit.

Macchia's treatment of glossolalia does not forsake the understanding of the Spirit as *active* in the experience of Spirit-baptism either. For him, this is most clearly evident in the fact that the diverse charismata both symbolize and effectively usher in the new creation. This broad construal of Spirit-baptism accommodates Lederle's insights and confirms Albrecht's assessment of Pentecostal ritual. It also cautions us against taking glossolalia, or any other single charism for that matter, as the only sign of the Spirit's presence and activity, something Macchia

theologian, Simon Tugwell, in answer to the question, 'is there a "Pentecostal" experience?':

> The reason why I think it is important to deny that there is any 'particular' 'Pentecostal experience' is that *all* our experience, if we are in Christ, must be 'Pentecostal'. What we have to learn from the Pentecostal churches is how to rediscover in ourselves and in our churches what it means to be so totally 'led by the Spirit' that every thought, even, is brought into subjection to Christ. The transformation of our whole experience will, of course, be articulated in fact into a wide variety of different experiences, and some of these may well be such that we shall want to speak of a special working of the Holy Spirit in our lives (1977: 9-10; cf. Hocken 1978).

Note also the Thomistic framework and language of the charismatic Catholic Francis Sullivan who interprets the experience of Spirit-baptism as 'a new sending...a real *innovatio* of that person's relationship with the indwelling Spirit. Therefore it has to mean a more intimate and "experiential" knowledge of God as present in the soul, a knowledge that "breaks out" into more ardent love' (1974: 66; cf. Gelpi 1992).

himself would want to be very careful about.[26] What it does is enable any interpretation of Spirit-baptism worth its name to account for the manifold expressions of the Spirit in the global Pentecostal–charismatic experience.

In other words, there is what Michael Green calls 'the reality behind the inaccurate description' of Spirit-baptism (1975: 146-47). Spirit-baptism for Pentecostals and charismatics points to an encounter with the divine (Spirit) such as that experienced when one undergoes a deluge or is swept by a whirlwind (baptism). Outwardly, Spirit-baptism could be accompanied by a variety of manifestations. One could be 'slain in the Spirit', whereby one falls to the ground either because one is powerless to sustain oneself, or because one passes from consciousness (cf. Rev. 1.17). One could burst forth in ecstatic or controlled glossolalic speech, or exuberant and melodious praise (Acts 10.16), or prophetic utterance (Acts 19.6). There have been those who have grunted, groaned, or laughed vociferously or quietly. Others have been motivated to take 'holy marches' around the sanctuary, or to dance innovatively 'in the Spirit', and so on. A pneumatological imagination enables these kinds of expressions. Through such a pneumatic orientation, Pentecostals and charismatics experience these phenomena as holistic encounters with the divine Spirit. By themselves, of course, none of these manifestations guarantee the special presence or activity of the Holy Spirit; they could be personally, or even on occasions, demonically inspired. Rather, the 'essence' of Pentecostalism on this view is best seen as a wide range of phenomena, many of which would occur in any Pentecostal–charismatic experience of Spirit-baptism, but none of which would transpire in all of them.[27]

---

26. I think Macchia's strategy a wise one on this point. My own theology of glossolalia is vague enough to account for the initial evidence doctrine even while it does not necessarily require it (Yong 1998a). Macchia and I both agree that the iconoclastic function of tongues is as important theologically since it underlines the Spirit as one who replaces that which is rote and tedious with creative novelty and advance. Timothy Gorringe also notes that the Spirit reveals precisely by taking us by surprise (1990: 9, 15); this is very much in line with how Peirce says we learn epistemologically and psychologically. Glossolalia is *par excellence* the vehicle of protest and transformation, although the fact that it can be routinized should also warn us about our 'domesticating the Spirit'. I think the verdict regarding tongues and how it functions as an evidential sign is far from closed and ecumenical discussion can only be beneficial for all sides.

27. Here, I follow J.Z. Smith's 'polythetic mode of classification' (1982: 1-5).

I would argue that this interpretation of Spirit-baptism is applicable to the global shape of Pentecostal–charismatic experience, including that of the African independent Spirit-type churches. Here is it useful to recall that since both Lederle and Albrecht consciously incorporate phenomenological and theological data from the broad spectrum of the Pentecostal–charismatic movement in their investigations, their conclusions should be applicable even to the experiences of the African churches to a greater or lesser degree. Further, it is not insignificant that Lederle's analysis come from a South African perspective although it is heavily slanted by the Reformed tradition that comprises his own theological background. While Lederle would most definitely emphasize the contrary (for all intents and purposes) religious frameworks which distinguish the pneumatologies of African Independent Churches from that of classical Pentecostal or charismatic interpretations of the Spirit, I would suggest with his South African former colleague and Pentecostal theologian Allan Anderson (1991) that the differences are more conceptual than real. The experience of the Spirit in the African independent Spirit-type churches is 'pentecostal' not only phenomenologically, Anderson argues, but experientially as well, insofar as the expectations and benefits of divine presence and activity is seemingly congruent whether one belongs to an independent or classical Pentecostal Church. I would add that this is the case because the experience of the Holy Spirit is guided by the pneumatological imagination. The point is that there is sufficient evidence for a convergent understanding of Spirit-baptism as the 'essence' of what it means to be Pentecostal or

Glossolalia as a charismatic phenomena would accompany perhaps the majority of the experiences of Spirit-baptism no matter which Pentecostal or charismatic community it occurs in, but not necessarily all of them (cf. Bennie 1980: 64). Gerald Pillay tells of the interesting case of the Bethesda Pentecostal Churches in South Africa which in fact attempt to downplay the significance of glossolalia even while they insist on their Pentecostal identity (1994: 197-202). These kinds of situations are probably not as uncommon as Pentecostals are inclined to think. Anderson and Otwang note that tongues-speech is emphasized more by Western and white Pentecostals while other 'tangible and intangible manifestations' are embraced by black or African ones (1993: 114-21). Dayton's classic *Theological Roots of Pentecostalism* does not even list glossolalia as among the central core doctrines of classical Pentecostalism (1987). All this goes to show that any talk about the 'essence' of Pentecostalism would need to be subtle and nuanced in order to be alert to the exceptions to the 'rule of classification' which real life always retains the right to insist on (cf. Wilson 1999: 105-108).

charismatic even if we do recognize, as we indeed should, the diversity of its manifestations.[28]

The foregoing has been selectively brief, given my immediate objective of arguing for the essential togetherness of the Pentecostal movement and various strands of charismatic groups. This has led me to attempt a 'Pentecostal–charismatic contribution to Christian theology of religions', rather than just a 'Pentecostal' one. In the next chapter, the results of such a joint effort should prove its worth. But before I accrue the evidence for this, however, a brief word needs to be said about how the Pentecostal–charismatic experience of the Spirit both conforms and contributes to the foundational pneumatology developed previously.

3. *Toward a Pentecostal–Charismatic Pneumatology*

The reality of the Holy Spirit, in the words of the distinguished Pentecostal biblical scholar, Gordon Fee, is 'God's way of being present, powerfully present, in our lives and communities as we await the consummation of the kingdom of God' (1994: xxi).[29] I would add that as an object of theological reflection, the Holy Spirit is a *symbol* of 'God's way of being present' *and* actively at work 'in our lives and communities' (cf. Lindbergh 1992). I have argued that Pentecostals and charismatics live according to this pneumatological imagination fostered in their encounters with the divine. Methodologically, two

---

28. I will return to Anderson's work in Chapter 6, but note here that his conclusions reflect an extensive background in both classical Pentecostal and independent Pentecostal–type African churches. Ultimately, this is a question concerning Pentecostal identity. Many Pentecostals reject indigenous movements in the two-thirds world as genuinely 'Pentecostal', saying that such only appear to have the form but not the substance. I am convinced, however, that such is wrong-headed and commend the openness of individuals like Paul Pomerville, an Assemblies of God missiologist, toward independent Christianity in Africa (1985: 27-35). In this work, I attempt to give theological reasons why experiences of certain kinds of charismatic phenomena qualifies persons and groups to the label 'Pentecostal' should they consider themselves such. There should not in any case be a priori theological barriers as to where, when, how and upon whom the Spirit can be present and active.

29. Fee's work represents a much more critical biblical pneumatology that is a marked advance over the work of other Pentecostals, e.g. Horton 1976, in this area.

strategies will be interwoven in what follows. First, I will initiate a four-way dialogue between the classical Pentecostal churches and the three streams of the contemporary charismatic movement as delineated earlier. Second, I will test the foundational pneumatological categories to see how they fare against the core Pentecostal–charismatic experience of the Holy Spirit. The overall objective is to arrive at a pneumatology that is a) theoretically of sufficient ecumenical amplitude such that it can potentially represent the broad spectrum of Pentecostal–charismatic churches and experiences worldwide, and b) empirically connected at key points to the vague categories of the foundational pneumatology so that it is potentially able to sustain its claims outside the Pentecostal–charismatic context.[30]

The thesis I am suggesting is that the experience of the Spirit informs the pneumatological imagination of the Pentecostal or charismatic and vice versa. Such an experiential vision is a holistic one which is integrative and transformative not only for individuals but also for whole communities. This holism can be explicated for individuals as the relationship between the cognitive, emotive and bodily components of Spirit-baptism; and it can be understood on the communal level as the charismatic relationship between individuals and the body of Christ. I submit this study as being at the heart of a theology of the Holy Spirit emerging from the ongoing dialogue between classical Pentecostalism

---

30. Note that I am *not* developing here a full-blown Pentecostal–charismatic theology of the Holy Spirit. My objective is to provide a sketch of the pneumatological imagination as derived from the classical Pentecostal dialogue with the charismatic movement (cf. Veenhof 1992) and in service of the interreligious dialogue which commences later. Of course, the interconnectedness of all theological loci means that what I outline here will have important repercussions in other areas. In this sense, Hollenweger is right to have persistently prodded Pentecostals and charismatics to rethink theology systematically from their experience of the Spirit (1978, 1984, 1991). Completing this project, however, is an interdisciplinary task beyond the pale of any one individual but thankfully already begun by the present generation of Pentecostals and charismatics, e.g., monographs which include the earlier work of Gelpi; on community, Jones (1975); on conversion, initiation and ecclesial life, Mühlen (1978); on theology of work, Volf (1991); on social ethics, Villafañe (1993); on spirituality, Land (1993); on pedagogy, Johns (1993); on eschatology, Faupel (1996a); and perhaps the most ambitiously comprehensive effort to date, Suurmond (1995). Some of what follows will draw from these pioneering reflections. My own desire is to contribute in some small measure both here and in future work to this collaborative task.

and the various strands of the charismatic movement.[31] To exemplify how this dialogue has enabled a more robust Pentecostal–charismatic pneumatology to emerge, it may be useful to highlight the theological presuppositions and emphases of classical Pentecostals, of which three in particular stand out. The first is the doctrine of subsequence whereby charismatic experiences of the spirit are understood to follow the experience of Christian conversion. The second is the assumed dualism between matter and spirit, especially in earlier classical Pentecostal thinking. The third is the functionality of Spirit-baptism as an endowment of power for witness (Acts 1.8). While there are obviously some truths to each of these doctrines, all undergo critical revision in the dialogue with the charismatic movement and global Pentecostalism.

To begin with, the classical Pentecostal doctrine of subsequence has come under heavy attack from neo-Pentecostals and Catholic charismatics. Theologically, the issue is that of the continuity or discontinuity between justification and sanctification. In Pentecostal–charismatic circles, this debate continues under the rubric of conversion–initiation and baptism in the Holy Spirit. In part because those who have pressed classical Pentecostals most on the issue of subsequence have been evangelicals and charismatics from mainline denominations, the discussion has focused on exegetical rather than theological issues.[32] At this level, a polarity has developed over interpreting pneumatology according to the didactic letters of St Paul or the historical material of Luke–Acts. Evangelicals and charismatics have generally insisted on giving priority to the Pauline theological framework while classical Pentecostals and those sympathetic to the subsequence position have responded that Luke has his own theological program that needs to be recognized and appreciated.

This issue is in part hermeneutical and in part derivative from the Pentecostal–charismatic experience. On the former point, some classical Pentecostal exegetes such as Gordon Fee have been led to concede the point that Spirit-baptism should not be considered as a second work

---

31. Examples of such a dialogue are found in Spittler (1976) and McGee (1991).

32. F.D. Bruner (1970) was one of the first to take on the Pentecostal doctrine of subsequence. His critique has since been taken over by James Dunn. The charismatic Baptist, Howard Ervin (1984, 1987) has been as staunch a defender of the doctrine of subsequence as any classical Pentecostal. For a review of key issues and players in the debate, see Dunn (1993).

of grace following conversion and Christian initiation (1991: 105-19). The truth of the subsequence emphasis, however, lies in its pointing to the 'more' that underlies any processive view of human experience. Thus neo-Pentecostals like J.R. Williams have understood Spirit-baptism as the 'actualization of a dynamic whereby the whole person is energized to fulfill *new possibilities*' (1972: 12), and Catholic charismatics like Gelpi have characterized the experience as a posture of openness to the divine (1971: 173-208). Spirit-baptism is thus fundamentally a transformative and reorienting experience in which novel elements are integrated into a personal force field thereby allowing new habits to eventuate. Theologically, Spirit-baptism emphasizes Christian life as that empowered by the Holy Spirit for witness and service, something which more and more classical Pentecostals and charismatics are coming to agreement on as being central to what I am calling the pneumatological imagination.[33] The point here is that whereas previous pneumatological discussions of Spirit-baptism have centered on its relationship to or distinction from conversion–initiation, it is now possible to focus on the experience itself—what it does in and for the individual, and derivatively, for whole communities.

The supposed dualism between the material and non-material realms has also been called into question by the ongoing Pentecostal–charismatic dialogue. The experience of the Holy Spirit led Pentecostals early on to understand God as both transcendent and yet immanent. The ongoing dialogue, however, has expanded the polemic against dualism in the direction both of theological anthropology and the theology of charisms, or charismology. In this expanded framework, the question is no longer whether human beings are bi- (body and soul/spirit) or tri- (body, soul and spirit) partite, or whether the charisms are natural endowments or supernatural gifts as in the older debates. Rather, what is important is whether or not any characterization gives us greater understanding of the interrelationship between the various dimensions of reality.

The Catholic charismatic priest and theologian, Peter Hocken, for example, has called for the further development of a theology of symbols given the Pentecostal–charismatic experience of the intimate connection between the physical and the spiritual (1989). Hocken's

---

33. That the Holy Spirit in Luke–Acts is the Spirit of prophecy has drawn widespread agreement among Pentecostal–charismatic biblical scholarship (see Stronstad 1984, 1995; Shelton 1991; Menzies 1994; Turner 1996).

suggestion comes in the midst of an energetic conversation about the sacramentality of the Pentecostal–charismatic experience wherein it is suggested that not only does the body receive and mediate the Spirit, but also that the body gives definition and expression to the Spirit's presence and activity.[34] His lead has more recently been taken up by Frank Macchia (1993) who attempts to interpret tongues sacramentally by drawing from the work of both Rahner and Tillich. He approves the former's emphasis of sacramental efficacy 'in the context of the *sign value* of the sacrament' (1993: 62) as well as Tillich's assertion of the divine self-disclosure through finite physical/audible forms. Wanting to avoid seeing the Pentecostal–charismatic experience of the Spirit as an unmediated encounter or as subjective emotionalism, Macchia is led to see the value of sacramental theology for explicating the presence and activity of the divine:

> …the experience of the Spirit for Pentecostals includes a visible/audible human response that signifies the divine presence in the sense of actually participating in making it present. Tongues as a sign is given in divine freedom but is also a visible [and audible, and kinesthetic, etc.] context in which the experience of God is received and manifested. It is both free and sacramental (1993: 70).

The value of Macchia's work for what is being accomplished here is not only that it lifts up the conjunction of Logos and Spirit in the Pentecostal–charismatic experience, but it also confirms our fundamental thesis that both Word and Spirit are constitutive elements of every thing, event or experience. Tongues-speech is a sign that the two hands of the Father are at work, albeit in different dimensions. While this can be parsed in different ways—i.e. Logos in the bodily expressions, Spirit in the emotive; or, Logos in the form of glossolalia, Spirit in its

---

34. See Hocken (1976); in this same volume, Tugwell said that Pentecostal glossolalia 'is a sacrament in the fullest catholic sense of that word, in that it is a human act given to men to do, in which however, according to their belief, we may unequivocally and without reserve identify an act of God himself' (1976: 151). Sacramental interpretations of Spirit-baptism among Catholics, however, tend to understand the experience as 'a "release" of the Spirit—a revitalization or flowering of the sacramental grace received in Christian initiation, breaking through into the personal conscious experience of the believer' (Lederle 1988: 105-106). As will be seen, I think this description on the whole fails to do justice to the powerfully transformative character of 'newness' intrinsic to the experience; on this point, see Sullivan (1974) over and against the mainstream of charismatic Catholic interpretations.

functions—these need not be dogmatically construed. Steven Land, Church of God (Cleveland, Tennessee) theologian, has submitted that from the human perspective, Word and Spirit come together in the affections (1993). The 'heart' is the unifying center for the human mind, will, emotions and body as shaped by the encounter with the Spirit. In this connection, charismatic experiences are initial signs of the believer's entry into the force field of the Spirit. The sacramentality of the Pentecostal–charismatic experience can then be taken further into the realm of what St Paul calls the 'fruits of the Spirit'. Dispositions that emerge from under the strong influence of the Spirit are expressed cognitively and somatically as being more integrative than those formed by the self or other spirits. In this way, charismatic experience and charismatic life continuously shape the pneumatological imagination, and vice versa.

Such a theological revision of anthropology from a Pentecostal–charismatic perspective goes hand in hand with Hollenweger's argument long ago that the charisms should be understood both as natural endowments as well as symbolic windows into the Spirit's presence and activity in the world (1978). According to Hollenweger, it was also Du Plessis's conviction 'that the Holy Spirit is also in the unbelievers, and that they too have charismata, although they might perhaps not understand or use them correctly' (1997: 352-53). I would add that this view supersedes the older notion of the charisms as a supernaturalistic in-breaking of the Spirit into the ecclesial order with the idea that they are spontaneous or gracious (i.e. *charis*-matic) appearances of the Spirit that integrate the various dimensions of human experience, both in and outside the institutional Church, into new wholes. In this sense, the charisms can be understood as affective dispositions that enable encounters of the Spirit which integrate the somatic, cognitive and emotional dimensions of human experience. On the one hand, they are informed by the Spirit to meet the needs of particular occasions (1 Cor. 12.7); on the other hand, they are shaped by the pre-existing psycho-socio-somatic force fields out of which they emerge. There is no room for metaphysical dualism in any theology of the Holy Spirit informed by the Pentecostal–charismatic experience.[35]

35. There are clear parallels here to the world-views of indigenous religious traditions which also deny any ultimate dualism between matter and spirit. This explains, in part, the success of Pentecostal–charismatic missions around the world. The difficulty here lies not in convincing either Pentecostals and charismatics or

The mention of charisms in this context leads to the third theological presupposition concerning the function of the Pentecostal–charismatic experience of the Spirit. The earliest Pentecostal understanding of the purpose of Spirit-baptism was thoroughly pragmatic: tongues were foreign languages supernaturally imparted by the Holy Spirit for the evangelistic task of the Church in the last days before the second advent of Christ. Levels of theological sophistication accrued as the Pentecostal movement developed and expanded over time.[36] Less emphasis was placed on glossolalia and more on prophetically inspired speech for the edification of the body following increased attention given to Paul's censure of Corinthian enthusiasm (1 Cor. 14). The emergence of the charismatic movement in the mainline churches brought about a renewed emphasis on the totality of the gifts of the Spirit: each charism was thought important and none was to be elevated above all the others. Meanwhile, the sacramental interpretation of Spirit-baptism especially among Roman Catholic charismatics yielded a more relational and ecclesiological understanding of the charisms. These diverse functions of the experience of the Spirit exemplify the richness of experience opened up by the pneumatological imagination of Pentecostals and charismatics.

At the same time, recognition also needs to be given to the various levels of functionality regarding the Pentecostal–charismatic experience of the Spirit, none of which should be seen apart from any of the others. Manifestation of any of the charisms, an ecstatic glossolalic utterance, let's say, is a potential sign of the Spirit's presence and activity in the individual in whom the phenomena is occurring. To the extent that the individual comes through the experience as a more integrated self bearing the fruits of the Spirit, to that extent we can say that the Spirit has been present and at work in his or her life. At a second level, glossolalia

indigenous peoples about the reality of the spirit-realm, but in preventing the reification of spirits and in enabling the discerning the spirits in the concreteness of the world. We are still in the formative stages of a global Pentecostal–charismatic theology of the Spirit, and this work is but a tentative step in that direction; more on this in Chapters 7 and 8.

36. My colleague, Frank Macchia, is working on a book in which he argues that the function of tongues in institutional Pentecostalism today is, of necessity, much different from that which operated amidst the missionary emphasis of early Pentecostalism. The issue is as much ecclesiological as it is pneumatological. I eagerly await the results of his work.

in a ritual context should be followed by interpretation which purpose is to ensure that the manifestations build up the congregation rather than misplace attention on the individual. To the extent that tongues and interpretation edify the congregation as a whole, to that extent the Spirit has been present and at work. At a third level, glossolalia could be a sign to unbelievers or non-Christians (1 Cor. 14.22), and the effects brought about by charismatic manifestations could also bring about a transformation of the relationship between Christians and non-Christians. To the extent that charismatic phenomena brings about more positive dispositions in the lives of Christians to the world, to such an extent it is possible to grant the Spirit's presence and activity in the world.[37]

At a final level, assuming as I do that Hollenweger is correct, charisms can be manifest in any human being open to the Spirit, regardless of their religious affiliation. To acknowledge the Spirit's universal presence and activity is to grant that signs of such should follow anywhere. In the words of Michael Welker, the charisms 'are not simply individual postures and attitudes, but forms of participation and of inclusion in public powers' (1994: 242). Living in the world by way of a pneumatological imagination simply means participating in the fields of force generated by the Spirit's presence and activity. We do not own the Spirit, but simply comply with what the Spirit is doing in the world. The Pentecostal–charismatic experience of the Spirit is thus a vivid and intensified form of this encounter and cooperation because it grasps the individual in the totality of his or her being and moves that person into a public force field, even while that field, the larger whole, is effectively transformed by the newly located presence of the Spirit-filled individual. Part of what Pentecostals and charismatics contribute to this larger field of force is the naming and identification of the forms of the Logos operating therein. In short, their witness explicitly names the transformative power of the Christ whose baptizing Spirit they have experienced.

Although the above discussion contains hints of how a pneumatology derived from the Pentecostal–charismatic experience of the Spirit connects with the foundational pneumatology being developed here, it is now time to make these connections explicit. Spirit-baptism, for instance, is explicable in terms both of the general categories of

---

37. The levels of interpretation for the experience of glossolalia are discussed in greater detail in Yong (1998a).

experience and of the specific pneumatological categories. Phenomenologically, Spirit-baptism is the conjunction (thirdness) of the simple
qualities of feeling (firstness) and fact (secondness), of emotion and the
body. At this level, what is manifest can be understood as no more than
enthusiastic expressions or perhaps even bodily convulsions. Yet there
is a difference between an epileptic fit and an experience of the Spirit.
The former can be explicated purely in terms of psycho-bio-physical
categories; the latter resists such reductionism and cries out for a
religious interpretation. This is not only because the experiences are so
intense but more so because the various dimensions of experience—
mental, emotional, somatic, affective *and spiritual*—are together and
separately brought to awareness in the experience itself resulting in the
religious intuition of a 'more'. Thus, glossolalia, for example, includes
cognitive (i.e. awareness one is speaking in tongues or praising God),
emotional (i.e. the rush of feelings), somatic (i.e. the movement of the
tongue) and affective (i.e. the choice to say words that make no sense)
elements. But there is also its inexplicability in which one feels engaged
with the boundaries of reality and in touch with something beyond.
Pentecostals and charismatics understand this 'more' as their experience of the resurrection power of Jesus Christ. Because the Spirit is
both the point of contact between the divine and the human, and is
relatedness, legality, rationality and harmony *par excellence*, it is theologically appropriate to interpret such manifestations as potential signs
of the Spirit's presence and activity.

It is important to underscore the qualifier 'potential' in every instance
of charismatic manifestation since the pneumatological categories
include *absence* alongside *presence* and *activity*. To reiterate, the
foundational pneumatology developed here posits every experience as,
at some level, that of the presence and activity of Word and Spirit.
Pentecostals and charismatics do not distinguish between the two
precisely. For them, the experience of the risen and exalted Jesus is the
experience of the Spirit and vice versa. This is the truth of St Paul's
statement that 'the Lord is the Spirit' (2 Cor. 3.17). Yet the scriptural
data also demands a non-identity between Word and Spirit, as when St
Paul discusses a disposition of the Spirit in the service of Christ (Rom.
14.17-18). This leads Ralph Del Colle to distinguish between the
Christus praesens and the *Spiritus praesens* with the help of three
principles: the former is the normative measure for human corporeality,
while the latter is the normative measure for human personality; the

former is modally anamnetic (based on remembrance and recollection of past events) and kerygmatic, while the latter is modally epicletic (based on the invitation toward presentness) and charismatic; the former focuses us on the fact of salvation through the life and death of Christ in anticipation of his parousia, while the latter focuses us on an empowered witness in the present as directed toward the eschaton (1993: 104; cf. 1992: 294-300).

While these principles are of some value for Christian discernment, they are incapable of recognizing the two hands of the Father in all experiences. Further, they are not at all beneficial in discerning the Spirit in other non-Christian traditions. Elsewhere, however, Del Colle makes a more helpful distinction in emphasizing that the two presences, while distinct, cannot be separated: 'at each level of the actualization of the *Christus praesens* in ecclesial faith, hope, and love the *Spiritus praesens* is the active modality—i.e. the agent—by which the former is realized without ever collapsing into it or vice versa' (1994: 179). I prefer to say that the *Christus praesens* is evident to a greater or lesser degree in all events or experiences as measured by their own existential norms, and that the *Spiritus praesens* is evident to a greater or lesser degree as any experience is moved toward or digresses from its ideal norm relative both to itself and to others. Persistent digression risks *ichabod*, or the Spirit's absence. A pneumatological imagination is sensitive to the diverse forms of both the Spirit's presence *and* absence. In the case of the latter, this imagination is, relatively speaking, much more equipped to discern the demonic features of our experience and world.

In more concrete terms, let me, as before, take a putative charismatic experience such as ecstatic tongues-speech. This phenomena can be assessed from a number of perspectives (e.g. Mills 1986; cf. Williams 1981). Physiologically and psychologically, the experience itself can be no more than a form of release from stress and tension. The question here is whether or not or to what extent this occurs in the glossolalist. The Spirit is deemed present and at work at this level to the extent that these purposes are accomplished.[38] Ecclesiologically, glossolalia may

38. There is some evidence, for instance, for positive personality changes that follow upon the experience of glossolalia. Behavioral scientists like Malony and Lovekin suggest that 'glossolalics become more open to feeling and to the affective dimension of their experience. They become more spontaneous and better able to cope with anxiety'; while the data is not conclusive as to whether 'this affectivity is

have a number of ideal forms such as being the vehicle for inspired prayer, the expression of doxological praise, or the means, along with interpretation, by which prophetic messages are initiated. In the last instance, tongues without interpretation in the congregation signifies a lesser degree of the Spirit's presence and activity either with regard to the glossolalist or to those who resist the Spirit's prompting to give the interpretation. On the other hand, tongues with interpretation that moves speaker and/or congregation into a more harmonious relationship with themselves and the world is evidence of the Spirit's activity.[39] On the theological level, finally, the claim that glossolalia is utterance under the inspiration of the Spirit can and will be adjudicated only eschatologically and then relative to the full appearance of the Word. Preliminary signs which give greater or lesser credence to this claim revolve around the extent to which glossolalists bear the fruits of the Spirit—i.e. whether or not their lives are ordered in lesser or greater degrees of harmony in relationship to others.

Glossolalia can thus be assessed from many other perspectives, but the preceding is suggestive at least of how the presence and activity of the Spirit can be discerned in any such manifestation. It is further suggestive of when the Spirit is absent. Glossolalia can become routinized as an end in itself; it can intensify rather than release tension; it can focus attention upon the glossolalist rather than upon what the Spirit is wanting to accomplish; it can estrange and alienate rather than bring about solidarity in a congregation; it can either fail to accomplish its objectives or overreach its purposes for being. In all of these ways, glossolalia ceases to point beyond itself, claiming instead the divine presence and activity in an unconditioned way. When this happens, it is

a precondition for becoming glossolalic or whether it results *from* the experience', it is undeniable that 'depression among glossolalics is reduced and remains low over time' (1985: 161-87, quotes from 185).

39. Theologically, one can insist that such harmonies be defined christologically. This is appropriate at one level, but not at all required. Harmonies can and should be assessed from as many vantage points as possible. It is best to assess harmonies first using their own self-defined categories, and then going on to other perspectives and frameworks of understanding. With regard to the interreligious dialogue, it may be best to withhold christological categories until later in the dialogue, and then only when ways have been found by which to make these categories meaningful to one's dialogue partner. Thus the value of a pneumatological approach for the interreligious dialogue is evident. More on this in Chapters 7 and 8.

evidence of a self-centered force field that is potentially demonic.

This very brief elaboration of a Pentecostal–charismatic experience of the Holy Spirit highlights the 'for us' character of pneumatology. This is in line with the metaphysical presuppositions outlined previously regarding the asymmetrical character of the divine act of creation: there is no point in asking about who or what the Holy Spirit is in himself. It does, however, raise the question of priority with regard to experience and interpretation. I took up the issue of interpretive categories (Chapter 4) before discussing the Pentecostal–charismatic experience of the Spirit. Does that mean that the latter experience has been forced into a foreign philosophical framework? If so, there is nothing that the experience contributes to the foundational pneumatological categories and this project as a whole can no longer claim to be a serious contribution to Christian theology of religions from a Pentecostal–charismatic perspective. On the other hand, if the response is given that the categories themselves arose from the experiential backdrop even if they were introduced first, then the resulting theology of religions runs the risk of being an imperialistic Pentecostal–charismatic (Christian) imposition on any other dialogue partners willing to be seated at the interreligious table.

Again, however, I need to reiterate that there is a dialectical process at work here, as there undoubtedly is in all questions of this sort. Experience and interpretation are mutually informing and correcting elements in any community of knowers.[40] Further, what I am proposing here is put forward tentatively for reflection, discussion and criticism. The theoretical and conceptual apparatus will always fall short of the richness of experience. The foundational pneumatology and Pentecostal–charismatic theology of the Spirit are both provisional and vulnerable to amplification, adjustment and correction. The pneumatological imagination of Pentecostals and charismatics is being constantly challenged, enlarged, transformed or exposed through their faithful attention to the Scriptures, participation in rituals of the Spirit and obedience to the divine Spirit in the world. I do, however, think that the

---

40. I am not alone among Pentecostals and charismatics on this point. The same or similar epistemological thesis has been argued with regard to the hermeneutical issue (e.g. Menzies 1979, Tate 1991, Stronstad 1992, Ellington 1996, Shuman 1997; cf. Hollenweger 1978). My approach extends the activity of interpretation to cover not only human engagement with texts, but with the reality of the world (cf. Neville 1989).

foundational categories generated from my interpretation of the Pente-costal–charismatic experience are correct in their general features in large part because these features are intrinsic to the human process. This is not to deny that the pneumatological imagination needs to be cultivated and that the Pentecostal–charismatic experience fosters such cultivation. It only asserts what has long been affirmed by the traditional doctrine of common grace: that human life and experience is dependent only on the prevenient grace and activity of God through the Holy Spirit, and that this should put us on the alert for possible experiences of the Spirit and alternative specifications of the pneumato-logical imagination outside of explicitly Christian contexts.

Since the Pentecostal–charismatic experience can be explicated in its specificity within the broader confines of our common humanity, I am therefore confident that the categoreal scheme developed here will show itself to be of value for the interreligious dialogue. I will elaborate further in Chapter 7 on how the foundational pneumatological cate-gories of presence, activity and absence can be productive for a Pentecostal–charismatic theology in general and theology of religions in particular even while developing there a discerning charismology for dialogue in the wider ecumenism. In the meanwhile, how Pentecostals and charismatics have related to religious others and why they should concern themselves with a theology of religions need to be detailed. It is therefore important that some effort be expended next on buying much needed theological space especially for those classical Pente-costals who would potentially be critical of this project.

Chapter 6

ON THE WAY TO A PENTECOSTAL–CHARISMATIC
THEOLOGY OF RELIGIONS

I was never pushed into Christian ministry. I saw the hardships my
parents faced as ministers, and when I shared with them during my early
teen years that such was not for me, they did not attempt to dissuade me.
However, God works in mysterious ways. When I was a high school
junior, I assumed responsibility for the youth group by default (our
congregation was small and lacked lay leaders). Through a series of
circumstances, I found myself as a ministerial major in Bible college. I
was drawn to academia (I remember reading biblical commentaries
during those days, 'just for the fun of it'), but felt the call on a number of
occasions to full-time Christian ministry. Because of my intellectualist
bent, I did not want to work with youth, per se. Yet when I was placed as
a pastoral intern under one of the most successful youth pastors in the
Northern California district of the Assemblies of God, I said to the Lord,
'OK, I'll do youth ministry, if you insist'. Sure enough, that is what I did
for a year after I graduated! Through all of this, however, I imbibed the
full range of hermeneutical and biblical studies, tools my father never
had, and cultivated what I considered to be a respectable preaching style.
I considered it part of my mission to show the world that real Pentecostal
preaching was not limited to charismatic passion and fire of the Holy
Ghost but that it necessarily included historico-grammatical criticism
and cultural sophistication. Yet in the back of my mind, I always felt
showed-up by Mormons and Jehovah Witnesses who went from home to
home to share their faith. I slowly learned about Muslim and Buddhist
missionaries (Jews and Hindus always seemed less aggressive in comparison) who also were committed to propagating the truths of their
sacred texts and sported an impressive hermeneutical tradition. For
awhile, I was grieved for their souls, 'if these people would only
listen…' or 'how sad that they have been blinded by the evil one…',
until it dawned on me that they were probably thinking similar things
about my type. I then realized that a hearing among these people must be
earned and that is done in part by listening to what they have to say. But
I am still a Pentecostal preacher, and more than that, a minister of the

Gospel of Jesus Christ. Are there not more profitable things to do than to spend time listening to what those who have preceded me in Pentecostal faith have called the 'doctrines of demons' without any guarantee that I will be granted an ear by these non-Christian missionaries when they are done? Or worse, would not my Christian witness be tainted if I were found to be only giving an appearance of interest all the while harboring the intent to proselytize? Maybe I should just not bother with those in other faiths and let the Lord reach them in His own way...

Introduction

A fairly recent article in *Advance*, a quarterly publication for American Assemblies of God ministers, summarizes the hurdles which any attempt to develop a Pentecostal–charismatic theology of religions has to face. Pentecostals ministers are reminded by Harold Carpenter of the threefold problem posed to the Church by advocates of a pluralistic approach to non-Christian faiths: (1) it is contrary to Scripture, e.g., Acts 4.12, Jn 3.18; (2) it replaces the obligation for world evangelism (Mt. 18.28, Mk 16.15) with interreligious dialogue; and (3) those who fail to fulfill the Great Commission are ultimately not living under the Lordship of Christ (Carpenter 1995). As Professor of Missions at Central Bible College in Springfield, Missouri, Carpenter's article comes with the approval of the Assemblies of God and undoubtedly claims to represent at least the denominational position on the subject if not the opinion of the vast majority of its constituency. The fact that the denomination voted as recently as its 47th General Council session in 1997 to retain the full force of its statement in the Constitution and Bylaws warning against the ecumenical movement does not bode well for Pentecostals who deem it important to rethink this question.[1]

It is therefore important at this juncture to put this matter in its proper historical context, and to provide some further justification for proceeding that would address specifically Pentecostal concerns. The former issue leads in Section 1 to a discussion of some of the many

---

1.   Article IX, Doctrines and Practices Disapproved, Section 11, gives the following grounds for caution: ecumenism invites theological liberalism, misplaces the biblical priority of salvation with social concern, and smacks too much of the 'world superchurch' (religious Babylon) of Revelation 17 and 18. Individual ministers, however, are not discouraged from giving Pentecostal witness 'on a local level with interdenominational activities'. That this is basically the stance of conservative evangelicalism and dispensationalist theology is evident.

reasons why Pentecostals have traditionally ignored developing a theology of religions or resisted participation in the modern ecumenical
movement. At the same time, it will also show that Pentecostal relationships with those in other faith traditions have often been much more
amicable than their rhetoric has let on. Such Pentecostal openness to
those in other faiths needs to be retrieved and reassessed. There are
signs that more and more Pentecostals see the need to conform their
theology to their ways of relating to religious others, even while they
have been nudged in that direction by theologians in the charismatic
movement. Section 2 then focuses on providing additional reasons for
Pentecostals to begin rethinking theologically about other religious traditions. Because I attempt in this chapter to deal with the classical
Pentecostal reluctance to engage in interreligious ecumenism, my
argument will focus more specifically on classical Pentecostalism than
on the charismatic movement.

1. *Pentecostal–Charismatic Responses to the Religions:*
An Historical Review

Classical Pentecostal Responses and More Recent Attitudes

There are a number of reasons why classical Pentecostals have generally been exclusivists with regard to other religious traditions.[2] First,
modern Pentecostalism developed during the era of fundamentalist–
liberal hostilities. A theological *via media* had not yet been staked out,
and the social location of many early Pentecostals led them to an alliance initially with fundamentalism and later with the emerging evangelical movement (Blumhofer 1989: II, 13-108). Like fundamentalists,
early Pentecostals were generally anti-intellectualists and communicated more through popular media such as magazines, newspapers and
periodicals than through systematically elaborated treatises. There is
much in the former genre of literature that identifies the religions with

---

2.   Because my own primary research of classical Pentecostal materials has
been in the archives of the Church of God, Cleveland, Tennessee, the journalistic
evidence submitted here will be drawn primarily from this denomination. I am convinced, however, that what I have observed in Church of God literature—an occasional display of openness to people of other faiths amidst a generally negative
overall attitude toward the religions as a whole—is an attitude that will be found to
be consistent across the broad spectrum of classical Pentecostalism regardless of the
denomination.

the devil and his minions. At the same time, when Pentecostals have attempted systematic theologies (e.g. Pearlman 1937, Williams 1953, P. Nelson 1981), they have duplicated both the form and content of conservative evangelical or even fundamentalist theologies, usually with the addition of a section on the baptism of the Holy Spirit and the charismata—the exception would be the emerging genre of doctrinal treatises from Oneness Pentecostals which usually include a lengthy apologetic against trinitarian theology—but rarely, if ever, mentioning the religions. The point is that all the bashing of other religious traditions may tell us something about how Pentecostals have *felt*, but do not really give us evidence that Pentecostals have thought through the subject.

A corollary and second reason is the Pentecostal commitment to the Bible as the inerrant and inspired Word of God. On the surface of it, a literalistic reading of Scripture leads to a dualism of God and Satan, spirit and flesh, salvation and damnation, a genuine relationship with God and idolatry (e.g. De Ridder 1978). The Jesus-centered spirituality of early Pentecostals quickly led them to highlight 'exclusivistic' texts as central to the good news.[3] Third, as an oral tradition, Pentecostals have perennially emphasized the testimony, verbal and prophetic witness, and evangelistic proclamation. Taking the Great Commission seriously has motivated Pentecostals to share their experience of salvation and of the Spirit with others. Their 'passion for the Kingdom' (Land 1993) has not allowed them to be passive toward those they consider eternally lost without the gospel of Christ.[4]

Other reasons for classical Pentecostalism's exclusivism can be enumerated, including their suspicion of the origins, motives and accomplishments of the ecumenical movement, derived in part from their

3.   A perusal of early periodical literature such as that from *The Church of God Evangel* (Church of God, Cleveland, Tennessee) quickly shows how often Acts 4.12 is quoted precisely in the context of discussing Christ as the only savior for the world, including those in other faiths. See, e.g., *The Church of God Evangel* (14 March 1919): 5; (13 July 1918): 4; (11 January 1919): 1; (8 November 1919): 3-4.

4.   Pentecostal literature is replete with salvation stories and missionary reports which testify to the superiority of Christ over other faiths. See, e.g., Barnes (1944); under the heading 'Christ the Savior for the Heathen', the 'Testimony of Brother S.B. Daniel, Convert from Brahminism', *The Church of God Evangel* (17 March 1945): 9, 14; and, in the 'News from the Mission Field' section, Zeno C. Tharp, Secretary of Mission Board, 'Heathen Worship in India', *The Church of God Evangel* (22 July 1959): 6, 16.

alignment with North American fundamentalism and conservative evangelicalism. What has gone almost unnoticed, however, is the strand of openness displayed by Pentecostals in their relationships with those in other faiths. Further, there also seems to be a perceptible shift in more recent Pentecostal attitudes towards the entire issue of the Spirit's presence and activity in the world and in other traditions. Recovering both of these aspects of Pentecostal life and thought is imperative for the project at hand.

Openness to those in other faiths has manifested itself among classical Pentecostals in a variety of ways. Thus in an article on Christian apologetics vis-à-vis the religions, Pentecostal missionary C.E. French grants that Hindus are 'true to their system of faith and manner of worship' even if they are wrong about the beliefs that they hold (1947: 5). 'Brotherhood Week' in September, 1950, was mentioned in the news release section in *The Church of God Evangel* followed by a listing of versions of the Golden Rule in ten other religious traditions (23 September 1950: 7).[5] An editor of the same *Evangel* had previously not only not disputed Gandhi's emphasis on love as the central doctrine of Christianity, but also underscored this statement without qualification (26 January 1946: 4). In the political arena during the turbulent Arab–Israeli wars of the late 1960s, Church of God officials were quick to respond sympathetically to a burning of a mosque in Israel, and to accept invitations to prayer and dialogue from King Hussein of Jordan.[6] More recently, while reasserting Mayan religiosity to be essentially pagan, missionary to Guatemala Richard Waldrop said, 'we would like to think that Pentecostals are closest to the ancient Maya religiosity of any Protestant movement' (quoted in Cook 1997: 90).

These examples of openness may be consistent with the Christian Gospel, but it begs the reconsideration of the classical Pentecostal rhetoric and theology concerning other faiths. There are now signs that

5.   The traditions included were, in order, Buddhism, Christianity, Confucianism, Hebraism, Hinduism, Islam, Jainism, Sikhism, Taoism and Zoroastrianism; credit was given to 'Dr. Selwyn Champion's book on the religions' (Champion 1945).

6.   See 'Jerusalem Report: Mid-East Superintendent Interviews High Priest of Al Aqsa Mosque', *The Church of God Evangel* (17 November 1969): 7; and 'Evangelist [T. L.] Lowery Meet's Jordan's King', and 'The King and His Country: A Sense of Destiny and Responsibility', both in the 5 May 1969 issue of *The Church of God Evangel*.

such rethinking is coming about. One of the earliest indications of this transformation of attitudes was actually a denominational guide to the religions published by the Church of God, Cleveland, Tennessee. *Is Christianity the Only Way?* (Anon.: 1975) is an introduction of Judaism, Hinduism, Buddhism and Islam (among the world religious traditions) to adult Sunday School participants. What is striking about this volume is the genuine effort made to present the non-Christian faiths on their own terms. Its objective is to furnish as unbiased a portrait as possible of other faiths even if it seeks in the end to uphold the supremacy of the Christian way.

The discussion of the Buddhist tradition, for example, shows an openness to other faiths unprecedented even to the present in classical Pentecostal denominational literature. Two chapters detail, in turn, the origins and teachings of Buddhism. After a presentation in the first chapter of the problematic confronting Gautama Buddha and the enlightenment he claimed to have experienced, the anonymous authors turn to a discussion of the Christian response: 'As Christians we may ask the question, "What can we show the Buddhists?" In another sense it is appropriate to ask, "What can the Buddhists show us?" ' (Anon.: 1975: 72). They go on to suggest that the Buddha's disciplined life, his concern or compassion for others, and his establishment of the *sangha*—the Buddhist order of monks dedicated to the quest of enlightenment and the personal witness of the Buddha's teaching—are deserving of praise and worthy of emulation. Of course, these examples are seen to be superseded in Jesus who is the light of the world, who gave his life as a sacrifice, and who also discipled and commissioned the twelve. Nevertheless, the fact is that the authors of *Is Christianity the Only Way?* were willing to appraise candidly a major religious tradition historically demonized by most Pentecostals. The openness displayed here is astounding given the fact that this book was distributed, for all intents and purposes, with the imprimatur of a classical Pentecostal denomination.[7]

---

7.   Another factor that may be contributing to this sea-change in classical Pentecostal attitudes is the arrival of foreign students to North American Pentecostal Bible colleges and seminaries. At least two Church of God Theological Seminary students, for example, are convinced that the Hindu Scriptures testify to Jesus (Gullapalli 1981: 102), and that 'the unknown Christ is there within Hinduism' (Sajja 1992: 41; see Panikkar 1964).

But even if it is granted that there is truth, goodness and righteous-ness of sorts in other faiths, is not such 'openness' finally compromised if Pentecostals persist in a staunch exclusivistic position regarding other religious traditions? Cornelia Scott Cree, a Pentecostal who has done work among the deaf, underscores the next question which needs to be asked: how does God save those who are unable to receive the gospel by the normal means of proclamation (cf. Rom. 10.13-15)? 'If we take Scripture seriously', she suggests, 'it appears that those who hear and reject the reality of Jesus are the ones truly liable to hell-fire [Jn 3:18]. Our Scriptures do not tell of the ONLY way but of a BETTER way [Hebs. 7:19; 8:6]' (1994: 4). Cree's inclusivism is sustained by the scriptural axiom that salvation comes by grace through faith. This response of faith is active at various levels, depending on whether the individual is Christian, Jew or otherwise. (Cree calls these 'parallel dis-pensations' in contrast to traditional dispensationalism which runs the various divine economies chronologically.) Cree therefore suggests that divine revelation is imparted directly by the Holy Spirit to non-cove-nant individuals. This unmediated revelation, she says, is the 'uniquely pentecostal paradigm, the acceptance and enlargement of special reve-lation' (1994: 19).

It is important to note that Cree's inclusivism is concerned solely with the question of the salvation of the unevangelized and not with the religions as such.[8] However, her invitation to Pentecostals to move from exclusivistic paradigm of conservative evangelical theology to a

---

8.   Regarding the religions, Cree's position is the standard Pentecostal one: the religions themselves are not revelatory of the divine but rather demonically inspired human efforts to compete with or co-opt God's program (1994: 26). Hints of how a Pentecostal theology of religions is possible can be seen in Frank Macchia's 'The Secular and the Religious under the Shadow of the Cross: Implications in Blum-hart's Kingdom Spirituality for a Christian Response to World Religions' (forth-coming). According to Macchia, there is a movement from Christology and eccle-siology to pneumatology and the Kingdom of God which allowed the nineteenth century German Pietist, Christoph Blumhardt, to anticipate Barth and others in relativizing both Christianity and other traditions under the judgment of the cross even while living under present and future transformative hope by the power of the Spirit. The logical step for Macchia is to move from a 'Blumhartian response to the religions' to a thoroughgoing Pentecostal *theologia religionum*. Macchia has all the qualifications to complete this move should he have the inkling to do so, and I can only hope that my own work will provide something of a stimulus to his thinking in this regard.

wider inclusivism is an important one. How she sustains her appeal, however, is debatable. While it is clear that the Holy Spirit works in the lives of non-believers, yet even among the deaf, it is arguable that all human experience is mediated in some way. If religious traditions are part of what informs our common humanity, it is not solely a theological question but also in some senses an empirical one whether or not and how the religions are truly revelatory of the divine.

Such considerations are behind the declaration by Jean-Jacques Suurmond that 'other religions, too, are not without gifts of grace' (1995: 199). A Dutch Reformed Pentecostal, Suurmond argues that the Pentecostal experience enables a theological understanding of God's Word and Spirit as present and active throughout creation.[9] Such presence and activity is evident particularly in the dimension of human experience characterized by playful celebration insofar as this leads to love of life and compassion for others (1995: 200). The Church's task is to name and participate in the universal reconciling work of God through Christ in the charismatic celebration of the Spirit. This leads Suurmond to say that what is important is 'the one Reality which the great religions all serve and worship,' and that 'Christ's Word and Spirit give everyone the power within their own cultures and religions to be liberated from the false self and take the way to God's kingdom' (1995: 201). These are bold statements considering both that the results of the interreligious dialogue are far from in and that the debate about the nature of ultimate reality is ongoing. That Suurmond is open to the interreligious dialogue should go without saying. He does, however, make some insightful theological and Pentecostal suggestions in support of interfaith ecumenism when he cites Acts 2.16-20 and Rom. 5.1-11 as suggestive of the relationship between the outpouring of the Holy Spirit and the increased human capacity for authentic interreligious encounter (1995: 201).[10]

---

9.   Suurmond grounds this thesis through an exegetical discussion of Word and Spirit as two aspects of the divine Wisdom (1995: 37-42). This complements my own foundational pneumatology developed in dialogue with a larger public.

10.   In this connection, there is a tantalizing statement made in 1983 by Harold Hunter of the International Pentecostal Holiness Church regarding the promise of Spirit-Christology for 'the multifaceted interfaith dialogue which has touched off a search for an effectual christological paradigm relevant to modern man' (1983: 127). Hunter, however, then goes on instead to consider the potential of Spirit-Christology relative to the Pentecostal–charismatic movement. He has, unfor-

More and more classical Pentecostals are beginning to see the value of interfaith ecumenism as evidenced by the official dialogues between Oneness Pentecostals and Muslims recently convened in Vancouver, British Columbia. This being, to my knowledge, the first formal inter-religious dialogue involving classical Pentecostals with academic back-grounds, it deserves to be recognized as an historic breakthrough.[11] Dialogue participants included United Pentecostal Church theologians, Dr David Bernard and Revd Jonathan Urshan, and co-founders of the Islamic Information Foundation, Imam Sabir Ally and Dr Jamal Badawi. Bernard's participation is less surprising when it is realized that he has gone on record as at least opening the door toward enter-taining an inclusivistic stance regarding the salvation of the unevangel-ized (1984: 308-12) even if he in the end insists on the traditional exclu-sivism.[12] In this case, the dialogue was not burdened by the doctrine of the Trinity (cf. Rahner 1983c), thus clearing the way for some produc-tive interreligious apologetics on the person of Jesus Christ. While par-tisan feelings ran high on both sides as measured by the fluctuating levels of cheers and applause from the congregation, the dialogue was a visible success in clearing away misunderstandings and stereotypes, and bringing Muslims and Pentecostal Christians together in civil discus-sion.

Why should this not be the result of interreligious ecumenism if the Holy Spirit is in fact the one who leads Christians to all truth? This premise is the first of five principles proposed by Samuel Solivan as undergirding Pentecostal participation in the interreligious dialogue (1998).[13] Other contributions Pentecostals bring to the dialogue table

tunately, not given further reflection to implications of Spirit-Christology for the interreligious dialogue.

11. My own second-hand exposure to the dialogue was via videotape: 'Who Was Jesus? According to the Qur'an and Bible' (produced by SNB Innovations, P.O. Box 4075, Vancouver, BC, V6B 3Z6, Canada. Videos are also available from Oneness Pastor Larry Sims, Maranatha Ministries, Vancouver, BC).

12. Given the fact that Bernard is the most theologically sophisticated and prolific Oneness Pentecostal theologian, I will have occasion to recur to his work periodically as has already been done. To my knowledge, however, he has been silent regarding the salvation of those in other faiths.

13. Solivan is a minister with the Hispanic American Assemblies of God and former Professor of Theology at Andover Newton Theological Seminary, Boston, Massachusetts. This paper, the first sustained consideration of the merits of inter-religious dialogue from a classical Pentecostal standpoint, was first presented to the

include the viewpoint 'from the underside' characteristic of the majority of the Pentecostal 'poor' from around the world, the conviction of the prevenient workings of the Holy Spirit in every human being, the empowerment of believers for witness by the Spirit, and the diverse and pluralistic character of the Spirit's manifestations across racial, class, gender, language and religious boundaries.[14] For these reasons, Solivan not only is compelled 'to recognize God's sovereign presence in grace in the world apart from a Christian expression' (1998: 41), but also feels liberated

> to examine the diverse ways the Holy Spirit is at work among other people of faith. It allows us to explore the variety of ways in which the human community seeks to express its longing and searching after God. A sharing of these expressions of spirituality can be informative and at times even transformative of our own models and modes of spirituality and their accompanying theological assumptions (1998: 43).

Solivan is clear to point out that these are his own thoughts but yet trusts them to be representative of the Pentecostal experience. He does briefly mention his reservations about the Pentecostal involvement in the wider ecumenism in his conclusion, all of which derive from four fundamental assumptions undergirding interfaith dialogue: that theological innovation is good, that dialogue is 'the preferred vehicle' for getting at religious truth, that prolonged study of and exposure to other faiths will lead one to the truth, and that all religious claims are relative and that no absolute truth exists (1998: 44). Together, Solivan's reservations and suggestions are illuminating guidelines for Pentecostals not only as they enter the interfaith arena, but also as they struggle to understand other religious traditions in light of their own convictions and experiences.

This process for achieving understanding of religious others is at the heart of the theology of religions and discerning charismology which Pentecostals need in the twenty-first century. It is, further, something

consultation 'Theological Resources for Responses to Religious Pluralism' which convened representatives of various interfaith organizations on 13–14 October, 1994 in Newark, New Jersey. Cf. also Robeck (1994a) for a Pentecostal response to the charge of 'interreligious proselytism' deriving from circles affiliated with the World Council of Churches.

14. With regard to this last principle, Solivan speaks of the implications of the 'multigender or androgynous identification of the Holy Spirit' for reconstructing an inclusive trinitarian understanding of God (1998: 43).

that can only emerge from the ongoing mutually informing inter- and intra-religious dialogue—dialogues between members of two or more traditions and internal 'dialogues' in the hearts and minds of Pentecostals about two or more traditions.[15] Pentecostals who seek to understand the role of the religions in the divine plan and how to discern the presence and activity of the Spirit in them need to be involved not only in formal and informal dialogues with those in other faiths, but also need to wrestle seriously within themselves about what possible truths found in other traditions mean for Pentecostal life and thought. A model of such a two-dimensional dialogue is to be found in the work of South African Pentecostal, Allan Anderson.

While of European extraction, Anderson was raised as a 'missionary kid' in Zimbabwe and Zambia and has spent most of his adult life since 1968 in classical Pentecostal and independent Pentecostal-type churches in southern Africa.[16] His first book, *Moya: The Holy Spirit in an*

15. Here, I follow the plain sense of the distinction as developed by Jochim (1995: 39). His, and my, use of *intra*-religious dialogue differs from Swidler's (1990) and Panikkar's (1978) uses of the term. Intra-religious dialogue for Swidler refers to either the 'intra-institutional' dialogue within Christian denominations or 'inter-institutional' dialogue among Christian denominations. My use is narrower than his but not as deep as Panikkar's whose *depth*-dialogue refers to the cross-over to and return from—interiorization of—another tradition in the individual soul. While I am sure that most Pentecostals and many charismatics are not ready for such an experiment, I am unsure that Panikkar's case can be made in some instances. I can see how one could maintain dual religious citizenship as Christian and Muslim if that means one is both a follower of Christ and a servant of the Almighty God. I can also see how one could be both a Christian and a Confucian if that means one loves both Jesus Christ and one's neighbor. But what could a Christian Buddhist or Christian Hindu mean? One would have to qualify severely the designation: Zen Christian, Vedantic Christian, etc. In any case, Pentecostals and charismatics will in time need to judge if and how such Panikkarian intra-religious depth-dialogue is possible. My goal here is the more modest one of getting them to the interreligious dialogue table.

16. For his background, see Anderson (1993: 1-3); his experience with the Holy Spirit is detailed in (1991: 46). It may be that Anderson is a 'post-classical Pentecostal' or charismatic. But since he calls himself a Pentecostal while being fully aware of these distinctions, I have therefore chosen to place him in this section. In the following discussion of Anderson's work, then, 'Pentecostal' and 'Pentecostal–type' will be used synonymously in accordance with his use of them to denote the broad spectrum of classical Pentecostal, charismatic and independent, indigenous

African Context (1991), was a master's thesis written under the supervision of Inus Daneel, expert on the African independent churches. Two sequels have since appeared focused more on South African Pentecostal churches than on pneumatology, although the elements of the latter are not completely absent (Anderson 1992; Anderson and Otwang 1993). Anderson's writings deserve careful consideration in that they converge at the intersections of theology and religious studies, Pentecostalism and African traditional religion, missiology and indigenization.

The dominant theological thread running throughout Anderson's work, however, is pneumatology. *Moya* asks the question of whether or not Pentecostalism is the first truly indigenous expression of the Christian experience of the Spirit in the African context. Against earlier detractors who urged that Pentecostal-type churches in African were syncretistic movements back toward traditional 'heathen' practices and beliefs (e.g. Oosthuizen 1968), Anderson has argued that Pentecostal expressions and manifestations are actually conduits toward a viable African Christianity, and this along three lines. First, whereas traditional Western pneumatology has suffered from a dualism between the spiritual and material world, Pentecostalism has advocated a practical belief in the immanence of God by the Holy Spirit. This accords much more congenially with the holism of the African world-view. Second, the Pentecostal emphasis on spiritual power also speaks to African religiosity. The difference between the two is the Pentecostal focus on the personal character of the divine initiative and empowerment by the Holy Spirit in contrast to the impersonal and manipulable 'life-force' of African religions (cf. Anderson 1990). Finally, the Pentecostal *Weltanschauung* recognizes spiritual realities such as that of the ancestors posited by African traditions. Again, however, the difference is that although there may be some ambiguity and misunderstanding of the relationship between the Holy Spirit and African nature and ancestor spirits among pockets of Pentecostal-type churches, on the whole, Pentecostal praxis insists on what Anderson calls 'confrontation, rejection and exorcism' of these entities rather than on placating and appeasing them (1991: 10). All in all then, Anderson advocates that we consider 'the African traditional spirit world to be the fertile ground

---

and Spirit-type African church movements that exhibit Pentecostal–type phenomena and religiosity.

that prepared the way for the "coming of the Holy Spirit" to Africa' (1991: 51).

Anderson does grant that there are innumerable counterfeit spiritual manifestations even among African Pentecostal-type churches. How then does he discern between the Holy Spirit and other spirits? In their collaborative effort, Anderson and Otwang describe prophetic practices as they occur in Pentecostal-type churches and how confusion exists in some cases regarding similarities and differences in the nature of diagnostic prophecy as used by Pentecostal prophet-healers and traditional diviners (1993: 122-33; cf. Oosthuizen 1992: 28-30). Further ambiguity persists in the theological praxis of many practitioners, both in leadership and among the laity, regarding the source of revelatory and healing power. There are laity who alternately consult either Christian prophets or traditional diviners depending on the kind of relief sought or their previous experiences of successes and failures. It seems that there is difficulty in distinguishing between the power and extent of ancestral spirits on the one hand and the Holy Spirit on the other.

When confronted with this broad spectrum of beliefs and practices in Pentecostal-type churches, the question of discernment arises again. To pursue the problem of the confusion between the Holy Spirit and ancestor spirits for a moment, how can Pentecostals be sure that ancestor spirits are 'demons' that need to be exorcised? Others such as Joseph Healey and Donald Sybertz (1996: 133) and Caleb Oladipo (1996) have suggested that this phenomena requires Christians to rethink pneumatology as a whole and that what is needed instead is a theology of the Holy Spirit that correlates biblical trinitarianism with traditional African concepts of ancestor spirits. There are, of course, numerous theological pitfalls one begins to encounter by proceeding down this path, not the least of which is the problem of whether or not the emergent construct is more adequately termed a pneumatology or an 'ancestorology'. Anderson's Pentecostal intuitions are on the alert when he cautions against such 'theological syncretism' (Anderson and Otwang 1993: 133; cf. Anderson 1993).[17]

17. On the other hand, I believe that this particular conversation is still in its infancy. While there are many that would second Anderson's advocacy of the exorcism thesis (e.g. Abijole 1988; Daneel 1990; Maxwell 1995; O'Donovan 1995), yet there is a strong attraction toward the cross-fertilization of ideas regarding ancestor spirits and the Holy Spirit via the category of power (Hammond-Tooke 1986). Contrary to those who have attempted to answer him, Gerhardus Oosthuizen's statement

To get at this problem, Anderson proposes a critical hermeneutical spiral (my term) which interprets African expressions of the Spirit 'in the light of the biblical revelation, the African spirit world, and [the] universal Christian experiences of the Spirit' (1991: 124). What is conspicuous by its absence in Anderson's discussion is the distinctively 'Pentecostal' experience of the Spirit. At the same time, it is clear that he wishes to make such experiences accountable to that of the Christian Church worldwide. Anderson is aware that the valid criticisms leveled against Pentecostalism need to be heeded and that bad theology needs to be corrected. Yet the presence of aberrations does not mean that the Pentecostal baby needs to be thrown out with the bath water. On the contrary, the Pentecostal experience—biblically based, critically understood and accountable to the larger Christian community—is precisely what is needed for a genuine African Christianity to emerge. Using this approach, then, Anderson's work represents an impressive inter-Christian and intra- and interreligious attempt to critically correlate biblical concepts and images of the Spirit with 'spiritual' manifestations in Pentecostal-type churches *and* traditional religions in Africa.

In this connection, it is instructive to mention the fascinating comparative study of traditional Filipino and Pentecostal world-views by the Korean Assemblies of God missionary and academic, Julie Ma (1997). Methodologically, Ma also proceeds via a three-way dialogue between the perspectives of a Filipino tribe, Kankana-ey (among whom she has served as missionary), classical Pentecostal orientations (with which she was raised) and Kankana-ey Pentecostals, this last being the result of successful Pentecostal missions over the years. This tri-logue on specific religious categories such as blessings, curses, healing, revelation and the Spirit world leads Ma to suggest that part of the reason for the success of the Pentecostal mission among this native group is

---

thirty years ago that one of the most difficult theological problems in Africa is precisely 'the confusion that exists with regard to the ancestral spirits and the Holy Spirit' (1968: 120) is still accurate. The difference is that the differing opinions now exist not only at the lay and pastoral level of praxis, but also, as Oladipo's thesis shows, at the sophisticated level of theological debate. The issues are complex and I have no intention of resolving them here. But I introduce them here because this discussion has a bearing on the theologies connected with folk Catholicism and indigenous Afro-American traditions. I will therefore return to this matter in Chapter 8 since I am of the firm opinion that Pentecostal participation is imperative if this particular dialogue is concerned with the truth of things.

that Kankana-ey animism functions in many ways as a *praeparatio evangelica* to the Pentecostal emphasis on God being present and at work by the power of the Holy Spirit (cf. Aigbe 1991). While Ma's primary interest is missiological and Anderson's concern is more so with theological inculturation, their contributions from these perspectives are crucial to the development of a Pentecostal theology of religions. Yet even at this stage, they have modeled the kind of intra- and interreligious dialogue that Pentecostals need to engage in.

Charismatic Contributions to Theology of Religions
That people like Anderson and Ma have given such extensive consideration to non-Christian traditions would be surprising only if their backgrounds and the emphasis Pentecostals place on contextualizing missions is forgotten. Therefore, given the diversity of charismatic movements worldwide, one would expect many to be involved in the interreligious dialogue and that the development of a theology of religions would be a well-worn theme. This, however, is not the case. There have been other matters which have occupied the concerns of neo-Pentecostals and Catholic charismatics, including the theological implications of the Pentecostal and charismatic experience of the Spirit and the larger question of the Spirit's activity and presence in the world generally.[18] Further, the initial reaction of many in the global Pente-

---

18. The examples of Arnold Bittlinger and James Jones bear this out. Bittlinger, a Swiss, has been heavily involved since the 1970s in the Reformed–Lutheran dialogue and the World Council of Churches as a representative of the European charismatic renewal. His theological work has therefore focused on the ecumenical implications of the charismatic experience of the Spirit (an excellent summary of which can be found in Lederle 1988: 171-78). Yet in an article written in anticipation of the 1991 World Council of Churches convention which adopted the theme, 'Come Holy Spirit—Renew the Whole Creation', Bittlinger recognizes three concentric spheres of the Spirit's work: in the individual Christian, in the Church, and in the world. His conclusion, which deserves to be quoted at length, is to suggest that an ecumenical pneumatology means

> the discovery and acceptance of the American Indian in us and, with them, the
> life of the rain forest and the singing of the birds: the discovery and acceptance
> of the African in us and, with them, the dance and rhythm; the discovery, too,
> of the Asian in us and, with them, stillness and meditation. As we let ourselves
> be renewed in this way by the Holy Spirit and led by him towards wholeness, a
> tiny part of the creation becomes healed. And if many people let themselves be

costal revival who have converted from other traditions has been to reject their original religious heritages *in toto*. The scarcity of charismatic writing on theology of religions, however, does not imply a complete dearth of reflection. There are signs of theological sophistication appearing on the horizon among these groups as seen in the work of people like Allan Anderson in the non-Western world and others in America. In what follows, I want to review briefly the work of three charismatics from diverse backgrounds: the Singaporean Presbyterian Yeow Choo Lak, the Canadian Baptist Clark Pinnock and the Roman Catholic Ralph Del Colle.

Yeow Choo Lak's charismatic identity has not played a major role in his theologizing over the years. While I am hopeful that this may change with his recent commitment to serve on the editorial board for the new *Asia Journal of Pentecostal Studies*, I am thankful that Yeow has been one of the few Asian charismatics who has been at the forefront of the movement to develop an authentic Asian Christian theology. This has marked his editorial work with the Association for Theological Education in South East Asia (ATESEA).[19]

An overview of Yeow's theology of religions is to be found in his *To God be the Glory! Doctrines on God and Creation* (1981: 9-27). Yeow has long been convinced that Christ is to be found in all cultures, which includes 'everything in life (human) and is learnt afresh by each generation through community activities' (1981: 49-50).[20] This theological

> led by the Holy Spirit in this way to renewal and wholeness, a network will begin to cover the whole earth, a network which will in the end bring about the renewal of all creation (Bittlinger 1990: 113).

Bittlinger's comments echo the work, which he did not reference, of James Jones who attempts to understand the work of the Spirit in community, social responsibility, politics and the Kingdom of God (1975). Jones's charismatic identity is clear, but his involvement in the charismatic movement as a whole has been minimal, at least since the publication of his book. Perhaps this explains the marginal attention his work has received in Pentecostal and charismatic circles.

19. Yeow has been general editor for the ATESEA Occasional Papers which have, to date, featured titles like *Doing Theology with Religions of Asia* (1986), *Doing Theology with People's Symbols and Images* (1989), *Doing Theology with God's Purpose in Asia* (1990), *Doing Theology with the Spirit's Movement in Asia* (1991), *Doing Christian Theology in Asian Ways* (1993), and *Doing Theology with the Festivals and Customs of Asia* (1994), all by ATESEA, Singapore.

20. Yeow's theology of 'Christ in cultures' is now accessible in a paper of the same title available on the Internet (1997).

openness has led him to understand revelation as historically mediated through human cultural institutions and engagements. General revelation (whether natural or historical), however, is only a prelude to special or Christian revelation. Yeow therefore insists that Christians have to begin with the revelation in Jesus Christ and proceed from there to 'discern the "partial truths" of other religions. Measured by Him the truth as well as the falsehood of all religion becomes discernible. God in nature, history, and conscience is only seen through the *a priori* of faith' (1981: 34).

This a priori approach in Rahner's transcendental theology has already been noted. While there are various types of religiosities, Yeow's position is that the difference between Christianity and the Asian traditions 'lies not in the questions asked, but in the answers given' (1981: 22). Yeow's theology of religions thus suffers from the same defect as Rahner's insofar as both seek dogmatic constructs by which to understand the religions rather than theologize about them from the empirical data. Yet, what he is after specifically theologically is a *via media* between Barth's absolutism or isolationism and Troeltsch's relativism. As a minority religion in Asia, Yeow knows that Christianity must avoid fanaticism and syncretism and can do so only by maintaining the tension between commitment to Christian faith and openness to other traditions. So Christians are committed to the Logos as the only-begotten of the Father without denying that the Logos also enlightens every person (Jn 1.9, 14); they are also committed to Peter's proclamation of 'no other name' even while holding to Paul's kerygma at Mars Hill based on 'common ground' (Acts 4.12; 17.22-31). In sum, Yeow's proposal, which deserves to be quoted in full, is to view

> all other religions from a double angle. On the one hand, it recognizes that gleams of the true light may, in spite of perversities and super-stitutions [*sic*], be detected everywhere. It would seem unlikely and unreasonable to think that God would reveal Himself to one tribe...only and leave all the rest of mankind in complete darkness. However, the recognition of the activity of the Spirit of God in men generally does not mean that all beliefs about God are equally true. All that I wish to say is that there are traces of God's image and likeness in man's conscience, emotional nature and personality, involving consciousness of obligation, desire for fellowship and craving for satisfaction. Also, 'God has not left Himself without witness' among the nations. On the other hand, Christianity also recognises a universal decay and degradation, including the sphere of religion. All religions stand under the judgement of God. It is in such contexts that we proclaim the Gospel (1981: 27).

Clark Pinnock's theology of religions, at least in its earlier forms, is in some ways handicapped by the a priori methodology that both Yeow and Rahner labor under. I have elsewhere (Yong 1999b) discussed Pinnock's failure to engage the religions empirically, even while treating in detail the development of his theology of religions beginning with the tension he poses between the two central axioms of the universality of God's salvific will and the provision of salvation in Jesus of Nazareth (Pinnock 1988, 1990, 1992), and proceeding to his turn to a pneumatological framework partly in light of the Pentecostal–charismatic experience (Pinnock 1993, 1995, 1996). In other ways, however, Pinnock's contribution is a significant advance for both evangelical theology of religions in particular and Christian *theologia religionum* in general. Evangelicals, Pinnock's target audience, have been challenged by his clear advocacy of theological inclusivism vis-à-vis traditional evangelical exclusivism while Christian theologians elsewhere have found much of value in his more recent reconstructive theology done within a pneumatological framework. In what follows, then, I want to outline how Pinnock's move from Christology to pneumatology has rejuvenated the Christian engagement with other faiths.

It is clear that Pinnock has long struggled with the empirical fact of religious pluralism. I think, however, that a genuine breakthrough has been accomplished in his latest book, *Flame of Love: A Theology of the Holy Spirit* (1996). The problem, as Pinnock has consistently posed and evangelical exclusivists have never been able to answer satisfactorily, is this: 'it would seem strange if the Spirit excused himself from the very arena of culture where people search for meaning. If God is reaching out to sinners, it is hard to comprehend why he would not do so in the sphere of religion' (1996: 203). The answer proposed by Pinnock is a thoroughgoing reconstruction of systematic theology from a pneumato-logical perspective. *Flame of Love* explores the doctrines of the Trinity, creation, Christology, ecclesiology and soteriology in light of pneuma-tology. The discussion of the non-Christian faiths toward the end of this volume is therefore set within this broad pneumatological framework. In this context, titled 'Spirit and Universality', Pinnock confidently asserts that the Holy Spirit, 'who is at work everywhere, is at work in the history of religions, and religions play a part in the history of grace, as the Spirit moves the world toward the kingdom' (1996: 203). Of course, this does not mean that there is no error or falsity in the religions. The pole of particularity in Christian faith means that God's decisive revelation is to be found in Jesus Christ. Yet the pneumatological pole is that of universality: 'there are elements of grace found in other religious traditions, and one hopes that they may mediate God's presence for people' (1996: 206).[21]

How can the divine presence and activity be discerned in the religions? This is the question that confronts any attempt to develop a pneumatological theology of religions. Pinnock goes the way of others discussed in Chapter 3 in proposing criteria that are primarily christological: the 'truth incarnate' of 1 Jn 4.2-3, the gospel narrative, Jesus himself. Yet he also refers to the ideals or Spirit of Jesus in more vague humanitarian terms: 'self-sacrificing love, care about community, longings for justice, wherever people love one another, care for the sick, make peace not war, wherever there is beauty and concord, generosity and forgiveness, the cup of cold water' (1996: 210). Recognizing the possibility here of confusing the human spirit with the Spirit of God, however, Pinnock retreats and reasserts that Jesus is 'the criterion of salvation...[and] of the Spirit's activity' (1996: 211).

Here again, however, it seems that Pinnock need not have succumbed so quickly to the theological pressure exerted by Christology. What is needed but lacking in *Flame of Love* is a metaphysics of divine presence and activity such as has been previously articulated. This would enable recognition of the different dimensions inhabited by the Christology and pneumatology, even as both can be related to each event. In such a framework, criteria appropriate to the integrity of each event or thing can be applied in the space created by pneumatology even while the christological moment is held at bay although never discarded. Yet perhaps Pinnock should not be faulted since his rhetoric in this book is more that of metaphorical and poetic imagery designed to evoke doxological praise and the experience of the Spirit, rather than that of tight rational argumentation contrived to resolve metaphysical puzzles or split theological hairs.[22]

---

21. Pinnock also says that the Spirit is 'at work in the sphere of religious life, so that religious experience may play a preparatory role for the coming of Christ' (1996: 207).

22. Pinnock's earlier *A Wideness in God's Mercy* (1992), for example, is much more of an argument in the strong sense of that word, especially with regard to presenting the biblical evidence for an inclusivistic theology of religions. *Flame of Love*, on the other hand, can rightly be said to herald the dawn of a new genre of

There is, however, one other conjunction of ideas in Pinnock's work that needs to be mentioned. He states that 'questions of access to salvation and religious pluralism can be approached profitably from the perspective of the future' (1996: 189). The future, after all, will reveal the place of the religions in light of the full glory of Christ. This revelation is the result of what Pinnock referred to in his earlier *A Wideness in God's Mercy* as the 'contest of the Gods' (1992: 122-24). This contest takes many forms: 'competition' or confrontation between religious traditions through which some die and some survive, but in which religious mutations inevitably occur; debate in interreligious apologetics on mutually contradictory truth claims; or other forms of 'spiritual warfare' such as that involving a broad spectrum of what Pinnock calls 'truth-seeking encounters': proclamation, works of love, church planting, healings, exorcisms, etc (1992: 129-33). As dynamic entities, religious traditions are continuously in the process of transformation. Pinnock believes that a pneumatological theology of religions, incorporating as it does the horizon of the *eschaton*, is supremely fit to negotiate the clash of religious traditions amid the vicissitudes of history. This does not warrant an exclusivistic *jihad* against religious others, but rather calls for a posture of humility combining Pentecostal testimony and Christ-like service toward the world even while anticipating the eschatological manifestation of truth (1996: 215-46). Pentecostals should find much of value here not only because of their sympathy with

systematic theology—one that is inspired by a pneumatological imagination. It makes for edifying and inspiring pentecostal reading, and I can only pray that more of my Pentecostal colleagues in Church and academy pay close attention to it even if they never get to the present work. It supplies the kind of theological vision that enables one to accept the argument presented in Pinnock's *Wideness*. This is why I do not offer a fully developed biblical justification for the theology of religions presented in this work even if many Pentecostals and charismatics would look first at how well I have done my exegetical homework. I have argued (Yong 1999b) that while Pinnock (and Sanders) have presented scriptural arguments, the debate between inclusivists and exclusivists would continue to be an ineffective exercise of proof-text hurling ad nauseam apart from a revisioning of theological presuppositions. What is attempted here therefore should be understood as complementing rather than supplanting Pinnock's labors toward such revisioning. It should also be seen as a response to Hollenweger's repeated challenge to Pentecostals and charismatics that they apply their 'pneumatological imagination' to their theological work.

Pinnock's eschatological orientation, but also because of his emphasis on the role of human beings in the ongoing subjugation of the demonic powers of the cosmos under the rule of the Spirit.

While Pinnock is having to defend his inclusivism as a charismatic evangelical against potential critics who are both evangelical and Pentecostal, Ralph Del Colle is under no such constraints operating as he is within the inclusivistic framework of the second Vatican Council. Rather than focusing on the argument for theological inclusivism, then, Del Colle has directed his energies toward developing a Christian model for the interreligious dialogue. His approach to this, however, is by way of Spirit-Christology and not as informed specifically by his charismatic experience. Yet reflection on the Pentecostal–charismatic experience has led him to identify it not as continuous with the first creation (Schleiermacher's *homo religiosus*) but as emerging from the new creation inaugurated by the resurrection, ascension and Pentecost events (the second Adam and the sending of the Spirit) (1995; 1996c). Within this framework, Del Colle suggests that divine agency must be considered in both pneumatological and filiological dimensions, neither separated nor made identical, but seen rather as mutually related. These are the 'two hands of God': the 'christological mission to a human nature [Jesus's] and the pneumatological mission to human persons' (1994: 206). He thus argues that 'Spirit-Christology is the most productive systematic model by which to understand and inform the unique contributions of Pentecostal–charismatic spirituality to the church catholic' (1993: 92-93). More specifically, 'the charismatic effusion of divine agency in Jesus and in the Church represents the eschatological intensification of temporality as the needed correlation between the divine sending (and kenosis) of the trinitarian missions and the perichoretic (and energetic) relations of the trinitarian processions' (1996b: 100). While Spirit-Christology means that the Spirit both anointed Christ and is sent by Christ, it also points to the convergence of divine and human actions in the Church since the Christ event. In short, Del Colle believes that the dogmatic construct of Spirit-Christology clarifies divine agency in the world which in turn illuminates the Pentecostal–charismatic experience and vice versa.

How does this connect to the interreligious dialogue? On this issue, Del Colle follows the model elucidated by the Sri Lankan Jesuit, Aloysius Pieris, in correlating the christological dimension of the interreligious dialogue with the collective memories of religious communities

(their founding texts) and the pneumatological dimension with their
primordial experiences (Del Colle 1994: 211). In the same way as the
experience of the Church, at Pentecost for example, combines both
divine agency and human reception, the religious dimension of experience in other traditions also can be seen to include these two components. What this means is that

> we may speak of the work of the Spirit in other than christological terms.
> This does not betray the instincts of Spirit-Christology, where we have
> sought the convergence without identity of the two missions. Rather, it
> enables us to theologize about the Spirit in either of two directions.
> Because Christ is the bearer and sender of the Spirit, we speak of the
> Spirit in relation to Christ and his work. However, because Christ is of
> the Spirit...we can also speak of the Spirit's work in creation, Israel, the
> secular order, and in other religions even as we still confess the unique
> work in Jesus Christ... In Christian faith it is the convergence of the ele-
> ments—e.g., Christ, Spirit, faith—that is significant; *in dialogue with
> other religions, this convergence allows its own elements to be focused
> at the point of inquiry where the dialogue will be most fruitful*' (1994:
> 212-13; my italics).

This last sentence shows how the theological distinction between
Word and Spirit as 'the two hands of the Father' leads to a crucial
insight and dialogic strategy. In a later article, Del Colle shows how
such a model pays dividends in a Christian dialogue with Judaism and
Islam (1996a). Here, he actually expands the pneumatological dimension to include not only the primordial experiences of a religious community, but also its 'ecclesial' or interpretive traditions. In the dialogue
he engages, these are the Rabbinic and halakhic traditions in Judaism
and the formation of the Abode or the *Ummah* in Islam. Because there
is no pneumatology without Christology and vice versa, and because
the pneumatic dimension correlates with human agency (in all persons,
including Jesus), Del Colle suggests that a fruitful dialogue can proceed
from a discussion of how the divine covenant has been deposited in the
founding prophetic persons and words and transmitted in the ensuing
communities. To say that the event of Jesus Christ (the christological
dimension for Christians) has given a new impulse to the Jewish
tradition resulting in Pentecost and the founding of the Church (the
pneumatological dimension) is not to deny the validity of the processes
of transformation traversed by Judaism by the power of the Holy Spirit
from the founding divine word of the Torah (by analogy, the christological dimension for Jews) to the Talmudic period (as an example of

the pneumatological dimension for Jews). Nor is this to deny the same processes in Islam from the initial giving of the Qur'an (by analogy, the christological dimension for Muslims) to the emergence of the diverse Islamic orders (the pneumatological dimension for Muslims). Signs of the Spirit are to be found in the convergence of the human and divine in each community's initial acceptance and ongoing reception of the divine word and in human praxis. This dialogue with Judaism and Islam would thus seem to support Del Colle's earlier contention that the goal of dialogue informed by Spirit-Christology is 'neither proselytism nor eclecticism but communion and mutual witness' (1994: 212).

Del Colle's concern to maintain continuity with the Catholic neo-scholastic tradition may at times result in his use of categories and terminology which Pentecostals like myself find difficult to digest. Further, especially in the interfaith encounter he overviews above, the details of particulars can and should be debated—e.g. if it is indeed possible, and if so, how, the Qur'an can be explicated in christological terms; or whether or not to do so would be to subsume Islam under the Christian rubric in an inappropriate manner. Yet on the whole, I think that his suggestions are sound. At the same time, I do not want to distinguish between the christological and pneumatological dimensions in quite the same way as Del Colle does. According to the metaphysical hypothesis adopted in this work, *every event* is informed to a greater or lesser degree by Word and Spirit, in different respects. We can therefore approach all matters in the interreligious dialogue pneumato-logically, including the christic, Sinaitic and Qur'anic events. At the same time, I agree with Del Colle that there are some matters that will pay greater dividends in the interreligious dialogue (those in which the pneumatological elements are most discernible) and others which we would do well to avoid (those in which the christological forms are most intensified), at least up front.[23]

---

23. Regardless of terminological and conceptual difficulties, however, there is much that Pentecostals can and need to learn from Del Colle. While I take issue with Del Colle on some things (e.g. the doctrine of the immanent Trinity, as mentioned in previous chapters), I see him overall as a comrade in arms. In the bigger picture of things, Del Colle is in a unique position to influence Pentecostals toward inclusivism by his involvement in such arenas as the Society for Pentecostal Studies or perhaps even formally in the Roman Catholic–Pentecostal dialogues. In this regard, mention should also be made of other Catholic charismatics like Gelpi, Killian McDonnell and Francis Sullivan, all of whom have made theological

This brief overview highlights the fact that Pentecostals look at the issues posed by other religious traditions more so as problems for missiology or theological contextualization while charismatics are more likely to engage directly in the construction of a theology of religions in a systematic manner or more apt to be involved in the interreligious dialogue. These concerns, among others, are suggestive of why the development of a theology of religions is an urgent task for Pentecostals and charismatics worldwide.

2. Why Pentecostals (and Charismatics) Need (and Should Desire) to Develop a Theology of Religions

The above considerations, however, may not be sufficient to motivate at least most classical Pentecostals toward either developing a theology of religions or participating in the interreligious dialogue. The fact that some Pentecostals or charismatics have been engaged in such reflections or dialogues is no proof for these detractors that these activities are valuable for the larger movement. I therefore want to argue specifically that Pentecostals and charismatics not only urgently need a theology of religions, but that they should also desire to partake in the interreligious dialogue. This argument proceeds along three lines: (1) the ecumenical roots and global presence of the Pentecostal–charismatic movement; (2) the classical Pentecostal emphasis on missions; and (3) the continued classical Pentecostal quest for theological identity and truth. I suggest that each of these factors not only requires serious reflection on theology of religions, but also that

---

contributions to charismatic theology. While Gelpi's and McDonnell's interests have been in other areas, there is much that they have done, and which I have tried to exploit at certain places in my own constructive argument, which have far-reaching implications for *theologia religionum*. Sullivan, whose background is patristics, has more recently written an erudite history of the *Extra Ecclesiam nulla salus* formula (1992). He is clearly on this side of Vatican II in positively delineating the shift from exclusivism and ecclesiocentrism to inclusivism and christocentrism in the Roman Catholic Church. There are indications throughout his work that he endorses an inclusivistic theology of religions, but this remains relatively undeveloped. He prefers instead to continue framing the soteriological question in ecclesiological terms (cf. Sullivan 1993). There may yet be something forthcoming from Sullivan that builds on this presentation of historical data. Such is my own hope, at any rate, since I am convinced that there is much that Pentecostals can glean from Catholic charismatic theologians like him.

the development of such a theology—which inevitably touches upon the entirety of the traditional loci of systematic and dogmatic theology—will enable especially classical Pentecostals to participate in and contribute to the ecumenical and interreligious dialogues.[24]

International Roots and Global Presence
In his most recent book, Walter Hollenweger delineates five contributing roots toward the global Pentecostal movement (1997). They are, in order, black oral, Catholic, evangelical, critical and ecumenical. The first derives from the contributions of Seymour and African–American spirituality and expression initially released from the Azusa Street revival and later given further impetus in the expansion of Pentecostal-type churches in the non-Western world (cf. Gerloff 1995). The second points both to the perfectionist spirituality of Wesley's Anglicanism as mediated to classical Pentecostalism by way of the nineteenth century Holiness movement, and the more recent contributions of the Catholic charismatic renewal. The third is that which has since become most dominant, at least in the North American Pentecostal and charismatic world: the Reformed 'higher life' spirituality as mediated through the English Keswick movement in the latter part of the nineteenth century, and the hermeneutics of fundamentalism as tempered by the Pentecostal–charismatic alliance with evangelicalism since the middle of the twentieth century. Hollenweger describes the critical root as the voice of protest—whether liturgically, politically, socially, or even theologically—which has been characteristic of Pentecostalism from its inception even if it has always been threatened by the ongoing processes of institutionalization that spiritual movements face.[25] Finally, there has always been an unpublicized group deriving from beyond the shores of the Americas (e.g. the South African Du Plessis, the Dutchman Gerrit Roelof Polman, the Swiss Louis Dallière, the German Jonathan Paul and the Briton Alexander Boddy) who have from the beginning of their ministries understood Pentecostalism as an international community with ecumenical significance (see Hollenweger

---

24. The argument presented in this section is a thoroughly expanded revision of portions of Yong (1999a).

25. Early Pentecostalism's rejection of 'enlightenment' Christian liturgical worship is well known; what is less well known are its advocacy of pacifism during the first World War, its social movements, and its struggle to articulate a theology able to account for the experience of the Spirit.

1997: 334-55). From this, Hollenweger cautions Pentecostals against allowing any regional, national or other kind of ideology to dominate the movement. Instead, a truly pluralistic Pentecostalism needs to be recognized, one that is in tune with the international movement of the Spirit and that is able to meet the needs of diverse cultures, societies and places.

This is all the more important given the fact that in less than one century, what transpired at Azusa Street has literally expanded across the globe. Over a decade ago, the statistician David Barrett (1988) presented Pentecostals and charismatics as comprising about one-fifth of all Christians and being active in over 8,000 ethnolinguistic cultures and 7,000 languages throughout more than 80 percent of the world's metropolises. At that time, over 360 million Pentecostals and charismatics in over 14,000 denominations rubbed shoulders with 95 percent of the world's population. Today, Pentecostals and charismatics number over 460 million worldwide (more than 25 percent of all Christians), and are situated in virtually every metropolitan area in the world (Barrett and Johnson 1998). Pentecostals and charismatics now belong to more denominations and even more denominationally-independent churches than they did in the mid-1980s, and daily engage the billions who are either non-Christians or members of other faiths.[26]

The point is not only that Pentecostals and charismatics in North America exist in a religiously plural melting pot and that there are Jews, Muslims, Hindus and Buddhists at their doorstep, although this is certainly true and of import. What is staggering for the imagination, however, is that members the world over have close contact with neighbors, co-workers, and even friends whose primary religious allegiances

---

26. Barrett and Johnson projected there would be well over 500 million Pentecostals and charismatics by the year 2000. This astonishing growth over the last quarter of a century can be attributed in part to Pentecostal–charismatic participation in global plans for world evangelization (megaplans). According to Barrett's calculations in the mid-1980s, 'of the world's 20 current megaplans launched since 1968, 13, or 65 per cent, are Pentecostal–charismatic. So are 8 (73 per cent) of the 11 current gigaplans (global plans to evangelize the world spending over one billion U.S. dollars) launched since 1968' (1988: 830; see Johnson 1992). It also follows from the demographic shift of the Pentecostal–charismatic movement from the West to the non-Western world that missionary activity from the latter, which is already well under way, will continue to increase. It has been projected that non-Western missionaries would outnumber Western ones by the end of the twentieth century (Pate 1991), a prognosis that appears to have been realized.

are non-Christian. The fact of the matter is that all of us operate with a 'theology of religions' even if such is unrecognized or unarticulated. These 'theologies' are what guide Pentecostal life and praxis, and for better or worse, their relations with those in other faiths. I am arguing that given the global presence of the Pentecostal–charismatic movement, those in Pentecostal leadership are obliged to reflect critically and theologically about their assumptions, attitudes and ideas concerning other faith traditions, and to incorporate such reflection systematically into their pedagogy and practice.

Urgent Missiological Issues

The global presence of the Pentecostals and charismatics also raises questions of import for the movement's enduring emphasis on missions.[27] While there are many issues of significance here, I want to focus on two: that related to contextualization and that related to missionary methods. Let me comment first on the former, more explosive subject.

The threat that accompanies any genuine attempt to contextualize the gospel message is that of syncretism.[28] To elaborate briefly on one concrete example, Pentecostalism in Korea has, on occasion, been charged with embracing the world-view of traditional Korean shamanism and incorporating elements of shamanistic practice. Boo Woong Yoo is one who has suggested that the emphasis placed by Yoido Full Gospel Church pastor, Yonggi Cho, on positive thinking, material prosperity,

---

27. Pentecostals have from the start considered the missionary mandate to be at the heart of their spirituality (cf. Pousson 1994; Bernard, *et al.* 1989: 139-50). An overview of contemporary Pentecostal theology of mission can be found in the work of missiologists like Gary McGee of the Assemblies of God (1986, 1989) and L. Grant McClung of the Church of God, Cleveland, Tennessee (1991, 1994, 1996).

28. I see 'contextualization' and 'syncretism' as contrast terms. Just as there are degrees of 'contextualization'—e.g. across the spectrum from toleration, translation, assimilation, Christianization, acculturation and incorporation, to use Steven Kaplan's typology (1995)—there are also degrees of 'syncretism' (cf. Gort, *et al.* 1989). Whereas both involve the fusion of Christian and non-Christian ideas and practices, I would distinguish them by saying that 'syncretism' results in the Christian being overcome by non-Christian elements, and is to be combated (cf. Wessels 1989), while 'contextualization' would attempt to redeem non-Christian elements within the Christian framework, and is to be encouraged. Pentecostals, however, are as concerned about the former as evangelicals (cf. Kato 1975), which explains why both groups are probably more conservative than others in their missiologies.

good health and bodily healing resonates with Koreans in part because they are central features of shamanistic practice in Korea. He concludes that Cho's 'role in Sunday morning worship looks exactly like that of a shaman or mudang. The only difference is that a shaman performs his wonders in the name of spirits while Rev. Cho exorcises evil spirits and heals the sick in the name of Jesus' (Yoo 1986: 74).[29] Pentecostals would be correct to argue, as Allan Anderson has done in the South African context, that the 'only difference' mentioned by Yoo is a crucial one. Other responses are also no doubt available to Pentecostal apologists.

My aim at present is not to resolve this controversy.[30] I am merely pointing out that there are many 'real life' issues at stake in the global expansion of Pentecostalism which are related to the anathemized word 'syncretism'. While the strategy of thoroughly denouncing all that pertains to local traditions may be a good one for Pentecostal administrators and missiologists, it is not viable in the long run for a number of reasons. First, it fails to account for the fact that there are at least phenomenological similarities between Pentecostal beliefs and practices and that of other local traditions. On the popular level, it is simply too easy for confusion to reign in doctrine and practice. Especially in Asia, Pentecostals and charismatics live and work in cultures steeped in the religious world-views of Hinduism, Buddhism, Taoism, Confucianism and Shintoism. Many who do not have formal connections to these traditions nevertheless either practice or have been influenced by their popular versions. It is practically impossible even for zealous Pentecostal or charismatic converts to isolate themselves from these 'religious others'. While their denunciations of past beliefs and practices are genuine, these serve more as rhetorical means by which to articulate

29. Harvey Cox also discusses this whole question of Pentecostalism and shamanism in Korea in some detail (1995: 213-41), as does Tai (1988); in the related contexts of Japan and Okinawa, see Mullins (1990, 1991) and Ikegami (1993) respectively. The fact that shamanism is so deeply embedded in Korean history, culture and society (cf. Guisso and Yu 1988) means, on the one hand, that the contextualization problem confronts not only the Pentecostals and charismatics, but also other Christian groups as well (cf. Adams 1995). On the other hand, however, shamanism has also served as a resource for liberative movements such as those associated with Minjung theologians (Tang 1991).

30. I will discuss this issue in much more detail in Chapter 8 as it exists in the Brazilian context.

new-found identities. They do not, in any case, provide the kind of discriminatory awareness which enables the old to be sifted out of the new.

Second, the denunciation of local traditions as a strategy assumes a dualism between gospel and culture (and religion) which makes genuine contextualization impossible. For Pentecostals to persist in the argument of dispensational theology that culture is irredeemable except at the parousia is for them to deny the reality of their holistic experience of the Spirit's presence and activity.[31] Third, and finally, this would be a much too simple response to a complex reality. Taking responsibility for the missionary task demands not only prolonged theological reflection but also the willingness to involve national and local leaders and laity in a process of mutual learning. The work of Del Tarr, former Assemblies of God missionary to West Africa, is a case in point. Tarr (1994) brings his years of missionary experience to argue for the legitimacy of an indigenous African hermeneutic of Scripture. He suggests that there is much in African culture that can contribute both methodologically and substantively to an understanding of the gospel. This kind of deep contextualization is rare among classical Pentecostals, which explains in part why there is a consciousness on the part of Tarr expressed throughout the book that what is proposed may be offensive or may sound suspicious to Western readers (he is referring to North American evangelicals as well as to his more conservative Pentecostal colleagues). Unfortunately, Tarr does not seriously consider the relationship between culture and religiosity. To do so would have led him from biblical exegesis to a recognition of the need for a more systematic treatment of *theologia religionum*.

What is therefore needed is what Hollenweger calls a 'theologically responsible syncretism' by which the old creation is challenged, renewed or transformed by the new (1997: 132-41). Pentecostals may be right to object to any attempt to salvage the idea of syncretism. But no matter what this process is labeled, the task of contextualization demands at least a critical and theological engagement with diverse

---

31. Not to mention the fact that this generation of Pentecostals has fought through the unsuccessful attempt to explicate their experience of the Spirit within the dispensational paradigm, and thus more or less rejected the latter as unsuitable for the theological task (cf., e.g., Sheppard 1984, Cargal 1993, Archer 1998).

cultures and the world of religions. Pentecostals are realizing that such is imperative if the movement is to remain viable in the long run since the ferment of practices and ideas are inevitable wherever the gospel has gone. Thus, in the Asian context, what is at stake is either a 'christianized' animism whereby indigenous religious traditions take in and transform the Christian message or an indigenous Christianity whereby the gospel redeems all that is good, true and holy in other local faith practices.

For many Pentecostals, this means other traditions are no more than *praeparatio evangelica*s in that they contain elements of the gospel which simply need to be brought out. In this scheme, non-Christians would convert to Christianity as soon as they see this truth. Conversion would thus be central to the missionary effort. However, there is another way in which the gospel can be seen to be redemptive for other faiths: by being a leaven toward that which is good, true, pure and holy—what John V. Taylor calls the fulfillment of any tradition in Christ 'in terms true to itself' (1973: 190). Gerald Pillay gives us a concrete example of how Pentecostalism has contributed in some ways to the purification of popular Hinduism in South Africa, and to a revitalization of that tradition in light of the gospel message (1994: 162-79). Of course, this is taking place quite apart from what Pentecostals think they are doing, almost as if it were a sovereign move of the Spirit. But the fact is the Pentecostal presence is causing religious leaders everywhere to re-examine critically their own traditions, leading to internal purification on the one hand, and to adoption of what is perceived to be good, true and useful from other traditions on the other. If Pentecostals are convinced that all truth is God's truth, *perhaps* these are occasions for thanking the Lord and acknowledging the Spirit's presence and activity in other faiths.

Recognizing this, Pentecostals like Wonsuk Ma are arguing for an 'Asian Pentecostal theology' that is evangelical and yet applicable to non-Western contexts, that is Christ-centered without neglecting the Spirit, and that is committed to the gospel and yet able to engage the spirit-world of Asia (1998). It is also significant that Ma is both a theologian and a missionary. That there is a clear connection between theology and missiology has long been recognized by Pentecostals. Operating within a theological framework dominated by apocalyptic and eschatological elements, Pentecostal missions have long emphasized personal witness, evangelistic zeal and kerygmatic proclamation.[32] What they have been slower to notice, and what the work of Ma implies but does not specify, is the intrinsic connection between theology *of religions* and theology *of mission*.[33] This connection has at least two important implications for Pentecostal missiology.

First, since all religions are about saving souls, Pentecostal missions should reflect the fact that there is a Christian difference focused on the saving of both souls *and lives* (cf. McGee 1994a). This more holistic approach to missions not only emerges out of the Pentecostal–charismatic experience of the Spirit but also serves to set the Christian gospel apart, at least in some respects, from what is offered in the religious marketplace. This means, in part, that a Pentecostal missiology will need to emphasize both proclamation and works of mercy and love. Missionary labor that is anointed by the Spirit will seek to do what Jesus did: heal the sick, open the eyes of the blind, release the oppressed, preach the gospel to the poor, and proclaim freedom for the captives (cf. Lk. 4.18 and Bosch 1991: 84-122). Historically, Pentecostal missions have actually been multi-faceted. On the one hand, there has been the preaching of the gospel with power (e.g. Sterk 1992). But, on the other, Pentecostals have also founded orphanages, provided health care, etc., in emphasizing what they have called 'ministries of compassion' (e.g. McGee 1989: 249-54). I am simply advocating that this aspect of missions needs to be considered, along with kergymatic proclamation, as central components to Pentecostalism's evangelistic and missionary task.

Second, because a holistic missionary focus covers both the personal

---

32. This is not to say that Pentecostal missions have not been innovative to some degree. Early on, Pentecostals realized that their experience of the Spirit had profound implications for theology of missions, especially with regard to the concept of indigenous leadership and indigenous expressions of the gospel. Mel Hodges, the Assemblies of God missiologist, argued for this as far back as 1957 (cf. also Hodges 1977 for a comprehensive statement). The present generation of Pentecostal missiologists have taken Hodges's legacy to the next level in attempting to develop a theology of mission in the broader context of the Kingdom of God. The focus, as Pentecostals have begun to realize, should emerge out of the theological tension between the task of the Church and the arrival of the Kingdom (e.g. Pomerville 1985; Petersen 1996). In this framework, the Church exists as a leaven in culture and, by implication I would add, in the religions, in anticipation of the full manifestation of the Kingdom of God. More on this in Chapter 7.

33. Missiologist Gerald Anderson has previously suggested that theology of religions is the 'epitome of mission theology' (1996).

and the socio-economic-political realms, and because advance in the latter is rarely successful if attempted apart from cooperative networks and coalitions, Pentecostal–charismatic missions need to be ecumenical to a larger degree than they currently are. This means, in part, that a Pentecostal missiology will need to emphasize both proclamation *and* dialogue. The fact is that the Pentecostal rhetoric of hellfire and brimstone that has motivated their evangelistic thrust is actually contrary to their experience of the Spirit. While the doctrine of eternal damnation remains a debated issue (e.g. Crockett 1992), the this-worldly character of the Kingdom of God and the intimate connection between its eschatological reality and the Spirit is beyond question. More important is that both Pentecostals and non-Pentecostals alike have recognized that Pentecostal missionary zeal derives first and foremost from their vital encounter with the Holy Spirit (Acts 1.8; Lk. 12.12; cf. Pomerville 1985; Boer 1961: 28-47). It is therefore appropriate for Pentecostals to look 'beyond triumphalism' (McGee 1994b), and conduct their missionary affairs in accordance with the belief that the Spirit has gone before them and is already at work in non-Christians. In this framework, mission is not undermined by dialogue, even of the interreligious kind, but actually even demands it![34]

Here is where a more robust theology of religions can contribute to the integrity of the Pentecostal missionary cause. Pentecostals have already begun to recognize both the need for dialogue and the need for

---

34. It is also important here to clarify briefly the place and role of conversion in this proposed revisioning of Pentecostal missiology. Two points need to be emphasized. First, conversion is God's business, not that of human beings. The Pentecostal obligation is to share the gospel as led by the Spirit. Second, conversion is not as much about increasing the size of the institutional Church as it is an invitation to a relationship with the Messiah of reconstituted Israel in the already-and-not-yet Kingdom of God (cf. Penney 1997). This is the truth behind the Pentecostal experience of the Spirit and its emphasis on the Church as a spiritual body. If the encounter with the Spirit is an eschatological experience, then this goes not only for the Pentecostal–charismatic experience proper but also for the experience of conversion. Conversion is therefore eschatological and cannot be regarded only as an historical act accomplished at a point in time, unless of course, history is understood to include the eschatological dimension of the Kingdom of God. In either view, there is no contradiction between emphasizing the importance of proclaiming the gospel and embracing a holistic view of salvation that sees conversion as a spiritual process in human hearts which is reflected in the transformation of human life (cf. Lord 1997; Schillebeeckx 1978).

a broader Pentecostal–charismatic–evangelical coalition with regard to fulfilling the Great Commission. Thus L. Grant McClung (1993) has called for a globalization of the doctrinal process whereby North American Pentecostals learn about socio-economic liberation from Latin American ones; about political engagement from South African ones; about ethics and totalitarianism from Eastern European ones; about the New Age movement from Indian ones; about Islam from Indonesian ones; and about non-Christian faiths from the worldwide Church, and so on. But if selective dialogues have been encouraged because they are seen to be helpful on some issues, what about further dialogues with others on other issues? Is not Walter Hollenweger correct in calling Pentecostals to a much more 'rigorous ecumenism'?

> Ecumenical means that we have not just to cooperate with all Christians, but also to listen to non-Christians's interpretations and criticisms. This is important if we are to deal constructively with the issues facing us; namely, the search for a just world order, the threat of nuclear war, the ecological crisis, the global drug mafia, and the widespread starvation with its devastating migration problems. All this needs understanding on a global scale (Hollenweger 1997: 292).

Although Pentecostals would grant that these concerns are valid, they would also say that interreligious cooperation places their commitment to the truth of the gospel in jeopardy. I would counter that while such may be possible, that does not necessarily have to be the case. On the contrary, I would argue that what is to be gained outweighs the risks taken since there are more strictly theological reasons for developing a Pentecostal theology of religions in addition to the preceding historical and missiological ones.

Pentecostal Identity and Theological Truth
In a recent plea before the Theology Working Group of the Society of Pentecostal Studies (SPS), Mel Robeck suggested three problem areas which Pentecostals need to address in order to move ahead:

> First among these questions is the issue of identity. After a full century, we haven't yet agreed upon what constitutes a Pentecostal. Second is the issue of how the Pentecostal movement is to view itself in relationship to all others who number themselves among the People of God. We do not know where we fit in God's ultimate work among His people. Third, is the question of how to relate to the world around us. What do we believe about God in the world, and how are we to discern His presence and, as a result, our role in God's creation (Robeck 1997b: 3-4).

While I think that Robeck's prognosis for Pentecostal theology in the twenty-first century is correct, I want to make explicit the connection that exists between all three of the concerns he outlines. Robeck himself understands that Pentecostal identity cannot be forged apart from her relationship with the larger Christian community. For this reason, among others, he has come to be recognized as the ecumenical heir apparent to Du Plessis as 'Mr Pentecost' through his long involvement in Christian ecumenical dialogue.[35] Yet because the identity of anything always involves its determinateness vis-à-vis other things, I would argue that the question of Pentecostal identity cannot be adequately treated if the even larger question of their relatedness to the world is not addressed. In this last category, as Robeck rightly notes, are not only secularists and atheists, but also those in other faiths. Not surprisingly, Robeck is led to raise the following fateful questions later in the same address to the SPS Theology Working Group:

> What role does the Spirit play in other religions? I am not here to argue for a relativistic approach to salvation. I hope you will understand me. But is the Holy Spirit present among the Muslims, and if so, in what ways? Is the Holy Spirit present among the Jews, and if so, how? And what about the animists, the Hindus, the Buddhists, and others?… How should I understand the work of God among them? Is He totally absent? I find that hard to believe, even though I am convinced that they need to know the one Lord that I confess as a Christian, Jesus Christ' (1997b: 8).[36]

35. See, e.g., Robeck (1987, 1994a, 1994c, 1999). Elsewhere, Robeck has retold the fascinating history of how the latent ecumenical potential in the Pentecostal experience was compromised in the Assemblies of God for ecclesial and political reasons (1997a). On a global level, however, Pentecostals have not been as reluctant to involve themselves in inter-Christian ecumenism (see Cole 1995). The Pentecostal Mission Church of Chile, for example, joined the World Council of Churches in 1961 (Palma 1985), while others have been involved in different ways at various levels (e.g. Hunter 1992). There has never been more of a consensus that Pentecostal involvement in inter-Christian ecumenical dialogue is long overdue for and helpful to both Pentecostals and the Church worldwide (see Lederle 1990; Moltmann and Kuschel 1996; Albrecht 1997).

36. Robeck had made a similar statement in his reflections on the seventh World Council of Churches convention in Canberra: 'I want to affirm those things I see in other religions that contribute to the dignity of humanity and to world peace, but I am also bound by God's revelation of himself in Jesus Christ to be faithful to the gospel' (1993: 111).

These are pointed questions which lie at the heart of the present work. What is important at this juncture, however, is to extend Peter Staples's suggestion with regard to Pentecostal ecumenism (1992). While Staples is correct to observe that Pentecostals will always be handicapped ecumenically so long as their ecclesiology remains relatively underdeveloped in comparison to their pneumatology, I think it important also to note that Pentecostal identity and missions will continue to be less than true to the gospel to some degree so long as serious reflection regarding their relationship to other cultures and religious traditions is avoided. I think that this is part of what Robeck is implicitly struggling to articulate. Developing a theology of religions is central not only to this wider (interreligious) ecumenism, but also to the forging of a Pentecostal identity over and against that of other Christian communions.

This leads, finally, to the issue of truth in religion. Truth, following Peirce's categories, is an interpretive activity deriving from the triadic relationship wherein knower and known are connected by signs.[37] As correspondence, truth is therefore the correlation between what is propositionally expressed via a potentially indefinite succession of signs and the reality they point to. As coherence, truth is the interconnectedness of all signs without express contradiction. As pragmatic, truth is not only what guides our engagement with the world correctly, but also that which is able to predict the behavior or habits of things. That truth emerges out of interpretation, however, means that signs have to be understood as related to what is known in their proper or appropriate respects. Knowers need to ask the right questions of signs and what is known, or they need to realize the specific respects in which signs point to what is known. In this scheme, then, Scripture asserts itself to point or reveal not, e.g., matters of science, but matters related to righteousness, morality and our salvation (2 Tim. 3.15-16). Interpreted properly (respecting the right things) it is truthful in enabling us to know the relationship between God, ourselves and the world accurately; and it is truthful in enabling us to navigate the processes of life and salvation. And yet, as those who are advocates of the Wesleyan quadrilateral point out, Scripture never exists in isolation but only in relation to the tradition of the Church, our exercise of reason and what we experience.

---

37. What follows is a condensation of Yong (2000b: 576-78). The essays in Dean (1995) should also be consulted as they are especially insightful with regard to the issue of truth and the interreligious dialogue.

By virtue of their experience of the Spirit, Pentecostals operate along similar premises even if they have not explicitly adopted the model of the quadrilateral.[38]

If for no other reason, Pentecostals should be aware that truth is a process guided by the Holy Spirit (Jn 16.13; 1 Jn 2.27) as they faithfully and communally study Scripture, and live out the dictates of the gospel. Clearly, Pentecostals believe that they have something of ultimate importance to share with those in other faiths. But is it conceivable that they have absolutely nothing even of relative import to learn from religious others? Are Pentecostals worried that what they believe to be true from Scripture and their experiences will not stand up to what they will confront in the interreligious arena? How can Scripture conflict with reality? If Pentecostals were indeed convinced that their experience of the Spirit is an experience of that which is absolutely true, why the anxiousness about a mutual sharing of this experience with those in other faiths? As familiar as they are to the strange and incomprehensible ways and movements of the Spirit (cf. Jn 3.8), they should be some of the first rather than last to not only acknowledge the possibility of the Spirit's presence and activity in other faiths, but also to then search out and 'test the spirits'.[39]

While it is true that Pentecostals have been known more for their ability to witness and testify than for their patient listening, yet all genuine and successful communication involves both elements. That Solivan is correct to insist that truth can never be decided by majority vote means only that Pentecostals should participate selectively and critically in the interreligious dialogue, not that they should avoid it at all costs. It is never too soon to realize that such involvement is part and

---

38. On this point, the essays on hermeneutics by Israel, Albrecht and McNally (1993), and Cargal (1993) show the convergence of the Pentecostal model with the Wesleyan one (cf. Gunter *et al.* 1997). However, since Pentecostals as a whole have generally understood truth solely in biblical terms (e.g. Bernard 1992: 63-72), they have given little consideration to the nature of truth. One exception is Harold Hunter's unpublished paper, 'What is Truth?' (1984). I appreciate Hunter's discussion of truth from a Pentecostal perspective as emerging from a tension between evangelical propositional and matters of ethos. At the same time, however, I would want to emphasize the respects or vantage points of interpretation no matter what is being discussed.

39. With regard to other faiths, then, Pentecostals and charismatics should engage the exegesis of this Johannine text by C.S. Song (1994: 36-38) and others rather than dismissing them out of hand.

parcel both to the success of missions that is holistic and multi-dimensional and to the quest for truth as revealed by the Holy Spirit. In point of fact, Pentecostals the world over are already involved in such informal conversations on a daily basis. They listen to their neighbors and share their experiences with them in turn. And since what they think about the religions influences how they respond and relate to adherents of other faiths, developing a theology of religions needs to be a priority. This can only provide an added dimension of versatility to their formal and informal interreligious discussions with 'religious others'.

It is unreasonable to think that all Pentecostal objections have been or can be answered. But I have shown here both that Pentecostals have demonstrated in times past an openness in their relations with non-Christians, and that there has been some willingness to rethink creatively the theological issues raised by their increasing awareness of the pluralistic character of the world of religions. More importantly, it is also clear that Pentecostals and charismatics are at a crucial historical juncture, one with dire implications not only for them but for Christianity as well insofar as they represent her to the world, and that formulating a critical theology of religions should be an urgent priority. It follows that I agree for the most part with Walter Hollenweger when he says that they should

> draw inspiration from its inter-cultural and ecumenical roots for the benefit of inter-religious dialogue. And this indeed seems to be a way out of the narrow, defensive, fundamentalistic position of many Christians. Pentecostal…inductive theology is not adequate to defend orthodoxy, but it is adequate for mission, testimony, and dialogue. Because a movement which understands itself from the third article…is essentially tolerant and open to new, so far unknown moves of the Spirit, such a return to the ecumenical roots of this movement could be a decisive contribution to a world conference on Religion and Peace, and to a global ethos of love (Hollenweger 1997: 399).

I would only want to add that the pneumatological imagination of Pentecostals and charismatics may not be as barren for theological orthodoxy as Hollenweger thinks. The next chapter therefore looks specifically at how this imagination connects their foundational categories with critical and theological norms so as to produce the kind of discerning charismology needed for a Pentecostal–charismatic theology of religions and for their participation in the interreligious dialogue.

Chapter 7

RESOURCES FOR A PENTECOSTAL–CHARISMATIC
THEOLOGY OF RELIGIONS

It was the summer of 1985, and I was completing a missions internship
at a church in Edmonton, Alberta. This was the first time that I had
strayed so far from home as to be in a foreign country, not knowing
anyone until I got there. About mid-summer, I came down one day with
terrible stomach pains, beyond description. I recall lying doubled-over in
my bed that afternoon for a few hours. I thought something was terribly
wrong, and I feared that I would not survive. I cried out to the Lord in
the midst of my pain, but it did not dissipate. When I thought I could no
longer endure the ordeal, I remembered that my mother periodically
called the Oral Roberts Prayer Tower in Tulsa, Oklahoma. The woman
who answered listened very sympathetically, read a passage from Scripture, and prayed 'in Jesus' name' that my stomach pains would be gone.
The moment she said the name of Jesus, I felt a release, a divine touch.
Within minutes, I was back to normal. This was as close as I have ever
come to experiencing a miraculous healing. I knew that we as Pentecostals believed in divine gifts of healing 'in the name of Jesus', so I was
not surprised, just grateful. But I also recalled asking my father when I
was in high school about how non-Pentecostal Christians could experience such success without having received the fulness of the Holy
Spirit. I never did get a straight answer from him. More recently, I have
come to a much greater awareness of healing traditions in other faiths.
How can we explain such phenomena? The typical Pentecostal response
to successful cures in other faiths has been to dismiss them as deceptive
maneuvers of the evil one so as to keep non-Christians from coming to
the light of Christ. Certainly, this possibility should not be dismissed.
But is that all that can be said from a Pentecostal perspective about healing and other related phenomena which are central to the spiritual quests
and religious practices of devoted and sincere non-Christians from time
immemorial?

Introduction

Let us briefly take stock of the ground gained so far. I argued in Chapters 2 and 3 that Christian theology of religions is at an impasse under the constraints imposed by Christology and that a pneumatological approach to the religions may be suggestive of a way out. I then proposed that this latter route can be best traversed if we cultivated a pneumatological imagination, a way of looking at reality that emerges out of the dialectical interplay between the Pentecostal–charismatic experience on the one hand and reflection on that experience on the other. I devoted most of Chapter 4 to a theoretical and systematic assessment of principal features of this imagination, features that allow us to conceptualize divine presence and activity in the world without denying the reality of divine absence. I have argued that since these categories are potentially universal, they can be considered as central elements of a foundational theology of the Holy Spirit.[1] My working hypothesis has been that the various dimensions of human experience, including the religious one, can be illuminated by such a foundational pneumatology. Returning in Chapter 5 to the experiential base of the pneumatological imagination, I sketched how the foundational categories emerge out of the Pentecostal–charismatic experience of the Holy Spirit on the one hand, and how the categories continue to guide and shape this experience on the other.

After pleading for the urgency of a Pentecostal–charismatic engagement with the religions (Chapter 6), the question at this point is what are the resources at their disposal by which to fashion a theological understanding of the non-Christian faiths. I submit that when the foundational categories developed in this book are applied to the phenomena of religion, three correlative categories emerge: religious experience, religious utility and religious cosmology. I will contend in the longer first section that these three sub-categories register features essential to the Pentecostal–charismatic tradition. Throughout, I also suggest that because the categories proposed are sufficiently vague so as to be rendered more specific by vastly contrasting phenomena, they may facilitate a more in-depth engagement with non-Christian faiths

---

1.   This would be true also for traditions which are not explicitly theistic since even these tend to exhibit theistic features when practiced at the folk or popular level.

precisely by highlighting the similarities-in-difference at the heart of comparisons across religious lines. In light of the vagueness of these comparative categories, however, further consideration should be given to the task of discerning the spirits. A Pentecostal–charismatic approach to discernment will therefore be set forth in Section 2.

1. *Revisioning Pentecostal–Charismatic Categories for the Interreligious Dialogue*

It is now time to return to the conversation taken up earlier with Harvey Cox. In moving from the categories of foundational pneumatology to categories designed explicitly to facilitate Pentecostal–charismatic participation in the interreligious dialogue, it is important to begin by conceding that Cox's theory of religion is suggestive in part because it derives from an analysis of the worldwide movement. Yet even though I agree with Cox that 'primal spirituality' is both appropriate and useful at some level, his sub-categories are either too restrictive or theologically ineffectual. Further, while his categories are primarily drawn from the cultural criticism and phenomenology of Pentecostal spirituality, I have argued throughout that the development of comparative categories needs to arise from the dialectical interplay between experience and theory. These factors suggest that a revision of Cox's categories may be required in order to conjoin cross-cultural theory, phenomenology and theology in the quest for an adequate Pentecostal–charismatic *theologia religionum*.

What I propose to do in the following, then, is expand the range, and hopefully relevancy, of Cox's 'primal' categories by relating them mutually with the previously developed categories drawn from foundational pneumatology. First, I will suggest that what Cox calls 'primal speech' can be understood as a specification of the category of divine presence; a mediating category, that of *religious experience*, will be submitted as more appropriate both to the Pentecostal–charismatic experience and to the interreligious dialogue. Second, what Cox calls 'primal piety' also can be understood as a specification of the category of divine activity; I will propose that a second mediating category, that of *religious utility*, better interprets the phenomena of religious spirituality and practice. Cox's third sub-category, 'primal hope,' correlates less naturally with our foundational category of divine absence. I am optimistic, however, that an alternative category, *religious cosmology*, sufficiently mediates the notion of hope which Cox understands as representative of *homo religiosus* with the category of divine absence so as to be of promise as a comparative theological category. Throughout, I will argue for the greater viability of these categoreal revisions for a pneumatological theology of religions along three lines: that they better reflect the Pentecostal–charismatic experience of the Spirit; that they both illuminate and confirm themselves as more specific categoreal elements of our foundational pneumatological imagination; and that their combined flexibility brings in to play the kind of normative theological interpretation of religious phenomena that is needed at some point both in comparative religious and theological studies and in the interreligious dialogue.

Divine Presence and the Religious Dimension of Experience
I have already noted (Chapter 5) that while glossolalia is a central element in the Pentecostal–charismatic experience, it is not necessarily the *sine qua non* for membership in the movement. A 1980 general survey suggested that even in North America, not much more than one fifth of all those who consider themselves generally as Pentecostals or charismatics speak in tongues; more astonishing, upwards of 50 percent of classical Pentecostals polled had never spoken in tongues (Synan 1984: 18-20).[2] Far from suggesting that glossolalia is unimportant for Pentecostals and charismatics, I am simply pointing out that what Cox calls 'primal speech' may be too restrictive with regard to the Pentecostal–charismatic experience, and too specific to serve as a comparative phenomenological or theological category. Cox himself is only minimally suggestive with regard to how primal speech is exemplified in non-Pentecostal traditions (1995: 91; but cf. May 1956 and C. Williams 1981: 192-212). What he does admit which is of significance, however, is that Pentecostals 'interpret tongue speaking as evidence of the wonderful nearness of the Spirit, as close as one's own larynx and vocal cords' (Cox 1995: 95). My point is that tongues, for most Pentecostals but especially for charismatics, is only one sign which points to the Spirit's presence. More precisely, tongues is a sign among others that embody for Pentecostals and charismatics the presence of the Spirit and shape their imaginative engagement with things of the Spirit.

2.   A much more recent study by R. Andrew Chestnut of Pentecostalism in Brazil shows that less than 47 percent of Pentecostal church-goers speak in tongues (1997: 80); this is close to what was discovered by earlier studies, in Chile for example, where only 57 percent spoke in tongues.

For this reason, I think it more productive to adopt a broader category for comparative purposes, that of *religious experience*. Building on our previous discussion of the religious dimension of experience (Chapter 4), I suggest that this category is able to register all that Pentecostal and charismatics feel and think in their encounter with the Spirit's presence. Phenomenologically, this encounter is manifest in a wide range of experiences: dreams and visions, the dance, the clap, the shout or chant, spontaneous (non-glossolalic) utterances, and the wave or lifting up of holy hands. Biblically, these experiences cover the entire range of the Pauline charismata: messages of wisdom and knowledge, faith, gifts of healing, miraculous powers, prophecies, discernment of spirits, tongues-speaking and interpretation of tongues (1 Cor. 12.8-10); functional charisms such as apostolic and teaching ministries, working of miracles, administrative gifts (1 Cor. 12.28); ecclesial charisms such as the offices of the evangelist and the pastor (Eph. 4.11); general personality charisms such as service, encouragement, almsgiving, leadership and the showing of mercy (Rom. 12.6-8).

More important, however, is that Pentecostals and charismatics understand these phenomena as palpable signs of the Spirit's presence in their midst. The operation of the charisms in the Pentecostal–charismatic experience signifies the conjunction of the divine and human in a manner such that there is a paradoxical tension between the recognition of the Spirit as a divine Thou over and against the I on the one hand, and yet a union between the Spirit and the self that obliterates the subject–object distinction on the other.[3] This tension highlights the special quality of the Pentecostal–charismatic encounter of the Spirit. To

3.   The pneumatological imagination recognizes and indeed celebrates in this tension. Both Steve Land's work on Pentecostal–charismatic affections and Tillich's idea of 'ecstatic reason' further illuminate how this tension is played out. Land's argument is that the affections are the unitive core of the Pentecostal experiential orientation (1993). For Land, the affections are rational, but not *only* rational; they give shape to rationality itself. His suggestion may be helpful in getting at what Tillich was trying to articulate in his notion of 'ecstasy' as 'reason beyond itself' and as transcending the finite subject–object structure of rationality (Tillich 1951: 111-18). The value of Tillich's discussion is that it shows how revelation occurs in the shock which moves us 'outside' of ourselves into the presence of and relationship with God. Both theologians are correct in their attempt to overcome dualism without doing away with it in all respects. I submit that this is, in part, the genius of what Pentecostals and charismatics can contribute to the formation of a Christian pneumatological imagination.

remove either pole of the tension is to either routinize the experience or succumb to all the excesses that tend to accompany what Ronald Knox in his analysis of enthusiastic movements throughout the history of Christianity has called 'ultrasupernaturalism' (1994: 2).

In addition, this element of corporeality in the Pentecostal–charismatic experience of the Spirit is central to the pneumatological imagination. The way that Pentecostals and charismatics engage God and the world derives from the impression made by the Spirit on the senses leaving the devotee no other explanation for their experience than that they have encountered the Holy Spirit. The pneumatological imagination is therefore the spectacles—continuously cleaned and tuned to greater precision through further spiritual experiences, it should be noted—through which Pentecostals and charismatics experience and engage the Spirit's presence in the world. What others would call the results of medical intervention, for example, Pentecostals and charismatics would be more apt to call a miraculous healing wrought by the Holy Spirit even if they would not deny the instrumental means of medicine and technology (cf. Poloma 1989: 51-65).[4]

Clearly, religious experience understood as encounter with the Holy Spirit is pivotal to the Pentecostal–charismatic way of being-in-the-world. It is arguable that this theological interpretation of the religious dimension of Pentecostal–charismatic experience is analogous to the central convictions of most, if not all, religious traditions. The religious dimension of human experience, focused as it is on the intersection between that which is transcendent and that which is of this world, is most clearly explicated in finite symbols which point to the infinite or enacted in rituals that serve to bridge the holy and the profane. The object of the religious quest is the experience of transcendence, whether such be defined in existential, psychological, social or more strictly theological and soteriological terms. In many traditions, such experiences of the transcendent are either also tangible or have implications for human corporeality. Our category of religious experience nicely captures this emphasis on the tangibility of the Spirit's presence for Pentecostals and charismatics and of the transcendent for other faiths.

It should go without saying that all experiences of transcendence are not like each other such that they can be abstracted from their concrete

---

4.   Pentecostals and charismatics are more apt to see 'the paranormal as normal' (Poloma 1989: 21-33).

expressions and christened 'primordial experiences' of the Holy Spirit. This is the truth behind the criticism that religious experience in itself is a vacuous category since all experience is 'of something' and shaped by social, cultural and linguistic forces. It is undeniable that most Pentecostals and charismatics consider their encounter with the Spirit (and, for that matter, any genuine encounters with the Holy Spirit) to be nothing less than the experience of Jesus. For this reason, Lederle and Clark are correct to note that 'Pentecostals are understandably skeptical of the dialogic elements in Christianity which claim to see the Holy Spirit active in non-Christian religions' (1983: 44). In order to begin to address this question, however, it would be helpful to recapitulate the metaphysical hypothesis undergirding our foundational pneumatology. With respect to their ontological status, all finite entities or events are, by virtue of their existential being and modality, the result of Word and Spirit as the two hands of the Father. With respect to the Christian interpretive scheme, however, the Spirit is intimately related to the sending of the Word incarnate just as the Spirit is pentecostally derivative from the ascension of the Word. The Spirit's modality, for Christians in general and for Pentecostals and charismatics in particular, is therefore as a field of force bearing the signature of Jesus the Christ.

The argument that is being developed here, however, is that a pneumatologically founded theology of religions does not need to begin the interreligious dialogue with the christological question. Rather, it allows Christians to approach the dialogue by focusing first on phenomenological commonalities (divine presence) and the other's understanding of these phenomena. Whenever theological categories are introduced into the dialogue (and note that this should necessarily occur sooner or later in order to keep the dialogue from degenerating into religious irrelevance), those procured from our foundational pneumatology can be pressed into service to query about the kinds of force fields that are present and active in other traditions. For Pentecostals and charismatics, the manifestation of the charismata and other related phenomena can be understood as the merging of the divine field of force with force fields within the human trajectory. This convergence, however, is not just a felt presence, but a transformative one. Force fields are by their very nature energetic modalities productive of change. In a similar way, then, spiritual force fields in other traditions need to be understood as both felt presences and transformative ones. In short, our pneumatological categories register not only the here- and thus-ness of the

Spirit's presence, but also the thence- and toward-ness of the Spirit's activity. The task of discernment therefore necessarily moves us both logically and existentially from categories of divine presence to categories of divine activity.

Divine Activity and Religious Utility
Whereas one might expect something like a phenomenology of spirituality in Cox's discussion of Pentecostal 'primal piety,' such will not be found. What is striking about primal piety as rehearsed by Cox is that it has enabled Pentecostals to provide a third alternative to the spiritualities of fundamentalism and liberalism in the late modern era, a spirituality that has retrieved and created religious space for primal experiences of mystery and ecstasy in the midst of a world undergoing massive urbanization and technologization. Such experiences are healing agents to those laboring under trials and tribulations ranging from personal illness and poverty to social and political marginalization (Cox 1995: 99-110). In short, Cox's primal piety is a 'working spirituality' by which Pentecostals find ways to comprehend meaning in their lives and articulate (testify of) their roles within the larger story of both the Church and the modern world.

This 'working spirituality' points to the paradox at the core of the Pentecostal–charismatic experience. On the one hand, the Pentecostal–charismatic encounter with the divine is often reported as a sovereign and gracious manifestation of the Holy Spirit. On the other hand, devotees do respond to the leading and working of the Spirit in their midst. As the discussion on Pentecostal–charismatic ritual (Chapter 5) showed, the experience of the Holy Spirit emerges out of the conjunction of divine initiative and human response. The fact that the pneumatological imagination senses the presence of Jesus' embracing love by his Spirit means that the Pentecostal or charismatic would be remiss if he or she did not respond in kind by lifting up holy hands and praising/embracing the Lord. The tangibility of this embrace, however, is for Pentecostals and charismatics the sign of divine presence which foreshadows something greater since the Spirit is not *merely* present, but is manifest to accomplish the transformation of soul. The upshot of this is that the experience of the Spirit's presence both leads to an expectation of the Spirit's activity and precipitates corresponding activity on the part of the devotee so that he or she is obliged to 'get in step with what the Spirit is doing'.

This activity of both the Spirit and of the believer leads me to suggest that Cox's primal piety may be appropriately re-categorized as *religious utility*. The gift of the Holy Spirit leads Pentecostals and charismatics to 'expect a miracle today,' the maxim introduced by the charismatic televangelist, Oral Roberts. This expectation at the same time transforms especially Pentecostals into pragmatists: what works is that which has been divinely ordained and brought about by the Holy Spirit, at times through human cooperation; what does not work is not the will of God and can be avoided by cultivating a sensitivity to the Spirit's leading. In his discussion of Pentecostal prayer, for example, Ed Rybarczyk talks of the 'deep vein of pragmatism common to most North-American Pentecostals. Increasingly this pragmatic vein runs not only to the heart of our spirituality, but to our very soul. We contemporary North-American Pentecostals are "wired" to get something done' (1996: 3). It is safe to say, however, that pragmatism is a feature of global Pentecostalism and not just of the prayer-strand in North-America (cf. Wilson 1988; Cleary 1997: 14-17).[5] I want to explore briefly further specifications of this category of religious utility in the Pentecostal–charismatic movement as seen in the personal experience of divine healing and in the notion of Pentecostalism not having but *being* a social ethic or policy.

Early Pentecostals emphasized a four-fold gospel: Jesus as savior, baptizer (in the Holy Spirit), healer and coming king.[6] While many Pentecostals brought into their experience of the Spirit the prominent Holiness doctrine that healing was included in the atonement of Christ (Dayton 1987: 127-32), the Pentecostal experience convinced them that

---

5.   It should no longer be so surprising that Peirce's categories have been as illuminative as they have been for the Pentecostal–charismatic experience given the fact that he is the recognized founder of the philosophy of pragmatism. Gelpi has noted that 'every version of pragmatism builds on the construct of experience' (1994: 1), and Pentecostal pragmatism is no exception to this general rule. I would only add that Peirce's philosophy can help Pentecostals understand their pragmatism better even while Pentecostal–charismatic pragmatism may in turn shed light on the truth of pragmatism; but that task will have to be reserved for another occasion.

6.   Hence the name International Church of the Foursquare Gospel, founded by the gifted evangelist, Aimee Semple McPherson; cf. Blumhofer (1993). Chris Thomas has reminded me, however, that there is some movement to reconceive early Pentecostalism as promoting a five-fold paradigm, adding the Wesleyan Holiness emphasis on Jesus as sanctifier (cf. Land 1993: 55-56; thus also the theme of the 26th annual meeting of the Society for Pentecostal Studies at Patten College, 13–15 March 1997: 'The Fivefold Gospel').

the entire range of the charismata, including the gifts of healing, was being fully restored to the Church despite the fundamentalist cessationist doctrine.[7] The physicality of glossolalia was an eschatological sign of the Spirit being poured out 'on all flesh' (Acts 2.17, KJV), thus heralding the fullness of salvation that emphasized the redemption of the body (Rom. 8.23) and the understanding of healing as included in the atonement (cf. 1 Pet. 2.24). Realizing that the work of the Holy Spirit in human life cannot be compartmentalized, Pentecostals developed a holistic understanding of divine healing that covers all manner of sickness, disease, psychosomatic illness, emotional affliction and mental disorder.[8]

A recent study of Pentecostalism in Brazil by R. Andrew Chestnut, a historian of religion, provides a window into how the Pentecostal belief in healing operates in practice. Chestnut's thesis is that 'the dialectic between poverty-related illness and faith healing provides the key to understanding the appeal of Pentecostalism in Brazil and much of Latin America' (1997: 6).[9] Whether illness be physically, socio-economically or spiritually classified, Chestnut argues that Pentecostal experience meets the needs of those suffering from crises of health along two lines.

---

7. For a survey of healing in the Christian tradition, see Kydd (1998a). Harrell (1975), Wacker (1986) and Taylor (1995) document the history of healing among Pentecostals and charismatics. For the Pentecostal response to the fundamentalist belief in the cessation of the charismata, see Ruthven (1990, 1993).

8. Theologies of healing vary across the Pentecostal–charismatic spectrum: for a biblical theology of healing, focused on the Christian Testament, but with the addition of clearly articulated implications for Pentecostal ministry, see Thomas (1998); classical Pentecostal statements include Duffield and Van Cleave (1983: 363-416) and Purdy (1995); the Oneness position is delineated by Bernard (1997: 123-72); a broad charismatic overview is Knight (1993); for a Catholic charismatic perspective, see Gelpi (1972: 1-58). For theologies of inner healing, see Kraft (1993) and Hummel (1993: 159-77). Of course, Pentecostals and charismatics recognize that healing does not occur in every instance (cf. Eutsler 1993; cf. Snook 1996). Further, they have also acknowledged that theological and practical excesses often accompany ministries focused on healing (e.g. Farah n.d.); outsider criticisms, especially of charismatic faith healing, include Moo (1988) and McConnell (1988).

9. That faith healing is central to global Pentecostal–charismatic success is beyond question. Cox himself notes this connection with regard to the African scene (1995: 245; cf. Oosthuizen 1992). For further evidence for the prominence of healing in the Pentecostal boom in Latin America, see, e.g., Conway (1980) on Haiti; Dirkson (1984) on Mexico; Kamsteeg (1991) on Peru; and Van Kessel (1992) on Chile.

First, conversion to and baptism in the Holy Spirit brings immediate relief from existential *angst* and provides empowerment over the forces of illness regnant in the life situation. The washing away of sins by the blood of Jesus includes the cleansing of infirmities from the body as well. Unaffected by historical-critical scholarship on the longer ending in St Mark, Pentecostals (especially in Latin America) regularly practice the laying on of hands in almost every service and believe that the sick will get well (Mk 16.18). Second, and more important, however, longer term remedies are provided by the Pentecostal community to nurture members to full health through a process of discipleship and the restructuring of social networks and relations. Pentecostal men, for example, are much less inclined to frequent the local bars where the temptation to squander resources on prostitution, alcohol and drugs is at its height, while Pentecostal women are taught health maintenance and sanitary techniques while being sustained—especially if they have unconverted spouses—by the solidarity and mutual aid provided in the ecclesial community.[10] For converts who have experienced the Spirit bodily and affectively, St Paul's injunction to 'offer your bodies as living sacrifices, holy and pleasing to God' (Rom. 12.1) is not too much to ask.

This connection between bodily healing and socio-economic well-being is what is behind Everett Wilson's comment that Pentecostals 'don't have a social policy, they are a social policy!' (quoted in Gros 1987: 12).[11] Clearly, the Pentecostal experience of the Spirit has not only engendered a strong conviction in the availability of divine healing to those afflicted, but has also been a generative source of transformation in socio-economic matters even if Pentecostals themselves have been slow to see the connections. But if Pentecostal pragmatism is

10. In this connection, sociologists have been intrigued by the social impact of Pentecostal gender relations in Latin America. While Pentecostals are generally patriarchal in theology, this has translated into a more egalitarian praxis; both Pentecostal men and women have gained, albeit in different ways, from their experience of the Holy Spirit. This has been borne out in numerous investigations such as that of Mariz and Machado (1997) in Brazil, Brusco (1995) in Colombia, and Austin-Broos (1997) in Jamaica.

11. It should also be noted that more and more Pentecostals are moving from a pragmatism regarding social policies toward seeing that the Pentecostal–charismatic experience of the Spirit has political social-ethical implications for activism as well. The apolitical stance of classical Pentecostalism is being reinterpreted even now (e.g. Cleary and Stewart-Gambino 1997).

understood as flowing out of a pneumatological imagination that sees what the Spirit is doing and seeks to emulate it, the utilitarian implications of the Pentecostal–charismatic experience of the Spirit cannot be denied. More and more Pentecostals and charismatics are convinced that their experience of the Spirit has personal and social ramifications, at both the micro- and macro-levels, and that sustained reflection on the meaning of the sending of the Spirit at Pentecost for socio-political issues is imperative. They are sensing the need to take the long-standing Pentecostal involvement in social welfare—ministries to the poor and hungry, the establishment of orphanages, the running of rescue missions, etc.—to the next step of social action devoted to reforming the larger social, economic and political structures that are at the root of the experience of sin, sickness and poverty. This step, however, cannot be taken apart from the articulation of a distinctively Pentecostal–charismatic social ethic.[12]

It is not by coincidence that the two major efforts to fulfill this task to date have come from Pentecostals living with and working among the socio-economically needy. Both Eldin Villafañe and Doug Petersen, who have been active in the ministry and training of urban Hispanic Americans and Latin American childcare provision and reform respectively, have probed the Pentecostal–charismatic experience for insights into a social ethic. Villafañe proposes a holistic ethical spirituality to correlate with the Pentecostal experience of the Spirit (1993). While the grieving of the Spirit (cf. Eph. 4.30) over personal and social sin should evoke responses of indignation, the working of the Spirit to bring about the eschatological reign of God should provoke believers to action in society and the world. This suggests a pneumatological paradigm for social spirituality whereby Christians are challenged to work with the Spirit in the larger realms of culture, history and creation. These various dimensions point to different challenges—e.g. institutional structures in the realm of culture, anti-theistic ideologies in the realm of history, principalities and powers in the created order—and call for special

---

12. Early Pentecostals were not oblivious to social concerns (e.g. Robeck 1992). More recently, however, there have been repeated calls for the development of a thoroughgoing Pentecostal–charismatic social ethic beginning with that by Lederle and Clark (1983: 85-95) as occasioned by their experience of apartheid in South Africa. Others include Bernard (1985: 275-302), Dempster (1987, 1993), Ford (1988), those in Sider (1988), Volf (1989), Jayasooria and Hathaway (1990), and Snell (1992).

methods appropriate to each task. While I will return below to pick up
on some of Villafañe's strategies for social engagement, it is important
to note at this point that in any of these areas, norms of the *regno Dei*
by which the Spirit's presence and activity are discerned can be appropriately applied: 'The Spirit is present as a "Helper" wherever good,
love, peace, justice—Signs of the Reign—are manifest in our world'
(Villafañe 1993: 183).[13]

In language similar to Villafañe's, Doug Petersen also draws on the
kingdom motif and writes of 'the ethos of justice, mercy, love and
peace as its principle moral features' (1996: 226). This is the work of
the Spirit from times immemorial, but exemplified most prolifically in
the charismatic work of the Hebrew prophets, and in the inaugural outpouring of the eschatological Spirit on the day of Pentecost. Given the
revitalization of this prophetic impulse in the modern Pentecostal–
charismatic movement, Petersen suggests that the distinctive Pentecostal contribution to social ethics lies in the empowering experience of
Spirit-baptism (1996: 204-209). Referring to Latin American Pentecostals, he writes:

> Because of Spirit-baptism they have access to empowerment not only to
> believe in and experience divine healing and miracles, but also for their
> social actions. These Pentecostals, dismayed by the misery and social
> injustice with which they are surrounded, can respond in constructive
> ways to resist spiritual, moral and social blight. Their efforts...should

13. Hauerwas and Saye (1995) fault Villafañe both for failing to provide more
of the Hispanic American Pentecostal story in support of his social ethic and for
being no more than a liberal Protestant in espousing just these signs as marks of the
Spirit. Yet I think this latter charge is methodologically misplaced and theologically
mistaken. Villafañe clearly recognizes the Spirit's presence and activity outside the
Church (1993: 183 n. 63), and his work is a prolegomena to discerning this reality;
his concluding chapter is therefore appropriately titled, '*Toward* an Hispanic
American Pentecostal Social Ethic' (my italics). I see the Pentecostal–charismatic
experience as formative of the kind of pneumatological imagination needed to
recognize more specific nuances of the Spirit's presence and activity under the more
general categories delineated by Villafañe (and, as will be seen below, by Petersen).
In that sense, I understand Hauerwas and Saye's complaint but refuse to equate that
with a sin. Liberal Protestantism was right to see justice, peace, etc., as the work of
the Spirit; but it was wrong and failed miserably in not taking into account the
reality of other spirits—the demonic—as complicating factors in that work. Villafañe, who pays detailed attention to the principalities and powers, does not fall into
that trap.

proceed, in the light of this Pentecostal social ethic, based upon theological foundations, not merely from a pragmatic reaction to suffering
and injustice (Petersen 1996: 204).[14]

Petersen's statement is revealing of the overall orientation of Pentecostalism and actually serves to confirm my study. The Pentecostal–
charismatic experience brings devotees into contact with the salvific
works of the divine Spirit. The devotee is effectively transferred from a
life of sin, infirmity and impotence to one in which he or she is empowered for prophetic witness, kerygmatic proclamation, compassion-
ate service and social action. These healing actions are sustained in
communities of faith by the continued practice of charismatic gifts and
training in the ways of the Spirit. Cheryl Bridges Johns calls these communities 'free spaces or zones of liberation created by the Holy Spirit'
(1996: 49). They are, according to the categories of foundational
pneumatology developed in this book, force fields of divine activity that
liberate individuals at the personal level even while equipping them
with charisms for the edification of the local community of faith and for
the transformation of the wider socio-political milieu (cf. Razu 1991).[15]
In the process of living out life-in-the-Spirit (praxis), Pentecostals have
come to see the possibility of providing greater guidance and structure

14. My only criticism of Petersen is that his theological method follows that of
evangelicalism too closely resulting in his view that a Pentecostal social ethic is
nothing more than an evangelical social ethic plus the empowerment of the Spirit to
actualize the kingdom (cf. Petersen 1996: 226). If I am methodologically correct,
however, Petersen has grossly underestimated the hermeneutical power attached to
the experience of the Spirit. His—and evangelicalism's, for that matter—problem is
that Word tends to overpower Spirit; rather, both need to be held in creative tension
in any fully trinitarian theology.

15. In this regard, it is also important to note Michael Welker's attribution of a
'public personality' to the Spirit (1997b: 31). By this, Welker means to amplify the
spacial and temporal dimensions of the Spirit's person implicit in his earlier
employment of the metaphor of force fields (1994) to include the cultural, ethical
and aesthetic domains. It should be noted that Welker's explication was provoked
by the response of Pentecostal theologian, Frank Macchia, to his book. While
appreciative of the pneumatological insights of Welker and his German colleague,
Jürgen Moltmann (1992, 1994, 1996b), in affirming the divine immanence in the
created order, Macchia (1994a, 1997) seeks to underscore the experience of radical
transcendence in the Pentecostal encounter of the Spirit and to preserve its
iconoclastic character. Macchia's work serves as a reminder that the Spirit's activity
is unpredictable and that the Spirit's field of force cannot be identified *in toto* with
the public forces of creation.

to their labors by reflecting on their experiences (theology). This does not, however, mean that Pentecostals and charismatics are first and foremost worshippers and doers and only secondly theologians (cf. G.L. Anderson 1990: 56).

The category of religious utility therefore enables both the public and pragmatic nature of the Pentecostal–charismatic experience of the Spirit. It allows the right questions to be asked about the cash value of religious experiences. For Pentecostals, the experience of divine presence is not the be-all and end-all of religiousness or spirituality. Rather it is the beginning of life in the Spirit, bearing the fruits of the Spirit, doing the work of the Spirit. Arguably, similar patterns can be demonstrated in other religious traditions. Devotional piety is practiced and communal rituals are performed for a variety of purposes: to please Allah and earn a spot in paradise; to alleviate suffering and escape from the wheel of *samsara*; to flow with the Tao; to placate one's ancestors, etc. Yet it is equally clear that while the kingdom criteria outlined by Villafañe and Petersen may be helpful in some instances (i.e. in the major religious traditions), they are not applicable across the board. It is also clear that the wide diversity of religious ends cannot be commensurate. The category of religious utility can help us identify in the abstract the general soteriological structures that devotees in different traditions strive to attain, but it is not as helpful in determining which are true or false at either the empirical or the theological levels. Our foundational category of divine absence may be of some assistance for this latter task.

Divine Absence and Religious Cosmology

Few, if any, Pentecostals have a communal Holocaust memory to draw from. Yet as a whole, Pentecostals have had their share in tasting the underside of history. It is because their experience of divine absence is so strong that Pentecostals have embraced divine presence with such fervor. It is also for this reason that a strong eschatological orientation has been a persistent feature of the Pentecostal mentality. It was, in Cox's terms, a 'millennial sensibility' that alerted early Pentecostals to the large-scale transformation of personal, social and cultural existence which they felt but could not articulate (1995: 116). By drawing from the primal springs of hope in a brighter future, Cox suggests that Pentecostalism was a millennial movement which was able to survive the transition between cultural and intellectual epochs without suffering extended religious losses. In this way, the absence of the divine in the present was conquered by a realized eschatology: the present thus served up a foretaste of the future and allowed its embrace.

Cox's analysis is correct so far as it goes regarding early Pentecostalism (cf. Faupel 1996a). However, as Steven Land has noted, not all early Pentecostals were socially marginalized and upward social mobility clearly characterizes much of the contemporary Pentecostal–charismatic landscape, both in the Euro-American West and elsewhere (1993: 71). What happens to primal hope and millennial sensibilities when apocalyptic expectations are replaced by this-worldly interests? Clearly there needs to be a revisioning of what hope aspires to if not the age to come. Equally clearly but rarely mentioned, however, is that hope not only concerns the future and gives rise to expectations, but also enables the identification and endurance of pain, emptiness and suffering (cf. Rom. 8.22-25). Hope enables the naming of both the present enemy to be defeated and, however inadequately, that of the victory to come. Hope is therefore a supreme mediating category that struggles with the tensions of divine presence and absence, of the eschatological 'now-and-not-yet' and the existential situation; in short, hope confronts and articulates the reality of both the divine and the demonic. Whereas Cox's primal hope would be useful as a historical, psychological or even cross-cultural category, I suggest that the category of *religious cosmology*, extrapolated from the notion of divine absence, would be more productive for the task at hand.

By *cosmology*, I am referring to our understanding of the created universe as a whole, or what Stephen Toulmin calls 'the Nature of the Whole' (1982: 3). Whereas cosmological speculation by scientific materialists or nominalists would reject the idea of 'spirits' or 'demons' out of hand, the metaphysical hypothesis developed in Chapter 4 in fact demands an acknowledgment of their reality in order to account for that which 'regulates' both the inexplicable and horrific features of human experience. The former could, in the Pentecostal–charismatic cosmology discussed in this chapter, be understood as angelic spirits while the latter would refer to the devil and his demons. While I will consider in the next chapter other religious cosmologies which do not divide the spirit world so neatly into angels and demons, I need to emphasize clearly here that with regard to cosmogony—the origins of the Whole and its parts—I reject an ultimate dualism. Ontologically, the demonic has no independent status apart from divine creation even if cosmologically, demons are real and destructive force fields interwoven with space and time.

The pneumatological imagination culled from the Pentecostal–charismatic experience is uniquely suited to capitalize on the usefulness of religious cosmology as a comparative religious and theological category. Whereas millennial hope accompanies only a select grouping of religious movements, spirit beings in general and the demonic in particular appear in many guises in all religious traditions almost without exception.[16] Unlike their secularized Christian counterparts, Pentecostals and charismatics are committed anti-nominalists who believe spirits and demons are just as real as rocks and persons.[17] A cosmology that includes spiritual beings recognizes, rather than explains away, the place of the uncanny, the unpredictable and the unquantifiable in human experience. Pentecostals and charismatics believe that these elements of the human experience are best accounted for within such a richly populated cosmology. They would also agree with the thesis that the category of the demonic has been a polemical, social and political tool used throughout the history of religion to exclude the religious other. But they would hasten to add that this does not necessarily mean demons are simply a figment or projection of the human imagination.[18] To name the demonic is to recognize the forces of destruction, sin and death which threaten human life; it is to allow protests from the margin, to embrace the cry of the poor, the sick, the downtrodden, the despicable, the prisoners as the cry of the Spirit. As a comparative religious

16. Unless I am mistaken, the Jain tradition may be the sole exception. Even non-theistic traditions like Theravada and Zen Buddhism have a place for demons in their cosmologies (cf. Long 1987).

17. According to missiologists like Charles Kraft (1989) and Paul Hiebert (1985b), this is one of the major reasons behind the success of the Pentecostal–charismatic missions in contrast to the languishing projects of mainline denominations. In this connection, see also Morton Kelsey's argument for the importance of what I have called the pneumatological imagination for Christian spirituality and life (1972).

18. For an interesting discussion of the social and political use of the rhetoric of the demonic relative to the history of Jewish–Christian relations, see Boys *et al.* (1997). At the same time, no matter how religious traditions have used such rhetoric to vilify others, demonic mythologies have also in each case served other cosmological functions with regard to the experience of evil, pain and suffering. Hence, as I endeavor to show, the value of religious cosmology as a comparative religious and theological category.

category, then, religious cosmology as an overarching framework, and the demonic as a particular specification of this may shed some light on issues of distributive justice and socio-economic politics. Such ethical issues may in turn serve as another point of entry to the interreligious dialogue table for Pentecostals and charismatics.

In order to appreciate fully the value of religious cosmology as a comparative category, however, some account needs to be rendered about the personal and social dimensions of Pentecostal–charismatic demonology.[19] The demonic is the means by which Pentecostals and charismatics understand the horror of divine absence, both on the individual and personal level and in larger contexts. On the former level, because Pentecostals and charismatics do not question the biblical account of the fall of Satan and his demonic hosts to the earth (e.g. Lk. 10.18; Rev. 12.7-17), they take seriously the Pauline injunction to engage in spiritual warfare against the 'powers of this dark world and against the spiritual forces of evil in the heavenly realms' (Eph. 6.12; cf. 2 Cor. 10.4-6). Resisting the devil who seeks to devour the unsuspecting (Jas 4.7, 1 Pet. 5.8) and spiritual warfare are necessary since to neglect vigilance in this respect is to open up oneself to various levels of demonic oppression and perhaps even possession. While Pentecostals and charismatics are divided on the question of whether or not a Christian can be possessed by demons, they are all agreed that Christians are not exempt from the assault of demonic forces.

One of the problems with regard to this whole issue is the difficulty in distinguishing between demonic influence as it relates to mental illness on the one hand (cf. Bufford 1989), and to ecstatic spiritual manifestations such as that which occurs in trance-like states on the other (cf. Goodman 1974; Kelsey 1978: 10-50). There are, of course, various norms which Pentecostals and charismatics have applied. Theologically, they often rely on the ability and willingness of the person in question to confess the Lordship of Christ (1 Cor. 12.3; 1 Jn 4.2-3). Phenomenologically, violent or uncontrollable behavior, voice changes, the dilation of the eyes and manifestation of hatred, frothing at the

---

19. For a bibliographic survey of Pentecostal–charismatic literature on the demonic, see Bolt (1994). Classical Pentecostal treatments include Duffield and Van Cleave (1983: 459-510), Möller (1987), Collins (1993–94), and Macchia (1995a); Thomas (1998) discusses the devil as related to disease and deliverance; a Oneness perspective is provided by Reynolds (1993: 97-106). The charismatic demonology I have found most balanced has been Wright (1990, 1996).

mouth, utterances of blasphemies and execrations, enduring bondage to destructive habits, compulsive fears, etc., have often been understood to signify at least demonic oppression if not possession (cf. Green 1981: 134-35; Shuster 1987: 186-90). I will return to a more detailed discussion of criteria for discernment later in this chapter. For now, however, suffice it to note that these phenomena exhibit the loss of self-control which is contrary to the biblical account whereby divine and human come together as counterbalanced forces in the pentecostal experience. As reported by St Luke, on the day of Pentecost, those gathered in the upper room 'were filled with the Holy Spirit and *began to speak* in other tongues *as the Spirit enabled* them' (Acts 2.4, my italics).[20]

While the majority of Pentecostals and charismatics think of the demonic in personal and individualistic terms, there has in the past decade or so been a marked increase in discussion within the movement of other categories by which to understand the biblical principalities and powers. This has come about in large part as a result of Third Wave interest in spiritual warfare directed toward identifying, addressing and overcoming strongholds of demonic oppression regnant over various kinds of social networks such as neighborhoods, people groups, cities and nations dispersed over specific geographic regions. Taking their cue

---

20. In this regard, Tillich's distinction between the ecstatic experience of the divine versus that of the demonic is noteworthy and deserves to be quoted at length: 'While demonic possession destroys the rational structure of the mind, divine ecstasy preserves and elevates it, although transcending it. Demonic possession destroys the ethical and logical principles of reason; divine ecstasy affirms them. Demonic "revelations" are exposed and rejected in many religious sources, especially in the Old Testament. An assumed revelation in which justice as the principle of practical reason is violated, is antidivine, and it is therefore judged a lie. The demonic blinds; it does not reveal. In the state of demonic possession the mind is not really "beside itself", but rather it is in the power of elements of itself which aspire to be the whole mind which grasp the center of the rational self and destroy it. There is, however, a point of identity between ecstasy and possession. In both cases the ordinary subject-object structure of the mind is put out of action. But divine ecstasy does not violate the wholeness of the rational mind, while demonic possession weakens or destroys it' (1951: 114).

Tillich's characterization is clearly in accord with the Pentecostal–charismatic intuitions regarding ecstatic experiences of the Spirit. While there are numerous accounts of trance-like behavior claimed by adherents of the movement, such are clearly not the norm if they are measured by the biblical account of the divine and human coming together synergistically—conjoined but never confused—in charismatic phenomena.

from biblical references to spiritual powers such as the 'prince of Persia' or the 'prince of Greece' (Dan. 10.13, 20), and to the implied regional assignment of Legion (Mk 5.9-10), Third Wavers have coined the phrase 'territorial spirits' to designate these forces of darkness which have as their objective the destruction of lives and the hindrance of the gospel message.[21] While territorial spirits have often been associated with specific vices—e.g. the spirit of greed, of rebellion, of pornography, of sexual perversion, or of the occult at work in various cities and metropolitan areas—there has also been a recognition of spirits at the socio-structural and institutional sphere. In commenting on the biblical ἐξουσία and ἀρχή, for example, Thomas White notes both their supernatural and natural connotations:

> In [Paul] the Apostle's understanding, there were supernatural forces that 'stood behind' human structures. Paul is no doubt voicing the Jewish apocalyptic notion of cosmic beings who were given authority by God to arbitrate human affairs. Presumably, the *dunamis* operate within countries and cultures to influence certain aspects of life... These insidious powers continue to work through human governments, religions, and powerful personalities to keep people in bondage to legalism, social ideology, and moral compromise (1991: 62).

There are undoubtedly many questionable assumptions and ambiguous concepts employed by Third Wave theorists, many of which have drawn critical responses and calls for further dialogue and investigation from classical Pentecostals.[22] I do, however, think there is sufficient latitude in the understanding of principalities and powers both among Third Wavers and classical Pentecostals to connect with the demonology developed under the category of divine absence. Villafañe, for example, has drawn from the work of the Anabaptist John Yoder (1972)

21. The literature is becoming extensive; for introductory surveys, see especially Wagner and Pennoyer (1990) and Wagner (1991). There is, of course, a wide range of popular level understandings of these doctrines such as those promulgated by the novelist Frank Peretti. Most Pentecostal–charismatic academics would endorse the critical response of Robert Guelich (1991) to such demonologies. In contrast, the 'territorial spirits' proposed by Third Wavers not only derives from their extensive pastoral and missionary experience but also includes a good dose of theological sophistication. Better for us to engage the latter in self-critical dialogue than to dismiss them along with the popularizers out of hand.

22. See, e.g., Pratt 1991; Menzies 1995; W. Ma 1997. Peter Wagner himself has expressed the need for caution in the research and application of this subject (in Wagner and Pennoyer 1990: 86-90).

in seeing the biblical powers to be 'religious structures, intellectual structures (-ologies and -isms), moral structures (codes and customs), political structures (the tyrant, the market, the school, the court, race, and nation)' (Villafañe 1993: 180). The fact that Yoder's work has been influential also in the development of Wink's theology of the powers may be coincidental, but it is not insignificant. A convergence can therefore be seen between the Pentecostal–charismatic theology of powers and demonology with the concept of the demonic in the metaphysical hypothesis employed in this book. The demonic can be understood as force fields that neutralize the presence of the Holy Spirit and counter his activity even while they originate and perpetuate destruction and evil in the world. They are legal vectors which shape the patterns and habits of human activity within cultural institutions, socio-economic networks and political structures. They wreck havoc in individual lives in part through personal incarnations that incite destructive habits and acts. While the demonic can be clearly regarded as real generals—laws, habits, tendencies or dispositions—in and of themselves, they can only be discerned from their effects on and instantiations in the concrete actualities of the world.

This growing awareness among Pentecostals and charismatics that there are larger dimensions to the demonic than the personal or individual level has led in turn to the development of appropriate strategies for engaging the enemy at the various levels in which it operates. Beginning with the presupposition that the powers of darkness have already been conquered by Jesus in the power of the Holy Spirit, Pentecostals and charismatics proceed to exercise this same authority in similar ways.[23] An expansion of the understanding of exorcism, one of the chief weapons employed by Pentecostals and charismatics in spiritual warfare, has been a part of this process.[24] Peter Wagner, for example,

---

23. F.P. Möller thus talks about Pentecostals having a 'particularly real experience of the Holy Spirit's dynamic working, which overcomes every power of evil' (1987: 173).

24. For overviews of Christian exorcism, see Linn and Linn (1981) and Olson (1992); a good exegetical treatment is Twelftree (1993). Representative Pentecostal-charismatic discussions include Hoy (1979), Reddin (1989), McClung (1990), Hunt (1995), Theron (1996) and Warrington (1997). The Pentecostal sensitivity to the realm of the demonic has been sharpened in part by the centrality that the Lukan narratives (Luke–Acts) play in their self-understanding. Exegetes such as Susan Garrett have shown that 'the struggle between Jesus (or the Holy Spirit) and Satan lies at the very heart of Luke's story' (1989: 58). This conflict has carried

has distinguished three levels of warfare corresponding to three realms of demonic activity (1996: 21-22). The first, ground-level warfare, concerns the casting out of demons from people.[25] Occult-level warfare deals with demonic forces behind structured occultism such as that seen in Satanism, witchcraft, New Age astrology and the like; Wagner does not specify how Christians should conduct warfare in this realm except to say that different approaches are called for.[26] Strategic- or cosmic-level warfare is Wagner's specialization. Wagner suggests biblical models for such warfare which include the fulfilling of the Great Commission, Jesus's example of binding or overcoming the strongman (cf. Lk. 11.21-22) and power confrontations—defined as visible and practical demonstrations 'that Jesus Christ is more powerful than the spirits, powers or false gods worshiped or feared by the members of a given people group' (Wagner 1996: 102)—in the ministry of the apostles.[27]

That the reality of territorial spirits calls forth appropriate strategies of spiritual warfare involving intensive fasting and intercessory prayer, power confrontations including the working of signs and wonders by the Holy Spirit, and various levels of exorcistic activity, is not to be denied. At the same time, Wagner seems to be less than aware of the fact that the powers are intricately and concretely connected to the socio-political structures of human existence. This demands both spiritual warfare, perhaps that promoted by Wagner but subject to some modification, and what Nigel Wright calls 'persuasive action' in the socio-political realm (1990: 131-53). Part of the process of exorcising

over in the day-to-day struggle of Pentecostals and charismatics whose attempt to find wholeness and healing, especially in the two-thirds world, has led many in search of the most powerful exorcist (e.g. Lartey 1986; Glazier 1980, Glazier [ed.] 1980).

25. I should note here one of the results from John Christopher Thomas's thorough research of the Christian Testament's understanding of the devil and deliverance: that exorcisms in the early Church were performed only on unbelievers—those 'outside' the Christian community (cf. Thomas 1998: 306-307, 317-18). The implications of this will be clear in the next chapter.

26. Later in his book, Wagner does suggest that a biblical example of occult-level warfare is to be found in the conversion of magicians at Ephesus (Acts 19). He admits, however, that it is difficult to separate ground-level from occult-level warfare when the two go together in real life.

27. A classic example from the Hebrew Bible is the confrontation between Elijah and the prophets of Baal at Mount Carmel resulting in the demonstration of the supremacy of Yahweh (1 Kgs 18).

the demonic has to involve, at a fundamental level, addressing the mechanisms which perpetuate its force fields of influence. While this involves the transformation of existing socio-political networks— which, in theological terms, is the redemption of the powers and their restoration to their original purposes according to the creative act— Pentecostals insist on beginning with the transformation of human lives whereby men and women in positions of power are turned from the darkness to the light of Christ.[28] In short, there is a growing recognition across the Pentecostal–charismatic–Third Wave spectrum that the salvation of souls is but the beginning of the uprooting of the kingdom of darkness and the establishment of the kingdom of God. Because sin, evil and the demonic reside and affect both the individual and the socio-structural realms, 'our spirituality, and the very Gospel that we preach, needs to be as big and ubiquitous as sin and evil. We will falter in our spirituality and thus grieve the Spirit if "our struggle with evil" does not "correspond to the geography of evil" ' (Villafañe 1993: 181).

The suggested revision of Harvey Cox's categories has emerged out of the preceding explication of the pneumatological imagination as imbibed by Pentecostals and charismatics. It has sought to accomplish three objectives. First, along with the discussion in Chapter 5, it has contributed to delivering on the promissory note issued earlier by providing further empirical evidence from the Pentecostal–charismatic experience for the foundational categories. Second, I have suggested throughout that the categories employed are sufficiently vague so as to be conducive to Pentecostal–charismatic participation in the interreligious dialogue. This hypothesis will be put to strenuous test in the next chapter.

Before this is done, however, the third and most important gain accomplished by the categorial scheme developed in this book must be noted. The above revision has confirmed the intuition that there is a normative process inherent in the foundational categories. The relationship between the categories of divine presence (religious experience)

---

28. This is the truth of Marguerite Shuster's argument that the most effective counter-attack against radical evil is through the demonstration of human weakness and reliance on the redemptive power of Word and Spirit (1987; cf. Wink 1992: 175-257). Shuster's advocacy of pacifism against the violence of the demonic not only needs to be given serious consideration as a viable alternative in various socio-political scenarios, but also serves to exemplify the personalistic category of the notion of the demonic.

and divine activity (religious utility) indicates that norms to measure the legitimacy of the former are to be found in the latter. Both, however, need points of contrast. This suggests, then, that there can be no discernment of either divine presence or of divine activity apart from the discernment of divine absence, which, of course, raises questions related to religious cosmology. In short, norms are built into the religious dimension of experience in that the processes of religious transformation eventually exhibit either relational harmonies that grow in spiritual grace or force fields of the demonic that terrify in their destructive capacity. Discernment is as much of the Holy Spirit as it is of other spirits; it is impossible to define the one apart from the other.

To demonstrate this, let me briefly discuss, as an example, glossolalia. In and of itself, glossolalia may not be conducive to social transformation (cf. Malony and Lovekin 1985: 244-45). As such, it is, on the one hand, only a potential sign of divine presence. However, both the processes of transformation traversed by the glossolalic and how glossolalic utterances affect and transform (edify) Christian communities come under the category of divine activity and are normative in various respects. It is the function of the charisms as a whole to bring about 'the common good' (1 Cor. 12.7) and in that sense, we can speak of the Spirit's presence and activity whenever such is noted. Such discernment, on the other hand, demands the capacity for recognizing the potentially demonic effects of glossolalia such as those which accompanied the Pentecostal revival in the Yucatán in the early 1970s (see Goodman's vivid account [1974]). This goes to show, then, that divine presence and divine absence are but two sides to the same coin. This means that at some level in the interreligious dialogue, issues of religious cosmology will need to be addressed in part to get at the norms of discernment.

2. *Discernment: A Pentecostal–Charismatic Approach*

The question of discernment has been repeatedly raised throughout this work. Central to the success of a Christian pneumatological theology of religions is the articulation of criteria by which to distinguish the Holy Spirit from other spirits in the non-Christian faiths. I will endeavor to do so by beginning specifically with a discussion of models of discernment suggested by Pentecostals and charismatics.

Classical Pentecostal and Charismatic Models
It is noteworthy that the clearest statements of discerning the demonic are to be found in discussions focused on that theme. Frank Macchia, for example, outlines criteria for discernment in his systematic discussion of Satan and demons which deserves to be quoted in full:

> The scriptural witness provides us with definite sources of guidance for discerning the forces of evil and oppression. There is a Christological criterion and a basis in the Spirit of God for discerning evil. For example, if God created humanity in the divine image and laid claim to humanity in the birth, death, and resurrection of Christ, then any attempt to dehumanize anyone for any reason contradicts God's love for humanity and serves the forces of darkness. If the Spirit anointed Christ to preach the good news to the poor, the blind, and the imprisoned (Luke 4:18), then those structures and forces that encourage poverty, sickness, and crime serve the forces of darkness. If Satan blinds the minds of the ungodly to the gospel (2 Cor. 4:4), then those things that discourage our gospel witness, both word and deed, to the needy also serve the forces of darkness (1995a: 211-12).

However, when one looks specifically at Pentecostal or charismatic discussions on the charism of discernment of spirits (1 Cor. 12.10), focus on the demonic is either the exception rather than the rule or it is only briefly mentioned as one of three sources of motives or impulses to human action (the other two being the human and the divine; e.g. Hamar 1980: 110; Bernard 1997: 114).[29] There are even some Pente-

---

29. Much of the literature on discernment by Pentecostals and charismatics is of one of two genres: either exegetical discussions found in scriptural commentaries on the corresponding passages, or studies on the charismatic gifts (e.g. R. Williams 1990: 388-94; Hernando 1992). For an overview, one can begin with Francis Martin's article on 'discernment' in the *Dictionary of Pentecostal and Charismatic Movements* (R.F. Martin 1988). Kelsey's (1978) excellent overview would be suspect to some Pentecostals due to his working from the standpoint of Jungian psychology. Other Pentecostal treatments tend to focus on specific issues, e.g., Robeck's (1994b) discussion of claims regarding prophetic inspiration and the ecumenical identity of the Church, and Wood's (1995) and Oropeza's (1995) focus on genuine versus aberrant revivalistic phenomena. The earlier work by Gelpi titled *Discerning the Spirit: Foundations and Futures of Religious Life* emphasizes getting 'behind some of the facts of religious living in order to discover the purposes and ideals which motivate them and give them life' (1970: vii); it does not touch directly on the kind of discernment which I am inquiring into here. It is fairly clear that the scantiness of literature specifically focused on discerning the demonic is probably a result of the Pentecostal–charismatic theological emphasis on the victory

costal commentators who hold that the gift of discernment of spirits applies not to 'spirits' but primarily to prophetic utterances (Fee 1994: 171). Those who do grant that the charism means 'the Spirit-given ability to distinguish between the Spirit of God from a demonic spirit' (Schatzman 1987: 41) often do not tell us how this occurs.[30]

What this suggests is that rather than limiting ourselves to literature specifically focused on the charism of discernment, a wider-ranging survey of Pentecostal–charismatic discussions of discernment in general may be necessary. At the same time, given the conclusion in the preceding section that discerning the demonic requires discerning the Spirit and vice versa, proceeding in this way may be more productive than initially supposed, especially if we keep our overall objective steadfastly in mind while examining this material. In what follows, then, I want to discuss briefly two models of discernment: an introductory sketch by Heribert Mühlen, a German Catholic charismatic, and a practical theology of discernment developed by Stephen Parker, a North American classical Pentecostal.

Mühlen, who has been heavily involved in the *Charismatische Gemeinde Erneuerung* in West Germany since his own experience of Spirit-baptism in 1973, discusses discernment in his lectures on *A Charismatic Theology: Initiation in the Spirit* (1978). He also emphasizes that there are divine, human and demonic impulses which lead to experiences of the Holy Spirit, of self, and of sin. Mühlen suggests that the convergence of self and Spirit brings about an intimacy regarding things divine whereby the Holy Spirit witnesses to our cry of 'Abba! Father!' (Rom. 8.14-16; Gal. 4.6). This means, as I have previously noted, that all experience of the Holy Spirit is indirectly mediated through human corporeality and affections. The discernment of spirits itself combines divine χάρις and the human capacity to discriminate (διακρίσεις, 1 Cor. 12.10).[31] Mühlen therefore concludes that the exer-

accomplished in and available through Jesus Christ by the power of the Holy Spirit; this is mentioned, oftentimes repeatedly, in almost all Pentecostal–charismatic discussions of the demonic without exception.

30. Schatzman in fact adopts criteria initially proposed by James Dunn: test of faithfulness to the kerygmatic tradition; test of character and fruitfulness; test of edification (cf. Dunn 1997: 293-97). But note that Dunn, while sympathetic to the Pentecostal–charismatic experience, writes as an outside commentator rather than as a participating observer (cf. Dunn 1998: 311-28).

31. Elsewhere, I arrive at some very similar conclusions as Mühlen's from an

cise of this gift (or, for that matter, any of the gifts) 'is always *neces-sarily* mingled with the tendency to sin, disruption and misuse...[and that] no one can know with absolute certainty, excluding all doubt, whether the Holy Spirit is active in him' (1978: 175-76; italics original).

Naturally endowed gifts therefore need to be subject to continual purification as the believer grows in grace. At the same time, however, each act of discernment is itself subject to judgment and testing (Mühlen 1978: 177-80). This brings the community of discerners into play. For Mühlen, the charismatic experience is necessarily a 'we-experience' that binds individuals in relationship. In language reminiscent of that employed in developing the foundational categories, Mühlen states that a charismatic group 'is so much more charismatic when it does not attach importance to itself, does not seek fellowship [for itself], does not want to remain self-centred' (1978: 181). The primary criterion for discerning the Spirit behind any exercise of the charismata is therefore whether or not the other is edified (1 Cor. 12.7; 14.26).

But what about criteria to discern the spirits in general? Mühlen distinguishes between 'universal' and 'personal' features of discernment (1978: 182-89). The former include agreement with Scripture and the teaching of the Church (which in Mühlen's case refers primarily to the Magisterium), and the building up of the Church and the world. The latter involve principally the manifestation of the fruit of the Spirit (Gal. 5.22-23). With regard to the criterion regarding the believer's relationship to the world, Mühlen writes, 'if...someone neglects the daily duties of his calling or appeals to his experience of the Spirit as a reason for being released from political and social obligation, he is not allowing himself to be led by the dynamism of the Holy Spirit, which seeks to direct all relationships between men' (1978: 185).

The subtitle of Stephen Parker's book, *Toward a Practical Theology of Pentecostal Discernment and Decision Making* (1996), indicates his interests more so in Christian praxis than in speculative charismology (theology of the charismatic gifts) or demonology. Rather than formulating abstract discernment criteria, Parker conducted an ethnographic survey of a classical Pentecostal congregation from the International Holiness Pentecostal Church in order to determine the concrete ways in which Pentecostals practice discernment. His investigation reveals four

exegetical approach to *diakriseis* and other biblical terms for discernment (see Yong, forthcoming).

primary means, all of which are functionally interrelated: retrospective judgment involving pragmatic considerations; reliance on tradition as mediated by Scripture and authority figures;[32] the presence of charismatic manifestations accompanying the discernment process; and the deeply-felt sense of rightness about the situation (1996: 104-11). This last feeling-of-rightness, Parker is careful to add, is not simply an emotional or physiological sensation. Rather, it is better described as an aesthetic experience: 'things feel harmonious and coherent; there is a sense that things are orderly and fit with what is transpiring' (1996: 109). One 'feels right' about something because one's cognitive, affective and practical senses combine to present an intuitively felt sense of harmony. In theological terms, Pentecostals call this being 'led by the Spirit' (cf. Gal. 5.18, 25).[33]

But Parker realizes what Mühlen had earlier suggested: that the processes of discernment themselves need to be queried for their accuracy and truthfulness. To so do, Pentecostal discernment is assessed from both psychological and theological perspectives. From psychology, Parker draws upon the concept of 'creative regression' as used in object relations psychology (1996: 117-44). He connects 'creative regression' with discernment by defining the former as 'behavior that taps into certain primal, foundational experiences associated with self-formation and is able to draw upon these earliest psychic experiences in creative and revitalizing ways to open up possibilities for growth, strength and guidance in the present, though also presenting opportunities for pathology' (1996: 117). Pentecostal–charismatic experiences of the Spirit, Parker suggests, are in part occasions of creative regression whereby relative degrees of innocence buried beneath the clutter accumulated by the consciousness in adult life are restored to the self. This process of purification in turn allows the self to be re-formed in the image of

32. This reliance on tradition draws heavily, of course, on the received wisdom of the Pentecostal-Holiness tradition. This wisdom emphasizes, at times, a strenuous moral dualism whereby right and wrong are clearly demarcated, and where that which is of the Spirit and that which is not are clearly defined; for a fairly recent classical Pentecostal exposition of this position, see Oneness Pentecostal authors Loretta and David Bernard (1981).

33. Later, Parker mentions an 'aesthetic hermeneutics' (following Gadamer 1994) whereby 'the good, the true, the right are discerned through a knowing that transcends the rational alone' (Parker 1996: 151). This is no guarantee that what is felt is of the Spirit of God; but for Pentecostals, this aesthetic sense is a good indicator that such is the case when critically combined with the other guidelines.

Christ and according to his mind. Discernment proceeds from the standpoint of these reconstituted selves, although such is never perfectly ordered due to the processive nature of human formation. In this way, Parker demonstrates how Pentecostal–charismatic experience can provide guidelines for discernment which while subjective (relative to each individual history), underscore the role of the non-rational subconscious in decision making and enables a more holistic assessment of psychological health (or imbalance, as the case may be).

Moving on to a theological dialogue with Paul Tillich, Parker suggests that the 'discernment criterion of things feeling right is a mediating symbol of the divine Presence, a revelatory moment in which one is "shaken, transformed, and grasped by ultimate concern" (or that which confronts one unconditionally' (1996: 145). Recall that revelation for Tillich is the partial manifestation of the mystery of the ultimate ground of being—God—which reception is possible only in a state of ecstatic reason. Going beyond the subject–object distinction posited by technical reason, ecstatic reason combines affective and cognitive dimensions of knowing into a more holistic rationality.[34] Parker proposes that the Pentecostal experience of the Spirit involves precisely this kind of ecstatic rationality and explores its connections with and implications for Tillich's later pneumatology (the doctrine of the Spiritual Presence developed in the last volume of the *Systematic Theology*). At the same time, Parker argues that true revelatory experiences of the Spirit can only be salvific in the Tillichian sense if experience itself is understood not only as a medium (Tillich) but also as a source for both empirical and theological knowledge. Tillich's hesitation to adopt this latter position derives in part because of his awareness of the temptation in human nature to equate the finite with the infinite (which equation, for Tillich, results in the demonic) and in part because of the need to preserve the uniqueness of the revelatory experience of the Christ event. Parker accepts Tillich's admonition regarding the former concern while pointing to the Pentecostal reliance on tradition as one of the checks and balances to the exercise of ecstatic rationality.

The model Parker proposes for Pentecostal discernment therefore combines four components: an acceptance of holistic ways of knowing; an insistence on integrating the needs of the individual and that of the community; a concern to respect the difference between finite and

---

34. See my discussion of Tillich's ecstatic reason in nn. 3 and 20.

ultimate concerns both so that the integrity of Spirit-led experiences are not ideologically corrupted and that the idolatrous stance toward the demonic absolutization of the finite is avoided; and a recognition of the ambiguity of the human experience and understanding of things of the Spirit. The ambiguity of the Spirit's comings and goings means that 'one cannot simply generate a list of guidelines that chart the ways the Spirit can and will move... Discerning the divine will always involve risk; there is no way to know for certain that one's choices or allegiances are ultimately the right ones... Human fallibility suggests that all decisions, even those made under the leading of the Holy Spirit, need periodic review' (Parker 1996: 202-203).[35] What is clear in Parker's discussion is that all of these are essential ingredients to discernment not only in decision making but also with regard to the divine revelation and the presence and activity of the Spirit. Implicitly, then, this model also addresses discerning situations of divine absence.

Three broad conclusions can be gleaned from the preceding discussion of Pentecostal–charismatic discernment. First, discerning the demonic is a derivative function of discerning the Holy Spirit; at the same time, however, proper discernment of the Holy Spirit is dependent in part on recognizing the other spirits at work. This dialectical process is the central tension of a discerning charismology. Second, the charism of discernment, as with all gifts of the Holy Spirit, is shot through and through with the human element. This factor of human complicity in all Pentecostal–charismatic encounters and experiences of the Spirit requires the continued subjection of individuals to the judgment of the larger community (cf. 1 Cor. 14.29-32).[36] Third, the pragmatist orienta-

---

35. Taken together, these elements in Parker's model shows how different the practice of discernment by a Pentecostal–charismatic insider can be when contrasted with that proposed by one outside of or critical toward the movement. As an example of the latter, David Middlemiss's criteria for discernment is dominated by rationalism, naturalistic assumptions and an intolerance of ambiguity (1996). Granted that his primary objective is the discernment of Pentecostal–charismatic phenomena rather than decision making, yet his model clearly demonstrates that even prolonged exposure to the movement (which he claims) does not provide the kind of pneumatological vision afforded by first hand experience of the Spirit.

36. This is also the conclusion of Chris Thomas in his exegetical treatment of the Christian Testament materials on the devil and discerning the demonic: 'The New Testament picture suggests that discernment requires a communal context, the involvement of the individual sufferer...as well as the leaders of the believing community' (1998: 316).

tion of Pentecostals and charismatics leads them to read past and present events as signs identifying activity in the spiritual realm. Unless otherwise corrected, that which is edifying and uplifting is understood to be of the Holy Spirit while that which is not is determined to be of the evil one. Finally, Pentecostals and charismatics embrace a holistic epistemology. Rational and non-rational (not irrational) ways of knowing combine to inform their charismology of discernment.[37]

The Holy Spirit and the Demonic in the Religions

It is now time to weave the various strands of the argument together and render a normative theology of discernment. In accordance with our categoreal scheme, I propose at least a three-tiered process of discernment—phenomenological–experiential, moral–ethical and theo-logical–soteriological—by which the pneumatological imagination of Pentecostals and charismatics can contribute to and engage in the inter-religious dialogue. It needs to be mentioned that this piecemeal approach should be recognized solely as a heuristic device for the sake of explicating the central elements of a discerning charismology, even if the actual practice of discernment intuitively integrates and syn-thesizes these activities under the unction of the Spirit.

37. The attentive reader will notice that I have not discussed a Third Wave model for discernment—an obvious oversight given my dependence on the contri-bution of the Third Wave to the Pentecostal–charismatic cosmology delineated above. The reason for this omission, however, is simple: Third Wavers have only recently begun to theologize about territorial spirits and have not, to my knowledge, produced a definitive work on the subject. Yet the elementary musings of Third Wave thinkers reveal all the elements outlined here in operation. Much of the theorizing on territorial spirits derive from accounts rendered by converted occult-ists, and from pastoral experiences and missionary praxis that is sensitive to both individual case situations and regional, metropolitan and structural hindrances to the advance of the gospel. Because they recognize that any inferences drawn from these growing number of case studies are inevitably inconclusive (as all results utilizing the inductive method are), Third Wavers confess that their belief in terri-torial spirits is in some senses best understood as a guiding hypothesis for pastoral and missionary action (Wagner 1990: 75-77). Their world-view is in large part a corollary to what many in that movement claim to have been a deliverance from the rationalistic and materialistic epistemology of the Enlightenment. The result is an openness to seeing beyond the natural world into the realm of the spirit. A pneuma-tological imagination is clearly at work, although it should continue to be cultivated for greater precision and critically subjected to the more mature judgment of the larger theological community.

The first level focuses on the comparative category of religious experience. Discernment here therefore necessarily involves the entire range of phenomena that is operative in the rituals, acts and symbols of religious experience.[38] At this level, the important questions concern not so much the symbols themselves but how they are experienced and engaged by the devotee or practitioner. What appears through the symbols to the devotee? How are these symbols understood, interpreted and assimilated by the devotee? What is the evidence of the power of these symbols to engage the devotee religiously in the long run? How is the devotee impacted by the experience? How does he or she respond to it? What is the aesthetic quality of the experience for the devotee? In short, aesthetic norms gauge the intensity and authenticity of personal religious experiences.

It is clear that at this level, the responses elicited to the question of whether or not the Spirit is present are inevitably subjective. This is due in part to the nature of religious experience which engages the ambiguous realm of the spirit in general, but also in part to human fallibility in the cognitive process. Nevertheless some clarity on these fundamental points needs to be achieved in order for accurate discernment to take place. The Buddhist *sartori* may be phenomenologically similar to the Pentecostal–charismatic baptism in the Holy Spirit, the different claims with regard to what is experienced notwithstanding. In fact, the Pentecostal or charismatic may be wrong—if so, they are speaking 'out of the flesh'—even while the Buddhist's experience is genuine. By focusing on the qualitative presentation of the experience itself and on how that transforms the individual, at least a tentative admission that the Spirit has been present in the respects specified may be ventured. Discerning the Spirit(s), however, cannot stop here.

The next level focuses on the comparative category of religious utility and looks for concrete signs that follow claims of experiencing the transcendent. The primary norms on this level are moral and ethical in nature. For the individual, signs of transformation of soul are

---

38. From here on, my use of the word *symbol* in either the singular or plural can be taken as a shorthand that includes all phenomena of religious import since it can be taken for granted that anything of religious significance has symbolic reference pointing beyond itself to a transcendent reality. It should not need to be mentioned that even the mystical experiences of religious contemplatives are replete with symbolic elements which clearly emerge in their efforts to communicate such experiences.

especially valuable. Have the religious symbols exhibited the power to affect the transformation of soul in the devotee? What are the fruits of the individual's change for the better? Is there any evidence of divine activity in the devotee's personal life, ecclesial community or wider networks of relationships? In short, moral–ethical norms gauge the extent of the Spirit's activity in the lives of individuals situated in religious communities and need to be applied to the entire range of human existence.

At this level of discernment, the references of religious symbols come into play. As previously discussed (Chapter 4), religious symbols are multivalent and have both network and content meaning. The former is the extensional references of religious symbols related to the multitude of historical phenomena within their religio-cultural-linguistic framework (a proximate reference), while the latter is the transcendental reference of the symbol as intended by the devotee (that which is of ultimate concern). The identification of network meaning is concerned specifically with the extensional references of symbols according to their functions and their various levels of interpretation. The questions that need to be asked here are, first, what devotees and communities of faith understand the symbol to disclose relative to the various dimensions of human life, e.g., the personal, ecclesial, material, economic, social or political; and second, how the symbols in question mediate the transformation of souls and communities into more cohesive relational harmonies in these dimensions. Discernment involves the ability to sort out both how devotees and religious communities use religious symbols to achieve mundane, existential or other goals, and how the symbols themselves affect such transformation in individual lives and communities. In short, the issue here is pragmatic: do the symbols work? If they do, two further questions arise: how do they work and what is accomplished by practicing with the religious symbols over time?

That Pentecostals and charismatics search for signs of the Spirit in the circumstances of history, in the practice of their faith, and in the manifestation of the fruits of the Spirit correlate well with the criterion of the *humanum* proposed by Hans Küng (Chapter 4). One clear scriptural sign of divine absence is the presence of destructive forces (Jn 10.10). Equally clear is the fact that the Christian view of moral and ethical uprightness is defined biblically and christologically. To the non-Christian objection that we have come this far only to impose

Christian categories, our response is both that we never anticipated doing away with our Christian stance to begin with nor would such be undesirable in the interreligious dialogue where the diverse perspectives should be laid out so that similarities *and* differences can be engaged. At the same time, however, this approach is specifically pneumato-logical in orientation.[39] The categories themselves are appropriate to the Spirit in the Spirit's own economy and therefore vague. The important question is whether or not they are able to register features of impor-tance in other traditions? Is there, in short, evidence of the Spirit's activity in the non-Christian faiths whereby lives are made whole and communal relationships are continually mended, formed and strength-ened? If yes, let the Christian say a tentative and yet hearty 'Amen'; if no, so much the worse for the other tradition and let the Christian then be led by the Spirit in developing further strategies for witness.

This being said, however, it should be acknowledged that the ethical criterion alone cannot be definitive. While the presuppositions of the pneumatological imagination can entertain as plausible the notion that the growing realization of the convergence of moral and ethical values to be found at the core of the various world religions is the work of the Holy Spirit (cf. Küng and Kuschel 1993), the fact of the matter is that the vigor of each global tradition resides precisely in its presenting itself as a legitimate alternative—contradictory at many points—to other world traditions including the Christian faith. What Pinnock called the 'contest of the gods' (Chapter 6) is far from over. Spiritual transformation for the better can always be succeeded by spiritual degradation. In short, the discernment of the Spirit involves the discern-ment of the demonic and vice versa.

At this level, our category of religious cosmology requires that we move to the content meaning of the religious symbols under consider-ation to determine their cosmological and transcendental reference. 'Cosmological' in this context can be taken either literally or as synonymous with 'transcendental' since what we are after, in effect, are

39. At issue for many Pentecostals and charismatics is the issue of whether there can be other norms for discernment such as christological or biblical ones. The question, however, should distinguish between norms that are extra-biblical versus unbiblical (cf. Oropeza 1995: 128-30). The latter, that which is explicitly condemned by Scripture, warrants our severest attention and rejection. The former, however, can be accepted on the grounds that 'all truth is God's truth no matter where it may be found'.

the references intended by devotees and religious communities that go beyond the human and finite realm. Demons may derive either from a lower or upper cosmos relative to the human sphere; their cosmological location, however, is not as important as the fact that they are immaterial forces of reality which thwart the divine plan of salvation. Discerning the spirits at this level therefore relates to the functional role of the demonic relative to soteriology.

Whereas previous levels attempt to trace how the symbols function and how they precipitate personal and social transformation, the issue at hand here is theological: to what transcendental reality, if any, do religious symbols refer? This is, of course, to confront the theological truth question straight on. It is also an efficient means to developing the Christian virtues of patience and humility since there is no guarantee that claims regarding the transcendent references of religious symbols can be successfully adjudicated anytime soon. The theological and soteriological norms that should be applied here are also, at least for Christians (as well as Jews and Muslims), eschatological in that they await complete illumination beyond our respective horizons.

Pentecostals and charismatics, however, are among those at the forefront of the contemporary Christian world whose strong convictions about the horror of the demonic are such that they would see it as an abrogation of their Christian faith to remain silent about radical evil. Discerning the Spirit(s) comes about in part from walking by faith and not by sight (2 Cor. 5.7). What this amounts to is that Pentecostal–charismatic discernment is guided and shaped but not dictated by aesthetic, ethical or theological norms which are cognitionally articulated. Even if precisely applied, these norms cannot pierce through the deceptiveness of radical evil since 'Satan himself masquerades as an angel of light' (2 Cor. 11.14). Rather, the discernment of spiritual things is ultimately a spiritual act that transcends purely rational ways of knowing (1 Cor. 2.10-15). The actual processes of discerning the Spirit(s) draws from and integrates perceptual feelings, affective impulses and cognitive judgments into spiritual insights. Even when the combination of evaluations at all of these levels in the end results in nothing more than an intuitive judgment that is inevitably imprecise, Pentecostals and charismatics are constrained to 'hold on to the good [and] avoid every kind of evil' (1 Thess. 5.21). At the same time, because they are cognizant that no human judgment is infallible, they are free to acknowledge that discerning the spirits in the religions is a profoundly complex and ambiguous affair (see Volf 1994). Responsible Christian engagement with those in other faiths, however, cannot avoid taking the risks involved in testing, naming and overcoming the spirits if it is to be true to the Spirit of God. Such engagement must, at the same time, be willing to submit its pronouncements to the judgment of the larger Christian community and be open to retracting such pronouncements either in light of evidence to the contrary or when it is clear that spiritual processes of transformation have unmasked and dissolved the force fields of darkness previously discerned.

Is such a charismology of discernment finally no more than fideistic? Perhaps ultimately yes, in the sense that all strictly theological convictions are finally verifiable or falsifiable only in the eschaton. At the same time, it is a chastened rather than incorrigible fideism that is also open to the correction of the Spirit whether that be through prayer and faithful meditation on Scripture, insights from the broader Christian community, the interreligious dialogue, or otherwise. Further, however, the Christian doctrine of creation insists that historical reality is just as valued in the eyes of God as what is eschatologically anticipated, and the pneumatological approach to other faiths operative here enables some agreement about where, when and how the Holy Spirit is present and active in the religions within the determinations of being in this present age. What needs to occur at this point, then, is what has been neglected by previous pneumatological approaches to the religions. Whereas others have remained contented with more or less general theological affirmations about the Spirit's presence and activity in the non-Christian world, I propose a detailed empirical investigation that tests the adequacy of the proposed categories and the perspicuity of the discerning charismology.

Chapter 8

PENTECOSTALISM AND UMBANDA: A TEST CASE

My mother is a first-generation Christian. She was raised in the practice of the popular form of Theravada Buddhism as found in the rural villages of West Malaysia. I recall her telling me about how, before her conversion to Christianity, she and grandmother were terrorized by demons associated with the popular Buddhist practices and beliefs.[1] These experiences, she reported triumphantly, began to fade upon their conversion to Christ, and eventually disappeared as they grew in their Christian faith. In my adulthood, I have been involved as a Pentecostal minister in a number of exorcisms and have experienced firsthand both the ugliness of evil and the demonic and the power of Christ by the Spirit. At the same time, however, I have come to realize not only that Christians have been troubled by demons in the same manner as Buddhists or those in other faiths, but also that Christians are not alone in their concern about putting the devil in his place; we do not have a monopoly on the business of exorcism.[2] But how can I reconcile these plain facts in the history of religions with my conviction that it is only the life, death and resurrection of Christ that has finally and decisively disarmed the principalities and powers and given us the authority over Satan and his minions (Col. 2.15; Lk. 10.18-19)? Is the Pentecostal experience of the Spirit able to shed any light on this matter?

1. What my mother called 'Buddhist idols' and 'Buddhist demons' as a Christian are referred to variously by Theravada Buddhists in South East Asia as *Mara* (equivalent to Satan) or *deva-ta* (divine beings), or regionally as *Khwan, Phī, Čhao*, or *Nat* (guardian or other kinds of spirit beings). For an overview of the kind of Buddhism formerly practiced both by my parents and their families, see Swearer (1995).

2. This was brought to my attention in a vivid way by Aloysius Pieris's description of a ritual exorcism performed by Buddhists (1995; cf. Shuster 1987: 75-77). More recently, I have come across a respected therapist with Christian leanings admitting that 'were I to conduct an exorcism, I would not exclude from the team any mature Hindu, Buddhist, Muslim, Jew, atheist, or agnostic who was a genuinely loving presence' (Peck 1983: 201).

Introduction

Is the metaphysical doctrine of creation adopted here true? Can it be said that the Holy Spirit is universally present and active, in both the proposed metaphysical sense and in the specifically Christian sense, even in the non-Christian faiths? If this is the case, how can it be demonstrated? Is the Pentecostal–charismatic experience of the Spirit suggestive of a Christian response to the fact of religious pluralism and does it shed any light on the process of discerning the Spirit in the world and in the religions? Does this experience provide a way of looking at the faith of those in other religious traditions which enables Pentecostals and charismatics to make a special contribution to the interreligious dialogue?

In order to begin to answer these questions, the abstract comparative theology developed so far in this book needs to be applied to a concrete interreligious dialogue with a non-Christian religious tradition. I have chosen to conduct such a dialogue with Umbanda, an Afro-Brazilian tradition. To some degree, this choice is an arbitrary one in that a dialogue with numerous other traditions could have been initiated.[3] Having begun down this road, however, second-guessing the decision would be counter-productive. Instead, the reasons leading to the consideration that such a dialogue will be fruitful need to be articulated in the hopes that potential critics will give them a fair hearing. This is especially important since Umbanda is considered by many Christians, including Pentecostals and charismatics, to be a spiritist cult.

---

3.   When I first began this project, for example, my intention was to pursue a Pentecostal dialogue with African traditional religions. That dialogue, however, has already been started by such Pentecostals as Allan Anderson even if his interests are shaped much more by missiological concerns than are mine (see my discussion of Anderson's work in Chapter 6). I also weighed the merits of conducting an interreligious dialogue with a world religious tradition as opposed to an indigenous or, in the case of Umbanda, a nationalistic religion. As an Afro-Brazilian tradition, however, it is arguable that Umbanda signifies in some sense a 'globalization' of African indigenous religiosity (cf. Yong 1998c). My initial intentions therefore have not been discarded completely. I was initially introduced to Umbanda in a seminar on Latin American Religion and Theology which I took under the direction of Professor Harvey Cox at Harvard University in the fall of 1997. As I hope to show, there are many good reasons that can be put forward in defense of a Pentecostal–Umbanda dialogue.

The task of Section 1, therefore, will focus on defending the decision to proceed with the dialogue between Pentecostalism and Umbanda.[4] A historical, sociological and anthropological overview of Umbanda is then sketched in Section 2, with specific attention given to the Umbandist ritual of spirit possession. Section 3 tests the adequacy of the proposed comparative categories while the final section seeks specifically to discern the Spirit(s) in Umbanda through the medium of the inter-religious dialogue. It may be that the Spirit is completely absent in Umbanda and that it has been infiltrated by other spirits including demonic ones. Let such, however, be a theological conclusion emerging from the dialogue rather than a presumption of guilt going in.

1. Pentecostalism and Umbanda: Grounds for Comparison?

Brazil is, nominally, a Catholic country. Most of her citizens are baptized into and buried by the Roman Catholic Church. The past few decades, however, have seen the conversion of many Catholics to Protestant churches, and the emergence of Afro-Brazilian religious traditions like Umbanda as legitimate religious alternatives for the Catholic masses (Leacock and Leacock 1972; Burdick 1993a). However, in part because of the centrality of spirit-mediums, spirit possession and trance to the practice of Umbanda, this movement has long been considered to be a form of witchcraft by Catholics.[5] This polemic has actually intensified with the growth of the Pentecostal movement in Brazil in that members of the latter consider the spirits in Afro-Brazilian traditions to be nothing less than demonic impersonations (e.g. Burdick 1993c: 38; Freston 1995: 130; Chestnut 1997: 84). Brazilian Pentecostals are therefore much more insistent on exorcising these demonic forces 'in

---

4. In this chapter, I will stay with the single adjective and noun 'Pentecostal' and forego the more cumbersome 'Pentecostal–charismatic' and its cognates since the former is inclusive of the latter in the Brazilian context. The even more comprehensive Brazilian designation is *crentes* (believers), which include both evangelical, Pentecostal and other kinds of generally conservative Protestants.

5. I use 'trance' and 'spirit possession' synonymously in the following discussion, following I.M. Lewis (1989: 25) and Esther Pressel (1974: 193-206). Technically, the former refers more to the notion of soul-loss while the latter emphasizes more the intrusion of an outside power—enthusiasm (ἐν θεός); Lewis does note that one can and does often occur without the other (1989: 39). Possession in Umbanda, however, normally features both elements, although I will later discuss specific nuances of the Umbandist experience of soul-loss.

the name of Jesus' than interested in dialoguing about or with them. Umbandist practitioners and adherents, on the other hand, are more tolerant than their Pentecostals rivals, even going so far as to grant Pentecostals a legitimate place in the Brazilian religious landscape. In order to understand the one-sidedness of this relationship and to assess further the grounds for proceeding with this dialogue, a brief look at the history of Pentecostalism in Brazil and the role that she has played and continues to play in Brazilian society may be helpful.

Paul Freston has charted the growth of Pentecostalism in Brazil, which now exceeds 16 million members, in three successive waves (Freston 1995).[6] The first goes back to the origins of Pentecostalism in Brazil during the first decade of the twentieth century when denominations such as the Assembléia de Deus (Assemblies of God) and Congregação Cristã (Congregation of Christ) were established. Of much greater impact, however, were the second and third waves stemming respectively from the 1950s–60s and the 1980s. During the former decades, massive modernization, industrialization and urbanization accelerated the break with existing models and allowed for the rise of denominations developed primarily to facilitate transitions from rural to mass-society such as the Igreja do Evangelho Quadrangular (Foursquare) and Brasil para Cristo (Brazil for Christ). The explosion of expectations regarding the 'economic miracle' led to the realization that the 'lost decade' had set in during the 1980s. These years saw the emergence of nationalist forms of Pentecostalism such as the Igreja Universal do Reino de Deus (Universal Church of the Reign of God) and the Deus de Amor (God of Love). Freston notes that the ideology of this third wave was in part a response to the development of slums, violence and gang activity in urban centers, deepening industrialization, the arrival of the high-tech age of mass media, increasing turmoil in the rural

6.   This is analogous to but not to be confused with the Third Wave charismatic movement in North America. For a complementary account of the history of Pentecostalism in Brazil, see Medcraft (1987). I should add the important point that understanding the development of Pentecostalism in Brazil is crucial not only because of the light this sheds on Umbanda itself, but also because it allows us to guard against comparing Umbanda in its Afro-Brazilian context to Pentecostalism in its North American or other forms. Much more effective, not to say equitable, would be to compare Umbanda and Brazilian Pentecostalism.

areas, and the crisis in Catholicism and the surging popularity of Afro-Brazilian spiritism (1995: 129).[7]

These factors tell us some important things about the diversity, ethos and vast spectrum of orientations in contemporary Brazilian Pentecostalism. The distinction between rural and urban pentecostalisms is a case in point. Rural Pentecostals tend to be much more influenced by popular Catholic and folk religiosities, even to the extent of seeking relief from some of their ills via Afro-Brazilian practices (Westra 1998; cf. Rolim 1991; Novaes 1994). Urban Pentecostals, on the other hand, are much less tolerant with regard to the Afro-Brazilian movements as well as much more diverse overall. There are, of course, those who identify themselves more with classical Pentecostalism in North America even though Brazilian Pentecostalism as a whole is relatively autonomous and boasts a following of up to eight times the number of North American Pentecostals (Stewart-Gambino and Wilson 1997: 229). But there are also those who have broken with the apolitical stance characteristic of classical Pentecostalism and have not only taken an active part in politics but also developed a social and political ethic appropriate to their situation in Brazil (Ireland 1991, 1995; Burdick 1993c; Freston 1994; Hess 1994: 158-59; Martin 1995). Further, however, the Brazilian Pentecostals riding the crest of their own third wave have not only developed distinctive styles and emphases but have also—like the Third Wave charismatics—made an impact in North America (Silva 1991). But whereas Third Wave charismatics have been developing overarching theologies of territorial spirits, third wave Brazilian Pentecostals have been busy exorcising the devil from the popular mentality and liberating the captives from the fear of demonic spirits (Lehmann 1996: 139-42).

While this brief characterization of Pentecostalism in Brazil enables us to detect features of our foundational categories, more important here is the recognition of the heterogeneity of pentecostalisms in Brazil which meet a variety of needs both in rural and urban settings, and among the lower, middle and upper middle classes. On the one hand,

---

7.   The term 'spiritism' has pejorative connotations for Pentecostals. It is undeniable, however, that it appropriately applies to Afro-Brazilian religiosity given the centrality of spirit possession to its beliefs and practices (cf. Hess 1994). My use of the term here draws from its currency in the history of religions and involves no conscious a priori bias against Umbanda.

this focus on the social functions of Pentecostalism places the Pentecostal rhetoric against Umbanda and other Afro-Brazilian traditions in a broader context. On the other hand, it provides a lens by which to understand the fact that Pentecostalism and Umbanda in particular (and Afro-Brazilian religions in general) have already been subjected to a number of detailed comparative analyses. It has been suggested, for example, that both traditions provide theologies and ideologies which enable their adherents to make the transition from rural to urban societies (Camargo 1970; Howe 1980); that both provide similar and yet different responses to poverty (Mariz 1994) and to religious pluralism (Droogers 1995) through a diversity of discourses; that both are politically alienated even while they alienate themselves from politics in different ways (Ireland 1980, 1991). However, while critics may grant that legitimate sociological analyses naturally follow from the fact that these two traditions have thrived in the same socio-economic context, they would also continue by insisting that as religious traditions, Pentecostalism and Umbanda are so different and diametrically opposed as to render any efforts at theological comparison ultimately futile.

Is this, however, the case? Other investigators, including anthropologists and psychologists, have pointed to the analogous phenomenological features that exist between the ecstatic rituals, trances and healing practices of Pentecostalism and Afro-Brazilian traditions including Umbanda (e.g. Goodman 1974 and Pressel 1974; cf. Goodman 1976). These similarities have been examined in detail across the broad scope of Afro-American spirituality and religiosity—including that of Candomblé, Santeria, Voodoo, etc.—by the historian of religion, Joseph Murphy (1994). As a professor in the Department of Theology at Georgetown University, Murphy's work on the bridge between religious studies and theology leads him to ask the pointed theological question: 'When African American Pentecostals affirm the unity of the Holy Spirit and *santeros* [devotees in Afro-Cuban tradition of Santeria] speak of a variety of spirits, could they be saying different things but experiencing something much the same when "the spirit" descends?' Murphy's response, and thesis of his book, is that the 'experience of "the spirit" in diasporan ceremonies may share important theological qualities without the traditions having to agree on the singularity or multiplicity of "the spirit" ' (1994: 8). He goes on to argue that 'spirit' points to activity and that the ritual and ceremonial liturgies of African diaspora communities can be interpreted as signs of 'spirit' at work.[8]

The point here is not only that Pentecostals and Umbandists share a common socio-economic struggle in Brazil or that their spiritualities express, at least in part, common African roots, but that the theological force of Murphy's question and answer should not, and indeed, cannot be avoided. It is not that we are disinterested in the moral-ethical and socio-economic assessments of Pentecostalism and Umbanda. In fact, I will argue that such analyses are crucial to discerning the Spirit(s) in Brazil. Ultimately, however, our interests here are theological: what is the truth of the Pentecostal–charismatic experience of the Holy Spirit and what is the truth of the Umbandist experience of spirit possession? Pentecostals (and charismatics) can take issue with or offense at Murphy's hypothesis. However, they are thereby obligated not simply to dismiss him but to engage his argument seriously. Given the wealth of new data bequeathed to us by the various sub-disciplines in religious studies, theologians need to re-examine the issues involved, ask better questions, and develop theological hypotheses and syntheses adequate to the evidence rather than persist in the old ones prejudiced by stereotypes from previous generations.[9]

The dialogue between Pentecostalism and Umbanda that follows, however, does not proceed from a vacuum but instead builds on the preliminary efforts of other Christians to engage the Afro-Brazilian tradition. The Jesuits and the Umbandists, for example, have had numerous engagements over the decades. The problem is that most of these encounters have been polemical in nature instead of dialogic. Further, the accounts of these conversations are recorded in Portuguese and little, if any, have been translated into English. Other efforts, however, may point the way forward. Franziska Rehbein, for example, is a Catholic theologian who has developed a Christian theology of Afro-

---

8.   In the end, however, Murphy does not really provide an answer to the question he raises. His definition of 'spirit' is too elastic to enable discerning the Spirit. In fact, he seems to confuse the Holy Spirit with almost any religious or even cultural *elán vital* whatsoever.

9.   Whereas former generations of researchers in the scientific study of religion disregarded theological questions as a valid part of the discipline, more recently, theology is being recognized as a vital and indispensable component of religious studies and history of religions (see Ogden 1978; Lee 1988; Neville 1993b). As a theologian trained in religious studies, I also want to emphasize this relationship as being two necessary sides to one conversation.

Brazilian religions. Her work was originally completed in Portuguese and later translated into German (1989). Her focus, however, is on Candomblé, the sister tradition to Umbanda, even while her Catholic conclusions are predictable: that the Afro-Brazilian traditions at best serve as a *praeparatio evangelica* to the gospel of the incarnation. Arnulf Camps, a Dutch theologian, was one of the first to ask if a Christian–Umbanda dialogue—alongside Christian dialogues with other indigenous or smaller religious traditions—could be fruitful, and his book was translated from French into English (1983: 125-33). Again, however, Camps's Catholic standpoint led to the rather confident assertion that 'the Holy Spirit is not much in evidence in Umbanda' (1983: 132). The evangelical missionary, Charles Uken, begins his article in a manner that suggests a serious effort to launch a dialogue (1992). Ultimately, however, he also is unable to see Umbanda as more than a spiritist and occultic movement and ends up searching for points of contact in Umbanda for the presentation of the Christian gospel. Uken does propose that Pentecostalism is more strategically equipped to engage in the missionary task in Brazil than other Protestant churches. I am encouraged by these who have preceded me to suggest that such a conversation may indeed be fruitful. I am thereby optimistic that Pentecostalism may be able to help launch the kind of depth dialogue with Umbanda that has been aspired to previously, and that such does not have to be only in lieu of fulfilling the Great Commission.

One final point before proceeding. Should this dialogue succeed in any way—and 'success' cannot be defined prematurely—it will, as a conversation with a tradition somewhat foreign to Christianity (at least to evangelical, Pentecostal and charismatic Christianity), testify to the potential fruitfulness of the categories developed here in particular and the pneumatological theology of religions as a whole for the continuing interreligious conversation. Discerning even slender rays of the Spirit's presence and activity in a tradition like Umbanda would be an encouraging sign for the wider ecumenism.[10] Let us see if the

---

10. Actually, painting Umbanda as a 'worst case' conversation partner is unfair and perpetuates the very stereotypes that should be avoided. Further, to do so is to forget that up until about a century ago, all other religious traditions were similarly conceived as having demonic origins or affiliations. In some quarters, of course, even the Jews are still branded as the demonically inspired murderers of the Messiah and as hostile to things divine. (On the whole, however, such opinions are no

pneumatological approach developed so far will advance the discussion substantially further than it has been taken to date.

2. *The Umbandist Tradition*

One of the keys to success in the interreligious dialogue is the ability to listen to the religious other. While my interests are primarily theological, any conclusions drawn without paying close attention to the empirical reality of the Umbandist tradition will be misguided. In what follows, then, an overview of the development of Umbanda will be presented along with a brief description of its central ritual of spirit possession.

A Brief History

Umbanda is a fairly recent spiritistic tradition uniquely rooted in the land of Brazil.[11] It is most well known by that name in São Paulo and in Rio de Janeiro where the first Umbandist federation—União Espírita de Umbando do Brasil (Spiritist Union of Umbanda in Brazil)—was organized in 1939. In other areas, Afro-Brazilian spiritism goes by other names—e.g. Macumba generally, Candomblé in the Bahia, Batuque in the state of Rio Grande do Sul, Xangô in the states of Alagôas and Pernambuco, Pajelança in the Amazonian region—each with its own distinctive styles and emphases. While 90 percent of the Brazilian population is nominally Catholic, well over 50 percent may be participating spiritists to some degree or other (Pressel 1974: 121).[12] How is the

---

longer widely entertained. Pentecostalism and Umbanda are fairly new traditions, and time will tell, God willing, whether and how attitudes will be transformed.) In reality, there is no 'worst' or 'best' conversation partner. Every tradition poses its own peculiar problems to Christianity. The challenge for the dialogue I am proposing is the utter strangeness and yet, at the same time, fascinating similarities between Umbanda and Pentecostalism.

11. The etymology of Umbanda is itself debated, deriving either from the Bantu root *ymbanda*—supreme head or unifying symbol of a cult—or from the Sanskrit *Aum-Bandhâ*—a Hindu metaphysical idea denoting the limit within what is limitless (Bastide 1978: 320-21). As will be clear later, however, this debate itself has been fueled by both political and ideological elements related to the development of Umbanda in the twentieth century. With regard to its nationalistic roots in Brazil, it should be pointed out that more recently, Umbanda has begun to spread across Latin America (cf. Pollak-Eltz 1993).

12. As of the mid-1980s, Umbandist adepts—priests and priestesses, initiates

popularity of spiritism in late twentieth-century Brazil to be explained?

Perhaps this phenomena is better understood in light of the religious history of Brazil.[13] This history, focused here especially on Umbanda, can also be conveniently sketched in three phases. The first phase, lasting from the middle of the sixteenth to the middle of the nineteenth centuries, saw the appearance of the Portuguese and the forced transplantation of upwards of three and a half million Africans to Brazil. The resulting fusion of Portuguese, African and indigenous cultures and religious traditions has been dubbed by Roger Bastide as the 'interpenetration of civilizations' (1978; cf. Raboteau 1978: 3-92). While racial purity was originally emphasized, it could not be maintained. The appearance of mestizos (of negro and Indian extraction) and mulattos (of European and negro blood) was inevitable. This gradual reconfiguration of Brazilian civilization was aided, over time, by the massive 'christianization' of both Africans and the indigenous population by the Roman Catholic Church. Forced conversions, however, often take on an outward form rather than transform the inner soul. The case with the African traditions in Brazil was no different. Bantu, Yoruba, Ewe/Fon and Dahoman religion from West and Central Africa continued in the new world. Spiritual songs, religious rhythms and ritual practices, along with entire lines of African deities were translated into the Brazilian context (cf. Flasche 1973; Megenney 1992). Slaves found ways to preserve their former beliefs and practices under Catholic guise when they identified the African High God—who while understood as creator of the world was aloof and uninvolved directly in human activities—with the Christian God the Father, and the lesser deities and ancestor spirits—emissaries of the High God—with the host of Catholic saints.[14]

---

and active members—numbered almost one-fourth of the Brazilian population: over 30 million in an overall population of 130 million (Pereira de Quieroz 1989: 95). This does not, of course, include the additional millions who frequent Umbanda centers for a variety of reasons.

13. I am not a historian of religion nor an anthropologist. Fortunately, there are excellent introductions to Umbanda and Afro-Brazilian spiritism such as the early work of McGregor and Smith (1967), St Clair (1971) and Langguth (1975). Bastide's (1978) historical overview is still unsurpassed in many respects. Brown (1986) provides a thorough introduction to Umbanda and remains the indispensable source for understanding its social, political and religious significance. My indebtedness to her reading of Umbanda will be evident in what follows.

14. This 'concealment theory' was first proposed by the anthropologist Melville Herskovits (1939). While there are clearly difficulties in this model, these are

By the time slavery was legally outlawed in Brazil in 1888, the fusion of African religion and Catholic spirituality was well-established, at least at the popular level of religious practice (cf. Ryle 1988, Omari 1994).

The latter half of the nineteenth century saw the addition of another element to the Afro-Brazilian religious situation: that of a European spiritualism better known as Kardecism. Named after a spirit who identified himself as Allan Kardec, a Druid, the central doctrines of Kardecism were dictated to a Parisian schoolteacher during seances and published, beginning with *Le livre des esprits* in 1857. The development of Kardecism featured the combination of a wide assortment of intellectual ideas. These included the scientistic rationalism and positivism of Comte, the newly discovered (for the French) Hindu doctrines of karma and reincarnation, evolutionary thought, the belief in the existence of spiritual bodies—including of those alive and those deceased—able to communicate through mediums with the material realm, the doctrines of astral bodies or fluids crucial for holistic health and healing, the teachings of esoteric traditions in the West—the spiritualism of Victor Cousins (1792–1867), the theosophic speculations of Annie Besant (1847–1933), Rosicrucianism, and the Kabbalah—and Christian ethical humanitarianism. Kardec's books were brought to Brazil by a returning traveler. They circulated widely especially among lighter skinned intellectuals and professionals, and were translated into Portuguese by the end of the nineteenth century.

This second phase, however, also saw, especially at the level of religious practice, the transformation of Kardecism by Brazilians to fit their religious needs and aspirations. Spiritualism became spiritism and mysticism, rationalism became pragmatism, and the importance of ethical humanism was transformed into an emphasis on physical healing and social well-being. Most important, perhaps, the spirits in the Kardecist cosmos which were shaped by evolutionary karma became the gods and saints of the Umbandist pantheon. This absorption of Kardecist doctrines was virtually complete by the 1910s. Although it is difficult to

generated only when Herskovits's theory is thought to be able to account on its own for the syncretistic nature of Afro-Brazilian religiosity. As the crucial component to a larger theory, however, the main lines of his argument remain intact (cf. Walker 1991). Its fruitfulness in explicating the development of Latin American religion as a whole can be seen in its successful application in other regions such as Inca-dominated Peru (e.g. Szemiński 1995).

comment with any degree of confidence on the religious character of Brazil during this time, it is safe to say that three types of spiritism were operative at various levels of society alongside official Catholicism: European-type Kardecism as practiced by whites and middle to upper-class professionals; a generic form of spiritism, Macumba, widespread throughout the middle to lower sectors of Brazilian society; and the deviant form of spiritism, Quimbanda, said to involve black magic, resorted to by a much smaller percentage of the lower-class population. Primarily because of the alleged practices of Quimbandists, formal spiritistic practices remained legally outlawed.

From this religious milieu, a third phase emerged during the 1920s which gave rise to ideologically driven agendas relative to the formation of Umbanda. Diana Brown (1986: 37-51) describes three such positions: the movement to de-Africanize Brazilian religiosity by becoming more Kardecist—Umbanda Pura or Branca (White Umbanda); the retaliatory movement to preserve the African lineage, elements and identity of the tradition—Afro-Brazilian Umbanda; and the movement to elevate the status of Umbanda as practiced by the masses by connecting its indigenous sources and religious ethos with the quest for an international Brazilian identity—nationalistic Umbanda. While the debates between these movements remain unresolved to the present, they accomplished a great deal for the development of Umbanda, including the convening of congresses, the formation of federations and organizations to provide legal protection and other kinds of assistance and guidance to practitioners, the articulation of doctrine and the publication of literature. In the meanwhile, the impetus for Umbanda Pura has taken a back-seat to the other two interpretations of the tradition in more rural areas even while it has become so much of a fabric of urban Umbanda as to be ideologically indistinguishable.[15]

The historical eclecticism of contemporary Umbanda is beyond question. Its adherents are quick to point out that Umbanda is a religious symbol for the syncretistic reality lived in Brazil. Why, they ask, should not the synthesis of European, African and Indian cultures also produce

---

15. The developments within Umbanda, however, cannot be divorced from those taking place within the larger context of Afro-Brazilian religions in general. Rowan Ireland's threefold typology—the traditional/Africanist, the autonomous-creative, and the co-opted whited groups—provide illuminating perspectives on the diversity of spiritisms in Brazil and can be readily applied to Umbanda (1991: 152-63).

an amalgamation of Catholic, African and indigenous religious traditions into a novel and coherent whole? At the same time, Umbandists
are also careful to add that their beliefs and practices are not only
social, political or ideological constructs. Rather, Umbanda more accurately reflects the truths contained in the traditions from which it drew,
not only for Brazilians but also for everyone. More than the cognitive
understanding of religious doctrines, Umbanda enables the experience
of religious truth. This is accomplished primarily in the ritual of spirit
possession.

Ritual in Umbandist Spiritism[16]
Umbandist rituals—also known as *sessões* (sessions)—are performed
up to three times a week at meeting places called *centros* or *terreiros*.[17]
Centro leaders include, in hierarchical order, the *pai-* or *mãe-de-santo*
(*chefes*, or father- and mother-of-saint), the *pai* or *mãe pequena* (fully
initiated ranking mediums who support the *chefes*), *Ogães* (caretakers
of the *centro* and *sessõe* organizers), *filhos-* and *filhas-de-santo* (sons-
and daughters-of-saints, or mediums who are in various stages of training), *atabaqueros* (drummers) and *cambones* (assistants to mediums).[18]
Mediums usually take a ritual bath of seven herbs at home before coming to the *centro*. They change into white ritual garments upon arrival,
and genuflect at the entryway into the ceremonial room before an altar
that holds food and drink to placate evil spirits called Exús.

16. I elaborate in this section on part of my earlier, 'Discerning the Spirit(s):
Toward Comparative Symbology of Healing in Pentecostalism and Umbanda'
(unpublished paper presented to the New England/Maritime Regional Meeting of
the American Academy of Religion, Newton Centre, Massachusetts, 17 April
1998). An excellent overview of spirit possession ceremonies is Walker (1972). The
most important studies on Umbandist rituals are Fischer (1970), Pressel (1977) and
Brown (1986: 79-92).

17. *Centro* is the term used more by groups oriented toward Kardecist spiritism
while *terreiro* generally denotes a group oriented toward the re-Africanization of
Umbanda (Hess 1994: 73). In what follows, I use *centro* in an inclusive sense for
the sake of convenience.

18. An excellent discussion of these agents and their responsibilities is provided
by Brumana and Martínez (1987: 98-138). Note also that mediums are mostly, but
by no means exclusively, women (cf. Lerch 1980; Pressel 1980; Burdick 1993a: 98-
101).

Centros are usually divided into a ritual area and a seating area by a railing. The ritual area consists of two or three drums, a large altar holding flowers, candles, a glass of water, and statues of Jesus, the Virgin and principal Umbandist spirits, and ritual space for dancing and client–medium consultations. The ceremony is formally opened with a *cambone* purifying the ritual area of malignant Exú spirits (or their female counterparts, Pombagiras) with a smoking 'astral perfume' and incense burner. This ritual, also called *defumação*, cleanses the congregation from contaminating fluids that they may have attracted during the course of the day or week, and protects the service from *espiritos sem luz* (the 'dark' Exú spirits). Catholic saints and the blessing of Jesus or the Virgin are also invoked. At times a passage is read from one of Kardec's books or the gospels.

Singing commences during the *defumação* when the congregation welcomes the spirits with sacred songs to the divinities (*pontos cantados*), and continues in the same mode after the prayers and readings. The mediums sway, dance and spin ritually to the songs, clapping at mixed paces to the expert polyrhythmic drumming of the *atabaqueros* (cf. Rouget 1985: 47-50). They are slowly possessed by various spirit-guides: Caboclos, unacculturated Indians traditionally recognized as warriors in the Amazonian forests; Pretos Velhos, African slaves who died in Brazil; and less frequently, Crianças, children who died between three and five years of age, and Orixás, farther removed divinities analogous to Catholic saints who, because of their power, send envoys to possess mediums in their place.[19] Different nights of the week are usually devoted specifically to each of the different groups of spirits.

The physical behavior of spirit-possessed mediums ranges across the spectrum from the wild and vulgar movements of less experienced mediums to the relatively controlled gestures of the older mediums. The latter tend to retain a greater degree of consciousness during trance than their newly-initiated colleagues (cf. Pressel 1974: 195-201). In contrast, the former may jerk uncontrollably, tremble, shuffle, weave, totter, twirl, wriggle and squirm; they may clench or claw with their fists or pull on their hair; verbally, gasps, moans, cries, shrieks, shouts,

19. For Umbandists, these emissaries are frequently the Caboclos or Preto Velhos. More recently, Oguns (soldiers), Bahianos (inhabitants of Northeastern Brazil), Boiadeiros (cowboys) and Cignanos (gypsies), have emerged in the Umbanda pantheon (cf. Brumana and Martínez 1987: 155-202). I will discuss the Umbanda cosmology further in the next section.

whispers, laughs, growls and barks are frequently heard; they often give a scowling look when their eyes are not glazed over or their eyeballs are not rolled up toward the back of their head leaving only the lower whites visible; deep trances are often accompanied by profuse sweating and salivating. These manifestations are usually allowed to run their course and the *pai-* or *mãe-de-santo* who oversees the *centro* helps to restore a certain degree of order so that mediums are able to sit relatively sedately and somberly during consultations listening to clients and dispensing cures. Clearly, the inexperienced mediums require time to learn both how to control their incorporated spirits and their own self-awareness during possession.[20]

During the ritual, however, the personalities of mediums are considered to be absent, the mediums themselves having surrendered to their possessing spirit. It is the spirits who are the actors in the ritual area, riding their 'horses' (mediums), greeting each other or members of the congregation, drinking rum, smoking pipes or cigars, and so on. The spirits tend to manifest themselves in identifiable behavioral patterns. Caboclos generally display strength, arrogance, bravado, aggressiveness and authoritativeness—traits related to their habits of survival in the forests. Pretos Velhos, on the other hand, are in stark contrast to the Caboclos. As spirits of enslaved, usually elderly blacks, they are characterized by humility, patience, kindness and *caridade* (charity).[21] Playfulness is the hallmark of Crianças, and aloofness and nobility that of the envoys for the Orixás. *Centro* leaders and *cambones* are especially schooled in how possession affects mediums, and therefore able to help both with maintaining order throughout the ritual and with ensuring that visitors and other members of the congregation are not accidentally hurt.

20. Equally clearly, there is strong evidence that the behavior of both mediums—whether it be loss of control or somber comportment—and *chefes* are culturally and socially structured within the Umbandist framework (cf. Pressel 1974: 194-95).

21. It should be mentioned that these generalizations admit of exceptions such as those uncovered by Burdick (1993b) in the spirits of Pretos Velhos whose exemplary traits are drawn from their participation in organized resistance to slave owners. The relationship between these Pretos Velhos and those who in former times were called 'bad negros' and understood to be 'crossed' with Exús remains unclear (cf. Bastide 1978: 317; Brown 1986: 75). The infamy of these latter spirits, however, may have been exaggerated by Umbanda purists.

While in the state of trance, *consultations* are conducted whereby the spirits give advice through their mediums to inquiring clients on a wide range of problems including family squabbles, unemployment, love relationships, business ventures, university studies and other matters. The exception to this are the Orixás who because of their removal from the mundane affairs of the world, generally do not speak or give direct council; messages from Orixás are interpreted more by their actions or translated with the help of *cambones*. The more important consultations, however, revolve around spiritual healing. This includes, in the Umbandist world-view, physical sickness, emotional trauma and mental illness within the broader framework of spiritual disorders. Physical or other kinds of symptoms which persist despite medical, psychological or psychiatric treatment are generally understood to evidence some sort of spiritual problem—a build-up of bad fluids within one's body. This build-up occurs for a variety of reasons usually related to the work of Exús.[22] Once the source of the problem is diagnosed during the consultation, healing is prescribed as appropriate through the performance of ritual obligations, the use of curative herbs, the means of ritual purification whereby the sickness is exorcised or drawn out from the body by the consulted medium (who is considered immune to 'infection' due to his or her possessed state), the neutralization of the power of the Exú responsible for the affliction, or initiation into the process of mediumship.[23]

Clients usually leave not too long after having their private consultation. After the needs of clients are met, the mediums come out of trance, often convulsively, as the spirits dis-incorporate. Umbandist ritual ceremonies tend to conclude around midnight with a spirited closing song, a moral homily, and the pronouncement of blessings by

---

22. Secondary causes include black magic as conjured in Quimbanda, what folk religious belief call the casting of an 'evil eye', resistance to developing one's mediumship, and the failure to perform one's obligations to the Orixás from either neglect or ignorance; or, it could simply be a case of karmic misfortune as stipulated by the Kardecist doctrine of reincarnation (see Pressel 1977: 339).

23. Some *centros* practice *roupas para firmar* (clothes for blessing) whereby clients who represent the problems of others—family members or friends who could not attend the service—usually bring clothes or other items that belong to the troubled person to the altar where they are blessed by 'astral perfume', thus discharging the evil fluids (Lerch 1980: 137).

the *centro* leader. After this, the mediums return to their dressing rooms to don street clothes and retire to their homes.[24]

3. *Unveiling the Spirits! Religious Symbolism in Umbanda*

The preceding discussion provides both a broad historical perspective and a more specific ritual viewpoint by which to understand Umbanda. My overarching concerns, however, are theological. More specifically, they are pneumatological: is the Holy Spirit present and active in Umbanda, and how is such presence and activity to be discerned?

In order to begin answering these questions, then, I propose to apply the comparative categories derived from foundational pneumatology to Umbanda. Three interrelated objectives shape the following discussion. First, this exercise represents an empirical test case for the suitability of the categories for the interreligious dialogue. If the categories register important features in Umbanda, our revisioning can be considered to be relatively successful—at least in this case. The second, related, goal is to achieve a better understanding of another tradition, in this case, Umbanda. According to the hypothesis operative here, the empirical specification of the categories in Umbanda will at the same time reveal much more about the tradition than a purely historical or phenomenological account. Attaining both of these aims will in turn place us in a much better position to accomplish the theological objective undergirding this project: discerning the Spirit(s). In this section, however, I will attempt to allow Umbanda to tell us what it can about the Spirit(s) in its own terms before asking the more explicit comparative and theological questions in the dialogue that follows.

24. This brief description of the Umbandist ritual may serve to reinforce the distinction originally drawn by Eliade (1972) between shamanism and spirit possession. Eliade defined the former as involving out-of-body experiences and other-worldly journeys (ecstasy; cf. Walsh 1990), and the latter as involving the incarnation or bodily reception of spiritual entities. While other-worlds are not entirely unknown in Brazilian mysticism, such occur more so in the context of Kardecist spiritism than in Umbanda (cf. Hess 1991). Spirit possession is the dominant feature in Umbanda, during which the displaced human personality is suspended in a state of limbo until allowed to return to the body. It is difficult to describe Umbandist possession as an ecstatic out-of-body experience because the alleged soul-loss may be literally that—the human personality being unconscious during trance—even if in semi-conscious states, mediums are usually engaged with clients and rarely, if ever, have the luxury of journeying to other worlds.

The Meaning of Spirit Possession

Religious experience plays a premier role in Umbandist spirit possession. In the words of Maria José, a widely respected *mãe-de-santo* in
Rio: 'we know the gods are alive because we see them all the time
incarnate in the bodies of men and women... They are here among us.
We know that our gods are full of energy—if they weren't there could
be no trances' (Bramly 1994: 38).[25] Umbandist possessions, it could be
hypothesized, are holistic experiences that mediate the human and the
divine, and the material and spiritual worlds. To what extent is this
hypothesis sustainable within the framework of the Umbandists' own
interpretation of their religious experience?

For Maria-José, trances are means by which the conflicting forces of
the world can be harmonized in the lives of individuals and communities. She describes the world as 'full of great floods of energy that
circulate and swirl in the greatest chaos imaginable'. These forces,
however, are not only without but within us. 'They push us, stop us,
throw us about or allow us to advance, and we go on completely
unaware of them. Some of them are positive, some negative.' Yet they
cannot simply be designated as mysterious supernatural forces; rather,
they may be better conceived of as the elemental forces of the cosmos,
'the most natural thing on earth!' (Bramly 1994: 64, 90, 166).

Yet human beings are for the most part oblivious to these trajectories
of force, or natural energies. Human life therefore becomes 'a battle of
forces'. Umbanda recognizes and studies these forces and provides the
rituals which enable people to 'live in harmony with those forces'
(Bramly 1994: 194, 119). Spirit possession and trance are moments in
these rituals that achieve the transference, stabilization and harmoni-
zation of these forces. This is accomplished primarily in the formation
and reconfiguration of personal identity. Thus Maria-José says that
these experiences are:

> desirable for anyone who has more energy than he or she can handle.
> People are like furnaces. If they are under-nourished they are cold and
> useless; they become leeches, parasites who feed on other people's
> energy. But if instead they are too full of magic forces, they can explode.
> Macumba takes the energy circulating in the world and channels it,

25. We are fortunate to have this insider's perspective presented in Serge
Bramly's interviews with Maria-José since reports by anthropologists and sociologists, no matter how skilled, are inevitably skewed by ethnographic presentation
and explanatory theory (cf. Lewis 1986: 1-22).

redistributes it according to need... Our work in the terreiro strives to
capture this energy, to tame it and use it. People criticize the violence of
our dances. But we don't create that violence. It exists. It's already there,
and it would quickly become very dangerous if it could not be expressed,
if it weren't freed... We accept the destructive side of the vital energy
within us: it is a force that has to be recognized (Bramly 1994: 64).

Elements of Kardecist doctrine adopted by Umbanda Pura are clearly
discernible in Maria-José's interpretation of spirit possession. Her two
central tenets—the world being full of forces of energy, and trance as
enabling individuals to harmonize and balance these conflicting forces—reflect this influence. What is also clear is that trance and spirit
possession in Umbanda are effective ordering experiences which have
cathartic and creative components.[26] They both allow the legitimate
release of frustration and stress and provide a venue for the expression
of creativity, the empowerment of selfhood and the reorientation of
spiritual life in the material world.

This reading of Umbandist spirit possession is especially persuasive
given the fact that a large percentage of mediums become initiates due
to 'some inability of the individual to operate successfully in his [more
appropriately, her] specific sociocultural environment' (Pressel 1974:
204). Their reasons for frequenting the *centro* in the first place are
typically related to some kind of dysfunctionality or illness. Experiences of spirit possession in the majority of these cases lead to initiation
into the cult and enable the individuals to lead normal and even successful social lives. The few cases where successful mediums become
pai and *mãe-de-santos* provide further testimony to the effectiveness of
trance in achieving personal health and social functionality.

There are, however, cases where occasional relapses occur or temporary difficulties later arise. Further, there is also evidence that the
behavior of the incorporated spirits can never be fully predicted or controlled and that unmanageable bouts of spirit possession—what Esther
Pressel calls 'negative spirit possession'—may be precipitated especially by the recurrence of stressful experiences. While this is especially
the case with the un-initiated or newly initiated mediums, spirit possession may at times provoke even expert mediums to acts of violence
such as flailing the arms wildly and pounding the head against the wall

26. Esther Pressel shows that disruptive pre- or early-trance behavior is usually
preceded by some kind of psychological stress, conflict or frustration for which
trance provides catharsis (1974: 199-201).

severely; less violent signs of an uncontrollable spirit include the aim-less wandering about of the medium around the *centro* rather than the willingness to enter into consultations (cf. Pressel 1977: 353).

Clearly, religious experience is central to Umbanda. On the basis of the discussion so far, can the Holy Spirit be said to be present and active in Umbanda, and if so, in what way? Joseph Murphy reads the phenomenological similarities between Afro-Brazilian traditions as evidence of 'spirit'. At the same time, Albert Raboteau is just as correct to insist on the difference between what he calls the elements of faith and belief that undergird ritual experience, and the patterns of motor behavior by which these experiences are expressed (1978: 62-65). The rhythmic dancing, singing and clapping are indeed carryovers from African religiosity to the Americas, but there is a theological chasm between what Pentecostal Shouters and devotees of Afro-American and Afro-Brazilian traditions believe are taking place in manifestations of spirit possession, namely, the Holy Spirit and other spirits. While I have not yet discussed the Umbandist cosmology in detail, there have been no indications so far that the Holy Spirit plays either a major or minor role in the Umbandist scheme of things. It is clearly hazardous to affirm the presence of activity of the Holy Spirit on Umbandist terms.

At the same time, it is equally clear, for example, that some trance experiences in Umbandist rituals are occasions for positive develop-ments in the lives of devotees. Mediums continue in their work in part due to the fear of offending their Orixás, but also because they find a certain amount of satisfaction and gratification in it. Further, spirit possession also imparts energy to devotees in the short term, even while it facilitates psycho-physiological and mental health in some cases in the long run. The extent and authenticity of these transformations will need to be further investigated. For now, however, spirit possession in Umbanda can be understood to bring about a relative degree of harmony in the lives of devotees. Because discerning the Holy Spirit is, after all, a Christian obligation, it is in this case incumbent on the Christian comparativist and theologian to make a preliminary judgment by discreetly applying the Christian pneumatological categories. To the extent that these effects accompany spirit possession in Umbanda, it may therefore be tentatively suggested that they are potentially signs of the Spirit's presence and activity.[27] To find further confirmation or

27. The benefits of Umbandist rituals seem to be consistent with the Afro-American experience across Latin America. Consider the following report from an

disconfirmation of this assertion requires that the other pneumatological categories be applied to Umbanda so as to shed further light on this question.

Healing and Salvation

The categorial hypothesis argued for in this book is that religious experience (the experience of the Holy Spirit) is followed by religious utility (the gifts and fruits of the Spirit manifest in personal lives and displayed in the socio-ethical realm). This connection has also been observed in anthropological terms by the British anthropologist, I.M. Lewis, who says: 'the ultimate force of symbols depends at least as much on their power to stir the emotions, moving men to action and reaction' (1977: 2). Significantly, Lewis's fieldwork has been spent on shamanism and spirit possession cults (cf. Lewis 1986; 1989). The case of Umbanda is again exemplary: spirit possession is not only a receiving of the gods, but is also an experience of healing that is not devoid of social implications. Regarding the latter, like Pentecostals, Umbandists have been slower to formulate a social ethic. But their experience of the gods has led them toward structural reconfigurations of communal networks and relationships. Let us see how this plays out.

The saying among converts that '*Umbandista entra pela porta do sofrimento*' ('People come to Umbanda through the gate of suffering') accurately describes the majority of Umbandist cases (Brown 1986: 94). Umbanda *centros*, no less than Pentecostal churches, Catholic priests and indigenous folk healers who practice *curandeirismo* (the arts of healing; see Williams 1979), are frequented by a people who, as Sidney Greenfield puts it, 'are ill, believe they are ill, fear they soon will be ill, or are very involved in an illness of an friend or relative'

---

observer/participant of Haitian Voodoo: 'We walk into the open air after 1:00 a.m. As we head for the highway to find transportation, I realize that I am utterly refreshed. Not in the least tired, not disturbed, not solemn, not giddy. Refreshed. This was my feeling after every one of the many Haitian *services* that I attended. Nothing that I had ever read or heard prepared me for this up-beat, cathartic effect from *vodou*. It was a gift.'

The fact that Haitian voodoo is a regional expression of what in Trinidad goes by Xangô, what in the Caribbean goes by Santeria, what in Brazil goes by Candomblé and Umbanda, etc., makes this a strong testimony to the edifying effects of Afro-American possession rituals. This account—from the Christian theologian, Tom Driver (1991: 69; italics original)—may be appealed to as evidence supporting our provisional conclusion.

(1987: 1105). The success of Umbanda is related specifically to the experience of physical healing and the betterment of a life situation, whether such be fairly instantaneous or gradual. While spirit possession itself is undoubtedly of direct benefit to many mediums, yet the over-arching purpose of Umbandist possession is to meet the needs of a needy clientele. In discussing the utilitarian features of Umbanda, we inevitably move from a focus on the spirit–medium relation to the spirit–client relation, and from the individual's trance experience to the *centro* as a collective and social phenomenon.

The *centro* as a healing community can be understood if assessed from multiple perspectives, including the sociological, political and doctrinal.[28] Sociologically, there is abundant evidence that Umbandist practice serves both ideologically and existentially to empower the powerless, whether the latter be the economically destitute, the socially marginalized, or women in a patriarchal society (e.g. Lerch 1980; Pressel 1980). In addition, it is also clear that Umbanda has formulated a counter-discourse to racism (Burdick 1993a: 146-81; 1993b). The assurance that comes with being a *filho-* or *filha-de-santo* serves in part as compensation for the socio-economic trials and tribulations Brazilians confront daily, while the fact that the gods themselves reflect the Brazilian fusion of cultures allows a certain transcendence over the endemic feeling of white (read Spanish/European) superiority.

The politics of healing in Umbanda have to be understood in the context of Brazil's history of clientelism. *Chefes* are paternalistic figures who mediate between the private lives of their clients and the public arena of economics and politics. Often, resources are marshaled by the *chefe* from a network of patrons and providers on behalf of clients as needs are brought to their attention. Clients who benefit from these services and goods often serve the *chefe* loyally which in turn increases the prestige of the *centro*. In addition, *chefes* frequently work with local and aspiring politicians, pledging their own support and that of their clients in exchange for personal, *centro* and other favors. While there are on occasion *chefes* who bilk their clients and take advantage of their positions of power and influence, for the most part, these *chefes* lead modest lifestyles, with some even giving self-sacrificially out of their own pocket to the work of the *centro* (cf. Brown 1986: 169-77). It is

28. Social and political analyses of healing have been successfully employed in the study of Candomblé (e.g. Westra 1991a; 1991b; Minz 1992) and, to a lesser extent, Umbanda (Pereira de Quieroz 1989).

customarily these same individuals who are instrumental in providing the kind of support network to those who are otherwise socially, economically and politically invisible, and who would otherwise fall through the cracks of society.[29]

In spite of this, however, there have been those who have voiced the complaint either that Umbanda lacks a ethical code, or that the ethic that does exist is based on manipulation above all else (e.g. Droogers 1998: 22-23). I would suggest that this is to focus so much on Umbanda as a social and political entity as to neglect that it is first and foremost a religious tradition concerned about relating things of the spirit world to the human arena. It is also to forget that Umbanda and other Afro-Brazilian traditions have emerged out of a fusion of Catholicism, Kardecist spiritism, and Amerindian and African cultures. What the former two contribute on the doctrinal level, the latter two put to work in a holistic understanding of salvation and healing that integrates the personal, the social or communal, and the natural realms of the cosmos.[30] In Brazil, then, the Catholic and Kardecist emphasis on charity takes on tangible features. It is not unusual for pharmacists, dentists, physicians, psychiatrists, lawyers, loan officers and other public service agents to offer free services on a regular basis as an expression of their religious commitment to practice *caridade* (charity). Many Umbandists work with a variety of spiritists in providing food for the hungry, maintaining preschool and daycare services, and establishing and running orphanages and hospitals.[31] This follows from the Umbandist motto: 'to give

29. In this connection, it is important to note that Brazil is not an exception to the general rule in Latin America where support systems are usually networks that combine extended family, folk healers, religious institutions and merchants (cf. Delgado and Humm-Delgado 1982). In urban Brazil, however, *centros* are fast filling in the gaps caused by movement from rural areas to the cities: the religious institution in this case is a source of healing, a reconstituted 'family,' a vast and intricate patronage system, and more. For a detailed treatment of the different levels at which Umbandist patronage functions, see Brown (1986: 167-94).

30. For African views of healing see Shorter (1985), Becken (1989), Thorpe (1993), Okorocha (1994) and Ephirim-Donkor (1997).

31. The perennially ill Brazilian population requires a large contingent of those skilled in medicine. It is not coincidental, then, that the spiritist milieu of Brazil should give rise to a professional class of alternative medical and healing practices including the notorious 'spirit surgeons' who perform operations without the use of anesthesia (cf. Greenfield 1987). At the same time, at least on the ideological level, there is a difference between the Umbanda and Kardecist practice of *caridade*. The

freely what is given to you. Charity is the *raison d'être*' (McGregor and Stratton Smith 1967: 197).

Ultimately, then, while it would be wrong to insist that Umbanda lacks an ethic, it would be more accurate to say that its operation in Brazilian culture takes the form of what Roberto da Matta calls a 'double ethic' (1981). Whereas outside the *centro* ambiguity prevails, within the *centro* and its system of patronage relations, the Christian rule of charity is reinforced by the Kardecist doctrine of karma. In this context, the Umbandist ethic as summarized by da Matta

> emphasizes tolerance, charity, acceptance of all with equal generosity, and compensation for all social and political differences. This ethic also creates an environment conducive to a moral recovery that otherwise would be difficult, especially during phases of acute social change... Thus it emphasizes social and moral relations, allowing for the salvation of individuals from all social categories. If a person is poor and destitute of all secular powers, being a true social nonentity with no acquaintances to protect him from the most violent forms of exploitation, his mystical relationships with the orixa let him be transformed into a 'saint's or god's horse'—into 'something' (1981: 257).

The main lines of the utilitarian features of Umbanda are now clearly identifiable. If in fact the movement toward personal authenticity in the lives of individuals and toward social solidarity in communities of faith are signs of the Holy Spirit's presence and activity, recognizing the greater or lesser degree of such allows the Christian to acknowledge the Spirit in other faiths to that same extent. As Sheila Walker puts it, 'socialized ceremonial possession, being of benefit to the whole community, is a positive phenomenon resulting in attention, respect, and admiration for the individuals involved. They serve their own personal interests, and vicariously those of the spectators, plus strengthening social solidarity through this collective religious experience' (1972: 149). The testimony of Umbandists themselves appear to confirm her findings when they report satisfactions derived from *centro* participation such as experiencing healing, receiving solutions to problems,

---

latter consists primarily in an impersonal relationship whereby the mostly white middle and upper-middle class Kardecist provides a non-reciprocated donation to the poor as an object of charity, while the former is 'a ritual form of spiritual aid that occurs in a reciprocal, personalized form of exchange and binds clients ritually into reciprocating through obligatory acts of ritual homage...in return for aid' (Brown 1986: 102).

obtaining peace, order and tranquility, and developing the ability to assume personal responsibility (cf. Brown 1986: 99). To the extent that all of these are genuinely mediated by the practice of Umbanda, can Christians conclude anything else than that at least in these instances, the Spirit has been present and at work?

It needs to be reinstated, however, that such a conclusion is the Christian's and not the Umbandist's. On the contrary, the latter would attribute their healing and well-being to their specific Orixás. Does that not flatly contradict the Christian assessment? In this case, to persist in the aforementioned judgment would be to commit theological imperialism in its most blatant form. In short, as has been indicated before, the Christian cannot adequately discern the Holy Spirit if there is no discernment of the many other spirits alleged to be operating in any given Umbandist situation. Our categoreal analysis of Umbanda therefore requires movement from religious utility to religious cosmology: what is the truth behind the deities and spirits of the Umbandist pantheon?

From Olorum to Exú: The Umbandist Cosmology
As will be clear in the following discussion, there are places in the Umbandist cosmos for God as creator (the Father) and God incarnate (the Son), even if reinterpreted in a spiritist framework. Mention of the Holy Spirit, however, is rare, not only in Umbandist literature but in the Afro-Brazilian traditions as a whole.[32] This is clearly related to the fact that there are many Orixás who descend in ritual trance, not just one (Holy) spirit. From the Umbandist perspective, then, discerning the spirits relates to the Orixás, Caboclos, Pretos Velhos and Exús. Who are these spirits and what kind of reality do they symbolize?

32. My inability to find the Holy Spirit in Umbanda may be related more to my lack of fluency in Portuguese—the language in which much of the doctrinal literature of Umbanda is published. The title, 'Les Orixás et le Saint-Esprit au secours de l'emploi (des stratégies d'insertion socio-économique dans le Nordest brésilien)' (M. Aubrée, in *Cahiers de Sciences Humaines, ORSTOM* 23.2 [1987]: 261-72), sounds fascinating, but unfortunately, I have been unable to track it down. I did, however, uncover one relatively pertinent secondary reference recorded by Jim Wafer in his discussion of the Candomblé tree-deity, Tempo. For the Candomblé, ' "Tempo is everything," and for this reason is like the Holy Spirit, who is *in* everything' (Wafer 1991: 173). There is probably room here for an analogous understanding in Umbanda (see the extended quotation from Maria-José below).

To get at this question, it will be helpful briefly to trace the tributaries that flow into the Umbandist cosmology, mainly the Catholic, the African, the spiritist and the Amerindian. To begin first with the fusion of Catholic and African cosmologies, it should be noted that their coming together is a complex story in the history of Afro-Brazilian religion. Suffice to say that the High God of African traditional religions was quickly identified with the Catholic creator God. More specifically, the Yoruba Olorum assumed the features of the Christian God the Father in Brazil as it did in Africa (cf. Parratt 1970). Following in the footsteps of the African cosmology, however, Afro-Brazilians also understood the high creator God to be so far above the created order as to be virtually inaccessible and thus practically dispensable relative to human affairs. In Umbanda, then, Olorum is no more than a symbol for the supreme power of the universe. Olorum's work must therefore be accomplished through intermediary deities and spirits.

Here is where the complication begins to exert itself. In the Yoruba pantheon, the mundane affairs of the human world belonged to the province of the spirits of the ancestors under various lines of deities—usually seven, in the Umbandist scheme of things, or, upwards of 400 by Yoruban count (cf. Thorpe 1991: 91). Needless to say, this is much more complex than the three-tiered Christian cosmology which is generally understood in terms of a trinitarian God, the realm of the principalities and powers (the demonic), and the material realm of human habitation. The clash of African and Christian cosmologies in Brazil, however, was mediated specifically by the status and function of saints in the Catholic understanding. The resulting synthesis accommodated both African deities and Catholic saints by identifying them based on their symbolic content. Thus Oxalá, the sky god, was identified with Jesus Christ; Yemanjá, the goddess of the sea, with the Virgin Mary; Xangô, the god of thunder and lightning, with St Jerome; Ogum, the god of iron, metal and war, with St George; and so on.[33] In short, the

33. Studies on these specific deities are beginning to appear, as in Bascom's portrait of Xangô (1972) and Ortiz's of Ogum (1997). With regard to the parallels between Olorum and Oxalá with God the Father and Jesus respectively, it should be noted that there are some discussions about an Umbandist version of the doctrine of the Trinity which identifies Ifa, a Yoruban god of divination, with the Holy Spirit. Rainer Flasche, for example, explicitly equates Ifa with *die Heilige Geist*—'die geistige Befähigung des Menschen, die in Umbanda wirkt, aufgefaßt wird' ('the spiritual gift of humanity that is Umbanda acts to compose and gather together';

middle cosmos between the high creator God and the human world was replete with deities and saints, and celebrated appropriately at the popular level in the various festivals and feast days.

These developments, however, were only the beginning. Under the influence of Kardecist spiritism, the Umbandist cosmos of high god, spirit world and human realm was transformed into the three tiers of astral spaces, the earth and the underworld. All three realms consist of spirits on the evolutionary process. Those that reside in the underworld are better identified as ignorant rather than evil spirits. The earth is an intermediate plane that serves as a temporary residence for spirits undergoing material purification. The astral plane, meanwhile, is inhabited by a host of spirits and deities at various, more advanced stages of evolution, but nevertheless still in process. The combination of Christian charity and Kardecist reincarnation is what 'provides the motor for spiritual evolution' (Brown 1986: 62).[34]

In its more sophisticated, Kardecist forms, Umbandist astral spirits, especially the Orixás, are understood as the elemental forces of nature and the universe. The various levels of spirits are hierarchically ordered and sub-divided from there, with seven sub-lines of spirits under each Orixá, seven legions under each sub-line, seven sub-legions under each legion, seven phalanxes under each sub-legion, and so on. The Umbandist appropriation of Kardecist cosmology amounts in the end to an Afro-Brazilian interpretation of the doctrine of the great chain of being.[35] Each line in the hierarchy is a complex arrangement of spirits

1973: 185; cf. 1973: 211)—while Bibolo Mubabinge writes that, 'C'est le Ifa qui agit dans le monde et en particulier dans le Umbanda; il donne vie, santé et paix' ('It is Ifa who moves in the world and in particular Umbanda; he gives life, health and peace'; 1983: 1452). Neither one, however, documents Umbandist sources for their statements, and I am wary that such analogies derive more from the Christian–African traditional religions dialogues than from an in depth engagement with Umbanda. To do this important subject justice, close attention needs to be focused on Umbandist theological and doctrinal tracts (in the Portuguese) which is beyond my competency.

34. David St Clair remarks that the belief in reincarnation is the most important contribution of Kardecism to Afro-Brazilian religion (1971: 102); van Rossum (1993: 60) seems to agree.

35. There is the further possibility that the Yoruban pantheon from which the Umbandist cosmology is derived may be just as ancient, if not more so, as that of Greco-Roman mythology; on this point, see St Clair (1971: 35-46) and Hess (1994: 43-44).

extending from the more impersonal and luminous natural forces to the more concrete material entities. Following theosophists like Annie Besant, Umbandists affirm that on the astral plane

> besides spirits of the dead on their way toward the light, there exist spirits of nature, grouped in countless legions—salamanders, water sprites, gnomes, etc.—which are linked with the seven elements of matter and direct their force, constituting channels through which divine energy can be transmitted to earth to nourish its life... [T]he forces of the heavenly bodies, the forces of nature, the lines, and the groups of spirits are all linked, so that the ultimate function of spiritism is to make magical use of these astral forces, which may help or harm man in his spiritual rise (Bastide 1978: 325, 327).

The more esoteric details are known only to those steeped in Kardecism.[36] From the perspective of lay practitioners of Umbanda, however, what is most important are the less evolved spirits such as the Caboclos and Pretos Velhos, since these are the ones that continue to descend and interact with the world of the living.

It is here that we see clearly the Amerindian contribution to the Umbandist cosmology and the traits which make Umbanda a syncretistic religion on the one hand and an original religious creation on the other. Whereas the Orixás still incorporate in Candomblé, they have been effectively displaced in Umbanda by the Caboclos and Pretos Velhos. It is, after all, the latter who are central to the Afro-Brazilian experience. Their prominence in spirit possession can therefore be understood as representing an active marginalization of both the Catholic and the African cosmologies in favor of an indigenous Brazilian world-view. As incorporating spirits, the Caboclos and Pretos Velhos symbolize all that is glorious, admirable and valued in the Amerindian and slave heritage as played out in the Brazilian historical context. Their continued presence in the Umbandist community specifically and in Brazilian society generally is the means by which Brazilians retain their ties to their past even while forging their own distinct social and national identity for the present and future. More importantly, their day to day appearances in the *centro* reinforces their connections with the Brazilian reality and invigorates both the religious and existential lives

---

36. Brown (1986: 54, 59) cautions about the importance of distinguishing between the specialist and lay interpretations of Umbandist cosmology. For her, specialists are federation members, authors of doctrinal tracts, those inclined toward the practice of Kardecist spiritism, and the more sophisticated *centro* leaders.

of their devotees. In a very real sense, it is legitimate to speak of a transfer of values in Umbandist trance—a transfer that shapes individuals particularly and Umbanda as a whole according to the ideal features of the Caboclos and Pretos Velhos.[37]

Although prominent in the Umbandist cosmos, Caboclos and Pretos Velhos are by no means the controlling spirits. As conspicuous, at least in the background if not in the foreground, is Exú. Within the Yoruban framework, Exú is an ambiguous trickster, a 'lesser' Orixá more closely related to the material world.[38] In fact, he is an amoral figure capable of good or harm, depending on the situation.[39] Under the influence of Catholicism in Brazil, Exú was equated with the devil (Lucifer) and relegated to the underworld. As such, he has been inexorably linked with the practice of the darker arts in Quimbanda. Undoubtedly responsible for the negative reputation of Exú, Quimbandist priests and priestesses are known to employ Exú spirits—Beelzebub Exú and Ashteroth

37. Here, it may be useful to reiterate the distinction between the more Kardecist-oriented practitioners and the more African-oriented *centros*. It is interesting to observe that the Caboclos and Pretos Velhos found in the former context are more cultured and linked with natural forces while those in the latter are less so. Sheila Walker has called attention to the fact that the classification of types of possession manifestations ranges across a spectrum from being predominantly cultural—featuring cosmic deities and natural elements—to the predominantly psychological—featuring spirits that express libidinous attitudes and pathologies— with those combining cultural and psychological traits in relative proportions somewhere in between (1972). Especially toward the psychological end of the spectrum, personalistic and idiosyncratic spirits tend to appear, often molded by individual likes, dislikes, expressions, etc. At the far end of this spectrum, Walker correctly notes that 'the god personalities are created by man in his own image, and they conform to the inclinations and needs of men, thus a man chooses his own deity in accordance with his needs and ideals' (1972: 164). This tendency, however, is played out across religious traditions, and especially so at the level of the popular imagination. It does not take away from more sophisticated renditions of religious traditions, and the interreligious dialogue must surely be conducted with representatives of the latter rather than with those of the former.

38. The 'trickster', of course, is an infamous figure in the history of religions. For a discussion of the archetype of the trickster in the Hebrew Bible itself, see Patterson (1999).

39. As David Bosch writes, 'There does not appear to be any figure in Africa truly comparable to the devil of the Christian Scriptures...the concept of Satan as absolutely and irrevocably evil and the final antithesis of God is...foreign to traditional Africa' (1987: 39-41).

Exú of the crossroads, Tarchimache Exú of the closed paths, Morail Exú of the shadows, and so on (cf. St Clair 1971: 172-78)—in the performance of evil. For a fee, hexes are cast, vengeance exacted, enemies punished, marriages destroyed, and even deaths arranged.

Within the main lines of Umbanda, however, Exú retains the ambiguity of the Yoruban symbol. On the one hand, Umbandists themselves claim to abhor Quimbanda and its works. They repudiate possession by Exús, insisting instead on placating him (recall that female Exús are known as Pombagiras) through sacrificial offerings of chickens, goats and other animals, and on keeping him away from the *centro* through the ritual of *defumação*. On the other hand, the undoing of the evils wrought by Exús are accomplished with the help of the Exús themselves. Experienced Umbandist mediums will often perform the ritual of *desobsessão* ('dis-obsession' or 'deobsession' treatments) which nullifies Quimbandist black magic by employing Exú against Exú. The result, predictably, is that the person initiating ill will receives double the trouble that was originally intended to be inflicted. Some Umbandists therefore see Exú as a servant of the higher Orixás, while others think of him as an attribute of the gods rather than as a 'separate' deity. In commenting on these opinions, Maria-José reveals the complexity of Exú:

> Exú doesn't work exclusively for evil. He works for anyone, anything, so long as he's handsomely rewarded and receives his share of liquor and cigars... It would be wrong to think that he's only involved with evil... Since he's the guardian of the ground and opener of paths, Exú is sometimes associated with Saint Peter. And as the intermediary between human beings and the gods...he's linked to the archangel Gabriel... Each god has his or her special domain. Exú is the only one who feels at home no matter where he is. He is the hyphen between gods. He knows no barriers, no borders, no limits. Whenever a god is unable to work, one of the Exús is employed (Bramly 1994: 200, 201, 202).[40]

This 'redemption' of Exú is even more pronounced among Umbandists oriented toward Kardecist spiritism. In this framework, Exú becomes 'the elemental force, the great cosmic fluid, "the subconscious

---

40. To the question of how Exú could be on the side of both good and evil simultaneously, Maria-José replies: 'good and evil are human constructs...values created by us. The gods have never heard of them...the gods are above all that. Our morality is of little concern to them' (Bramly 1994: 202).

of God." It was he who was created when God said: "Let there be light." So he is ultimately the perpetual vibration of the ether, the life of the universe, and hence the great magical agent who can be used for good as well as evil. "Without him no one can do anything" ' (Bastide 1978: 330). These comments reveal the Umbandist understanding of Exú as life force, equated with ontological light and linked to a saying of Jesus (Jn 15.5). Discernment in this scheme of things is less about good and evil and more about relative degrees of ignorance, material obfuscation, evolutionary purification and spiritual illumination.

It is time to assess how the foundational categories developed here fare in this interfaith context. Undeniably, many of the important elements of Umbanda practice and doctrine are ascertainable through the categoreal lenses of religious experience, religious utility and religious cosmology, although it would certainly be going too far to claim that nothing of importance has been left out. Perhaps the opposite charge may be laid: that the categories are too vague and all-inclusive. The vagueness of categories, however, are their virtue rather than their fault. The latter begin to accrue only when the categories fail to illuminate their objects in the intended respects. Ultimately, then, only further comparative efforts and the ongoing interreligious dialogue can adjudicate this allegation. At this point, however, it is safe to say that the categories drawn from pneumatology have been flexible, illuminating and up to the task at hand to the degree that they have allowed Umbanda to speak for itself.

But what about the question of discerning the Spirit(s) which I have repeatedly insisted is at the center of a viable pneumatological approach to the religions? Clearly, there is a legitimate place for discerning the demonic in Umbanda since this is both conceptually available and existentially plausible in the Umbandist cosmology. Yet the ambiguity of Exú is itself a stumbling-block in the process of discernment. What kind of spirit or reality is Exú? Is Exú evil, or evil and yet capable of good? Or is Exú an arm or attribute of divinity? Going further, is Exú just an elemental force in nature? Or, perhaps, is Exú no more than a symbol projected from the human psyche? This ambiguity is pervasive throughout the Umbandist cosmos. Even the Orixás, on account of their distance from the human reality, are open to the kind of doubt that is not easily dispelled in the experience of ritual possession. As one devotee put it in reflecting on the ontological status of the possessing spirit: 'it exists?, it doesn't exist?, there is?, there doesn't? I don't know...

Sometimes I feel that I have (*Orixas*), but I don't. I don't know' (quoted in Brumana and Martínez 1989: 224).

The categories do provide a normative form of progression whereby the spirits behind the phenomena of Umbanda can be assessed both on the individual and the social level. They also enable us to ask the right kinds of questions regarding the forces that are present and at work at both the ontological and theological levels. In the end, however, the 'proof' of the Holy Spirit's presence and activity may lie in the positive and negative events that follow spirit possession in the long run: positively in resulting healings, material prosperity, existential serenity, etc., and negatively in the destructive consequences that are inevitably seen as punishments handed down by the gods to doubters and dissenters. Regardless of what has been discerned along the way, however, the categories themselves have demonstrated their usefulness and flexibility. They have brought us a long way toward a sympathetic understanding of the Umbandist reality. They have enabled a positive appreciation of the Umbandist creed:

> I believe in God, the omnipotent and highest, in the Orixas and in the divine spirits which according to God's will brought us to life; I believe in the rebirth of the soul and the divine righteousness in conformity with the law of return; I believe in communication with the leaders who went before us on the way of love of neighbour by practising the good; I believe in invocation and the prayer of intercession, and in sacrifices as well as in the practices of faith; I believe in Umbanda as a religion of redemption which can bring us on the way of development to Orixa Father (quoted in van Rossum 1993: 61).

4. *A Pentecostal Dialogue with Umbanda*

The preceding discussion has both facilitated a greater understanding of Umbanda on its own terms, and confirmed that the categoreal norms are effective to the degree that they are understood as pointing to a process of transformation. Herewith lies the importance and, indeed, indispensability of the ongoing interreligious dialogue. Discernment is always of concrete situations, and can never be in general. What is discerned as the Holy Spirit or some other spirit in this or that particular situation today, may be decidedly reversed or no longer applicable when the situation is examined tomorrow. Such may be part and parcel of life in the Spirit, and if so, then the dialogue always commences *in via* and should never be prematurely terminated.

In approaching the dialogue then, two points need to be underscored. First, an equitable and viable dialogue trades on similarities and differences. The preceding analyses of Umbanda and Pentecostalism put us in a good position to recapitulate quickly the comparisons and contrasts illuminated by the pneumatological categories. This leads to the second, perhaps more important task of asking what each tradition can learn from the other. Genuine dialogue will stimulate critical self-reflection on both sides leading to a process of mutual transformation (e.g. Cobb 1982). In proceeding, keep in mind the thesis underlying this entire project. I have argued that in contrast to an approach to the non-Christian faiths dominated by Christology, a pneumatological theology of religions provides a better theological framework for understanding religious plurality and is more adequate to the demands of the inter-religious dialogue. Can I now deliver the goods promised in my argument?

What Can Pentecostals Learn from Umbanda?

I want to suggest three areas where Pentecostals can learn from Umbanda: they can learn to appreciate better the diversity of religious expressions in responding to the transcendent; they can learn something about developing a theology of ancestors, one that provides a deeper understanding of the correlation between healing and community; they can also learn about the ambiguity at the heart of the intersection between the finite and the infinite, at least with respect to the relationship between the divine and the demonic. [41] Let me take each of these in turn.

First, the religious experience of Pentecostals and Umbandists have in common many phenomenological features. What the former calls Spirit-baptism, the latter calls spirit possession. Beyond that, students of

41. For the remaining dissenters who doubt Pentecostals have anything to learn from a dialogue with Umbanda, I suggest taking a few lessons from George Mulrain's courageous effort to learn from Haitian Voodoo (1984). Learning from those in other faiths derives as much from the universal presence and activity of the Spirit as it does from our openness to hearing what that same Spirit is saying to the churches. Furthermore, as Wink stipulates, in a God-bereft world, Christians have now developed the kinds of tools by which to relate to other gods and religious traditions 'without lapsing into their worship...[so that] Christianity can at last open itself to receive gifts from the other religions of the world' (1986: 123). This exercise hopes to convince the skeptics that Pentecostals have some of these important tools.

both traditions have been struck by other similarities. David Lehman, for example, has pointed out that newer Brazilian Pentecostals such as those in the Igreja Universal 'seem to engage in systematic borrowing of ritual elements and procedures, gestures and symbols, from popular and official Catholicism, most notoriously from possession cults' (1996: 137). The elements of Afro-Brazilian practices that stand out in Pentecostalism, ironically, are to be found in their practice of exorcism. Phenomenologically, on the Pentecostal side, the rhythmic music and clapping used to invite and cheer on the Holy Spirit, the interrogation of the possessed by the pastor, and the physical gestures used to expel demons, among other similarities, bring to mind on the Umbandist side the *pontos cantados*, the *consultados*, and the jerky movements caused when the spirits dis-incorporate (Lehman 1996: 149). Part of the question here may be either an interpretive or historical one: are Brazilian Pentecostals borrowing from Umbandists or are they simply reclaiming a more ancient, perhaps biblical spirituality which has made its way into Umbanda through the Catholic Church? Umbandist apologists can counter the latter claim by attempting to trace the genealogies of both traditions even farther back to ancient Yoruban religiosity.

The point, however, is that at least on the level of phenomenology, Pentecostals and Umbandists are not as far off as Pentecostal rhetoric has let on. This commonality is clearly due in part to their roots in the oral spirituality of black Africa. Two issues of theological import can be isolated for discussion in this connection. First is the question of how white Pentecostals, specifically in the North American context, relate to this phenomenological mutuality between Pentecostal spirituality and that of other Afro-American traditions such as Umbanda.[42] White Pentecostals may dispute the evidence of such commonality, whether it be presented by historians of religion (e.g. Jenkins 1978; Raboteau 1978), or by students of Pentecostalism (e.g. Paris 1982; MacRobert 1988; Hollenweger 1972; 1997). To attempt to do so, however, is to begin moving away from what is part of the essence of Pentecostalism itself. As previously noted, this is the complaint registered against much of the more recent white Pentecostal establishment—that it has become so 'evangelicalized' as to have lost its dis-

42. In what follows, 'white Pentecostals' is a shorthand label that refers specifically to North American Pentecostals—whether white, Asian, Hispanic or whatever—who prefer the more evangelical type of Pentecostalism prevalent especially among white Protestants over and against a more African style.

tinctive Pentecostal flavor. Perhaps the recent 'Memphis reconciliation' between white and black Pentecostals in North America will prove to be a providential catalyst for the former to recognize and reaffirm that part of their identity which is ecumenical and, indeed, African. In any case, exposure to the varieties of global Pentecostalism and the ways in which each have been influenced by local religio-cultural elements should at least give white Pentecostals pause before they conclude that its expression in the North American context is normative for what occurs worldwide under that name. White Pentecostals need to resist the temptation, exerted probably unconsciously through stereotypical thinking and ideological rhetoric, that non-American or African forms of spirituality are antagonistic to the Pentecostal experience. On the contrary, Africa is, in fact, intrinsic to the Pentecostal orientation, and norms for Pentecostalism in Africa or Latin America should be derived, at least in part, from these regions. There is no a priori or valid theological reason to suppose that the heritage of African traditional religiosity is any less capable than the culture of Hellenism or the Euro-American West of nurturing an authentic form of Christianity.[43]

The other theological point worth exploring regarding the phenomenological similarities between Pentecostalism and Umbanda relates to the question of how human beings in diverse religio-cultural contexts respond to things transcendent or divine. The fact is that the orality of Pentecostal worship and glossolalia is not far from the glossolalia-like orality of Umbandist singing and chanting. This observation fits what the anthropologist Cyril Williams has called a 'mysticism of sound' that includes, in its global forms, shamanistic language, the repetitive Sufi *dhikr*, spontaneous Kabbalistic utterances, certain forms of Hindu mantras and Tibetan tantrism (1981: 192-212).[44] Leaving aside for the moment the question of what it is that is on the other side of such experiences, I want to propose that the Pentecostal claim of encounter-

---

43. On this point, see the pertinent argument of Emmanuel Twesigye (1987, 1996) that the spirituality, philosophy and even theology of African traditional religions is not just a *praeparatio evangelica* to the Christian gospel but may be a necessary means by which the gospel is to be lived out in that continent.

44. Williams therefore wisely concludes his study by calling for a multidisciplinary approach to the experience of glossolalia in its affective, cognitional, somatic and other dimensions. Such approaches to the entire phenomenon of Pentecostal–charismatic experience are still needed; that they need to be conducted in a global, comparative context should go without saying.

ing the Holy Spirit in glossolalia should at least create a framework of plausibility whereby Pentecostals can entertain the notion that other analogous experiences in the non-Christian faiths are symbolic of authentic engagements with transcendence as well. If this is in fact possible, then such phenomena do not necessarily have to be either only human efforts to reach God or demonic intrusions into the human realm. They could be genuine instances of people responding to the Holy Spirit. This is not to say that all such experiences are that of the Spirit. Again, the argument throughout this work has been that religious experiences need to be evaluated on a case by case basis and the Spirit(s) need to be discerned. The point that needs to be emphasized is that discernment needs to be open to the possibility of encountering the Holy Spirit at the most unexpected places, and that the awe and wonder that accompanies Pentecostal experiences of the Spirit should enable them to be the first to break out of preconceived understandings of how, when and where the Spirit should be present and at work.[45] In short, the time may be right for Pentecostals the world over to begin appreciating, affirming and critically appropriating the diverse manifestations of spiritual and religious life as manifest both within and without the Christian tradition.

Second, Pentecostals can also learn from Umbanda about the importance of developing a broader theology of community and healing, one that includes recognition of the relationship between the living and the dead. The beginning of such a theology of ancestors and of community is to be found in reinterpreting Umbandist healing within a more holistic framework. In a perceptive article, Gerrit Huizer discusses nontraditional forms of healing including that of spirit possession in Umbanda. Umbandist healing, Huizer suggests, 'can no longer be ignored as "superstitions", but may fit within newer and broader paradigms, presently being developed among scientists, which go beyond those of the current newtonian cartesian views' (1987: 85). I am open to the suggestion that what the West has traditionally ignored as superstitious dabbling with spirits of previous generations is in fact a means by which human beings live out and express the reverence they feel for their progenitors that comes from an intuitive sense of

45. Pentecostals who now consider themselves in some regions to be the vanguard of Christianity should not too quickly forget that their own charismatic experiences were suspected by fundamentalists to be of demonic inspiration during the first few decades of the modern Pentecostal movement!

connectedness. Whatever else the Caboclos and Pretos Velhos are to Umbandist practitioners, they symbolize the proud heritage of a courageous and free people, and of resisting slaves. To receive these ancestral spirits in trance is to participate in their liberative power and to draw strength for the trials and tribulations that come with the vicissitudes of existential life. On the other hand, of course, Umbandists generally take every precaution against incorporating Exú spirits. These are ignorant spirits at best or malevolent ones at worst which continue to wander around in the underworld because their previous incarnations were devoid of the charity and light that move spirits up the evolutionary ladder. There is here a correct sense that not all ancestors have performed immaculately and that those who have failed continue to haunt the realm of the living by their failures and threaten to perpetuate their sin and destructiveness through those who are alive.

What are Pentecostals to make of all this? Let me clearly state at this point that I am not advocating practices denounced in Scripture such as divination, sorcery, witchcraft, the interpretation of omens, the holding of seances to consult the dead, and so on (cf. Deut. 18.10-12; 1 Chron. 10.13). Clearly, some of the more Kardecist-oriented Umbandists hold seances with the spirits of the dead; equally clear is that at the popular level the belief prevails that possessing spirits are literally those of dead ancestors (Caboclos and Pretos Velhos).[46] Insofar as this is the case, to that extent, Umbandist belief and practice are at odds with the biblical prohibitions and are to be denounced.[47] Further, while Umbandists do not generally claim to worship their possessing spirits, I am convinced on one level that their venerating their pantheon of deities is fundamentally misguided in the same way as are some versions of the Catholic veneration of saints. The question before us, however, is what Pentecostals can learn from Umbanda. I propose that the symbolic

46. The question of whether or not possessing spirits and spirit guides are deceased ancestors is a knotty one in Umbandist theology. For Umbandist specialists, the spirits are either natural forces or symbolic and archetypal representations of things divine rather than those of the departed dead (e.g. St Clair 1971: 76, 133; Bastide 1978: 325). A more literal understanding, however, persists at the lay level.

47. For the Pentecostal argument that channeling spirits are demonic, see Duffield and Van Cleave (1983: 492-94) and Bernard (1985: 303-12). On this point, most Pentecostals agree with evangelicals who also link the practice of channeling to demonic activity (e.g. Hillstrom 1995: 176-94; Newport 1998: 209-10). A more progressive Protestant view of these and related matters is suggested by Peters (1991, 1994).

representation of the interconnectedness between the living and the dead in Umbandist spirit possession points to an aspect of reality that Pentecostals understand in a relatively undeveloped and somewhat confused way.

Take, for example, the Pentecostal insistence on interceding by prayer and fasting against what they call 'generational curses'. In some circles, it is customary to 'break the power' of the past over the present, whether such be cycles of poverty, habits of violence learned from parental abuse, or genetically transmitted dispositions—e.g. vulnerability to physical diseases, propensities toward alcoholic consumption, or homosexual inclinations. In some of these cases, fasting and prayer may be the appropriate or only response. In others, however, healing needs to be recognized as a multi-generational affair that comes about not just by denouncing what is inherited from the past, but perhaps by affirming generational connections and forgiving the wrong-doings perpetrated by one's ancestors. This is suggested in different words by Walter Hollenweger who draws from the psychological sciences in suggesting that 'we have to develop a critical relationship to our ancestors (to tradition, to father- and mother-complexes), otherwise we become the slaves of the past' (1997: 266).[48] Is it not plausible that Pentecostals have erred by labeling such broken relationships as 'generational curses' and then attempting to flee from them, when the proper response might be to bring about reconciliation, acceptance and affirmation? Clearly much theological work remains to be done. Reflection on the healing function of the Caboclo and Preto Velho symbols in Umbanda is one way by which such can be stimulated.[49]

This leads, thirdly, to the question concerning the ontological status of Umbandist spirits. I suggest that there is much Pentecostals can learn from the Umbandist understanding of Exú about dealing with the

48. Hollenweger makes a number of other references in his most recent book to the need for Pentecostals to develop a theology of ancestors (cf. Hollenweger 1997: 77, 266-67, 383).

49. That this call for a theology of ancestors is not a passing theological fad can be seen from the fact that it had been articulated as far back as twenty to thirty years ago (e.g. Fasholé-Luke 1974; Sawyerr 1994: 43-55) and that its more recent advocates include theologians the stature of Jürgen Moltmann. In Moltmann's theology of 'community with the dead,' the connection between the living and those of previous generations is bridged by the reconciling work of Christ and the hope of resurrection (1996a: 104-10). His theology of ancestors thus emphasizes redemption from the torment of the past through the blessed hope.

ambiguity of the demonic relative to the divine. Generally, however, Pentecostals are uncomfortable with ambiguity. As David Lehmann puts it, 'Pentecostals trade in absolutes' (1996: 154). This translates, on the practical level, into a Pentecostal world that is not a *universe*, but rather a dual-cosmos wherein God and Satan battle for the souls of human beings, and where the identities of the Holy Spirit and of Satan and his demonic hosts are clearly demarcated. In this framework, Pentecostals would often find themselves in wholehearted agreement with the kind of syllogistic argument proposed by Michael Green (1981: 177). Building on the major premise that 'all the gods of the nations are idols', or to be more specific according to the Septuagint, 'all the gods of the nations are demons' (Ps. 96.5), and the minor premise that the lines of deities in both Yoruban and Umbandist religion are no more than regional and national formulations of the spiritual cosmos, Pentecostals quickly conclude that these pantheons are no more than idols at best and demonic at worst. There is something to be said for this interpretation which I will pursue in the next sub-section. At this point, however, it should be noted that 'idol' and 'demon' in this verse derive from the Hebrew root *'elîl*, which means primarily 'to be weak, deficient', and secondarily to be worthless as an object of worship (Harris, Archer and Waltke 1980: I, 46). On one level, this would not be applicable to Umbanda insofar as it 'is not a religion of worship or adoration' (Howe 1980: 129) but rather one of placating the gods or negotiating with them. On another, more theological level, while weakness and deficiency certainly do not deserve worship, when applied to the spiritual realm, they could instead be mere indicators of chaotic fields of force rather than references to strictly demonic ones.[50]

I want to suggest that the ambiguity of Exú points in one respect to the fallibility of human cognition regarding things divine, and in another more important theological respect to an ambiguity within the divine order of things itself. It is important to recall that Exú is only one member of the Umbandist pantheon, albeit the one who is the most ambiguous in terms of his interactions with the human realm. He and the other Orixás, however, ultimately serve as envoys or emissaries of

---

50. This goes for understanding the references to the demonic in the Christian Testament as well. In the early Christian era, *daimons* were equated with ghosts and the demonic in the popular mentality. At the same time, however, among more philosophically oriented circles, they would have been recognized as intermediate beings, forces or realities in a multi-level cosmos (cf. Bolt 1996: 96).

Olorum. Similarly, in the biblical world-view, the principalities and powers need to be understood in a dual sense. On the one hand, they are, potentially in some cases and actually in others, demonic in their destructive effects. On the other hand, it must not be forgotten that they are in the Hebrew Bible forces and agents under the command of Yahweh (e.g. Deut. 4.19; 32.8-9; Ps. 82.1; 86.8; 89.6-7; 138.1; the Satan of Job) and in the Christian Scriptures authorities established by God for divine purposes (e.g. Rom. 13.1-6; the various angels throughout the Apocalypse). By the time of the early Christian era, the equation of what the ancient Hebrews called the 'gods of the nations' with the demons of the heathen was sufficiently established so as to provide 'the new formula by which paganism would be eradicated by the church' (Wink 1986: 113). The fact is, however, that early Christian rhetoric created a dualism that obscured rather than clarified the theological relationship between the divine and the demonic.[51]

The point I am calling attention to is that allowed, in fact demanded, by the metaphysical hypothesis developed earlier. The various fields of force and trajectories of energies in the world are realities created for the purpose of providing order to the natural cosmos. Due to the existential spontaneity at the heart of each thing and event, however, created realities develop habits and tendencies which have the divine or demonic imprint to a greater or lesser degree. The spirits, in other words, range across a spectrum from that of being ministering servants of God to that of being rebellious or fallen angels. Yet even in the latter case, they remain subservient to the purposes of the God whose transcendent creative act provides the context within which the temporal

---

51. Here again, Wink's succinctly stated argument is helpful: 'Worship of the gods of a nation was the spiritual expression of what it meant to *be* a nation, tribe, tongue, or people. The gods of the nations—later depotentiated by being demoted to angelic rank by Jews and Christians—were conceived of in a projected way as possessing a separate existence as heavenly transcendent beings... [Rather], *they were the actual inner spirituality of the social entity itself.* I will argue...that the gods or angels of the nations have a discernible personality and vocation; that they too, though fallen, pernicious, and insatiable, are a part of the redemptive plan of God; and that our role in this redemptive activity is to acknowledge their existence, love them as creatures of God, unmask their idolatries, and stir them up in their heavenly vocation' (1986: 88; cf. 1984: 26-35; 1986: 87-127).

This present work can be understood as one effort to respond to Wink's challenge and to follow through on his suggestions on a concrete level.

affairs of the world flow. Perhaps this demonological revision allows for a better understanding of what is referred to as the 'evil spirit from the Lord' (1 Sam. 16.14; 19.9; cf. 2 Sam. 24.1 and 1 Chron. 21.1). The best interpretation that harmonizes the contradictory reports of what incited David to conduct the census would be to see Satan's action as being at least allowed, if not inspired, by Yahweh. Further, on this reading, it would be legitimate hermeneutically to speculate that enigmatic actions such as Yahweh's alleged attempt to kill Moses (Exod. 4.24) were simplistically identified as Yahweh's when they should have been more clearly specified as Satan's conducted under the divine provenance. Of course, early Israelite conceptions of the demonic were still rather vague; clearly, however, there is recognition here that evil is somehow connected to the creator, Yahweh, even if its precise name(s) were yet to be known (cf. Routledge 1998). What needs to be emphasized here is that which Walter Hollenweger has called attention to in his book on pneumatology: for the non-Western mentality, 'die Grenze zwischen Gott und Teufel nicht so scharf ziehen will' ('The lines between God and the devil cannot be so sharply drawn'; 1988: 115).

In this connection, should it not be surprising that there are Brazilian Pentecostals, for example, who believe that the prayers and efforts of both the Jesuits *and* the spiritists help, especially when these are directed to God. This is not a case of some marginal, sectarian Pentecostal itinerant, but that of Reverend Nasser Bandeira, a minister affiliated with the Igreja do Evangelho Quadrangular (Foursquare) (cf. Hess 1994: 163). While Bandeira himself practices exorcism Pentecostal style, yet his attitude is consistent with the behavior demonstrated at certain levels of popular practice where Pentecostals may be just as inclined to seek cures from spiritist groups as they are from their local churches. In these cases, it is not uncommon that Pentecostals at least act in agreement with the belief of Afro-Brazilian mediums—that 'all *orixás* have to obey God too. Without God they can't do anything for you'—even if they may not voice such a doctrine themselves (cf. Westra 1998: 122). The interesting question, perhaps enabled by recent advances in archetypal depth psychology, is whether or not such actions, even at the level of 'folk-Pentecostalism', reveal correct human intuitions into the divine order of things. My point is not to confuse the divine and the demonic to the extent that neither can be distinguished from the other. It is to call for both cautious discernment with regard to the Spirit(s) that may be at work in any given situation, and the recognition that the principalities, powers and the demonic have their ordained places within the divine providence.

In light of the foregoing, I believe the question, What can Pentecostals learn from Umbanda? has been justifiably asked. Such sincere questioning can be seen as an inquiry into the declaration by Vatican II that there are elements of truth and goodness to be found in all traditions which the Church needs to search out, acknowledge and respect (*Nostra aetate* §2).[52] Certainly, the pneumatological approach developed here has enabled Pentecostals to begin identifying just such elements and learning from Umbanda. Yet the conciliar decree also states that whatever is found needs to be related to the fullness of the Christian revelation in Christ. This requires that the reverse question be posed in order to complete at least this round of the dialogue.

What Can Umbandists Learn from Pentecostalism?

I hereby propose three areas of theological deficiency whereby Umbandists can learn something from Pentecostals. They can learn more about discerning the spirit-world both at the level of spirit possession and in the larger context of Brazilian society. Further, relative to the latter, they can learn more about healing, both in terms of its means and in terms of the socio-ethical dimension of health and wholeness. Finally, they can learn about the further implications of the battle of and against Exú spirits. As with the preceding discussion, let me take these in turn.

To begin, I want to pick up on my passing comment in the previous section that there is a sense in which the Pentecostal view of the Umbandist pantheon as being idolatrous at best and demonic at worst is potentially, at least in some cases, correct. This can be assessed on both the individual and the more corporate or social levels. With regard to

---

52. Vatican II has, in effect, transformed even Catholic theological opinion with regard to Afro-Brazilian traditions. Whereas blanket condemnation was the norm prior to the Council, post-conciliar attitudes included the acknowledgment by Bonaventura Kloppenburg that 'by his nature the Negro man demands his own ritual litanies. We must respect, rise up and consummate in Christ everything that we discover as being truly good, beautiful, just, holy and lovable in Umbanda... As the Church, at the Council, changed its attitude and its mentality, so have I. I must now feel as the Church feels and so have changed my attitude and mentality as well' (quoted in St Clair 1971: 269). Note that this comes from a man who had been, during his tenure as priest in Petrópolis before the Council, the most outspoken crusader against Afro-Brazilian spiritism.

the individual, the critical questions that Pentecostals would raise of the Umbandist experience of trance derive from their own continuous internal encounter with the more extreme phenomenal manifestations of the Pentecostal–charismatic experience itself. This question has been acutely posed to the Pentecostal theological conscience by the recent Holy Laughter revivals on the North American continent.[53] It has not been unusual for services within this stream of Pentecostal–charismatic spirituality to exhibit manifestations such as 'barking, roaring like a lion and "holy drunkenness" ' (Kydd 1998b: 73; cf. also the list of manifestations in Dempster, Klaus and Petersen 1999: 382-83). The classical Pentecostal response has been to confirm that since such manifestations are not biblically normative, they should be understood as mere human expressions at best rather than as irrefutable evidence of the Holy Spirit's presence and activity (cf. Wood 1995).

In this context, it is useful to draw once again from the work of Walter Wink. Wink distinguishes between what he calls an 'inner personal' demonic and 'outer personal possession'. The latter is 'the possession of an individual by something that is alien and extrinsic to the self' while the former is best seen in 'the struggle to integrate a split-off or repressed aspect that is intrinsic to the personality, an aspect that is only made evil by its rejection' (1986: 43). What is alien in outer personal possession is what Wink calls the personalized actualization of 'the collective malady afflicting an entire society' (1986: 50). In these cases, the appropriate response would be to exorcise the demonic spirit, although Wink is by no means convinced that the diagnosis in most cases of exorcism is accurate with regard to the problem. Much more extensive, he claims, is the situation whereby the individual presents evidence of some disturbance which is related to the fact that essential elements of his or her being have been suppressed due to social constraints or rejected as socially unacceptable. In these cases, what needs to be exorcised, if anything, is the fears that keep the individual repressed and inhibited. This then needs to be followed by the demonstration of 'accepting love. It is finally love, love alone, that heals the [inner] demonic' (1986: 57).

---

53. The literature is becoming enormous. The two primary Euro-American Pentecostal academic journals, *Pneuma: The Journal of the Society for Pentecostal Studies*, and the *Journal of Pentecostal Theology*, have both featured numerous articles in the past half-decade on Laughing Revival, also known as the Toronto Blessing. For a fair book-length assessment, see Oropeza (1995).

I think this discussion is useful and applicable in providing a theological framework to understand Umbandist possession. Clearly, much of the behavior brought upon those possessed by Umbandist spirits can be explicated in terms of Wink's inner personal demonic. At the same time, I am surprised that Wink makes such a clear cut distinction between the inner and outer demonic based on his own overall theology of the demonic. It is important to recall that for him, the demonic has *both* inner and outer aspects. I am more inclined to see the 'inner demonic' as personal aspects of the individual which have been contaminated by social and other larger-than-life forces resulting in a perverted disposition of habits, tendencies and values originally created in the image of God. As previously discussed, symptoms of the demonic influence which are applicable at this level include the loss of personal rationality, integrity and authenticity. As the charismatic Episcopalian priest and theologian, Morton Kelsey, observes, the 'one characteristic of the demonic psychic content is that it tries to possess the human psyche, while the angelic actually tries to relate to it. No matter how positive and good a psychic content appears, if it tries to take possession of the personality, its ultimate results are destructive and one is led into further unconsciousness rather than consciousness' (1972: 157).

At this point, it is important to recall that Pentecostals emphasize their experience of the Holy Spirit to be a conjunction of the divine and the human rather than a subjugation of the latter to the former. In contrast with the destructive frenzy that demonic forces initiate, the presence and activity of the Holy Spirit implies that 'everything should be done in a fitting and orderly way' (1 Cor. 14.40). Within this framework, 'the baptism in the Holy Spirit is therefore seen as the pneumatological antithesis of demon possession' (Möller 1987: 184). While psychotherapy can be helpful (as suggested by Wink 1986: 53), complete deliverance can only come about as a gift of the Spirit enabling repentance and discipleship in truth and righteousness.

It is within this framework that the Pentecostal critique of Umbandist trance needs to be understood. The liminal state of Umbandist spirit possession reveals various elements of a phenomenology of the demonic. This may be blamed, on the one hand, on the presence of Exú spirits, or, it may also be alleged that the mediums have simply not learned to work with their possessing spirits. Yet, as previously noted, even seasoned Umbandist mediums experience negative bouts with their Orixás, Caboclos and Pretos Velhos resulting in loss of personal self-control and rationality. Further evidence of the demonic element in the Umbandist experience is found in the prevalence of fear as a fundamental orientation and attitude in the Umbandist psyche. Umbanda is not a religious tradition that inspires worship. Rather, religious actions are motivated by the fear of the unknown spiritual world and of their after effects in the mundane realm of human existence. This is, of course, part of the rationale behind the sacrifices offered to appease the Exús. For these reasons, Pentecostals respond by quoting St Paul to the effect that 'the sacrifices of pagans are offered to demons, not to God' (cf. 1 Cor. 10.20), and exorcising the evil spirit in the name of Jesus. As has been pointed out by Key Yuasa, a Japanese Brazilian familiar with Pentecostalism in Brazil, Pentecostal exorcisms and the 'involvement of the Pentecostal with the spirits leads to a kind of demythologizing of their [the Orixás's] power, a power which is feared by the people because it is uncontrollable' (quoted in Hollenweger 1972: 97). Instead of the spirit of fear of the unknown, there is the spirit of power, of love, and of a sound mind (2 Tim. 1.7) that enables the joyous celebration of Pentecostal services.

It could well be that despite our previous efforts to understand the world of Umbanda, it is as a religious tradition so foreign to Pentecostalism that we have not succeeded in fully appreciating its paradoxes and are nowhere near to possessing the capability of discerning Umbandist spirit possession objectively. Such a possibility needs to be granted.[54] At the same time, the purpose of the interreligious dialogue is partly to provide a critical outsider's perspective which the receiving tradition can either reject as missing the mark or apply as appropriate. The mature Pentecostal community has not been reluctant to judge certain charismatic manifestations within its own movement as aberrations at best and demonic at worst when individual authenticity is not achieved and the larger community of the faithful is not edified. The question, for example, of how barking enables spiritual and personal integration has not been forthcoming from those who allow or advocate

---

54. Recall that Pentecostal discernment involves an intuitive sense of 'feeling right' (Chapter 7). Rather than this being an excuse for Pentecostal imperialism, however, I would suggest that a similar intuition can be detected in the 'pneumatological imagination' of Umbandists in their overall recognition that Exú is better avoided than engaged. What I am doing here, in part, is putting Pentecostal discernment to the test in the broader public involving Umbandist adepts and practitioners.

its presence in the Pentecostal experience. In a similar way, then, the Pentecostal queries Umbandists with the question of how the various spirits can be deities on the one possession while inspiring demonic behaviors in the next. This may not mean that Caboclos and Pretos Velhos are demonic impersonations. They may be. But the critical question is whether or not Umbandists have the spiritual tools to discern between their Caboclos, Pretos Velhos (and other spirits) and Exús, and to identify clearly the divine from the demonic. It does not appear so far that they do.[55]

This inability to discern relates also to the question of the relationship between the gods in the Umbandist pantheon and healing in its larger contexts. On the one hand, the metaphysical hypothesis suggested above not only allows but demands the acknowledgment of a plurality of spirits or spiritual entities in the world. On the other hand, it is a perennial human temptation to reify these spirits and gods even if they had been correctly identified previously. This is especially troublesome given the capability of the spirits and deities to proliferate in the human imagination.[56] In order to discern better the Spirit(s), both evidence and the ability to interpret such evidence are required. I suggest that on both counts, Umbandists can learn from Pentecostals. They have neither developed the kind of holistic understanding of healing implied in the idea of healing as a divine work nor have they been discerning of spirits in these larger contexts. In short, if the healing spirits in Umbanda do not accomplish the kind of healing expected of them, then perhaps this is as much evidence for the demonic as it is for any other spirit. In order to get at this question in a systematic way, I propose to move the dialogue to the level of the presuppositions undergirding the idea of

55. A related question is whether or not I am imposing a foreign rationality on Umbandists in asking about their ability to discern critically. I think not since Umbandists already do distinguish between helpful and dangerous spirits—the good and the evil. The question is therefore justified. Yet my negative response, even if generally correct for the present situation, should be considered as provisional since, as Al Raboteau notes, African gods in America 'have shown an amazing resiliency because of their ability to absorb and transform traditions from other sources' (1986: 559). Self-critical inquiry may yet be forthcoming in the Afro-Brazilian religious landscape.

56. This is evidenced in the Brazilian context by the earlier quote relating to the Umbandist appropriation of theosophical speculations of Annie Besant. Pentecostals themselves are not immune to such fantastic speculations (see Pratt 1991: 28-29).

healing, and discuss how the Umbandist understanding of the means, nature and implications of healing can be enriched and corrected.

In the first place, there is clearly a magical element in Umbandist healing. Even among those who detest Quimbanda, there is agreement that the curses wrought by Exús can only be dispelled by appropriate magical acts performed by Umbandist mediums. But what is magic? M. Scott Peck succinctly notes that magic is the attempt to procure, maintain and enhance the charisms or gifts of the Spirit for selfish purposes (1983: 190). These charisms are given by God for the edification of others. Yet, they are also natural endowments within the human constitution that are stirred up by the Spirit when necessary. Magical acts, however, ignore the gratuitousness of the divine gifts, and abuse them for personal gain at the expense of others. Within Umbanda, such assumptions are evidenced in 'cures' dispensed by mediums in the name of spirit guides during consultation. While some aspects of human freedom are preserved—i.e. 'if you follow this prescription...'—the divine freedom is muted in that the curative result is *guaranteed* to follow. Ultimately, however, magic cannot be countered with magic without destructive consequences (cf. Lk. 11.17-18). Perhaps this explains why the curses of Exú have to be reversed rather than just neutralized. This not to say that the Umbandist reversal of the Quimbandist curse cannot be 'effectual'. It is to say that this kind of 'resolution' only serves to perpetuate the demonic element of fear and destruction that is at the heart of the human predicament in general and the Brazilian existence specifically. What is ultimately healing can only be a divine gift that is positively affirming. As Erazim Kohák notes, 'the demonic will-to-evil can only be countered by an equally resolute will-to-good: by a consistent affirmation of the life which the demonic negates' (1975: 55). In contrast to the use of magical remedies and the reliance on previously incarnated spirits or at least spirits allegedly at the higher levels of the evolutionary scale, Pentecostals emphasize the graciousness of God and the gift of the Holy Spirit as the source of healing and human health.[57]

---

57. In this connection, Susan Garrett makes an important point regarding Jesus: 'Jesus qualified as a *biaiothanatos* (a person who had died a violent death), and the spirits of such persons were thought to be eager to return to earth. Such spirits were regarded by many persons as readily available to do the magician's work' (1989: 3; cf. 1989: 44). As Garrett later points out, however, there is a qualitative difference between the power of Christ through the Holy Spirit and that of other spirits:

The dominance of the magical component in Umbanda thereby contributes to obscuring a more holistic vision of healing. In this regard, while the Brazilian admixture of African, Catholic, spiritist and indigenous traditions has produced a social understanding of healing to some extent, this has been understood much more in terms of patronage networks operating within the background of an emphasis on individual health. The result has been a rather skewed Umbandist theology of healing that has been unable to integrate the individual and society within a more holistic framework. I suggest that this failure can be attributed in part to the idolatrous element operative in Umbanda.

Idolatry, as used here, follows Tillich's definition regarding the elevation of any preliminary concern to ultimacy (1951: 13; cf. Smith 1987). Clearly, at both the specialist and lay levels, there is some agreement that Umbanda is a religious innovation specific to Brazil, that the transplantation of Yoruban deities to Brazilian soil has, over the course of time, resulted in the Brazilians claiming them as their own, and that the spirit of Umbanda reflects the destiny of Brazil and foreshadows the universal potency of its religious power for the world (cf. Brown 1986: 48-51).[58] At the individual level, the beliefs and practices of Umbanda have, to some extent, allowed for the transition of Brazil as a rural to an urban nation, especially in the basic areas of fundamental human needs. At another level, however, the question needs to be asked: what have the Caboclos, Pretos Velhos and more distant Orixás done for the souls of their devotees and for the soul of the nation? What kind of healing has been delivered or experienced?

This problem relates to what Helmut Thielicke long ago attached to the development of a 'a nationalistic polytheism' (1963: 188). There are philosophical and theological problems with a multiplicity of gods, both of which have social and political implications. On the philosophical level, there is the recurring problem of the one and the many. A nationalistic religion held together by a pantheon of deities, each

---

'Christian authority is in no way like magical-satanic authority, for the latter can be bought but the former is solely a gift of God' (1989: 77). Simon Magus certainly could not purchase the power of the Holy Spirit, and neither could the seven sons of Sceva simply apply the name of Jesus and expect automatic (magical) results! (cf. Acts 8.9-24; 19.13-16). In contrast, it is certainly appropriate to assert that Umbanda 'sublimates Christianity in a higher magic' (Bastide 1978: 328).

58. I discuss the global diffusion of African traditional religiosity and the theological questions that are raised elsewhere (Yong 1998c: esp. 225-27).

demanding to be placated at one point or other, or each being concerned with the pleasures of corporeality, points to a disintegrating center pulled apart by conflicting interests. This same struggle is replicated in various levels all the way down to the personal and idiosyncratic clashes that occur between individuals. To get one's way, one has to appease specific deities in a manner appropriate to that deity's preferences. What this amounts to is that Umbandists acquire the traits of their warring gods, live in fear of human and divine retaliation, and act in a manner consistent with the characteristics of their spirits. In short, Olorum's removal from the realm of the human necessitates that lesser deities manage these affairs. The human relationship is therefore never with Olorum but with the unpredictable and often reckless forces of the many deities in the astral realm.[59]

Now this elaborate cosmological theology certainly has the merit of explaining both the diversity of competing human interests and the turmoil inherent in human life. It does not, however, provide any reasonable faith or assurance that one can obtain existential security. Further, it provides no theological resources to undergird the belief in the possibility of a better world nor does it do much to motivate the fight for such a world. In short, Umbandist theology supports only a limited vision of healing focused on the individual. The lines of influence of Umbandist deities are clearly demarcated, leading to a compartmentalized world. Healing can only come about piecemeal, and that without long-term guarantee. Ultimately, because of the ephemeral nature of health and the fickleness of the gods, emphasis calcifies on that which brings immediate relief and satisfaction above all else. Idolatry develops in that the finite is elevated above its reach. The gods have become no more than a means to get one's way.

In Pentecostalism, on the other hand, there is only one God with whom all have to deal. At the same time, there is also the clearly evidenced notion that 'God does not show favoritism' (Acts 10.34).[60]

---

59. This is admitted by no less than a Candomblé priest: 'Candomblé doesn't save anybody. Candomblé is no more than a duty, an obligation to the spirits, but the safest road is of course the path to God. He is the only one who is able to oppose the many evil things that we do. God sets us free, Candomblé does not. In my religion, you are always busy making offerings and serving the [lesser] spirits. In the Pentecostal church, they do that better' (quoted in Westra 1998: 129-30; brackets original).

60. While the Umbandist experience of the gods is theoretically available to all,

Also known as the doctrine of the priesthood of the believer, this egalitarianism is embraced and realized in far-reaching ways by the Pentecostal mentality. The result, however, has been that Pentecostal experience of the Spirit has led especially in the Latin American context to a heightened understanding of the practical effects of healing and liberation recognizable in everyday life. This transformation itself is evidence of the triumph of the divine over the demonic. In the words of Michel Bergmann, a Taizé sociologist,

> For the Pentecostal believer, one of the most appealing points is deliverance from fear. If this liberation is to be truly successful, the Pentecostal church has to have credibility. That can be demonstrated in visible signals, such as when someone quits drinking alcohol, when someone leads a monogamous life, and so forth. Only then is it convincing. This conviction is necessary to be freed from fear [of black magic]. The new life must remain visible, manifest in daily life (quoted in Westra 1998: 128; brackets original).

However, the Pentecostal encounter with the Holy Spirit not only produces the kind of transformation of soul that leads to righteous living (cf. Westra 1998: 128, 140), but also leads to the recognition that the reception of personal healing has far reaching implications for interpersonal and social reconciliation. Now, it should come as no surprise that Pentecostalism in Brazil also operates to some degree within the system of patronage given the history of Brazil as a clientelist state. As David Stoll reports, Pentecostal leaders in Brazil 'were joining political machines to obtain building and parade permits, neighborhood improvements, and government jobs for their members' (1990: 111). For both Pentecostals and Umbandists, patronage does, to some degree, meet the urgent physical and material needs of a marginalized population. The difference for Pentecostals, however, is the sense of community engendered among its members. Within the ranks of Pentecostalism, there is the daily mutual encouragement and exhortation not only that one can make sense and meaning out of life but that one can also aspire to and experience success as socially measured. For Umbandists, on the other hand, the sense of community remains much more like that between patron and client. The *centro* is frequented primarily when needs arise, and left to its own when things are going well. The predictable result is that 'Umbandistas consistently showed far less

it is practically confined to spirit–mediums and those elected by the spirits to mediumship.

concern than Pentecostals with occupational upward mobility and achievement' (Brown 1986: 194).

This in itself, as Brown notes, is inconclusive evidence regarding the gods. Taken as a whole, however, I suggest that the hedonistic concerns of the Umbandist pantheon allow for a transfer of similar values into the lives of devotees. While this does not necessarily mean that the Umbandist spirits are demonic entities, functionally at least, they occupy an idolatrous place in the Brazilian mentality and ethos. There is further evidence that such idolatry may be demonic in that while the Umbandist clearly provides an avenue of relief for individuals seeking resolution to existential problems, it is not productive of the kind of vision needed to transform the larger structures of the socio-political status quo. Instead, Umbandist theology serves to keep people in their place rather than putting them in a position to identify and deal with the root, systemic causes of their problems. In this case, the continued practice of Umbanda becomes the means by which servitude within the patronage system is ensured. The point is that such systems are demonic precisely because they hold their devotees captive within networks of destruction which do not allow escape.

Evidence for this can be accumulated from a few different sources. From a sociological perspective, Kaja Finkler, for example, argues that spiritist systems of healing lead to networks of patronage that are not subversive but retentive of the status quo (1987). Her assessment of Mexican spiritism is equally applicable to Umbanda. In more straight-forward theological language, demonic forces repress creative advance and temporal development. They are hostile to all modalities of creative transformation. It is fair to conclude, in the words of Ted Peters, that rituals and symbols that 'prevent others from gaining access to the God of love and salvation' are demonic (1994: 218). At the same time, of course, it should be said that the religious rituals and symbols of non-Christian faiths are not the only ones capable of keeping people from God; Christian ones work just as well in many instances. Having said that, however, Christians still need to be discerning about such things, and to raise the question whether or not such idolatry and demonism can be overcome.[61]

---

61. This is the truth behind the comment of my father, Revd Joseph Yong—a model classical Pentecostal, if there ever was or is one—that to allow the possibility that other religious traditions are redemptive in any measure is to allow the possibility that adherents and members of these traditions may, because of these

This leads to the third area in which I foresee Umbanda learning from Pentecostalism. Just as Pentecostals can learn something about the divine from the symbol of Exú, they may in turn also be able to teach Umbandists something about dealing with the Exú spirits of the world. Umbandists both fight against the Exús on the one hand and employ them in their daily struggle to survive on the other. Exús thus symbolize the stakes involved in the cosmic realm of the divine and the perennial hostilities featured in human relationships with each other and with the transcendent. The parallel notion in Pentecostalism is the doctrine of spiritual warfare, entailing both the human struggle with the divine on the one hand (Gen. 32.22-32), and against the demonic on the other (Eph. 6.11-18). I do not intend to focus here on the Pentecostal activity of exorcism as practiced upon individuals. Such occurs routinely in Brazilian Pentecostal churches. Rather, what I want to do here is bring together the Third Wave theory of territorial spirits and Clark Pinnock's notion of the eschatological 'battle of the gods'.

To some degree, the lesson is a mutual one for both Pentecostals and Umbandists that comes in the form of a challenge. It begins by asking the following question: Who among the gods has both the authority, power and interest in correcting the wrongs, reconciling hostilities, healing the world and its sufferings, and establishing justice, peace and righteousness? Does this better describe the God of Jesus Christ or perhaps one of the Orixás and their envoys? It may be objected that this is an unfair question on two grounds. First, Umbandists have never made such grandiose claims on behalf of any of the Orixás, much less the lesser deities. Second, within the scheme of Umbandist theology, these larger questions are either of secondary or of no concern to these second-ranked Orixás who are primarily symbols of the forces of nature. I insist, however, that this is not only a fair question but one that is by no means weighted on the side of Pentecostals. In fact, should Pentecostals take up the challenge and fail to deliver the goods, it could

experiences of redemption (however such be defined), forever remain captive within that tradition's grip, thus effectively eliminating the possibility that they may at some point see its limitations and their need for specifically Christian redemption. My response is that while this is a risk that cannot be avoided, that does not mean we adjust our theology (and pneumatology, etc.) to fit our missiology or to address our pragmatic concerns. Rather, we make missiological adjustments precisely in order to account for the diversity of existential situations that we encounter and explicate at various theological levels.

instead provide damning evidence that their own conception of the divine is just as faulty as that of anyone else's.

The challenge for Pentecostals comes down to what I call spiritual warfare waged on social and indeed cosmic territory. Pentecostals are firmly convinced that Christ has vanquished the Devil and his minions. Does such conviction carry over into the social and political world? Do Pentecostals believe strongly enough in the victory of Christ over the diabolical forces at work in human history to raise up an intercessory banner against all forms of injustice, oppression, unrighteousness and corruption? Can Pentecostals muster the kind of spiritual determination and social vision to fight against the gods of this age? Is the Pentecostal conviction in the power of Christ over the demonic large enough to believe for and work toward the liberation of human life from the powers of destruction (cf. Comblin 1989)?

This challenge therefore requires that Pentecostals take their stand as did Elijah on Mount Carmel against the prophets of Baal (1 Kgs 18.16-40). This is an urgent call to arms in the Brazilian context. Territorial spirits of destruction are continuously at work, from those inspiring governmental corruption to those operating in trans-national companies unleashed over the virgin Amazon forests. In both urban and rural contexts, there is a battle of the gods. Umbandists may invoke the Orixás, their envoys, or even Exús. Among those oriented toward Kardecism, innumerable spirit-guides will be among those available to be called upon. Will the spirits that respond reveal themselves as salvific or demonic? Or, if they remain silent, should that be interpreted as evidence of their impotence or as an indication that they have been misnamed?

This same complex of questions follow Pentecostals as they march into battle. For them, either the God of Jesus Christ is the solution to these many problems, or this is no God at all. This is part of the ambiguity of the life of faith. Which God will ultimately meet the needs, struggles and sufferings of modern Brazilians (cf. Hess 1992)? Will Pentecostals or Umbandists, or both, arise to the challenge and respond to the divine call to wage a comprehensive assault on the forces and spiritual strongholds that hold institutions and social structures in corruption and injustice? The gods of this age must be dethroned. Who is up to the task? The final verdict is not in. On the one side, Pentecostals are much more open today than before to this kind of warfare, yet such openness does not guarantee any action since spiritual warfare includes individual and socio-political acts of the will as much as it does the activity of intercessory prayer and fasting. On the other side, I am unsure that the Umbandist framework of belief can sustain this kind of activity. Perhaps the Orixás will prove me a false prophet or at least a lousy prognosticator. For the sake of the Brazilian people, I hope that they do.

There is much that remains to be proposed for discussion on the Christian side, including the strengths and weaknesses of the Umbandist doctrine of reincarnation, the relatively syncretistic nature of Umbanda and its attending theological implications, and the tradition's reliance on the principles and practices of spiritism. These matters point to the root issue that separates Christianity and Umbanda regarding the human predicament at its most fundamental level: is the human problem that of ignorance to be resolved by karma and evolution or is it sin that can only be removed by a mediating agent between God and humankind? This requires the introduction of christological categories and criteria. I raise these questions, however, not in order to launch into a second volume for this project at the present time, but to acknowledge that the Christian dialogue with Umbanda is far from exhausted by the preceding discussion. My focus thus far in this first round of the Pentecostal–Umbanda dialogue has been to examine the fertility of the pneumatological imagination derived from the Pentecostal–charismatic experience of the Holy Spirit when thrust into a theological engagement with a non-Christian faith. Clearly, Pentecostals have something unique to contribute to this dialogue that supplements the gains made previously. Equally clear is that the fulness of the Christian revelation in Christ has only been tangentially discussed so far. Given, however, that Pentecostals have an inexhaustible capacity to speak as the Spirit gives utterance, this conversation is far from over. Future discussions will provide opportunities for Pentecostals to share further how their own pneumatological approach to the issues of Christology can complement and challenge the Umbandist understanding of the person and work of Jesus Christ.[62]

62. Again, the evidence suggests mutual fertilization and transformation since Umbanda is not entirely bereft of Christology (cf. St Clair 1971: 190). This would be the case especially if the conversation involves those Umbandists who are more oriented toward Roustaingist Kardecism, after the Spiritist Jean-Baptiste Roustaing, a contemporary of Kardec (on Roustaingism in Umbanda, see Hess 1994: 78-80).

Chapter 9

THEOLOGICAL QUESTIONS INSTEAD OF A CONCLUSION

A Pentecostal life of the mind? Two generations ago, this would have been an oxymoron. Today, Pentecostals still place much more emphasis on life in the Spirit than on a life of the mind. But what about a life of the mind led by the Spirit? This is what I had envisioned I was searching for when I embarked on graduate studies almost ten years ago in 1989. Two masters degrees later, I was still committed to this ideal and left a brand new home and financially secure position in the state of Washington. With my wife and three young children, we moved across the country to further my quest by beginning doctoral studies. There were no guarantees when we left except an older, small apartment, job-hunting, and the continued quest. Many thought we were crazy, and at times, we were convinced that they were right! Well, things have providentially worked themselves out. We have not gone hungry, and our children have always had a roof (even if it was a leaky one) over their heads, been well-clothed, and had more than their share of toys. The PhD has been signed, sealed and delivered. But, if I were honest, I would have to admit that I am still unsure that I understand what a life of the mind led by the Spirit is all about. At the same time, maybe this uncertainty itself is a sign of the Spirit's presence and activity since none are able to tell where he is coming from nor where he is going (Jn 3.8). Is it the case, then, that a life of the mind led by the Spirit is precisely that uncanny intuition that hears the Spirit saying, 'This is the way; walk in it' (Isa. 30.21)? Is this Kierkegaard's 'leap of faith' even if it is not a leap completely into the dark? Is this not the knowing that transcends but does not transgress against rationality? There have been many in the history of the Christian Church who were feared to have lost their minds in their enthusiasm for things of the Spirit. Will I struggle to keep mine, or perhaps it is only by losing it that it can be gained...?

Introduction

The interreligious dialogue has only just begun. We have, however, completed the opening exchange between two traditions and are at a rest area along our own road to Emmaus.[1] It is therefore a good place to stop and chart the gains that have been made. I begin with ten theses that have emerged so far in this quest for a Pentecostal–charismatic theology of religions. The implications of these theses will then be explored. This project concludes by outlining the many directions that this study has opened up for further research and dialogue.

1. *A Pentecostal–Charismatic* Theologia Religionum: *Some Exploratory Theses*

Thesis One: A Pentecostal–charismatic theology of religions should complement rather than displace other Christian theological efforts to comprehend the non-Christian faiths.

Thesis Two: A Pentecostal–charismatic theology of religions should be founded on a robust trinitarianism that recognizes the Son and the Spirit as the two hands of the Father even while it avoids the popular and lay-level tripersonalistic understanding of the Trinity rejected by Oneness Pentecostals. Such a trinitarian theology allows for both christological and pneumatological approaches to the phenomenon of human religiosity, albeit in different respects.

Thesis Three: A Pentecostal–charismatic theology of religions should be capable of establishing the relationship between the economy of the Holy Spirit and the religions not only at a theological level, but also at a philosophical or metaphysical level of generality. At the former level, the religions can be understood as created by God through Word and Spirit. At the latter level, the religions can be understood to be dynamic historical realities that are in processes of transformation, and through which human beings potentially experience ultimate transformation.

Thesis Four: A Pentecostal–charismatic theology of religions should be able to provide a pneumatological account for the transformative character of human experience in general and the experience of ultimate

---

1.   This reference is, of course, to the city Cleopas and another disciple were on their way to when they were joined by the risen Christ. It is interesting to note, however, that modern scholarship has been unable to confirm the historicity of this city even though Luke clearly states that it was 'about seven miles from Jerusalem' (Lk. 24.13; cf. Liefeld 1984: 1054-55). My reference to this 'mystery city' is therefore an apt metaphor for our own contemporary interreligious journey: we may not know exactly where we are headed, but we sense the presence and leading of the Spirit who raised Jesus from the dead.

salvation in particular. This is retrieved from the Pentecostal–charismatic encounter with the Holy Spirit which in turn shapes their engagement with the world. Such a way of looking at the world—a pneumatological imagination—enables the instantiation of the divine symbol of the Holy Spirit in the human experience of the world. This is to acknowledge the divine presence and activity in creation. The former relates to the constitution of the harmonies of things in their own authenticity and integrity, and the latter relates to the constitution of things in their networks of relationships with others. Divine presence is evidenced by a thing's fulfilling its created purpose while divine activity can be said to occur when greater and greater degrees of harmony are realized in the processes of history. Non-Christian faiths can be regarded as salvific in the Christian sense when the Spirit's presence and activity in and through them are evident as hereby defined.

Thesis Five: A Pentecostal–charismatic theology of religions should also be able to account for processes that are not transformative but rather destructive. This it does by way of combining pneumatology and anthropology: it recognizes that human beings are free and that their lives are influenced not only by the Holy Spirit but also by other spiritually destructive fields of force symbolized by divine absence or the demonic. The pneumatological imagination enables the recognition of religions as a complex welter of spiritual forces, all of which are ambiguous in and of themselves but tend either toward the divine or the demonic, although never fully so in either case.

Thesis Six: A Pentecostal–charismatic theology of religions should therefore provide a means by which to discern the divine from the demonic in the religions. The modality of the pneumatological imagination—from divine presence to divine activity to divine absence—provides *a* normative measure by which such discernment is exercised. The religious symbols, practices and doctrines of other faiths can be assessed as modalities which lead either to divine blessedness or to demonic condemnation and destruction.

Thesis Seven: A Pentecostal–charismatic theology of religions should be open to learning more about the world and the religions from the Spirit. Such epistemological openness is intrinsic to a genuine pneumatological orientation. This reflects both the fact that the Spirit leads fallible human beings into a greater and greater grasp of the truth and the fact that the Spirit is continuously at work in the world of religions and transforming them. Discerning the Spirit(s) in the religions is there-

fore always provisional, subject to both the enlargement of epistemological horizons and to the facts as revealed by the transformative work
of the Spirit.

Thesis Eight: A Pentecostal–charismatic theology of religions should
therefore free human beings for participation in the interreligious dialogue. The goal of such dialogues is not a mere agreement on similarities that ignores serious differences. Rather, the activity of apologetics needs to be included in acknowledging such conversations to be
in the service of the righteousness, peace and truth that characterize the
Kingdom of God. Dialogue is thus ultimately about providing the kind
of self-criticism that leads to the mutual and, ultimately, eschatological
transformation of religious traditions, including the Christian faith.

Thesis Nine: A Pentecostal–charismatic theology of religions should
also free human beings to follow the leading of the Spirit into the
world, to work with all those who bear the marks of the Spirit for the
transformation of the world and for the counteraction of demonic forces
in anticipation of the impending Kingdom of God. To the extent that
the religions are discerned to be working toward these objectives, they
can be acknowledged to be fulfilling their divine mandate for being.

Thesis Ten: A Pentecostal–charismatic theology of religions should,
finally, invigorate the proclamation of the Christian gospel even as it
recognizes the eschatological horizon of the Holy Spirit's presence and
activity. Dialogue as truth-seeking-encounters, service as labors-of-
Christian-love, and proclamation of the redemption of the world from
the forces of the demonic and of the reconciliation of the creation to the
creator through Jesus Christ, all need to be combined. In this way,
Christian faith in Christ is put to public test whereby the power of the
Holy Spirit can be demonstrated throughout the course of human history. Ultimately, however, no empirical evidence suffices to establish
the validity of Christian truth claims beyond doubt vis-à-vis that of
other religious traditions since such confirmation can only be obtained
at the eschaton. A pneumatological orientation to this reality is therefore able to embrace the ambiguities of history without succumbing to a
nihilistic relativism. Instead, it allows itself to be led by the Spirit who
is believed to have raised Christ from the dead and will do so also for
religious persons now and in the end.

2. *Implications of this Study*

The above theses report the provisional findings of this study. Allow me briefly to tease out three implications emerging from them.

First, recall the statement at the conclusion of Chapter 1 regarding this being a 'pneumatology of quest'. Such a pneumatology allows only a provisional certitude at every turn, beginning with the theological and metaphysical presuppositions and hypotheses, continuing with the interpretation of empirical data, and including (but not terminating at) the discernment of Spirit(s). Needless to say, nothing can be prejudged. This is not so much because our subject is pneumatology as it is that the creation of the world through Word and Spirit provides the open context within which human beings live and know.

Such provisional certitude pertains also to our knowledge and discernment of the non-Christian faiths (cf. Volf 1994). It may be that the Spirit's presence is evident only on Christian terms; but it may also be that the Spirit's presence and activity can be confirmed on grounds delineated by both traditions. Alternatively, it may be that the Spirit is here present in this religious symbol but not in that one, here active in this ritual but not in that one, here at work in this religious process but not in that one. Or perhaps the comparative process or conversation will reveal areas under the control of the demonic within either tradition. This of course, requires repentance and the righting of wrongs, much more so if Christians discover themselves to be guilty as has been the case in so many instances previously. But it also may be that there is a relative void of the Spirit's presence and activity in other traditions. Even in this case, however, who is to say that the Spirit's entrance into these traditions has not been providentially arranged through a genuine interreligious dialogical interchange?

Because of human fallibility, understanding the ways of the Spirit can never be an individualistic effort. A pneumatology of quest requires that discernment be subject to public examination, either for ratification or for correction. This is the reason for the interim nature of my concluding theses. They are hereby submitted to the review of my peers, colleagues and partners in Christian ministry generally, and Pentecostal-charismatic ministry specifically. As Lederle and Clark say,

> in the final event it is the Spirit himself who grants the people of God the ability to recognise in the lives of others the working of God (cf. Acts 10). Pentecostal theology may thus attempt to pinpoint criteria for doc-

trine and experience—but in the long run it will be that discernment
which is given the community of Spirit-filled believers at large which
will approve or disprove the matter (1983: 63; cf. McQueen 1995: 15-
16).

A second theological implication of the foregoing study relates to the
proposed criteria for discernment. According to the metaphysical hypothesis developed here, all things and events can and should be evaluated
both pneumatologically and christologically. In fact, a more thorough
understanding of any thing or event cannot be attained apart from the
acknowledgment and assessment of the contributions of both hands of
the Father. In this work, I have developed some criteria to test the
Spirit(s) by focusing on the character and nature of pneumatology. All
pneumatological criteria, however, have their corresponding christological dimension. The latter has not been seriously examined in this
project for two reasons. First, as previously noted, the dialogue between
Umbanda and Pentecostalism conducted in the preceding chapter is the
first of its kind. It seems right that the full implications of a pneumatological theology of religions should be allowed to exert themselves
before resorting to christological criteria. I suggested at the end of
Chapter 8 some other areas of dialogue which require the employment
of christological categories, and these will need to be brought into play
in future dialogues.

The second reason for delaying the application of Christology to this
dialogue is that the approach to other faiths proposed here is one of the
first to explore the viability of a theology of religions within a systematically developed pneumatological framework. Relatively new models
need to be severely tested on their own terms for their coherence,
plausibility and adaptability. It is best to proceed with such probation
piecemeal so that categorial confusion is kept to a minimum. There
comes a point in the application of the model that it is recognized to
have exhausted its ability to provide further insights. I did not sense that
to be the case in the above dialogue between Pentecostalism and
Umbanda. That said, however, at some point in any interreligious dialogue, Christians will need to correlate the findings provided by a
pneumatological approach with christological categories and criteria in
order to complete the dialogue and be faithful to the fully trinitarian
structure of their faith.

This said, I need to reiterate my commitment to Christology as an
essential feature of all things and events. There is no better way to do so

than by acknowledging my own theological inclusivism, following the
model developed by Clark Pinnock and John Sanders, among others.
Ultimately, as Gerald Finnegan indicates, I suspect that perhaps my
metaphysical intuitions have been so shaped by the Christian story that
I have thus far been unable to read reality other than through a trinitarian lens. In discussing the question of Jesus Christ as the unique or
only savior of the world, Finnegan comments that

> the uniqueness of all things historical and the ability to distinguish and
> evaluate such realities may be the underlying question here. We return
> here to intuition and the ancient question of the one and the many. For
> those who favor pluralism seem to be opting for multiplicity over unity,
> whereas those who accept the traditional understanding of Christian faith
> seem to presume the unity exists at a deeper level of reality, indeed at the
> deepest level, and multiplicity is a phenomenon which arises from it and
> returns to it in the end (1991: 149).

Clearly, my adherence to the metaphysical hypothesis of God as
creator of all things *ex nihilo* predisposes me ultimately toward a christological inclusivism within a trinitarian framework. For that reason, I
can understand the meaningfulness of ultimate salvation expressed in
the *Christ*-ian way and through the name of Jesus (cf. Surin 1983).

Yet the metaphysical hypothesis undergirding this study also provides for a 'pneumatological inclusivism' that enables me to defend
pluralism in terms of the created order. As a Pentecostal Christian, the
pneumatological imagination does make the world a much more adven-
turous place to live in, even as it frees me to look for evidence of both
hands of the Father in other religious traditions. In the long run, perhaps
the pneumatological imagination will require a fundamental reorientation of Christology. Karl Rahner suggests as much in reflecting on the
trinitarian and pneumatological framework of Eastern theology toward
the end of his life:

> Perhaps an Eastern theology will one day reverse this perspective [of
> Western christocentrism]. Because of the universal salvific will of God
> and in legitimate respect for all the major world religions outside of
> Christianity, it may perhaps make a pneumatology, a teaching of the
> inmost, divinizing gift of grace for all human beings (as an offer to their
> freedom), the fundamental point of departure for its entire theology, and
> then attempt from this point—and this is something that might be
> achieved only with considerable effort—to gain a real and radical under-
> standing of Christology. For a theology of this kind John 7:39 ('There
> was no Spirit as yet because Jesus had not yet been glorified') will

perhaps be less suitable and intelligible than scriptural passages which extol the universal salvific will of God and which let the Spirit speak through all the prophets and know that the Spirit has been poured out on all flesh (1988: 97-98).[2]

The third, and perhaps most important theological implication of this study is that the turn to pneumatology in the formation of a Christian theology of religions necessarily transforms the character of Christian theology for two related reasons. To begin with, if it is acknowledged that the Holy Spirit is at work perhaps even in the non-Christian religious traditions of humankind, it becomes incumbent on Christian theologians to cease ignoring other faiths in the doing of theology. The possible presence and activity of the Spirit in other traditions means the possible existence of theological insights in other traditions that may have a positive impact on Christian theology. To deny this latter possibility is to lapse to an extremely anemic pneumatology even on biblical grounds. Perhaps the pneumatological approach to other religions developed here can provide the impetus toward a theological appropriation of the insights of other traditions that has been suggested but rarely accomplished.[3]

Following from this, the universal presence and activity of the Holy Spirit speaks of the universality of truth. Christian theology that claims to be true and universally applicable cannot continue operating according to the parochial categories of a Western, institutionalized Christendom (cf. Stackhouse 1988). Theoretically, it is certainly possible and legitimate, from a Christian standpoint, to insist on divine revelation as being given in the form of the Hebrew Bible and the Christian Testament. Two caveats, however, should be registered. First, a pneumatological orientation cannot arbitrarily deny that other canonical traditions

---

2.   In this connection, see also Stan Burgess's suggestions about the value of bringing Eastern Orthodox pneumatology into dialogue with Pentecostalism (1991).

3.   For a valiant beginning effort, see Smart and Konstantine (1991). One of the more celebrated 'failures' to follow through with the program of deriving theological insights from other faiths is Wolfhart Pannenberg's three-volume *Systematic Theology* (1991, 1994, 1997). Whereas he clearly suggests in part one of the first volume that such is imperative for Christian theology at the present time, what we find throughout the second part and the remaining two volumes is a systematic and thoroughgoing engagement with the Christian tradition in a manner reminiscent of Barth! Pannenberg's *Systematic Theology* does not live up to the expectations generated in the theological community both by his methodological claims and by his previous work (e.g. 1971; cf. Bollinger 1982; Braaten 1988; Grenz 1989).

may also be divinely inspired in some way (cf. Dupuis 1977: 211-28).
Such must be the conclusion of an extended investigation, not an assumption at the beginning. Second, even to insist that Christian scripture is divinely inspired and normative does not do away with the
requirement for careful exegesis and interpretation of both the Christian
Bible and non-Christian canonical texts. Such processes inevitably involve the religio-cultural lenses of the interpreter and interpreting community in the hermeneutical spiral. To say that revelation is scriptural
does not obviate the reality that the revelation that counts—i.e. that
saves and transforms—emerges from the dialectical encounter between
the text (or ritual, or symbol, etc.) and the person-in-community (more
accurately, person with various levels of membership in multiple communities).[4] In the same way, Christian theology inevitably results from
the interface between Christian Scripture and the context of interpretation. In a multi-religio-cultural world, a Christian theology aware of the
universal and prevenient presence and activity of the Spirit cannot but
be open to the truths of the Spirit wherever they may be found. In that
sense, a pneumatological theology of religions will therefore both require and enable a reconstruction of Christian systematic theology that
engages the truths that are discovered in the global interreligious context.

4.   This is Henry Knight's primary error (1997). Knight clearly recognizes the
contextuality of all interpretation. But he seems unaware that it is a purely semantic
move to privilege the biblical narrative over the contemporary horizon. He is right
to insist on guarding revelation against 'cultural accommodation, ideological captivity, and reductionism' (1997: 165). But such comes about by playing out the dialectic between text and context rather than simply asserting the priority of the
former. It is unrealistic and self-deceiving to think oneself and one's community
able to preserve the priority of biblical revelation since it is precisely such mechanisms which allow the ideological captivity Knight fears. The pneumatological
dimension of revelation is precisely the open-endedness that temporally situated
beings negotiate. It is therefore better, and more accurate, to say that the form of
revelation is 'influenced by the cultures and histories in which it occurs... It is a
blend of human imagination and reflection and Divine...co-operative persuasion'
(Ward 1994: 343; cf. D'Costa 1994). The traditional Christian argument that general revelation leaves human beings without excuse (Rom. 1.20; cf. Oden 1998) is
valid not because general revelation is only damning, but because general revelation
imparts sufficient knowledge about the divine reality such that one neglects it to
one's peril. To say that human beings are unable to appropriate general revelation
salvifically due to total depravity is to go down the road to the kind of five-point
Calvinism that finds no resonance with the Pentecostal–charismatic experience.

In sum, a Pentecostal–charismatic theology of religions embraces the tensions between pneumatology and Christology, between inclusivism and exclusivism, between divine presence and divine absence. The explosion of the Pentecostal–charismatic movement attests to the vitality of its pneumatocentric spirituality and the promise of such spirituality for the wider ecumenism. I have therefore argued in this study that this imagination signifies a latent ability to engage religious 'others' theologically. If it is in fact true that meaningful, engaging and relevant theology has inevitably been founded upon authentic and vibrant spirituality, then Pentecostal theology has plenty of pneumatological capital to draw from and is therefore under obligation to provide the kind of reflection that matches its life and practice. This theological potency has led some observers to anticipate that Pentecostalism 'will play a prominent role in the next millennium's Christian vision' (Cleary 1997: 15). I suggest that this role includes the forging of a more holistic and trinitarian theology, one which gives proper place and emphasis to both Word and Spirit and that refuses to allow either to be dominated by the other. It is therefore correct to say that Pentecostal–charismatic imagination is empowered by the Spirit to insist on both singularity and multiplicity, unity and plurality, the one and the many. In the words of Peter Hodgson, 'I affirm a quest for a more radical pluralism, but let it be a pluralism of solidarity rather than of separation… Confidence in the possibility of mutual transformation through dialogue is properly grounded not in an optimistic humanism but in a realistic theology of spiritual presence: Spirit is the third, the Interpreter who interprets all in all' (1994: 306).

3. *Suggestions for Further Research*

This study should be considered to be nothing more than an important first step toward a much larger project. In the first place, I am in agreement with many current thinkers that anthropological, sociological, historical and psychological studies of religion need to be supplemented by theological analyses. Herein lies the potential not only for theological dialogue about religious traditions among representatives of these traditions but also critical dialogue between observers and careful students of traditions and their practitioners. Religion is, after all, about that which is of ultimate concern; the subject of God can thus never be only penultimate. Harvey Cox's theory of religion has led me to push the theological questions. While this query can never admit of a final answer, that does not justify its neglect.

Secondly, this study helps fill the relative dearth of reflection on a Christian theology of indigenous religious traditions in general. The dialogue with the major world religions has been underway for some time. Yet for the most part, indigenous traditions have continued to be understood within the framework of *praeparatio evangelica*—as preliminary to the gospel analogous to the way in which Hebrew religion was traditionally understood to have been preliminary to Christ. While I am agreement with this, to understand indigenous traditions *solely* on these terms leads to the kind of restrictive christological quests that continue to denigrate the Holy Spirit as having less-than-equal status as a trinitarian member.

Better, I think, to allow the pneumatological dimension to highlight the distinctive features of indigenous traditions before rushing into comparative analyses. This requires that each tradition be examined on a case by case basis. I have provided one example of such an assessment in comparing Pentecostalism and Umbanda in Brazil. Further dialogue between Umbandists and Christians is called for, one which involves or takes into consideration the ongoing relationship and discussions between Brazilian Jesuits and Umbandists. Perhaps this study will be a catalyst for some broader conversations between Christians, Umbandists and other Afro-Brazilian traditions as a whole.[5] Perhaps it will also stimulate thinking on a Christian theology of Umbanda within the broader framework of a theology of indigenous religious traditions.

Thirdly, in order to practice what I preach, I need to acknowledge the fallibility of my own analyses beginning with presuppositional and methodological issues. Perhaps other Pentecostals and charismatics remain unconvinced by my arguments, whether they be suspicious about my adopting the concept of a pneumatological imagination or even for my use of sources—biblical, Pentecostal, charismatic or otherwise. I hereby open myself to correction and present my ideas to the theological public for consumption and debate.

Further, I am sure that my categorial vision is severely inadequate despite efforts to be fully ecumenical in taking account of the global Pentecostal–charismatic movement. Better categories can and need to

---

5.   I am thinking here about the recent developments in Africa where African traditionalists, Muslims and Christians have begun multi-lateral conversations; see Nkulu-N'Sengha (1996).

be brought into play, some of which may be less abstract, others more so. Further, the probability is that in depth engagement with the broad diversity of religious traditions will demand both a flexible and adaptable categorial scheme. I hope this work will stimulate all interested parties, whether they be Pentecostals, charismatics, or those who are pneumatologically oriented, to think further about the viability of the categories proposed and how they may be best revised in service of the discipline of comparative theology and the interreligious dialogue.

Regarding the fallibility of my own proposals, finally, I need to clearly state that other means of theological discernment exist besides the more general phenomenological and symbolic methods of inquiry and the more specific Pentecostal-inspired intuitions I am applying here. I trust that this effort will encourage my Pentecostal and charismatic colleagues to open themselves to discerning the Spirit(s) in the world of religions, and to allow that gift to operate through them. In any case, it is clear that much further thought is needed in order for the Christian Church to even begin the kind of 'discernment of spirits' that is required for our contemporary experience of religious pluralism.

A fourth consequence of this study is that regardless of the outcome of my test case, it is only one case. Other comparative projects need to be undertaken, the most difficult and pressing of which may be that between Pentecostalism and shamanism in Korea. How Pentecostal spirituality compares and contrasts with folk traditions that are part of world religious traditions should also be examined. This kind of work needs eventually to engage the world religions themselves, especially if the discussions can focus on pneumatological themes. Peter Lee's relating Christian pneumatology to the Confucian idea of *Ch'i* comes to mind as one project worth pursuing immediately (see my comments in Chapter 4). Other undertakings may include updating the findings of a previous generation of scholars who sought to compare ideas of the Holy Spirit as found in the Islamic Qur'an with those in the Christian tradition. Other projects may query how a Pentecostal–charismatic pneumatology would or would not correlate with the Bliss (*-ānanda*) of the Hindu trinity, or whether or not Christian pneumatology can contribute toward a better understanding of the Buddhist doctrines of *anatta* (no self) or dependent co-origination.[6] Part of the objective of

6. I am already working on a follow-up manuscript tentatively titled *The Holy Spirit and Other Faiths*, whereby I engage each of the major religious traditions of the world from a pneumatological perspective.

this study is to encourage Christian thinkers from within and without the Pentecostal–charismatic movement to reconsider the viability of a pneumatological approach to the interreligious dialogue, and perhaps to reconceive *theologia religionum* along these lines (cf. Haire 1992).

Fifthly, I have introduced what has traditionally been a marginal subject in theology as a major part both of the pneumatological imagination of Pentecostals and charismatics and of this monograph, namely, the demonic. Much more theological reflection needs to be given to the reality symbolized by the demonic, and its relation to the divine. The above dialogue between Pentecostalism and Umbanda has helped me reformulate some of the questions regarding the demonic, but it has also raised many others in the process. For those committed to developing *theologia religionum* either in the direction of or in conjunction with liberation theology, the category of the demonic appears to be an important but largely missing link. On a related note, normative measures cannot be posited without contrasts or polar opposites. As repeatedly emphasized in Chapters 7 and 8, theological discernment of the Spirit(s) requires engaging both the Holy Spirit and other spirits including the demonic. In short, the category of the demonic is as necessary to pneumatology as the Holy Spirit is to demonology. The implications of this not only for theology of religions but also for the systematic reconstruction of Christian theology in the global context of the twenty-first century have yet to be seriously explored.

Sixthly, along the way to a Pentecostal–charismatic theology of religions, I have sought to bring the latest in Pentecostal–charismatic scholarship and thought into dialogue with the larger Christian and academic communities. Throughout, my focus has been on the doctrine of the Holy Spirit and on pneumatological issues related to Christian theology of religions and the interreligious dialogue. Clearly, what has been said on these topics is far from exhaustive, not only in term of theology, but also perhaps in terms of religious studies and even philosophy and metaphysics, especially as I developed the latter themes in Chapter 4. Beyond that, however, there is much more that can be gleaned on other loci of theology from the ongoing intra-Christian dialogue between those within and without the Pentecostal–charismatic movement. A glimpse of how a pneumatological orientation to systematic theology reorders things methodologically and effects a transformation of theological content itself can be found in Clark Pinnock's *Flame of Love* (1996, see Chapter 6 above; cf. Rosato 1978 and Rusch 1987).[7]

Other clues to the difference a pneumatological imagination makes to the doing of systematic theology can be gleaned from this work. The most obvious one for Pentecostals and charismatics is the suggestion that theology has to take into account the musings about God or that which is transcendent that are undertaken in the non-Christian faiths.[8] No theology of religions or theology worth its name can be complete until all of its parts—truths from whatever their source, including that of other faiths—fit coherently and systematically together. This means that in the long run, Pentecostal–charismatic *summas* such as that of Guy Duffield and Nathaniel Van Cleave, French Arrington, Stanley Horton and company, or even J. Rodman Williams need to be updated in part through the interreligious dialogue. Perhaps the dialogical and heuristic method employed in this study can be refined and be found useful by the present or next generation of Pentecostal and charismatic theologians.

Seventh, and finally, I wish to conclude provisionally, where I began, by issuing a call for a pneumatology of quest. Emmaus itself may not be locatable here on earth; nevertheless our task as Christians is to walk along that road, and to believe that the Spirit will lead us to where we should go. The Spirit has gone before us, and calls us to hear what he is saying. Should we miss the mark, he will be there to assist us back onto the path. The road is full of treacherous curves, and dangerous cliffs

---

7.   In this connection, see also the call by Debra Moody of the Ohio Council of Churches for 'an interfaith theology of the Holy Spirit' (quoted in Heim 1998: 220).

8.   This is the one missing item from David Bundy's list of nine characteristics enumerated as 'essential components of a Pentecostal systematic theology' (1993: 106-107). They include (1) an understanding of Pentecostal experience and tradition; (2) an awareness of Pentecostal theological sources; (3) an awareness of Pentecostalism as a global phenomenon; (4) a consistent interaction with charismatic theology and theologians; (5) a knowledge of and engagement with the larger Christian tradition; (6) a thoroughly biblical foundation and approach; (7) missions as axiomatic; (8) the inclusion of an ethical component; and (9) a methodological and analytic presentation consistent with and appropriate to Pentecostal life, thought and values (read orality). Upon reflection on Bundy's inventory at the concluding juncture of this book, I am somewhat gratified to think that what is presented here meets all of his requirements—even if I did not embark on this journey with the specific intention of satisfying Bundy—with the one addition of having a pneumatological imagination rich enough to take into account the truths that reside in other religious traditions as revealed by the Spirit.

often appear suddenly, threatening to swallow us up as in an abyss. However, there is an intuition that just as often warns us of impending doom, and we swerve in time to avoid destruction and continue within the Spirit's field of force. The religions of the world can be either curves, cliffs or rest stops; but they are also dynamic realities whose contours undergo transformation from one day to the next. The Spirit, however, is at work in the religions, shaping and reshaping them, or else mollifying their resisting spirits. Should we not follow his lead and work with him to do the same?

BIBLIOGRAPHY

Abijole, Bayo
    1988   'St. Paul's Concept of Principalities and Powers in African Context',
        African Theological Journal 17: 118-29.

Adams, Daniel J.
    1991   'Reflections on an Indigenous Movement: The Yoido Full Gospel
        Church', The Japan Christian Quarterly 57: 36-45.
    1995   'Ancestors, Folk Religion, and Korean Christianity' in Mark R. Mullins
        and Richard Fox Young (eds.), *Perspectives on Christianity in Korea and
        Japan: The Gospel and Culture in East Asia* (Lewiston, NY: Edwin
        Mellen Press): 95-113.

Aigbe, Sunday
    1991   'Pentecostal Mission and Tribal People Groups', in Murray W. Dempster,
        Byron D. Klaus and Douglas Petersen (eds.), *Called and Empowered:
        Global Mission in Pentecostal Perspective* (Peabody, MA: Hendrickson):
        165-79.

Albrecht, Daniel E.
    1992   'Pentecostal Spirituality: Looking Through the Lens of Ritual', *Pneuma*
        14: 107-26.
    1997   'Pentecostal Spirituality: Ecumenical Potential and Challenge', *CPCR* 2
        [http://www.pctii.org/cybertab.html].
    1999   *Rites in the Spirit: A Ritual Approach to Pentecostal/Charismatic Spiri-
        tuality* (JPTSup, 17; Sheffield: Sheffield Academic Press).

Aldwinckle, Russell F.
    1982   *Jesus—A Savior or the Savior? Religious Pluralism in Christian Perspec-
        tive* (Macon, GA: Mercer University Press).

Anderson, Allan
    1990   'Pentecostal Pneumatology and African Power Concepts: Continuity or
        Change?', *Missionalia* 19: 65-74.
    1991   *Moya: The Holy Spirit in an African Context* (Pretoria: University of
        South Africa Press).
    1992   *Bazalwane: African Pentecostalism in South Africa* (Pretoria: University
        of South Africa Press).
    1993   'African Pentecostalism and the Ancestor Cult: Confrontation or Com-
        promise?', *Missionalia* 21: 26-39.

Anderson, Allan, and Samuel Otwang
    1993   *Tumelo: The Faith of African Pentecostals in South Africa* (Pretoria: Uni-
        versity of South Africa Press).

Anderson, Gerald H.

1996 'Theology of Religions: The Epitome of Mission Theology', in Willem Saayman and Klippies Kritzinger (eds.), *Mission in Bold Humility: David Bosch's Work Considered* (Maryknoll, NY: Orbis Books): 113-20.

Anderson, Gerald H., and Thomas E. Stransky (eds.)

1981 *Christ's Lordship and Religious Pluralism* (Maryknoll, NY: Orbis Books).

Anderson, Gordon L.

1990 'Pentecostals Believe in More Than Tongues', in Harold B. Smith (ed.), *Pentecostals from the Inside Out* (Wheaton, IL: Victor Books): 53-64.

Anderson, Norman

1984 *Christians and World Religions: The Challenge of Pluralism* (Downers Grove, IL: InterVarsity Press).

Anderson, Robert M.

1992 *Vision of the Disinherited: The Making of American Pentecostalism* (Peabody, MA: Hendrickson [1979]).

Anon.

1975 *Is Christianity the Only Way?* (Cleveland, TN: Pathway Press).

Archer, Kenneth J.

1998 'Pentecostal Babblings: The Narrative Hermeneutic of the Marginalized, Paper presented to 27th Meeting of the SPS (Church of God Theological Seminary, Cleveland, TN, 12–14 March).

Ariarajah, S. Wesley

1991 *Hindus and Christians: A Century of Protestant Ecumenical Thought* (Amsterdam: Editions Rodopi; Grand Rapids: Eerdmans).

1992 *The Bible and People of Other Faiths* (Maryknoll, NY: Orbis Books [1985]).

Arrington, French L.

1992 *Christian Doctrine: A Pentecostal Perspective*, I (Cleveland, TN: Pathway Press).

1993 *Christian Doctrine: A Pentecostal Perspective*, II (Cleveland, TN: Pathway Press).

1994 *Christian Doctrine: A Pentecostal Perspective*, III (Cleveland, TN: Pathway Press).

Austin-Broos, Diane J.

1997 *Jamaica Genesis: Religion and the Politics of Moral Orders* (Chicago: University of Chicago Press).

Badcock, Gary

1997a *Light of Truth and Fire of Love: A Theology of the Holy Spirit* (Grand Rapids: Eerdmans).

1997b 'Karl Rahner, the Trinity, and Pluralism', in Kevin J. Vanhoozer (ed.), *The Trinity in a Pluralistic Age: Theological Essays on Culture and Religion* (Grand Rapids: Eerdmans): 143-54.

Barnes, D.C.

1944 'Is There is Difference?', *The Church of God Evangel* (12 August): 6-7.

Barrett, David B.

1988 'Statistics, Global', in Stanley M. Burgess, Gary B. McGee and Patrick H. Alexander (eds.), *Dictionary of Pentecostal and Charismatic Movements* (Grand Rapids: Regency Reference Library): 810-30.

Barrett, David B., and Todd M. Johnson
1998   'Annual Statistical Table on Global Mission: 1998', *IBMR* 22: 26-27.
Bartleman, Frank
1980   *Azusa Street: The Roots of Modern-Day Pentecost* (Plainfield, NJ: Logos International [1925]).
Bascom, William
1972   *Shango in the New World* (Austin, TX: African and Afro-American Research Institute).
Bastide, Roger
1978   *The African Religions of Brazil: Toward a Sociology of the Interpenetration of Civilizations* (trans. Helen Sebba; Baltimore: The Johns Hopkins University Press).
Bayart, J.
1966   'The Cosmic Christ and Other Religions', *Indian Journal of Theology* 15: 145-49.
Becken, H. Jürgen
1989   'African Independent Churches as Healing Communities', in G.C. Oosthuizen *et al.*, *Afro-Christian Religion and Healing in Southern Africa* (Lewiston, NY: Edwin Mellen Press): 229-39.
Bennie, Christopher
1980   'Personal Meaning in the Charismatic Renewal Movement: A *Verstehen* Approach', in Victor C. Hayes (ed.), *Religious Experience in World Religions* (Bedford Park, Australia: The Australian Association for the Study of Religions): 60-77.
Berkhof, Louis
1975   *The History of Christian Doctrines* (Grand Rapids: Baker Book House [1937]).
Bernard, David K.
1984   *The New Birth* (Hazelwood, MO: Word Aflame Press).
1985   *Practical Holiness: A Second Look* (Hazelwood, MO: Word Aflame Press).
1992   *God's Infallible Word* (Hazelwood, MO: Word Aflame Press).
1996   *A History of Christian Doctrine* (2 vols.; Hazelwood, MO: Word Aflame Press).
1997   *Spiritual Gifts: A Practical Study with Inspirational Accounts of God's Supernatural Gifts to His Church* (Hazelwood, MO: Word Aflame Press).
Bernard, David K., *et al.*
1989   *Meet the United Pentecostal Church International* (Hazelwood, MO: Word Aflame Press; Pentecostal Publishing House).
Bernard, Loretta A., and David K. Bernard
1981   *In Search of Holiness: A Practical Guide for Today* (Hazelwood, MO: Word Aflame Press).
Binyon, Pamela M.
1977   *The Concepts of 'Spirit' and 'Demon': A Study on the Use of Different Languages Describing the Same Phenomena* (Studies in the Intercultural History of Christianity, 8; Bern: Peter Lang).
Bittlinger, Arnold
1990   'A "Charismatic" Approach to the Theme', *EcRev* 42: 107-13.

Blue, J. Ronald
    1981   'Untold Billions: Are They Really Lost?', *BSac* 138: 338-50.
Blumhofer, Edith L.
    1989   *The Assemblies of God: A Chapter in the Story of American Pente-costalism* (2 vols.; Springfield, MO: Gospel Publishing House).
    1993   *Aimee Semple McPherson: Everybody's Sister* (Grand Rapids: Eerdmans).
Bockmuehl, M.
    1996   Review of *Shekinah-Spirit: Divine Presence in Jewish and Christian Religion* (New York: Paulist Press, 1992), by Michael E. Lodahl, in *Themelios* 21.2: 28-29.
Boer, Harry R.
    1961   *Pentecost and Missions* (Grand Rapids: Eerdmans).
Bollinger, Gary
    1982   'Pannenberg's Theology of the Religions and the Claim to Christian Superiority', *Encounter* 43: 273-85.
Bolt, John
    1994   'Satan is Alive and Well in Contemporary Imagination: A Bibliographic Essay with Notes on "Hell" and "Spiritual Warfare" ', *Calvin Theological Journal* 29: 497-506.
Bolt, Peter
    1996   'Jesus, the Daimons and the Dead', in Anthony N.S. Lane (ed.), *The Unseen World: Christian Reflections on Angels, Demons, and the Heavenly Realm* (Grand Rapids: Baker Book House; Carlisle: Paternoster Press): 75-102.
Boros, Ladislaus
    1978   'Discernment of the Spirit', in Christian Duquoc and Casiano Floristan (eds.), *Charisms in the Church* (New York: Seabury): 78-86.
Bosch, David J.
    1987   'The Problem of Evil in Africa: A Survey of African Views on Witchcraft and the Response of the Christian Church', in Pieter G.R. de Villiers (ed.), *Like a Roaring Lion...: Essays on the Bible, the Church and Demonic Powers* (Pretoria: C.B. Power Bible Centre/University of South Africa): 38-62.
    1991   *Transforming Mission: Paradigm Shifts in Theology of Mission* (Maryknoll, NY: Orbis Books).
Bouchet, Jean-René
    1979   'The Discernment of Spirits', in Hans Küng and Jürgen Moltmann (eds.), *Conflicts About the Holy Spirit* (New York: Seabury): 103-106.
Boys, Mary C., *et al.*
    1997   'Authenticity without Demonization', *JES* 34: 334-55.
Braaten, Carl E.
    1987   'Christocentric Trinitarianism vs Unitarian Theocentrism: A Response to S. Mark Heim', *JES* 24: 17-21.
    1987–88   'The Meaning of Evangelism in the Context of God's Universal Grace', *Journal of the Academy for Evangelism* 3: 9-19.
    1988   'The Place of Christianity among the World Religions: Wolfhart Pannenberg's Theology of Religion and the History of Religions', in Carl E. Braaten and Philip Clayton (eds.), *The Theology of Wolfhart Pannenberg:*

Twelve American Critiques, with an Autobiographical Essay and Response (Minneapolis: Augsburg): 287-312.

Bracken, Joseph
1995   *The Divine Matrix: Creativity as Link Between East and West* (Maryknoll, NY: Orbis Books).

Bramlett, Bruce R.
1993   Review of *Shekinah-Spirit: Divine Presence in Jewish and Christian Religion* (New York: Paulist Press, 1992), by Michael E. Lodahl, in *JES* 30: 286-87.

Bramly, Serge
1994   *Macumba: The Teachings of Maria-Jose, Mother of the Gods* (San Francisco: City Lights Books [1977]).

Brouwer, Steve, Paul Gifford and Susan D. Rose
1996   *Exporting the American Gospel: Global Christian Fundamentalism* (London: Routledge).

Brown, Diana DeG.
1986   *Umbanda: Religion and Politics in Urban Brazil* (Ann Arbor, MI: UMI Research Press).

Brumana, Fernando Giobellina, and Elda González Martínez
1987   *Spirits from the Margin. Umbanda in São Paulo: A Study on Popular Religion and Social Experience* (Uppsala, Sweden: Acta Universitatis Upsaliensis).

Bruner, Frederick Dale
1970   *A Theology of the Holy Spirit: The Pentecostal Experience and the New Testament Witness* (Grand Rapids: Eerdmans).

Brusco, Elizabeth E.
1995   *The Reformation of Machismo: Evangelical Conversion and Gender in Colombia* (Austin: University of Texas Press).

Bufford, Rodger K.
1989   'Demonic Influence and Mental Disorders', *Journal of Psychology and Christianity* 8: 35-48.

Bundy, David
1993   'The Genre of Systematic Theology in Pentecostalism', *Pneuma* 15: 89-108.

Burdick, John
1993a   *Looking for God in Brazil: The Progressive Catholic Church in Urban Brazil's Religious Arena* (Berkeley: University of California Press).
1993b   'The Spirit of Rebel and Docile Slaves: The Black Version of Brazilian Umbanda', *Journal of Latin American Lore* 18: 163-87.
1993c   'Struggling Against the Devil: Pentecostalism and Social Movements in Brazil', in Virginia Garrard-Burnett and David Stoll (eds.), *Rethinking Protestantism in Latin America* (Philadelphia: Temple University Press): 20-44.

Burgess, Stanley M.
1984   *The Spirit and the Church: Antiquity* (Peabody, MA: Hendrickson).
1989   *The Holy Spirit: Eastern Christian Traditions* (Peabody, MA: Hendrickson).

1991   'Implications of Eastern Christian Pneumatology for Western Pentecostal
                Doctrine and Practice', in Jan A.B. Jongeneel (ed.), *Experiences of the
                Spirit: Conference on Pentecostal and Charismatic Research in Europe
                at Utrecht University, 1989* (Studies in the Intercultural History of Chris-
                tianity, 68; Frankfurt: Peter Lang): 23-34.

1997   *The Holy Spirit: Medieval and Reformation Traditions* (Peabody, MA:
                Hendrickson).

Burgess, Stanley M., Gary B. McGee and Patrick H. Alexander (eds.)

1988   *Dictionary of Pentecostal and Charismatic Movements* (Grand Rapids:
                Regency Reference Library).

Caldwell, Wayne E.

1983   'Angelology and Demonology: Intelligent Nonhuman Creatures', in
                Charles W. Carter (ed.), *A Contemporary Wesleyan Theology*, II (Grand
                Rapids: Francis Asbury Press): 1043-97.

Camargo, Cândido Procópio Ferreira de

1970   'Amérique latine—Latin America', *Social Compass* 17: 263-67.

Camps, Arnulf

1983   *Partners in Dialogue: Christianity and Other World Religions* (trans.
                John Drury; Maryknoll, NY: Orbis Books).

Cargal, Timothy B.

1993   'Beyond the Fundamentalist–Modernist Controversy: Pentecostals and
                Hermeneutics in a Postmodern Age', *Pneuma* 15: 163-87.

Carman, John B.

1994   *Majesty and Meekness: A Comparative Study of Contrast and Harmony
                in the Concept of God* (Grand Rapids: Eerdmans).

Caron, Charlotte

1993   *To Make and Make Again: Feminist Ritual Thealogy* (New York: Cross-
                road).

Carpenter, Harold R.

1995   'Tolerance or Irresponsibility: The Problem of Pluralism in Missions',
                Advance 31.2: 19.

Carruthers, Gregory H.

1990   *The Uniqueness of Jesus Christ in the Theocentric Model of the Christian
                Theology of World Religions: An Elaboration and Evaluation of the Posi-
                tion of John Hick* (Lanham, MD: University Press of America).

Carson, D.A.

1996   *The Gagging of God: Christianity Confronts Pluralism* (Grand Rapids:
                Zondervan).

Champion, Selwyn Gurney

1945   *The Eleven Religions and their Proverbial Love* (New York: E.P. Dutton).

Charlesworth, Max

1980   'On the Notion of Religious Experience', in Victor C. Hayes (ed.), *Reli-
                gious Experience in World Religions* (Bedford Park, Australia: The
                Australian Association for the Study of Religions): 16-24.

Chestnut, R. Andrew

1997   *Born Again in Brazil: The Pentecostal Boom and the Pathogens of
                Poverty* (New Brunswick, NJ: Rutgers University Press).

Ching, Julia
 1977 *Confucianism and Christianity: A Comparative Study* (Tokyo: Kodansha International).

Christian, William C.
 1987 *Doctrines of Religious Communities* (New Haven: Yale University Press).

Clanton, Arthur L.
 1970 *United We Stand: A History of Oneness Organizations* (Hazelwood, MO: Pentecostal Publishing House).

Cleary, Edward L.
 1997 'Introduction: Pentecostals, Prominence, and Politics', in Edward L. Cleary and Hannah W. Stewart-Gambino (eds.), *Power, Politics, and Pentecostals in Latin America* (Boulder, CO: Westview Press): 1-24.

Cleary, Edward L., and Hannah W. Stewart-Gambino (eds.)
 1997 *Power, Politics, and Pentecostals in Latin America* (Boulder, CO: Westview Press).

Clooney, Francis X.
 1993 *Theology After Vedanta: An Experiment in Comparative Theology* (Albany, NY: State University New York Press).

Cobb, John B., Jr
 1982 *Beyond Dialogue: Toward a Mutual Transformation of Christianity and Buddhism* (Philadelphia: Fortress Press).

Coffey, David
 1979 *Grace: The Gift of the Holy Spirit* (Manly, Australia: Catholic Institute of Sydney/St Patrick's College).

Cole, David
 1995 'Current Pentecostal/Ecumenical Tensions', *Ecumenical Trends* 24: 1-2, 9-15.

Collins, W. Duane
 1993–94 'An Assemblies of God Perspective on Demonology', Part I, *Paraclete* 27.4: 23-30; Part II, *Paraclete* 28.1: 18-22.

Camargo, Cândido Procópio Ferreira de
 1970 'Amérique latine—Latin America', *Social Compass* 17: 263-67.

Comblin, José
 1989 *The Holy Spirit and Liberation* (trans. Paul Burns; Maryknoll, NY: Orbis Books).

Congar, Yves
 1961 *The Wide World My Parish: Salvation and its Problems* (trans. Donald Atwater; Baltimore: Helicon Press).
 1983 *I Believe in the Holy Spirit* (trans. David Smith; 3 vols.; New York: Seabury; London: Geoffrey Chapman).
 1986 *The Word and the Spirit* (trans. David Smith; London: Geoffrey Chapman; San Francisco: Harper & Row).

Conway, Frederick J.
 1980 'Pentecostalism in Haiti: Healing and Hierarchy', in Stephen D. Glazier (ed.), *Perspectives on Pentecostalism: Case Studies from the Caribbean and Latin America* (Washington, DC: University Press of America): 7-26.

Cook, Guillermo
 1997 'Interchurch Relations: Exclusion, Ecumenism, and the Poor', in Edward

L. Cleary and Hannah W. Stewart-Gambino (eds.), *Power, Politics, and Pentecostals in Latin America* (Boulder, CO: Westview Press): 77-96.

Cooper, John Charles

1997   *The 'Spiritual Presence' in the Theology of Paul Tillich* (Macon, GA: Mercer University Press).

Corten, André

1997   'The Growth of the Literature on Afro-American, Latin American, and African Pentecostalism', *Journal of Contemporary Religion* 12.3: 11-34.

Covell, Ralph R.

1986   *Confucius, The Buddha, and Christ: A History of the Gospel in Chinese* (Maryknoll, NY: Orbis Books).

Coward, Harold

1985   *Pluralism: Challenge to World Religions* (Maryknoll, NY: Orbis Books).

Cox, Harvey

1972   *The Feast of Fools: A Theological Essay on Festivity and Fantasy* (New York: Perennial Library [1969]).

1995   *Fire from Heaven: The Rise of Pentecostal Spirituality and the Reshaping of Religion in the Twenty-First Century* (Reading, MA: Addison-Wesley).

1997   'Jesus and Pentecostals', in Leonard Swidler and Paul Mojzes (eds.), *The Uniqueness of Jesus: A Dialogue with Paul F. Knitter* (Maryknoll, NY: Orbis Books): 55-60.

Cracknell, Kenneth

1986   *Towards a New Relationship: Christians and People of Other Faith* (London: Epworth Press).

Cragg, Kenneth

1986   *The Christ and the Faiths: Theology in Cross-Reference* (London: SPCK).

Cree, Cornelia Scott

1994   'A Theology of Mission: God's Autonomous Invitation to Non-Covenant Individuals', Paper presented to the 24th Meeting of the SPS (Wheaton College, Wheaton, IL, 10–12 November).

Crockett, William (ed.)

1992   *Four Views on Hell* (Grand Rapids: Zondervan).

Cupitt, Don

1990   *Creation Out of Nothing* (London: SCM Press; Philadelphia: Trinity Press International).

da Matta, Roberto

1981   'The Ethic of Umbanda and the Spirit of Messianism: Reflections on the Brazilian Model', in Thomas C. Bruneau and Philippe Faucher (eds.), *Authoritarian Capitalism: Brazil's Contemporary Economic and Political Development* (Boulder, CO: Westview Press): 239-64.

Daneel, M.L.

1987   *Quest for Belonging: Introduction to a Study of African Independent Churches* (Gweru, Zimbabwe: Mambo Press).

1990   'Exorcism as a Means of Combating Wizardry: Liberation or Enslavement?', *Missionalia* 18: 220-47.

1993   'African Independent Church Pneumatology and the Salvation of All Creation', *IRM* 87: 143-66.

Davies, Paul
    1992   *The Mind of God: The Scientific Basis for a Rational World* (New York: Simon & Schuster).

Dayton, Donald W.
    1987   *Theological Roots of Pentecostalism* (Peabody, MA: Hendrickson).

D'Costa, Gavin
    1985   'Karl Rahner's Anonymous Christian—A Reappraisal', *Modern Theology* 1: 131-48.
    1986   *Theology and Religious Pluralism: The Challenge of Other Religions* (Oxford: Basil Blackwell).
    1994   'Revelation and Revelations: Discerning God in Other Religions Beyond a Static Valuation', *Modern Theology* 10: 165-83.

D'Costa, Gavin (ed.)
    1990   *Christian Uniqueness Reconsidered: The Myth of a Pluralistic Theology of Religions* (Maryknoll, NY: Orbis Books).

Dean, Thomas (ed.)
    1995   *Religious Pluralism and Truth: Essays on Cross-Cultural Philosophy of Religion* (Albany, NY: State University New York Press).

Del Colle, Ralph
    1992   'The Experience of the Divine', *Chicago Studies* 31: 290-300.
    1993   'Spirit-Christology: Dogmatic Foundations for Pentecostal–Charismatic Spirituality', *JPT* 3: 91-112
    1994   *Christ and the Spirit: Spirit-Christology in Trinitarian Perspective* (New York: Oxford University Press).
    1995   'Postmodernism and the Pentecostal/Charismatic Experience', Paper presented to the North American Congress on the Holy Spirit and World Evangelization (Academic Track), Orlando, FL, 27 July.
    1996a   'The Two-Handed God: Communion, Community and Contours for Dialogue', in Gerard S. Sloyan (ed.), *Religions of the Book* (Lanham, MD: University Press of America): 35-48.
    1996b   'Trinity and Temporality: A Pentecostal/Charismatic Perspective', *JPT* 8: 99-113.
    1996c   'Pentecostalism and Apocalyptic Passion: A Review of Steve Land's *Pentecostal Spirituality: A Passion for the Kingdom* (A Roman Catholic Response)', Paper presented to the 25th Annual Meeting of the SPS (Wycliffe College, Toronto, Ontario, 7–9 March).
    1997   'Reflections on the *Filioque*', *JES* 34: 202-17.

Delgado, Melvin, and Denise Humm-Delgado
    1982   'Natural Support Systems: Source of Strength in Hispanic Communities', *Social Work* 27: 83-89.

Dempster, Murray W.
    1987   'Pentecostal Social Concern and the Biblical Mandate of Social Justice', *Pneuma* 9: 129-63.
    1993   'Christian Social Concern in Pentecostal Perspective: Reformulating Pentecostal Eschatology', *JPT* 2: 51-64.

Dempster, Murray W., Byron D. Klaus and Douglas Petersen (eds.)
    1999   *The Globalization of Pentecostalism: A Religion Made to Travel* (Oxford: Regnum Books International).

Deng, Zhaoming
        1993   'Miracles or Misguided Faith? Stories of Healing in China', *Areopagus:*
                    A Living Encounter with Today's Religious World 6: 27-31.
De Ridder, Richard R.
        1978   'God and the Gods: Reviewing the Biblical Roots', *Missiology* 6: 11-28.
Dhavamony, Mariasusai
        1983   'The Holy Spirit and Hinduism', in *Credo in Spiritum Sanctum*, II (Vati-
                    can City: Libreria Editrice Vaticana): 1427-36.
        1998   *Christian Theology of Religions: A Systematic Reflection on the Christian*
                    Understanding of World Religions (Studies in the Intercultural History of
                    Christianity, 108; Bern: Peter Lang).
Dinoia, Joseph A.
        1992   *The Diversity of Religions: A Christian Perspective* (Washington: Catho-
                    lic University of America Press).
Dirkson, Murl Owen
        1984   'Pentecostal Healing: A Facet of the Personalistic Health System in
                    Pakal-Na, a Village in Southern Mexico' (PhD dissertation, University of
                    Tennessee).
Donovan, Peter
        1986   'Do Different Religions Share Moral Common Ground?', *RelS* 22: 367-
                    75.
Drescher, Hans-Georg
        1993   *Ernst Troeltsch: His Life and Work* (trans. John Bowden; Minneapolis:
                    Fortress Press).
Driver, Tom F.
        1991   *The Magic of Ritual* (New York: HarperSanFrancisco).
Droogers, André
        1995   'Identity, Religious Pluralism and Ritual in Brazil: Umbanda and Pente-
                    costalism', in Jan Platvoet and Karel van der Toorn (eds.), *Pluralism and*
                    Identity: Studies in Ritual Behaviour (Leiden: E.J. Brill): 91-113.
        1998   'Paradoxical Views on a Paradoxical Religion: Models for the Expla-
                    nation of Pentecostal Expansion in Brazil and Chile', in André Droogers,
                    Barbara Boudewijnse and Frans Kamsteeg (eds.), *More than Opium: An*
                    Anthropological Approach to Latin American and Caribbean Pentecostal
                    Praxis (Lanham, MD: Scarecrow Press): 1-34.
Duffield, Guy P., and Nathaniel M. Van Cleave
        1983   *Foundations of Pentecostal Theology* (Los Angeles: Life Bible College).
Dunn, James D.G.
        1993   'Baptism in the Holy Spirit: A Response to Pentecostal Scholarship on
                    Luke–Acts', *JPT* 3: 3-27.
        1997   *Jesus and the Spirit* (Grand Rapids: Eerdmans, 2nd edn).
        1998   *The Christ and the Spirit*. II. *Pneumatology* (Grand Rapids: Eerdmans).
Dunuwila, Rohan A.
        1985   *Saiva Siddhanta Theology: A Context for Hindu–Christian Dialogue*
                    (Delhi: Motilal Banarsidass).
Du Plessis, David J.
        1970   *The Spirit Bade Me Go* (Plainfield, NJ: Logos International, rev. edn).

Dupré, Louis
    1998   *Religious Mystery and Rational Reflection* (Grand Rapids: Eerdmans).

Dupuis, Jacques
    1966   'The Cosmic Christ in the Early Fathers', *Indian Journal of Theology* 15: 106-20.
    1977   *Jesus Christ and His Spirit: Theological Approaches* (Bangalore: Theological Publications in India).
    1991   *Jesus Christ at the Encounter of World Religions* (trans. Robert R. Barr; Maryknoll, NY: Orbis Books).
    1997   *Toward a Christian Theology of Religious Pluralism* (Maryknoll, NY: Orbis Books).

Durkheim, Emile
    1915   *The Elementary Forms of Religious Life* (trans. Joseph Ward Swain; New York: Free Press).

Eddy, Paul Rhodes
    1999   'John Hick's Pluralist Philosophy of World Religions: An Exposition and Response' (PhD dissertation, Marquette University).

Edwards, Jonathan
    1988   *The Works of Jonathan Edwards*, II (ed. Edward Hickman; Carlisle, PA: Banner of Truth Trust [1834]).

Eliade, Mircea
    1972   *Shamanism: Archaic Techniques in Ecstasy* (trans. Willard R. Trask; Princeton: Princeton University Press [1964]).
    1974   *Patterns in Comparative Religion* (trans. Rosemary Sheed; New York: New American Library [1958]).
    1987   *The Sacred and the Profane: The Nature of Religion* (trans. Willard R. Trask; New York: Harcourt Brace Jovanovich [1957]).

Ellington, Scott A.
    1996   'Pentecostalism and the Authority of Scripture', *JPT* 9: 16-38.

England, John C., and Alan J. Torrance (eds.)
    1991   *Doing Theology with the Spirit's Movement in Asia* (Singapore: ATESEA).

Ephirim-Donkor, Anthony
    1997   *African Spirituality: On Becoming Ancestors* (Trenton, NJ: Africa World Press).

Erickson, Millard J.
    1996   *How Shall They Be Saved? The Destiny of Those Who Do Not Hear of Jesus* (Grand Rapids: Baker Book House).

Ervin, Howard M.
    1984   *Conversion-Initiation and the Baptism in the Holy Spirit: An Engaging Critique of James D.G. Dunn's* Baptism in the Holy Spirit (Peabody, MA: Hendrickson).
    1987   *Spirit-Baptism: A Biblical Investigation* (Peabody, MA: Hendrickson).

Eutsler, Steve D.
    1993   'Why Are Not All Christians Healed?', *Paraclete* 27.2: 15-23.

Fackre, Gabriel
    1995   'Divine Perseverance', in John Sanders (ed.), *What About Those Who Have Never Heard? Three Views on the Destiny of the Unevangelized* (Downers Grove, IL: InterVarsity Press): 71-95.

Fallon, P.
1966   'The Cosmic Christ and the Asian Revolution', *Indian Journal of Theology* 15: 150-53.

Farah, Charles, Jr
n.d.   *From the Pinnacle of the Temple: Faith or Presumption?* (Plainfield, NJ: Logos International).

Fasholé-Luke, Edward W.
1974   'Ancestor Veneration and the Communion of Saints', in Mark E. Glasswell and Edward W. Fasholé-Luke (eds.), *New Testament Christianity for Africa and the World: Essays in Honour of Harry Sawyerr* (London: SPCK): 209-21.

Faupel, William D.
1996a   *The Everlasting Gospel: The Significance of Eschatology in the Development of Pentecostal Thought* (JPTSup, 10; Sheffield: Sheffield Academic Press).
1996b   'Glossolalia as Foreign Language: An Investigation of the Early Twentieth Century Pentecostal Claim', *WesTJ* 31: 95-109.

Fee, Gordon D.
1991   *Gospel and Spirit: Issues in New Testament Hermeneutics* (Peabody, MA: Hendrickson).
1994   *God's Empowering Presence: The Holy Spirit in the Letters of Paul* (Peabody, MA: Hendrickson).

Fernando, Ajith
1987   *The Christian's Attitude Toward World Religions* (Wheaton, IL: Tyndale House).

Finkler, Kaja
1987   'Spiritualist Healing Outcomes and the Status Quo: A Micro and Macro Analysis', *Social Compass* 34: 381-95.

Finnegan, Gerald F.
1991   'Jesus as Saviour of the World', in Paul F. Knitter (ed.), *Pluralism and Oppression: Theology in World Perspective* (Lanham, MD: University Press of America): 141-50.

Fisch, Max H.
1983   'The Range of Peirce's Relevance', in Eugene Freeman (ed.), *The Relevance of Charles Peirce* (La Salle, IL: The Hegeler Institute): 11-37.

Fischer, Ulrich
1970   *Zur Liturgie des Umbandakultes: Eine Untersuchung zu den Kultriten oder Amtshandlungen der synkretistischen Neureligion der Umbanda in Brasilien* (Leiden: E.J. Brill).

Flasche, Rainer
1973   *Geschichte und Typologie afrikanischer Religiosität in Brasilien* (Marburg: Universitäts-Bibliothek Marburg-Lahn).

Ford, Josephine M.
1988   'The Social and Political Implications of the Miraculous in Acts', in Paul Elbert (ed.), *Faces of Renewal: Studies in Honor of Stanley M. Horton Presented on his 70th Birthday* (Peabody, MA: Hendrickson): 137-60.

Frankenberry, Nancy
    1987   *Religion and Radical Empiricism* (Albany, NY: State University New York Press).

Franklin, Stephen T.
    1993   'Theological Foundations for the Uniqueness of Christ as Hope and Judge', *Evangelical Review of Theology* 17: 29-53.

French, C.E.
    1947   'Christianity Among Religions', *The Church of God Evangel* (1 March): 5, 14.

Freston, Paul
    1994   'Popular Protestants in Brazilian Politics: A Novel Turn in Sect-State Relations', *Social Compass* 41: 537-70.
    1995   'Pentecostalism in Brazil: A Brief History', *Rel* 25: 119-33.

Friesen, J. Stanley
    1996   *Missionary Responses to Tribal Religions at Edinburgh, 1910* (New York: Peter Lang).

Gadamer, Hans-Georg
    1994   *Truth and Method* (trans. Joel Weinsheimer and Donald G. Marshall; New York: Continuum, 2nd rev. edn).

Gangadean, Ashok K.
    1995   'The Hermeneutics of Comparative Ontology and Comparative Theology', in Thomas Dean (ed.), *Religious Pluralism and Truth: Cross-Cultural Philosophy of Religions* (Albany, NY: State University New York Press): 225-46.

Garrett, Susan R.
    1989   *The Demise of the Devil: Magic and the Demonic in Luke's Writings* (Minneapolis: Fortress Press).

Gaxiola-Gaxiola, Manuel J.
    1991   'Latin American Pentecostalism: A Mosaic within a Mosaic', *Pneuma* 13: 107-30.

Geerts, Henri
    1990   'An Inquiry into the Meaning of Ritual Symbolism: Turner and Peirce', in Hans-Günter Heimbrock and H. Barbara Boudewijnse (eds.), *Current Studies in Rituals: Perspectives for the Psychology of Religion* (Amsterdam: Editions Rodopi): 19-32.

Geertz, Clifford
    1973   *The Interpretation of Cultures* (New York: Basic Books).

Geivett, R. Douglas, and W. Gary Phillips
    1995   'A Particularist View: An Evidentialist Approach', in Dennis L. Ockholm and Timothy R. Phillips (eds.), *More than One Way? Four Views on Salvation in a Pluralistic World* (Grand Rapids: Zondervan): 211-45, 259-70.

Gelpi, Donald L.
    1970   *Discerning the Spirit: Foundations and Futures of Religious Life* (New York: Sheed & Ward).
    1971   *Pentecostalism: A Theological Viewpoint* (New York: Paulist Press).
    1972   *Pentecostal Piety* (New York: Paulist Press).

1978   *Experiencing God: A Theology of Human Emergence* (New York: Paulist Press).

1984   *The Divine Mother: A Trinitarian Theology of the Holy Spirit* (Lanham, MD: University Press of America).

1988   *God Breathes the Holy Spirit in the World* (Wilmington, DE: Michael Glazier).

1992   'The Theological Challenge of Charismatic Spirituality', *Pneuma* 14: 185-97.

1994   *The Turn to Experience in Contemporary Theology* (New York: Paulist Press).

Gerloff, Roswith

1995   'The Holy Spirit and the African Diaspora', *JEPTA* 14: 85-100.

Gifford, Paul

1994   'Ghana's Charismatic Churches', *Journal of Religion in Africa* 24: 241-65.

Gill, Kenneth

1989   'Toward a Contextualized Theology for the Third World: The Emergence and Development of Jesus' Name Pentecostalism in Mexico' (PhD dissertation, University of Birmingham, UK).

Gillis, Chester

1989   *A Question of Final Belief: John Hick's Pluralistic Theory of Salvation* (New York: Macmillan).

Githieya, Francis Kimani

1997   *The Freedom of the Spirit: African Indigenous Churches in Kenya* (Atlanta: Scholars Press).

Glasser, Arthur F.

1981   'A Paradigm Shift? Evangelicals and Interreligious Dialogue', *Missiology* 9: 392-408.

Glazier, Stephen D.

1980   'Pentecostal Exorcism and Modernization in Trinadad, West Indies', in Stephen D. Glazier (ed.), *Perspectives on Pentecostalism: Case Studies from the Caribbean and Latin America* (Washington, DC: University Press of America): 67-80.

Glazier, Stephen D. (ed.)

1980   *Perspectives on Pentecostalism: Case Studies from the Caribbean and Latin America* (Washington, DC: University Press of America).

Goff, James R., Jr

1988   *Fields White unto Harvest: Charles F. Parham and the Missionary Origins of Pentecostalism* (Fayetteville, AR: University of Arkansas Press).

1991   'Initial Tongues in the Theology of Charles Fox Parham', in Gary M. McGee (ed.), *Initial Evidence: Historical and Biblical Perspectives on the Pentecostal Doctrine of Spirit Baptism* (Peabody, MA: Hendrickson): 57-71.

Goodman, Felicitas D.

1974   'Disturbances in the Apostolic Church: A Trance-Based Upheaval in Yucatán', in Felicitos D. Goodman, Jeannette H. Henney and Esther Pressel, *Trance, Healing, and Hallucination: Three Field Studies in Religious Experience* (New York: John Wiley & Sons): 227-364.

1976   'Shaman and Priest in Yucatán Pentecostalism', in Agehananda Bharati (ed.), *The Realm of the Extra-Human: Agents and Audiences* (The Hague: Mouton): 159-65.

Gorringe, Timothy J.
1990   *Discerning Spirit: A Theology of Revelation* (London: SCM Press; Philadelphia: Trinity Press International).

Gort, Jerald, *et al.* (eds.)
1989   *Dialogue and Syncretism: An Interdisciplinary Approach* (Amsterdam: Editions Rodopi; Grand Rapids: Eerdmans).

Green, Michael
1975   *I Believe in the Holy Spirit* (Grand Rapids: Eerdmans).
1981   *I Believe in Satan's Downfall* (Grand Rapids: Eerdmans).

Greenfield, Sidney M.
1987   'The Return of Dr Fritz: Spiritist Healing and Patronage Networks in Urban, Industrial Brazil', *Social Science and Medicine* 24: 1095-1108.

Grenz, Stanley J.
1989   'Commitment and Dialogue: Pannenberg on Christianity and the Religions', *JES* 26: 196-210.
1994   'Toward an Evangelical Theology of the Religions', *JES* 31: 49-65.

Griffin, David Ray
1991   *Evil Revisited: Responses and Reconsiderations* (Albany, NY: State University New York Press).

Griffiths, Paul J.
1991   *An Apology for Apologetics: A Study in the Logic of Interreligious Dialogue* (Maryknoll, NY: Orbis Books).
1993   'Modalizing the Theology of Religions', *JR* 73: 382-89.

Griffiths, Paul J., and Delmas Lewis
1983   'On Grading Religions, Seeking Truth, and Being Nice to People—A Reply to Professor Hick', *RelS* 19: 75-80.

Gros, Jeffrey
1987   'Confessing the Apostolic Faith from the Perspective of the Pentecostal Churches', *Pneuma* 9: 5-16.

Gruenler, Royce
1983   *The Inexhaustible God: Biblical Faith and the Challenge of Process Theism* (Grand Rapids: Baker Book House).

Guelich, Robert A.
1991   'Spiritual Warfare: Jesus, Paul and Peretti', *Pneuma* 13: 33-64.

Guisso, Richard W.I., and Chai-Shin Yu (eds.)
1988   *Shamanism: The Spirit World in Korea* (Berkeley: Asian Humanities Press).

Gullapalli, Vinayak
1981   'Establishing *Christu Samajamulu* in Unreached Communities of Andhra Pradesh India' (MA thesis, Church of God School of Theology, Cleveland, TN).

Gunter, W. Stephen, *et al.*
1997   *Wesley and the Quadrilateral: Renewing the Conversation* (Nashville: Abingdon Press).

Gunton, Colin
    1993   *The One, the Three and the Many: God, Creation and the Culture of Modernity* (Cambridge: Cambridge University Press).
Hackett, Rosalind I.J.
    1996   'New Directions and Connections for African and Asian Charismatics', *Pneuma* 18: 69-78.
Haight, Roger
    1979   *The Language and Experience of Grace* (New York: Paulist Press).
Haire, I. James M.
    1992   'Animism in Indonesia and Christian Pneumatology', in Jan A.B. Jongeneel *et al.* (eds.), *Pentecost, Mission and Ecumenism: Essays on Intercultural Theology: Festschrift in Honour of Professor Walter J. Hollenweger* (Studies in the Intercultural History of Christianity, 75; New York: Peter Lang): 177-88.
Hamar, Paul A.
    1980   *The Book of First Corinthians* (Springfield, MO: Gospel Publishing House).
Hammond-Tooke, W.D.
    1986   'The Aetiology of Spirits in Southern Africa', *African Studies* 45: 157-70.
Harrell, David Edwin, Jr
    1975   *All Things are Possible: The Healing and Charismatic Revivals in Modern America* (Bloomington: Indiana University Press).
Harris, R. Laird, Gleason L. Archer, Jr and Bruce K. Waltke (eds.)
    1980   *Theological Workbook of the Old Testament* (2 vols.; Chicago: Moody Press).
Hart, Ray L.
    1985   *Unfinished Man and the Imagination: Toward an Ontology and a Rhetoric of Revelation* (Atlanta: Scholars Press [1968]).
Hauerwas, Stanley, and Scott Saye
    1995   'Domesticating the Spirit: Eldin Villafañe's *The Liberating Spirit: Toward an Hispanic American Pentecostal Social Ethic'*, *JPT* 7: 5-10.
Healey, Joseph, and Donald Sybertz
    1996   *Towards an African Narrative Theology* (Maryknoll, NY: Orbis Books).
Heim, S. Mark
    1987   'Thinking about Theocentric Christology', *JES* 24: 1-16.
    1995   *Salvations: Truth and Difference in Religion* (Maryknoll, NY: Orbis Books).
    1998   'Elements of a Conversation', in S. Mark Heim (ed.), *Grounds for Understanding: Ecumenical Resources for Responses to Religious Pluralism* (Grand Rapids: Eerdmans): 208-23.
Heim, S. Mark (ed.)
    1998   *Grounds for Understanding: Ecumenical Resources for Responses to Religious Pluralism* (Grand Rapids: Eerdmans).
Hernando, James D.
    1992   'Discerning of Spirits', *Paraclete* 26.2: 6-9
Heron, Alasdair
    1980   'The *Filioque* Clause', in Peter Toon and James D. Spiceland (eds.), *One God in Trinity* (Westchester, IL: Cornerstone Books): 62-77.

Herskovits, Melville J.
    1937   'African Gods and Catholic Saints in New World Negro Belief', *American Anthropologist* 39: 635-43.

Hess, David J.
    1991   'On Earth as it is in Heaven: Spiritist Other Worldly Ethnographies', in Roberto Reis (ed.), *Toward Socio-Criticism: Selected Proceedings from the Conference 'Luso-Brazilian Literatures, a Socio-Critical Approach'* (Tempe, AZ: Center for Latin American Studies, Arizona State University): 219-28
    1992   'New Sciences, New Gods: Spiritism and Questions of Religious Pluralism in Latin America', in Gerard Behague *et al.*, *Competing Gods: Religious Pluralism in Latin America* (Providence: Thomas J. Watson Jr Institute for International Studies, Brown University): 26-40.
    1994   *Samba in the Night: Spiritism in Brazil* (New York: Columbia University Press).

Hesselgrave, David J.
    1990   'Christian Communication and Religious Pluralism: Capitalizing on Differences', *Missiology* 18: 131-38.

Hick, John
    1980   *God Has Many Names* (Philadelphia: Westminster Press).
    1981   'On Grading Religions', *RelS* 17: 451-67.
    1984   'Religious Pluralism and Absolute Claims', in Leroy S. Rouner (ed.), *Religious Pluralism* (Notre Dame: University of Notre Dame Press): 193-213.
    1989a   *An Interpretation of Religion: Human Responses to the Transcendent* (New Haven: Yale University Press).
    1989b   'Trinity and Incarnation in the Light of Religious Pluralism', in John Hick and Edmund S. Meltzer (eds.), *Three Faiths—One God: A Jewish, Christian, Muslim Encounter* (New York: State University New York Press): 197-210.
    1989c   'The Logic of God Incarnate', *RelS* 25: 409-23.
    1995   'A Pluralist View', in Dennis L. Ockholm and Timothy R. Phillips (eds.), *More Than One Way? Four Views on Salvation in a Pluralist World* (Grand Rapids: Zondervan): 27-59.

Hick, John (ed.)
    1977   *The Myth of God Incarnate* (London: SCM Press).

Hick, John, and Paul F. Knitter (eds.)
    1987   *The Myth of Christian Uniqueness: Toward a Pluralistic Theology of Religions* (Maryknoll, NY: Orbis Books).

Hiebert, Paul G.
    1985a   'Discerning the Work of God', in Cecil M. Robeck, Jr (ed.), *Charismatic Experiences in History* (Peabody, MA: Hendrickson): 147-63.
    1985b   'The Missiological Implications of an Epistemological Shift', *TSF Bulletin* (May–June): 12-18.

Hillman, Eugene
    1966   ' "Anonymous Christianity" and the Missions', *The Downside Review* 84: 361-79.

Hillstrom, Elizabeth L.
    1995   *Testing the Spirits* (Downers Grove, IL: InterVarsity Press).
Hocken, Peter
    1976   'The Significance and Potential of Pentecostalism', in Walter Hollen-
                weger *et al.*, *New Heaven? New Earth?: An Encounter with Pentecostal-
                ism* (Springfield, IL: Templegate): 15-68.
    1978   'The Charismatic Experience', *The Way* 18: 43-55.
    1989   'Signs and Evidence: The Need for Catholic–Pentecostal Dialogue on the
                Relationship between the Physical and Spiritual', *Pneuma* 11: 123-33.
Hocken, Peter C., *et al.*
    1994   'The Charismatic Movement', *Pneuma* 16: 167-270.
Hodges, Melvin L.
    1957   *Build My Church* (Springfield, MO: Gospel Publishing House).
    1977   *A Theology of the Church and its Mission: A Pentecostal Perspective*
                (Springfield, MO: Gospel Publishing House).
Hodgson, Peter C.
    1994   *Winds of the Spirit: A Constructive Christian Theology* (Louisville: West-
                minster/John Knox Press).
Hollenweger, Walter
    1972   *The Pentecostals: The Charismatic Movement in the Churches* (trans.
                R.A. Wilson; Minneapolis: Augsburg).
    1978   '*Creator Spiritus*: The Challenge of Pentecostal Experience to Pentecostal
                Theology', *Theology* 81: 32-40.
    1984   'All Creatures Great and Small: Towards a Pneumatology of Life', in
                David Martin and Peter Mullen (eds.), *Strange Gifts? A Guide to Charis-
                matic Renewal* (Oxford: Basil Blackwell): 41-53.
    1986   'Pentecostals and the Charismatic Movement', in Cheslyn Jones,
                Geoffrey Wainwright and Edward Yarnold (eds.), *The Study of Spiritu-
                ality* (New York: Oxford University Press): 549-54.
    1987   'Towards an History of Christianity', *IRM* 76: 526-56.
    1988   *Geist und Materie. III. Interkulturelle Theologie* (Munich: Kaiser Verlag).
    1991   'Priorities in Pentecostal Research: Historiography, Missiology, Herme-
                neutics and Pneumatology', in Jan A.B. Jongeneel (ed.), *Experiences of
                the Spirit: Conference on Pentecostal and Charismatic Research in
                Europe at Utrecht University 1989* (Frankfurt: Peter Lang): 7-22.
    1992   'The Critical Tradition of Pentecostalism', *JPT* 1: 7-17.
    1997   *Pentecostalism: Origins and Developments Worldwide* (Peabody, MA:
                Hendrickson).
    1998   'Fire from Heaven: A Testimony by Harvey Cox', *Pneuma* 20: 197-204.
Horst, Mark
    1986   'The Problem with Theological Pluralism', *The Christian Century* 5: 971-
                74.
Horton, Stanley M.
    1976   *What the Bible Says about the Holy Spirit* (Springfield, MO: Gospel Pub-
                lishing House).
Horton, Stanley M. (ed.)
    1995   *Systematic Theology* (Springfield, MO: Logion Press, rev. edn).

Howe, Gary Nigel
    1980   'Capitalism and Religion at the Periphery: Pentecostalism and Umbanda in Brazil', in Stephen D. Glazier (ed.), *Perspectives on Pentecostalism: Case Studies from the Caribbean and Latin America* (Washington, DC: University Press of America): 125-41.

Hoy, Albert L.
    1979   'The Holy Spirit in Exorcism', *Paraclete* 13.1: 9-13.

Hughes, Edward J.
    1986   *Wilfred Cantwell Smith: A Theology for the World* (London: SCM Press).

Huizer, Gerrit
    1987   'Health and Healing in Global Perspective: Should the Rich Learn from the Poor?', *Mission Studies* 6: 75-99.

Hummel, Charles E.
    1993   *Fire in the Fireplace: Charismatic Renewal in the Nineties* (Downers Grove, IL: InterVarsity Press, 2nd edn).

Hunt, Stephen
    1995   'Deliverance: The Evolution of a Doctrine', *Themelios* 21: 10-13.

Hunter, Harold D.
    1983   'Spirit Christology: Dilemma and Promise (1)', *HeyJ* 26: 127-40.
    1984   'What is Truth?' Paper presented to the 13th Annual Meeting of the SPS (Gordon-Conwell Theological Seminary, South Hamilton, MA, 15–17 November).
    1992   'Reflections by a Pentecostalist on Aspects of *BEM*', *JES* 29: 317-45.
    n.d.   Review of *Fire from Heaven: The Rise of Pentecostal Spirituality and the Reshaping of Religion in the Twenty-First Century* (Reading, MA: Addison-Wesley), by Harvey Cox, Research page of the Pentecostal–Charismatic Theological Inquiry International web site [http://www.pctii.org].

Ikegami, Yoshimasa
    1993   'Okinawan Shamanism and Charismatic Christianity', *The Japan Christian Quarterly* 59: 69-78.

Ireland, Rowan
    1980   'Getting It Right: The Everyday Experience of Pentecostalism and Spiritualism in a Northeast Brazilian Town', in Victor C. Hayes (ed.), *Religious Experience in World Religions* (Bedford Park, Australia: The Australian Association for the Study of Religions): 145-59.
    1991   *Kingdoms Come: Religion and Politics in Brazil* (Pittsburgh: University of Pittsburgh Press).
    1995   'Pentecostalism, Conversions, and Politics in Brazil', *Rel* 25: 135-45.

Irvin, Dale T.
    1995   ' "Drawing All Together in One Bond of Love": The Ecumenical Vision of William J. Seymour and the Azusa Street Revival', *JPT* 6: 25-53.

Isaacs, Marie E.
    1976   *The Concept of Spirit: A Study of Pneuma in Hellenistic Judaism and its Bearing on the New Testament* (London: Heythrop College).

Israel, Richard D., Daniel E. Albrecht and Randal G. McNally
    1993   'Pentecostals and Hermeneutics: Texts, Rituals and Community', *Pneuma* 15: 137-162.

Jayasooria, Denison, and Brian Hathaway
1990   'Spirit and Kingdom/The Kingdom Manifesto: A Charismatic, Pente-
        costal, Evangelical Dialogue on Kingdom Christianity', *Transformation*
        7.3: 5-11.

Jenkins, Ulysses Duke
1978   *Ancient African Religion and the African-American Church* (Jacksonville,
        NC: Flame International).

Jochim, Christian
1995   'The Contemporary Confucian-Christian Encounter: Interreligious or In-
        trareligious Dialogue?' *JES* 32: 35-62.

Johns, Cheryl Bridges
1993   *Pentecostal Formation: A Pedagogy Among the Oppressed* (JPTSup, 2;
        Sheffield: Sheffield Academic Press).
1996   'Healing and Deliverance: A Pentecostal Perspective', in Jürgen Molt-
        mann and Karl-Josef Kuschel (eds.), *Pentecostal Movements as an Ecu-
        menical Challenge* (Maryknoll, NY: Orbis Books): 45-50.

Johns, Donald A.
1991   'Some New Directions in the Hermeneutics of Classical Pentecostalism's
        Doctrine of Initial Evidence', in Gary B. McGee (ed.), *Initial Evidence:
        Historical and Biblical Perspectives on the Pentecostal Doctrine of Spirit
        Baptism* (Peabody, MA: Hendrickson): 145-67.

Johnson, Todd M.
1992   'Global Plans in the Pentecostal/Charismatic Tradition and the Challenge
        of the Unevangelized World, World A', in J.A.B. Jongeneel *et al.* (eds.),
        *Pentecost, Mission and Ecumenism: Essays on Intercultural Theology:
        Festschrift in Honour of Professor Walter J. Hollenweger* (Studies in the
        Intercultural History of Christianity, 75; New York: Peter Lang): 197-206.

Jones, James
1975   *The Spirit and the World* (New York: Hawthorn Books).

Kamsteeg, Frans
1991   'Pentecostal Healing and Power: A Peruvian Case', in A. Droogers,
        G. Huizer and H. Siebers (eds.), *Popular Power in Latin American Reli-
        gions* (Saarbrücken: Verlag Breitenbach): 196-218.

Kaplan, Steven
1995   'The Africanization of Missionary Christianity: History and Typology', in
        Steven Kaplan (ed.), *Indigenous Responses to Western Christianity* (New
        York: New York University Press): 9-28.

Kato, Byang H.
1975   'The Gospel, Cultural Context and Religious Syncretism', in J.D. Douglas
        (ed.), *Let the Earth Hear His Voice: Official Papers and Responses from
        the International Congress on World Evangelization, Lausanne, Switzer-
        land* (Minneapolis: World Wide Publications): 1216-23.

Keenan, John P.
1989   *The Meaning of Christ: A Mahāyāna Theology* (Maryknoll, NY: Orbis
        Books).
1995   *The Gospel of Mark: A Mahāyāna Reading* (Maryknoll, NY: Orbis Books).

Keith, Graham A.
1992   'Justin Martyr and Religious Exclusivism', in Andrew D. Clarke and

Bruce W. Winter (eds.), *One God, One Lord: Christianity in a World of Religious Pluralism* (Grand Rapids: Baker Book House; London: Paternoster Press): 161-85.

Kelsey, Morton T.
1972   *Encounter with God: A Theology of Christian Experience* (Minneapolis: Bethany).
1978   *Discernment: A Study in Ecstasy and Evil* (Mahwah, NJ: Paulist Press).

Kendrick, Klaude
1961   *The Promise Fulfilled: A History of the Modern Pentecostal Movement* (Springfield, MO: Gospel Publishing House).

Keshishian, Aram
1992   *Orthodox Perspectives on Mission* (Oxford: Regnum Books).

Khodr, Georg
1971   'Christianity in a Pluralistic World—The Economy of the Holy Spirit', *EcRev* 23: 118-28.

Khoury, Joseph
1983   'L'Esprit dans le Coran', *Credo in Spiritum Sanctum*, II (Vatican City: Libreria Editrice Vaticana): 1405-10.

Klootwijk, Eeuwout
1992   *Commitment and Openness: The Interreligious Dialogue and Theology of Religions in the Work of Stanley J. Samartha* (Zoetermeer, The Netherlands: Uitgeverij Boekencentrum).

Knight, Henry H. III
1993   'God's Faithfulness and God's Freedom: A Comparison of Contemporary Theologies of Healing', *JPT* 2: 65-89.
1997   *A Future for Truth: Evangelical Theology in a Postmodern World* (Nashville: Abingdon Press).

Knitter, Paul
1974   *Towards a Protestant Theology of Religions: A Case Study of Paul Althaus and Contemporary Attitudes* (Marburg: N.G. Elwert Verlag).
1978   'World Religions and the Finality of Christ: A Critique of Hans Küng's *On Being a Christian*', *Horizons: The Journal of the College Theology Society* 5: 151-64.
1979   'Jesus—Buddha—Krishna: Still Present?' *JES* 16: 651-71.
1985   *No Other Name? A Critical Survey of Christian Attitudes Toward the World Religions* (Maryknoll, NY: Orbis Books).
1987   'Theocentric Christology: Defended and Transcended', *JES* 24: 41-52.
1988   'Dialogue and Liberation: Foundations for a Pluralist Theology of Religions', *The Drew Gateway* 58: 1-53.
1989   'Missionary Activity in a Theocentric-Soteriocentric Approach to Dialogue', in Leonardo N. Mercado and James J. Knight (eds.), *Mission and Dialogue: Theory and Practice* (Manila: Divine Word Publications): 186-221.
1991   'A New Pentecost? A Pneumatological Theology of Religions', *Current Dialogue* 19: 32-41.
1994   'Christian Salvation: Its Nature and Uniqueness—An Interreligious Proposal', *New Theology Review* 7: 33-46

1995   *One Earth Many Religions: Multifaith Dialogue and Global Respon-sibility* (Maryknoll, NY: Orbis Books).

1996   *Jesus and the Other Names: Christian Mission and Global Responsibility* (Maryknoll, NY: Orbis Books).

Knox, Ronald A.

1994   *Enthusiasm: A Chapter in the History of Religion* (Notre Dame: University of Notre Dame Press [1950]).

Kohák, Erazim V.

1975   'Speaking of the Devil: A Modest Methodological Proposal', in Alan M. Olson (ed.), *Disguises of the Demonic: Contemporary Perspectives on the Power of Evil* (New York: Association Press): 48-56.

Kraemer, Hendrik

1938   *The Christian Message in a Non-Christian World* (London: International Missionary Council).

Kraft, Charles H.

1989   *Christianity with Power: Your Worldview and Your Experience of the Supernatural* (Ann Arbor, MI: Servant Publications; Vine Books).

1993   *Deep Wounds, Deep Healing: Discovering the Vital Link Between Spiritual Warfare and Inner Healing* (Ann Arbor, MI: Servant Publications; Vine Books).

Krieger, David

1991   *The New Universalism: Foundations for a Global Theology* (Maryknoll, NY: Orbis Books).

Kritzeck, James

1975   'Holy Spirit in Islam', in Edward D. O'Connor (ed.), *Perspectives on Charismatic Renewal* (Notre Dame: University of Notre Dame Press): 100-11.

Kruse, Heinz

1967   'Die "Anonymen Christen" exegetisch gesehen', *MTZ* 18: 2-29.

Küng, Hans

1965   'The World Religions in God's Plan of Salvation', *Indian Ecclesiastical Studies* 4: 182-222.

1967   *The Church* (trans. Ray and Rosaleen Ockenden; New York: Sheed & Ward).

1973   'Die Religionen als Frage an die Theologie des Kreuzes', *EvT* 33: 401-23.

1976   *On Being a Christian* (trans. Edward Quinn; Garden City, NY: Doubleday).

1987   'What is True Religion? Toward an Ecumenical Criteriology', in Leonard Swidler (ed.), *Toward a Universal Theology of Religion* (Maryknoll, NY: Orbis Books): 231-50.

Küng, Hans, and Karl-Josef Kuschel (eds.)

1993   *A Global Ethic: The Declaration of the Parliament of the World's Religions* (New York: Continuum).

Kydd, Ronald A.N.

1998a   *Healing Through the Centuries: Models for Understanding* (Peabody, MA: Hendrickson).

1998b   'A Retrospectus/Prospectus on Physical Phenomena Centered in the "Toronto Blessing" ', *JPT* 12: 73-81.

LaCugna, Catherine M.
  1991   *God For Us: The Trinity and Christian Life* (San Francisco: HarperSan-
          Francisco).
Lai, Pan-Chiu
  1994   *Towards a Trinitarian Theology of Religions: A Study in Paul Tillich's
          Thought* (Kampen: Kok).
Lampe, G.W.H.
  1977   *God as Spirit* (Oxford: Clarendon Press).
Land, Steven J.
  1993   *Pentecostal Spirituality: A Passion for the Kingdom* (JPTSup, 1; Shef-
          field: Sheffield Academic Press).
Lane, Anthony N.S. (ed.)
  1996   *The Unseen World: Christian Reflections on Angels, Demons, and the
          Heavenly Realm* (Grand Rapids: Baker Book House; Carlisle: Paternoster
          Press).
Langguth, A.J.
  1975   *Macumba: White and Black Magic in Brazil* (New York: Harper & Row).
Lartey, E.Y.
  1986   'Healing: Tradition and Pentecostalism in Africa Today', *IRM* 75: 72-81.
Laurentin, René
  1977   *Catholic Pentecostalism* (trans. Matthew J. O'Connell; Garden City, NY:
          Doubleday).
Lawless, Susan
  1980   ' "What Did She Say?" An Application of Peirce's General Theory of
          Signs to Glossolalia in the Pentecostal Religion', *Folklore Forum* 3: 23-37.
Leacock, Seth, and Ruth Leacock
  1972   *Spirits of the Deep: A Study of an Afro-Brazilian Cult* (Garden City, NY:
          Doubleday).
Lederle, Henry I.
  1987   'Better the Devil You Know? Seeking a Biblical Basis for the Societal
          Dimension of Evil and/or the Demonic in the Pauline Concept of the
          "Powers" ', in Pieter G.R. de Villiers (ed.), *Like a Roaring Lion...: Essays
          on the Bible, the Church and Demonic Powers* (Pretoria: C.B. Power
          Bible Centre/University of South Africa): 102-20.
  1988   *Treasures Old and New: Interpretations of 'Spirit-Baptism' in the Charis-
          matic Renewal Movement* (Peabody, MA: Hendrickson).
  1990   'The Spirit of Unity: A Discomforting Comforter: Some Reflections on
          the Holy Spirit, Ecumenism and the Pentecostal–Charismatic Move-
          ments', *EcRev* 42: 279-87.
Lederle, Henry I., and Mathew Clark
  1983   *What is Distinctive About Pentecostal Theology?* (Pretoria: University of
          South Africa).
Lee, Peter K.H.
  1988   'World Religions—Ecumenical Theology—Religious Studies in a Global
          Context', *Ching Feng* 31.1: 70-86.
  1994   'Dancing, *Ch'i*, and the Holy Spirit', in R.S. Sugirtharajah (ed.), *Fron-
          tiers in Asian Christian Theology: Emerging Trends* (Maryknoll, NY:
          Orbis Books): 65-79.

Lehmann, David
     1996   *Struggle for the Spirit: Religious Transformation and Popular Culture in
               Brazil and Latin America* (Cambridge: Polity Press).
Lerch, Patricia Barker
     1980   'Spirit Mediums in Umbanda Evangelizada of Porto Alegre, Brazil:
               Dimensions of Power and Authority', in Erika Bourguignon (ed.), *A
               World of Women: Anthropological Studies of Women in the Societies of
               the World* (New York: Praeger; J.F. Bergin): 129-59.
Lewis, Gilbert
     1980   *Day of Shining Red: An Essay on Understanding Ritual* (Cambridge:
               Cambridge University Press).
Lewis, I.M.
     1986   *Religions in Context: Cults and Charisma* (Cambridge: Cambridge University Press).
     1989   *Ecstatic Religion: A Study of Shamanism and Spirit Possession* (London:
               Routledge, 2nd edn).
Lewis, I.M. (ed.)
     1977   *Symbols and Sentiments: Cross-Cultural Studies in Symbolism* (London:
               Academic Press).
Liefeld, Walter L.
     1984   *The Expositor's Bible Commentary.* VIII. *Luke* (ed. Frank E. Gaebelein;
               Grand Rapids: Regency Reference Library): 797-1059.
Lindbeck, George
     1984   *The Nature of Doctrine: Religion and Theology in a Postliberal Age*
               (Philadelphia: Westminster Press).
Lindberg, Carter
     1975   'Mask of God and Prince of Lies: Luther's Theology of the Demonic', in
               Alan M. Olson (ed.), *Disguises of the Demonic: Contemporary Perspectives on the Power of Evil* (New York: Association Press): 87-103.
Lindbergh, Thomas
     1992   'The Holy Spirit—God at Work', *Paraclete* 26.3: 10-13.
Lindsell, Harold
     1975   'Universalism', in J.D. Douglas (ed.), *Let the Earth Hear His Voice: Official Papers and Responses from the International Congress on World
               Evangelization, Lausanne, Switzerland* (Minneapolis: World Wide Publications): 1206-13.
Linn, Matthew, and Dennis Linn
     1981   *Deliverance Prayer: Experiential, Psychological, and Theological Approaches* (New York: Paulist Press).
Lodahl, Michael E.
     1992   *Shekhinah/Spirit: Divine Presence in Jewish and Christian Religion* (New
               York: Paulist Press).
     1994   *The Story of God: Wesleyan Theology and Biblical Narrative* (Kansas
               City, MO: Beacon Hill Press).
Lonergan, Bernard J.F.
     1979   *Method in Theology* (Minneapolis: Seabury [1972]).

Long, Bruce
    1987   'Demons: An Overview', in Mircea Eliade (ed.), *The Encyclopedia of Religion*, IV (16 vols.; New York: Macmillan): 282-88.

Lord, Andrew M.
    1997   'Mission Eschatology: A Framework for Mission in the Spirit', *JPT* 11: 111-23.

Lossky, Vladimir
    1957   *The Mystical Theology of the Eastern Church* (London: James Clarke).

Ma, Julie
    1997   'A Comparison of Two Worldviews: Kankana-Ey and Pentecostal', in Wonsuk Ma and Robert P. Menzies (eds.), *Pentecostalism in Context: Essays in Honor of William W. Menzies* (JPTSup, 11; Sheffield: Sheffield Academic Press): 265-90.

Ma, Wonsuk
    1997   'A "First Waver" Looks at the "Third Wave": A Pentecostal Reflection on Charles Kraft's Power Encounter Terminology', *Pneuma* 19: 189-206.
    1998   'Toward an Asian Pentecostal Theology', *AJPS* 1: 15-41.

Macchia, Frank D.
    1992   'Sighs Too Deep for Words: Toward a Theology of Glossolalia', *JPT* 1: 47-73.
    1993   'Tongues as a Sign: Toward a Sacramental Understanding of Pentecostal Experience', *Pneuma* 15: 61-76.
    1994a   'The Spirit and Life: A Further Response to Jürgen Moltmann', *JPT* 5: 121-27.
    1994b   'Revitalizing Theological Categories: A Classical Pentecostal Response to J. Rodman Williams's *Renewal Theology*', *Pneuma* 16: 293-304.
    1995a   'Created Spirit Beings: Satan and Demons', in Stanley M. Horton (ed.), *Systematic Theology* (Springfield, MO: Logion Press, rev. edn): 194-213.
    1995b   'From Azusa to Memphis: Evaluating the Racial Reconciliation Dialogue Among Pentecostals', *Pneuma* 17: 208-18.
    1997   'Discerning the Spirit in Life: A Review of *God the Spirit* by Michael Walker', *JPT* 10: 3-28.
    Forthcoming   'The Secular and the Religious under the Shadow of the Cross: Implications in Blumhardt's Kingdom Spirituality for a Christian Response to World Religions', in Arvind Sharma (ed.), *Religion in a Secular City* (Festschrift H. Cox; Harrisburg, PA: Trinity International Press).

MacPherson, Camilia Gangasingh
    1996   *A Critical Reading of the Development of Raimon Panikkar's Thought on the Trinity* (Lanham, MD: University Press of America).

MacRobert, Iain
    1988   *The Black Roots and White Racism of Early Pentecostalism in the USA* (New York: St Martin's Press).

Malony, H. Newton, and A. Adams Lovekin
    1985   *Glossolalia: Behavioral Science Perspectives on Speaking in Tongues* (New York: Oxford University Press).

Mariz, Cecília Loreto
    1994   *Coping with Poverty: Pentecostals and Christian Base Communities in Brazil* (Philadelphia: Temple University).

Mariz, Cecília Loreto, and María das Dores Campos Machado
    1997   'Pentecostalism and Women in Brazil', in Edward L. Cleary and Hannah W. Stewart-Gambino (eds.), *Power, Politics, and Pentecostals in Latin America* (Boulder, CO: Westview Press): 41-53.

Marshall, Molly Truman
    1993   *No Salvation Outside the Church? A Critical Inquiry* (Lewiston, NY: Edwin Mellen Press).

Martin, Bernice
    1995   'New Mutations of the Protestant Ethic among Latin American Pentecostals', *Rel* 25: 101-17.

Martin, David
    1990   *Tongues of Fire: The Explosion of Protestantism in Latin America* (Oxford: Basil Blackwell).

Martin, M.-L.
    1975   *Kimbangu: An African Prophet and His Church* (Oxford: Basil Blackwell).

Martin, R.F.
    1988   'Discernment of Spirits, Gift of', in Stanley M. Burgess, Gary B. McGee and Patrick H. Alexander (eds.), *Dictionary of Pentecostal and Charismatic Movements* (Grand Rapids: Regency Reference Library): 244-47.

Martinson, Paul Varo
    1987   *A Theology of World Religions: Interpreting God, Self, and World in Semitic, Indian and Chinese Thought* (Minneapolis: Augsburg).
    1988   'The Protestant Church in Post-Mao China', *Ching Feng* 31: 3-23.

Maxwell, David
    1995   'Witches, Prophets and Avenging Spirits in the Second Christian Movement in North-East Zimbabwe', *Journal of Religion in Africa* 25: 309-39.

May, L. Carlyle
    1956   'A Survey of Glossolalia and Related Phenomena in Non-Christian Religions', *American Anthropologist* 58: 75-96.

McAlpine, Thomas H.
    1991   *Facing the Powers: What are the Options?* (Monrovia, CA: MARC).

McClung, L. Grant, Jr
    1990   'Pentecostal/Charismatic Understanding of Exorcism', in Peter Wagner and F. Douglas Pennoyer (eds.), *Wrestling Dark Angels: Toward a Deeper Understanding of Supernatural Forces in Spiritual Warfare* (Ventura, CA: Regal Books): 195-214.
    1991   'The Pentecostal/Charismatic Contribution to World Evangelization', in Gerald H. Anderson, James Phillips and Robert T. Coote (eds.), *Mission in the Nineteen 90s* (Grand Rapids: Eerdmans): 65-71.
    1993   'The Pentecostal "Trunk" must Learn from its 'Branches" ', *Evangelical Missions Quarterly* 29.1: 34-9.
    1994   'Pentecostal/Charismatic Perspectives on a Missiology for the Twenty-First Century', *Pneuma* 16: 3-10.
    1996   'Pentecostal/Charismatic Perspectives on Missiological Education', in J. Dudley Woodberry, Charles Van Engen and Edgar J. Elliston (eds.), *Missiological Education for the Twenty-First Century: The Book, the*

Circle, and the Sandals: Essays in Honor of Paul E. Pierson (Maryknoll, NY: Orbis Books): 57-66.

McConnell, D.R.
1988   *A Different Gospel: A Historical and Biblical Analysis of the Modern Faith Movement* (Peabody, MA: Hendrickson).

McDonnell, Killian
1979   'The Experience of the Holy Spirit in the Catholic Charismatic Renewal', in Hans Küng and Jürgen Moltmann (eds.), *Conflicts about the Holy Spirit* (New York: Seabury): 95-102.

1982   'The Determinative Doctrine of the Holy Spirit', *TTod* 39: 142-61.

1985   'A Trinitarian Theology of the Holy Spirit?', *TS* 46: 191-227.

McDonnell, Killian, and Catherine M. LaCugna
1988   'Returning from "The Far Country": Theses for a Contemporary Trinitarian Theology', *SJT* 41: 191-215.

McGee, Gary B.
1986   *This Gospel Shall Be Preached: A History and Theology of Assemblies of God Foreign Missions*, I (Springfield, MO: Gospel Publishing House).

1989   *This Gospel Shall Be Preached: A History and Theology of Assemblies of God Foreign Missions*, II (Springfield, MO: Gospel Publishing House).

1994a   'Saving Souls Or Saving Lives? The Tension Between Ministries of Word and Deed in Assemblies of God Missiology', *Paraclete* 28.4: 11-23.

1994b   'Pentecostal Missiology: Moving Beyond Triumphalism to Face the Issues', *Pneuma* 16: 275-81.

1996   Review of *Fire from Heaven: The Rise of Pentecostal Spirituality and the Reshaping of Religion in the Twenty-first Century* (Reading, MA: Addison-Wesley), by Harvey Cox, in *Missiology* 24: 421.

McGee, Gary B. (ed.)
1991   *Initial Evidence: Historical and Biblical Perspectives on the Pentecostal Doctrine of Spirit Baptism* (Peabody, MA: Hendrickson).

McGrath, Alistair E.
1995   'A Particularist View: A Post-Enlightenment Approach', in Dennis L. Ockholm and Timothy R. Phillips (eds.), *More Than One Way? Four Views on Salvation in a Pluralistic World* (Grand Rapids: Zondervan): 149-80.

McGregor, Pedro, and T. Stratton Smith
1967   *Jesus of the Spirits* (New York: Stein & Day).

McQueen, Larry R.
1995   *Joel and the Spirit: The Cry of a Prophetic Hermeneutic* (JPTSup, 8; Sheffield: Sheffield Academic Press).

Medcraft, John P.
1987   'The Roots and Fruits of Brazilian Pentecostalism', *Vox Evangelica* 17: 67-94.

Megenney, William W.
1992   'West Africa in Brazil: The Case of Ewe–Yoruba Syncretism', *Anthropos* 87: 459-74.

Menzies, Robert P.
1994   *Empowered for Witness: The Spirit in Luke–Acts* (JPTSup, 6; Sheffield: Sheffield Academic Press).

1995	'A Pentecostal Perspective on "Signs and Wonders" ', *Pneuma* 17: 265-78.

Menzies, William W.

1971	*Anointed to Serve: The Story of the Assemblies of God* (Springfield, MO: Gospel Publishing House).
1979	'Synoptic Theology: An Essay on Pentecostal Hermeneutics', *Paraclete* 13.1: 14-21.

Meynell, Hugo

1985	'The Idea of a World Theology', *Modern Theology* 1: 149-61.

Michel, Thomas

1983	'Criteria for Discerning the Movement of Holy Spirit in Islam', *Credo in Spiritum Sanctum*, II (Vatican City: Libreria Editrice Vaticana): 1411-26.

Middlemiss, David

1996	*Interpreting Charismatic Experience* (London: SCM Press).

Mills, Watson E. (ed.)

1986	*Speaking in Tongues: A Guide to Research on Glossolalia* (Grand Rapids: Eerdmans).

Minz, Lioba

1992	*Krankheit als Niederlage und die Rückkehr zur Stärke: Candomblé als Heilungsprozess* (Bonn: Holos Verlag).

Möller, F.P.

1987	'Pentecostal Perspectives on the Activity of Demonic Powers', in Pieter G.R. de Villiers (ed.), *Like a Roaring Lion...: Essays on the Bible, the Church and Demonic Powers* (Pretoria: C.B. Power Bible Centre/University of South Africa): 173-91.

Moltmann, Jürgen

1981a	*The Trinity and the Kingdom: The Doctrine of God* (trans. Margaret Kohl; San Francisco: Harper & Row).
1981b	'Theological Proposals towards the Resolution of the *Filioque* Controversy', in Lukas Vischer (ed.), *Spirit of God, Spirit of Christ: Ecumenical Reflections on the* Filioque *Controversy* (Geneva: World Council of Churches): 164-73.
1992	*The Spirit of Life: A Universal Affirmation* (trans. Margaret Kohl; London: SCM Press).
1994	'A Response to my Pentecostal Dialogue Partners', *JPT* 4: 59-70.
1996a	*The Coming of God: Christian Eschatology* (trans. Margaret Kohl; Minneapolis: Fortress Press).
1996b	'A Pentecostal Theology of Life', *JPT* 9: 3-15.

Moltmann, Jürgen, and Karl-Josef Kuschel (eds.)

1996	*Pentecostal Movements as an Ecumenical Challenge* (London: SCM Press; Maryknoll, NY: Orbis Books).

Montague, George T.

1974	*Riding the Wind: Learning the Ways of the Spirit* (Ann Arbor, MI: Word of Life).
1994	*Holy Spirit: Growth of a Biblical Tradition* (Peabody, MA: Hendrickson [1976]).

Moo, Douglas
    1988   'Divine Healing in the Health and Wealth Gospel', *Trinity Journal* 9: 191-209.

Moran, Gabriel
    1992   *Uniqueness: Problems or Paradox in Jewish and Christian Traditions* (Maryknoll, NY: Orbis Books).

Morse, Christopher
    1994   *Not Every Spirit: The Dogmatics of Christian Disbelief* (Valley Forge, PA: Trinity Press International).

Mountcastle, William W., Jr
    1978   *Religion in Planetary Perspective: A Philosophy of Comparative Religion* (Nashville: Abingdon Press).

Mouw, Richard J., and Sander Griffioen
    1993   *Pluralisms and Horizons: An Essay in Christian Public Philosophy* (Grand Rapids: Eerdmans).

Mubabinge, Bibolo
    1983   'La notion de l'Esprit-Saint et de la Trinité face à la tradition religieuse africaine', *Credo in Spiritum Sanctum*, II (Vatican City: Libreria Editrice Vaticana): 1437-54.

Mühlen, Heribert
    1978   *A Charismatic Theology: Initiation in the Spirit* (trans. Edward Quinn and Thomas Linton; London: Burns & Oates; New York: Paulist Press).

Mullins, Mark R.
    1990   'Japanese Pentecostalism and the World of the Dead: A Study in Cultural Adaptation in Iesu no Mitama Kyokai', *Japanese Journal of Religious Studies* 17: 353-74.
    1991   'Magic, Ancestors, and Indigenous Christianity', *The Japan Christian Quarterly* 57: 60-62.
    1994   'The Empire Strikes Back: Korean Pentecostal Mission in Japan', in Karla Poewe (ed.), *Charismatic Christianity as Global Culture* (Columbia: University of South Carolina Press): 87-102.

Mulrain, George M.
    1984   *Theology in Folk Culture: A Study of the Theological Significance of Haitian Folk Religion* (Studies in the Intercultural History of Christianity, 22; Frankfurt: Peter Lang).

Murphy, Joseph M.
    1994   *Working the Spirit: Ceremonies of the African Diaspora* (Boston: Beacon Press).

Nash, Ronald H.
    1994   *Is Jesus the Only Savior?* (Grand Rapids: Zondervan).

Nelson, Douglas J.
    1981   'For Such a Time as This: The Story of Bishop William J. Seymour and the Azusa Street Revival' (PhD dissertation, University of Birmingham, UK).

Nelson, P.C.
    1981   *Bible Doctrines* (Springfield, MO: Gospel Publishing House, rev. edn [1948]).

Netland, Harold

1987   'Exclusivism, Tolerance, and Truth', *Missiology* 15: 77-95.

1991   *Dissonant Voices: Religious Pluralism and the Question of Truth* (Grand Rapids: Eerdmans).

Neuner, Joseph

1968   'The Place of World Religions in Theology', *The Clergy Monthly* (March): 102-15.

Neuner, Joseph (ed.)

1967   *Christian Revelation and World Religions* (London: Burns & Oates).

Neville, Robert Cummings

1974   *The Cosmology of Freedom* (New Haven: Yale University Press).

1978   *Soldier, Sage, Saint* (New York: Fordham University Press).

1981   *Reconstruction of Thinking* (Albany, NY: State University New York Press).

1982   *The Tao and the Daimon: Segments of a Religious Inquiry* (Albany, NY: State University New York Press).

1989   *Recovery of the Measure: Interpretation and Nature* (Albany, NY: State University New York Press).

1991a   *A Theology Primer* (Albany, NY: State University New York Press).

1991b   *Behind the Masks of God: An Essay Toward Comparative Theology* (Albany, NY: State University New York Press).

1992   *God the Creator: On the Transcendence and Presence of God* (Albany, NY: State University New York Press [1968]).

1993a   *Eternity and Time's Flow* (Albany, NY: State University New York Press).

1993b   'Religious Studies and Theological Studies: The 1992 Presidential Address to the American Academy of Religion', *JAAR* 61: 185-200.

1995a   *Creativity and God: A Challenge to Process Theology* (Albany, NY: State University New York Press, rev. edn [1980]).

1995b   *Normative Cultures* (Albany, NY: State University New York Press).

1996   *The Truth of Broken Symbols* (Albany, NY: State University New York Press).

Newbigin, Lesslie

1989   'Religious Pluralism and the Uniqueness of Jesus Christ', *IBMR* 13: 50-4

Newport, John P.

1998   *The New Age Movement and the Biblical Worldview: Conflict and Dialogue* (Grand Rapids: Eerdmans).

Nicholls, Bruce J. (ed.)

1994   *The Unique Christ in Our Pluralist World* (Grand Rapids: Baker Book House; Carlisle: Paternoster Press).

Nkulu-N'Sengha, Mutombo

1996   'Interreligious Dialogue in Black Africa among Christianity, Islam, and African Traditional Religion', *JES* 33: 528-56.

Norris, Frederick W.

1994   'Gregory the Theologian and Other Religions', *Greek Orthodox Theological Review* 39: 131-40.

Novaes, Regina Celia Reyes

1994   'Pentecostal Identity in Rural Brazil', *Social Compass* 41: 525-35.

Ockholm, Dennis L., and Timothy R. Phillips (eds.)
    1995   *More Than One Way? Four Views of Salvation in a Pluralistic World* (Grand Rapids: Zondervan).

O'Connor, Edward D.
    1971   *The Pentecostal Movement in the Catholic Church* (Notre Dame: Ave Maria Press).

Oden, Thomas C.
    1998   'Without Excuse: Classical Christian Exegesis of General Revelation', *JETS* 41: 69-84.

O'Donovan, Wilbur
    1995   *Biblical Christianity in African Perspective* (Carlisle: Paternoster Press).

Ogden, Schubert M.
    1978   'Theology and Religious Studies: Their Difference and the Difference It Makes', *JAAR* 46.1: 3-15.
    1988   'Problems in the Case for a Pluralistic Theology of Religions', *JR* 68: 493-507.
    1992   *Is There Only One True Religion or Are There Many?* (Dallas: Southern Methodist University Press).

Ojo, Matthews A.
    1988   'Deeper Christian Life Ministry: A Case Study of the Charismatic Movements in Western Nigeria', *Journal of Religion in Africa* 18: 141-62.
    1995   'The Charismatic Movement in Nigeria Today', *IBMR* 19: 114-18.

Okorocha, Cyril
    1994   'The Meaning of Salvation: An African Perspective', in William A. Dyrness (ed.), *Emerging Voices in Global Christian Theology* (Grand Rapids: Zondervan): 59-92.

Oladipo, Caleb Oluremi
    1996   *The Development of the Doctrine of the Holy Spirit in the Yoruba (African) Indigenous Christian Movement* (New York: Peter Lang).

Olson, Alan M. (ed.)
    1975   *Disguises of the Demonic: Contemporary Perspectives on the Power of Evil* (New York: Association Press).

Olson, Ken
    1992   *Exorcism: Fact or Fiction?* (Nashville: Thomas Nelson).

Omari, Mikelle Smith
    1994   'Candomblé: A Socio-Political Examination of African Religion and Art in Brazil', in Thomas D. Blakely, Walter E.A. van Beek and Dennis L. Thomson (eds.), *Religion in Africa: Experience and Expression* (Provo, UT: Brigham Young University; London: James Currey; Portsmouth, NH: Heinemann/Reed): 135-59.

Oosthuizen, G.C.
    1968   *Post-Christianity in Africa: A Theological and Anthropological Study* (London: C. Hurst).
    1975   *Pentecostal Penetration into the Indian Community in Metropolitan Durban, South Africa* (Pretoria: Human Science Research Council).
    1992   *The Healer-Prophet in Afro-Christian Churches* (Leiden: E.J. Brill).

Oropeza, B.J.
    1995   *A Time to Laugh: The Holy Laughter Phenomenon Examined* (Peabody, MA: Hendrickson).

Ortiz, Renato
    1997   'Ogum and the Umbandista Religion', in Sandra T. Barnes (ed.), *Africa's Ogun: Old World and New* (Bloomington: Indiana University Press, 2nd edn): 90-102.

Osburn, Evert D.
    1989   'Those Who Have Never Heard: Have They No Hope?', *JETS* 32: 367-72.

Outler, Albert C.
    1989   'Pneumatology as an Ecumenical Frontier', *EcRev* 41: 363-74.

Paden, William E.
    1988   *Religious Worlds: The Comparative Study of Religion* (Boston: Beacon Press).

Pagels, Elaine
    1995   *The Origins of Satan* (New York: Random House).

Palma, Marta
    1985   'A Pentecostal Church in the Ecumenical Movement', *EcRev* 37: 223-29.

Panikkar, R.
    1964   *The Unknown Christ of Hinduism* (London: Darton, Longman & Todd).
    1973   *The Trinity and the Religious Experience of Man* (Maryknoll, NY: Orbis Books).
    1978   *The Intrareligious Dialogue* (New York: Paulist Press).
    1980   'Aporias in the Comparative Philosophy of Religion', *Man and World* 13: 357-83.
    1987a   'The Jordan, the Tiber, and the Ganges: Three Kairological Moments in Christic Self-Consciousness', in John Hick and Paul Knitter (eds.), *The Myth of Christian Uniqueness: Toward a Pluralistic Theology of Religions* (Maryknoll, NY: Orbis Books): 89-116.
    1987b   'The Invisible Harmony: A Universal Theory of Religion or a Cosmic Confidence in Reality?', in Leonard Swidler (ed.), *Toward a Universal Theology of Religion* (Maryknoll, NY: Orbis Books): 118-53.
    1993   *The Cosmotheandric Experience: Emerging Religious Consciousness* (Maryknoll, NY: Orbis Books).

Pannenberg, Wolfhart
    1971   *Basic Questions in Theology: Collected Essays*, II (trans. George H. Kehm; Philadelphia: Fortress Press).
    1991   *Systematic Theology*, I (trans. Geoffrey W. Bromiley; Grand Rapids: Eerdmans).
    1994   Systematic Theology, II (trans. Geoffrey W. Bromiley; Grand Rapids: Eerdmans).
    1997   Systematic Theology, III (trans. Geoffrey W. Bromiley; Grand Rapids: Eerdmans).

Paris, Arthur E.
    1982   *Black Pentecostalism: Southern Religion in an Urban World* (Amherst, MA: University of Massachusetts Press).

Parker, Stephen E.
    1996   *Led by the Spirit: Toward a Practical Theology of Pentecostal Discern-*
                ment and Decision Making (JPTSup, 2; Sheffield: Sheffield Academic
                Press).
Parratt, John K.
    1970   'Olorum and the High God Pattern', *Ghana Bulletin of Theology* 3: 1-10.
Parthenios, Patriarch of Alexandria
    1991   'The Holy Spirit', in Michael Kinnamon (ed.), *Signs of the Spirit: Official*
                Report of the Seventh Assembly of the World Council of Churches, Can-
                berra, Australia, 7–20 February 1991 (Geneva: WCC Publications; Grand
                Rapids: Eerdmans): 28-36.
Pate, Larry D.
    1991   'Pentecostal Missions from the Two-Thirds World', in Murray W. Demp-
                ster, Byron Klaus and Douglas Petersen (eds.), *Called and Empowered:*
                Global Mission in Pentecostal Perspective (Peabody, MA: Hendrickson):
                242-58.
Patterson, Richard D.
    1999   'The Old Testament Use of an Archetype: The Trickster', *JETS* 42.3:
                385-94.
Pearlman, Myer
    1937   *Knowing the Doctrines of the Bible* (Springfield, MO: Gospel Publishing
                House).
Peck, M. Scott
    1983   *People of the Lie: The Hope for Healing Human Evil* (New York: Touch-
                stone; Simon & Schuster).
Peirce, Charles Sanders
    1931   *Collected Papers of Charles Sanders Peirce*, I (eds. Charles Hartshorne
                and Paul Weiss; Cambridge: Harvard University Press).
    1934   *Collected Papers of Charles Sanders Peirce*, V (eds. Charles Hartshorne
                and Paul Weiss; Cambridge: Harvard University Press).
    1935   *Collected Papers of Charles Sanders Peirce*, VI (eds. Charles Hartshorne
                and Paul Weiss; Cambridge: Harvard University Press).
Pelikan, Jaroslav
    1971   *The Christian Tradition: A History of the Development of Doctrine*, I
                (Chicago: University of Chicago Press).
Penney, John Michael
    1997   *The Missionary Emphasis of Lukan Pneumatology* (JPTSup, 12; Shef-
                field: Sheffield Academic Press).
Pereira de Queiroz, Maria Isaura
    1989   'Afro-Brazilian Cults and Religious Change in Brazil', in James A. Beck-
                ford and Thomas Luckman (eds.), *The Changing Face of Religion* (SAGE
                Studies in International Sociology, 37; London: SAGE Publications): 88-
                108.
Peters, Ted
    1991   *The Cosmic Self: A Penetrating Look at Today's New Age Movements*
                (San Francisco: HarperSanFrancisco).
    1994   *Sin: Radical Evil in Soul and Society* (Grand Rapids: Eerdmans).

Petersen, Douglas
  1996   *Not by Might nor by Power: A Pentecostal Theology of Social Concern in Latin America* (Oxford: Regnum Books).
Pieris, Aloysius
  1986   'A Theology of Liberation in Asian Churches?' *Vidyajyoti* 50: 330-51.
  1995   'Prophetic Humor and the Exposure of Demons: Christian Hope in the Light of a Buddhist Exorcism', *East Asian Pastoral Review* 32: 178-91.
  1996   *Fire and Water: Basic Issues in Asian Buddhism and Christianity* (Maryknoll, NY: Orbis Books).
Pillay, Gerald J.
  1994   *Religion at the Limits: Pentecostalism Among Indian South Africans* (Pretoria: University of South Africa).
Pinnock, Clark H.
  1988   'The Finality of Jesus Christ in a World of Religions', in Mark A. Noll and David F. Wells (eds.), *Christian Faith and Practice in the Modern World: Theology from an Evangelical Point of View* (Grand Rapids: Eerdmans): 152-68.
  1990   'Toward an Evangelical Theology of Religions', *JETS* 33: 359-68.
  1992   *A Wideness in God's Mercy: The Finality of Jesus Christ in a World of Religions* (Grand Rapids: Zondervan).
  1993   'Evangelism and Other Living Faiths: An Evangelical Charismatic Perspective', in Peter Hocken and Harold D. Hunter (eds.), *All Together in One Place: Theological Papers from the Brighton Conference on World Evangelism* (JPTSup, 4; Sheffield: Sheffield Academic Press): 208-18.
  1995   'An Inclusivist View', in Dennis L. Ockholm and Timothy R. Phillips (eds.), *More Than One Way? Four Views of Salvation in a Pluralistic World* (Grand Rapids: Zondervan): 93-148.
  1996   *Flame of Love: A Theology of the Holy Spirit* (Downers Grove, IL: InterVarsity Press).
Pittman, Don A., Ruben L.F. Habito and Terry C. Muck (eds.)
  1996   *Ministry and Theology in Global Perspective: Contemporary Challenges for the Church* (Grand Rapids: Eerdmans).
Plüss, Jean-Daniel
  1996   Review of *Fire from Heaven: The Rise of Pentecostal Spirituality and the Reshaping of Religion in the Twenty-First Century* (Reading, MA: Addison-Wesley), by Harvey Cox, in *JEPTA* 16: 103-105.
Poewe, Karla (ed.)
  1994   *Charismatic Christianity as Global Culture* (Columbia: University of South Carolina Press).
Pollak-Eltz, Angelina
  1993   *Umbanda en Venezuela* (Caracas, Venezuela: Fondo Editorial Acta Cientifica Verezotana; Consorcio de Ediciones Capriles, C.A.).
Poloma, Margaret M.
  1989   *The Assemblies of God at the Crossroads: Charisma and Institutional Dilemmas* (Knoxville: University of Tennessee Press).
Pomerville, Paul A.
  1985   *The Third Force in Missions: A Pentecostal Contribution to Contemporary Mission Theology* (Peabody, MA: Hendrickson).

Pousson, Edward Keith
    1994   'A "Great Century" of Pentecostal/Charismatic Renewal and Missions', *Pneuma* 16: 81-100.

Prabhu, Joseph (ed.)
    1996   *The Intercultural Challenge of Raimon Panikkar* (Maryknoll, NY: Orbis Books).

Pratt, Thomas D.
    1991   'The Need to Dialogue: A Review of the Debate on Signs, Wonders, Miracles and Spiritual Warfare in the Literature of the Third Wave Movement', *Pneuma* 13: 7-32.

Pressel, Esther
    1974   'Umbanda, Trance, and Possession in São Paulo, Brazil', in Felicitas Goodman, Jeannette H. Henney and Esther Pressel, *Trance, Healing, and Hallucination: Three Field Studies in Religious Experience* (New York: John Wiley & Sons): 113-226.
    1977   'Negative Spirit Possession in Experienced Brazilian Umbanda Spirit Mediums', in Vincent Crapanzano and Vivian Garrison (eds.), *Case Studies in Spirit Possession* (New York: John Wiley & Sons): 333-64.
    1980   'Spirit Magic in the Social Relations between Men and Women (São Paulo, Brazil)', in Erika Bourguignon (ed.), *A World of Women: Anthropological Studies of Women in the Societies of the World* (New York: Praeger; J.F. Bergin): 107-28.

Price, Leslie
    1980   'What is Meant by Testing the Spirits?' *The Journal of the Academy of Religion and Psychical Research* 3: 210-13.

Proudfoot, Wayne
    1985   *Religious Experience* (Berkeley: University of California Press).

Pruitt, Raymond
    1981   *Fundamentals of the Faith* (Cleveland, TN: White Wing Publishing House).

Pulikottil, Paulson
    1998   'Pentecostalisms in Independent India', Paper presented to the Pentecostal World Conference (Seoul, Korea, 19–23 September).

Punt, Neal
    1980   *Unconditional Good News: Toward an Understanding of Biblical Universalism* (Grand Rapids: Eerdmans).

Purdy, Vernon L.
    1995   'Divine Healing', in Stanley M. Horton (ed.), *Systematic Theology* (Springfield, MO: Gospel Publishing House): 489-524.

Quebedeaux, Richard
    1983   *The New Charismatics II* (San Francisco: Harper & Row).

Raboteau, Albert J.
    1978   *Slave Religion* (New York: Oxford University Press).
    1986   'The Afro-American Traditions', in Ronald L. Numbers and Darrell W. Amundsen (eds.), *Caring and Curing: Health and Medicine in the Western Religious Traditions* (New York: Macmillan): 539-62.

Race, Alan

1982   *Christians and Religious Pluralism: Patterns in the Christian Theology of Religions* (Maryknoll, NY: Orbis Books).

Rahner, Karl

1966   'The Theology of the Symbol', in *idem*, *Theological Investigations,* IV (trans. Kevin Smyth; London: Darton, Longman & Todd): 221-52.

1968   *Spirit in the World* (trans. William Dych; New York: Herder & Herder)

1969   'Anonymous Christians', in *idem*, *Theological Investigations*, VI (trans. Karl and Boniface Kruger; Baltimore: Helicon Press; London: Darton, Longman & Todd): 390-98.

1970   *The Trinity* (trans. Joseph Donceel; New York: Herder & Herder).

1971a   'The Church as the Subject of the Sending of the Spirit', in *idem*, *Theological Investigations*, VII (trans. David Bourke; London: Darton, Longman & Todd; New York: Herder & Herder): 186-92.

1971b   'The Spirit that is All Over Life', in *idem*, *Theological Investigations*, VII (trans. David Bourke; London: Darton, Longman & Todd; New York: Herder & Herder): 193-201.

1974   'Anonymous Christianity and the Missionary Task of the Church', in *idem*, *Theological Investigations*, XII (trans. David Bourke; New York: Seabury): 161-80.

1976   'Observations on the Problem of the "Anonymous Christian" ', in *idem*, *Theological Investigations*, XIV (trans. David Bourke; New York: Seabury): 280-94.

1977   'Church, Churches, and Religions', in *idem*, *Theological Investigations*, X (trans. David Bourke; New York: Seabury [1973]): 30-49.

1979a   'Religious Enthusiasm and the Experience of Grace', in *idem*, *Theological Investigations*, XVI (trans. David Morland; New York: Crossroad): 35-51.

1979b   'Anonymous and Explicit Faith', in *idem*, *Theological Investigations*, XVI (trans. David Morland; New York: Crossroad): 52-59.

1979c   'The One Christ and the Universality of Salvation', in *idem*, *Theological Investigations*, XVI (trans. David Morland; New York: Crossroad): 199-226.

1981   'Jesus Christ in the Non-Christian Religions', in *idem*, *Theological Investigations*, XVII (trans. Margaret Kohl; New York: Crossroad): 39-50.

1982   *Foundations of Christian Faith: An Introduction to the Idea of Christianity* (trans. William V. Dych; New York: Crossroad).

1983a   'Christianity and the Non-Christian Religions', in *idem*, *Theological Investigations*, V (trans. Karl Kruger; New York: Crossroad [1966]): 115-34.

1983b   'On the Importance of the Non-Christian Religions for Salvation', in *idem*, *Theological Investigations,* XVIII (trans. Edward Quinn; New York: Crossroad): 288-95.

1983c   'Oneness and Threefoldness of God in Discussion with Islam', in *idem*, *Theological Investigations*, XVIII (trans. Edward Quinn; New York: Crossroad): 105-21.

1983d   'Experience of the Holy Spirit', in *idem*, *Theological Investigations*, XVIII (trans. Edward Quinn; New York: Crossroad): 189-210.

1988   'Aspects of European Theology', in *idem*, *Theological Investigations*, XXI (New York: Crossroad): 78-98.

Railey, James H., Jr, and Benny C. Aker

1995   'Theological Foundations', in Stanley M. Horton (ed.), *Systematic Theology* (Springfield, MO: Logion Press): 39-60.

Raiser, Konrad

1989   'The Holy Spirit in Modern Ecumenical Thought', *EcRev* 41: 375-87.

Ramachandra, Vinoth

1996   *The Recovery of Mission: Beyond the Pluralist Paradigm* (Grand Rapids: Eerdmans).

Raposa, Michael L.

1989   *Peirce's Philosophy of Religion* (Bloomington: Indiana University Press).

Razu, John Mohan

1991   'Signs of the Movement of the Spirit in People's Struggles—Toward a Fusion', in John C. England and Alan J. Torrance (eds.), *Doing Theology With the Spirit's Movement in Asia* (Singapore: ATESEA): 85-99.

Reat, N. Ross, and Edmund F. Perry

1991   *A World Theology: The Central Spiritual Reality of Humankind* (Cambridge: Cambridge University Press).

Reddin, Opal (ed.)

1989   *Power Encounter: A Pentecostal Perspective* (Springfield, MO: Central Bible College Press).

Reed, David A.

1975   'Aspects of the Origins of Oneness Pentecostalism', in Vinson Synan (ed.), *Aspects of Pentecostal–Charismatic Origins* (Plainfield, NJ: Logos International): 143-68.

1978   'The Origins and Development of the Theology of Oneness Pentecostalism in the United States' (PhD dissertation, Boston University).

1997   'Oneness Pentecostalism: Problems and Possibilities for Pentecostal Theology', *JPT* 11: 73-93

Rehbein, Franziska C.

1989   *Heil in Christentum und afro-brasilianischen Kulten: Ein Vergleich am Beispel des Candomblé* (Bonn: Berengässer).

Reno, R.R.

1995   *The Ordinary Transformed: Karl Rahner and the Christian Vision of Transcendence* (Grand Rapids: Eerdmans).

Reynolds, Blair

1990   *Toward a Process Pneumatology* (Selinsgrove, PA: Susquehanna University Press; London: Associated University Presses).

Reynolds, Ralph V.

1993   'Angels', in L.J. Hall and David K. Bernard (eds.), *Doctrines of the Bible* (Hazelwood, MO: Word Aflame Press): 83-106.

Richard, Lucien

1981   *What Are They Saying About Christ and World Religions?* (New York: Paulist Press).

Richard, Ramesh P.

    1994   *The Population of Heaven: A Biblical Response to the Inclusivist Position on Who Will Be Saved* (Chicago: Moody).

Richardson, Don

    1974   *Peace Child* (Glendale, CA: Regal Books; G/L Publications).

    1981   *Eternity in Their Hearts* (Ventura, CA: Regal Books).

Riedl, Johann

    1965   'Rom 2, 14 ff. und das Heil der Heiden bei Augustinus und Thomas', *Scholastik* 40: 189-213.

Riesenhuber, Klaus

    1964   'Der Anonyme Christ, Nach Karl Rahner', *ZKT* 86: 286-303.

Robeck, Cecil M., Jr

    1987   'David du Plessis and the Challenge of Dialogue', *Pneuma* 9: 1-4.

    1991   'William J. Seymour and "the Bible Evidence" ', in Gary M. McGee (ed.), *Initial Evidence: Historical and Biblical Perspectives on the Pentecostal Doctrine of Spirit Baptism* (Peabody, MA: Hendrickson): 72-95.

    1992   'The Social Concern of Early American Pentecostalism', in Jan A.B. Jongeneel *et al.* (eds.), *Pentecost, Mission and Ecumenism: Essays on Intercultural Theology: Festschrift in Honour of Professor Walter J. Hollenweger* (Studies in the Intercultural History of Christianity, 75; New York: Peter Lang): 97-106.

    1993   'A Pentecostal Reflects on Canberra', in Bruce J. Nicholls and Bong Rin Ro (eds.), *Beyond Canberra: Evangelical Responses to Contemporary Ecumenical Issues* (Oxford: Regnum Books): 108-20.

    1994a   'Evangelization, Proselytizing and Common Witness: A Pentecostal Perspective', Paper presented to the Roman Catholic–Pentecostal Dialogue (Kappel, Switzerland, 23 July).

    1994b   'Discerning the Spirit in the Life of the Church', in William R. Barr and Rena M. Yocum (eds.), *The Church in the Movement of the Spirit* (Grand Rapids: Eerdmans): 29-49.

    1994c   'Pentecostals and Visible Church Unity', *One World* (January–February): 11-14.

    1997a   'The Assemblies of God and Ecumenical Cooperation: 1920–1965', in Wonsuk Ma and Robert P. Menzies (eds.), *Pentecostalism in Context: Essays in Honor of William W. Menzies* (JPTSup, 11; Sheffield: Sheffield Academic Press): 107-50.

    1997b   'A Pentecostal Theology for a New Millennium', Paper presented to the 26th Annual Meeting of the SPS (Patten College, Oakland, CA, March 13–15).

    1999   'Pentecostals and Ecumenism in a Pluralistic World', in Douglas Petersen, Murray Dempster and Byron Klaus (eds.), *The Globalization of Pentecostalism: A Religion Made to Travel* (Oxford: Regnum Books International): 338-62.

Robeck, Cecil M., Jr (ed.)

    1985   *Charismatic Experiences in History* (Peabody, MA: Hendrickson).

Rogers, Delores J.

    1994   Review of *Shekinah-Spirit: Divine Presence in Jewish and Christian*

Religion (New York: Paulist Press, 1992), by Michael E. Lodahl, in *American Journal of Theology and Philosophy* 15: 103-8.

Rolim, Francisco Cartaxo
    1991   'Popular Religion and Pentecostalism', in Jacques van Nieuwenhove and Berma Klein Goldewijk (eds.), *Popular Religion, Liberation and Contextual Theology* (Kampen: Kok): 126-37.

Rosato, Philip J.
    1977   'Spirit Christology: Ambiguity and Promise', *TS* 38: 423-49.
    1978   'Called by God, in the Holy Spirit: Pneumatological Insights into Ecumenism', *EcRev* 30: 110-26.

Rose, Kenneth
    1996   *Knowing the Real: John Hick on the Cognitivity of Religions and Religious Pluralism* (New York: Peter Lang).

Rouget, Gilbert
    1985   *Music and Trance: A Theory of the Relations Between Music and Possession* (rev. and trans. Brunhilde Biebuyck; Chicago: University of Chicago Press).

Routledge, Robin
    1998   ' "An Evil Spirit from the Lord"—Demonic Influence or Divine Instrument?', *EvQ* 70: 3-22.

Royce, Josiah
    1968   *The Problem of Christianity* (2 vols.; Chicago: Henry Regnery [1913]).

Rubinstein, Murray A.
    1988   'Taiwan's Churches of the Holy Spirit', *The American Asian Review* 6: 23-58.

Ruokanen, Miikka
    1992   *The Catholic Doctrine of Non-Christian Religions According to the Second Vatican Council* (Leiden: E.J. Brill).

Rusch, William G.
    1978   'The Doctrine of the Holy Spirit in the Patristic and Medieval Church', in Paul D. Opsahl (ed.), *The Holy Spirit in the Life of the Church* (Minneapolis: Augsburg): 66-98.
    1987   'The Theology of the Holy Spirit and Pentecostal Churches in the Ecumenical Movement', *Pneuma* 9: 17-30.

Russell, Jeffrey Burton
    1988   *The Prince of Darkness: Radical Evil and the Power of Good in History* (Ithaca, NY: Cornell University Press).

Ruthven, Jon
    1990   'On the Cessation of the Charismata: The Protestant Polemic of Benjamin B. Warfield', *Pneuma* 12: 14-31.
    1993   *On the Cessation of the Charismata: The Protestant Polemic on Post-biblical Miracles* (JPTSup, 3; Sheffield: Sheffield Academic Press).

Rybarczyk, Ed
    1996   'Pentecostals and the Eastern Orthodox: Prayer as a Window for Self-understanding', Paper presented to the 25th Annual Meeting of the SPS (Wycliffe College, Toronto, Ontario, 7–9 March).

Ryle, John
    1988   'Miracles of the People: Attitudes to Catholicism in an Afro-Brazilian

Religious Centre in Salvador Da Bahia', in Wendy James and Douglas H. Johnson (eds.), *Vernacular Christianity: Essays in the Social Anthropology of Religion Presented to Godfrey Lienhardt* (Oxford: JASO; New York: Lillian Barber Press): 41-50.

Sajja, Ratna Kumar
    1992   'My Journey from Hinduism to Christianity' (MDiv thesis, Church of God School of Theology, Cleveland, TN).

Samartha, Stanley J.
    1974   'The Holy Spirit and People of Various Faiths, Cultures, and Ideologies', in Dow Kirkpatrick (ed.), *The Holy Spirit* (Nashville: Tidings): 20-39
    1990   'The Holy Spirit and People of Other Faiths', *EcRev* 42: 250-63.
    1991   *One Christ—Many Religions: Toward a Revised Christology* (Maryknoll, NY: Orbis Books).

Samuel, Vinay
    1999   'Pentecostalism as a Global Culture: A Response', in Douglas Petersen, Murray Dempster and Byron Klaus (eds.), *The Globalization of Pentecostalism: A Religion Made to Travel* (Oxford: Regnum Books International): 253-58.

Sanders, Cheryl J.
    1996   *Saints in Exile: The Holiness-Pentecostal Experience in African-American Religion and Culture* (New York: Oxford University Press).

Sanders, John (ed.)
    1995   *What About Those Who Have Never Heard? Three Views on the Destiny of the Unevangelized* (Downers Grove, IL: InterVarsity Press).

Sanders, John E.
    1988   'Is Belief in Christ Necessary for Salvation?', *EvQ* 60: 241-59.
    1992   *No Other Name: An Investigation into the Destiny of the Unevangelized* (Grand Rapids: Eerdmans).

Sawyerr, Harry
    1994   *The Practice of Presence: Shorter Writings of Harry Sawyerr* (ed. John Parratt; Grand Rapids: Eerdmans).

Schatzmann, Siegfried S.
    1987   *A Pauline Theology of Charismata* (Peabody, MA: Hendrickson).

Scheff, T.J.
    1979   *Catharsis in Healing, Ritual, and Drama* (Berkeley: University of California Press).

Schillebeeckx, Edward
    1978   'Questions on Christian Salvation of and for Man', in David Tracy, Hans Küng and Johann B. Metz (eds.), *Toward Vatican III: The Work that Needs to be Done* (Nijmegen: Concilium; New York: Seabury): 27-44.

Schineller, J. Peter
    1976   'Christ and Church: A Spectrum of Views', *TS* 37: 545-66.

Schlette, Heinz Robert
    1963   *Die Religionen als Thema der Theologie* (Freiburg: Herder).

Schoonenberg, Piet J.A.M.
    1975   'Trinity—The Consummated Covenant: Theses on the Doctrine of the Trinitarian God', *SR* 5: 112-16.

Schwarz, Hans
    1983   'Reflexion on the Work of the Spirit Outside the Church', *Credo in Spiritum Sanctum*, II (Vatican City: Libreria Editrice Vaticana): 1455-72.

Schweizer, Eduard
    1989   'On Distinguishing Between Spirits', *EcRev* 41: 406-15.

Sepúlveda, Juan
    1994   'The Pentecostal Movement in Latin America', in Guillermo Cook (ed.), *New Face of the Church in Latin America: Between Tradition and Change* (Maryknoll, NY: Orbis Books): 68-74.

Sharpe, Eric J.
    1986   *Comparative Religion: A History* (La Salle, IL: Open Court, 2nd edn).

Sheard, Robert B.
    1987   *Interreligious Dialogue in the Catholic Church Since Vatican II: An Historical and Theological Study* (Lewiston, NY: Edwin Mellen Press).

Shelton, James M.
    1991   *Mighty in Word and Deed: The Role of the Holy Spirit in Luke–Acts* (Peabody, MA: Hendrickson).

Sheppard, Gerald T.
    1984   'Pentecostalism and the Hermeneutics of Dispensationalism: Anatomy of an Uneasy Relationship', *Pneuma* 6: 5-33.
    1986   'The Nicean Creed, Filioque, and Pentecostal Movements in the United States', *Greek Orthodox Theological Review* 31: 401-16.

Shorter, Aylward
    1985   *Jesus and the Witchdoctor: An Approach to Healing and Wholeness* (London: Geoffrey Chapman; Maryknoll, NY: Orbis Books).

Shuman, Joel
    1997   'Toward a Cultural-Linguistic Account of the Pentecostal Doctrine of the Baptism in the Holy Spirit', *Pneuma* 19: 207-23.

Shuster, Marguerite
    1987   *Power, Pathology, Paradox: The Dynamics of Good and Evil* (Grand Rapids: Zondervan).

Sider, Ronald (ed.)
    1988   *Words, Works and Wonders: Papers from an International Dialogue Between the Pentecostal/Charismatic Renewal and Evangelical Social Action* (*Transformation* 5.4).

Silva, Manuel
    1991   'A Brazilian Church Comes to New York', *Pneuma* 13: 161-66.

Smart, Ninian
    1996   *Dimensions of the Sacred: An Anatomy of the World's Beliefs* (Berkeley: University of California Press).

Smart, Ninian, and Steven Konstantine
    1991   *Christian Systematic Theology in a World Context* (Minneapolis: Fortress Press).

Smith, John E.
    1995   *Experience and God* (New York: Fordham University Press [1968]).

Smith, Jonathan Z.
    1982   *Imagining Religion: From Jonestown to Babylon* (Chicago: University of Chicago Press).

Smith, Wilfred Cantwell
  1959   'Comparative Religion: Whither—and Why?', in Mircea Eliade and
          Joseph M. Kitagawa (eds.), *The History of Religions: Essays in Metho-
          dology* (Chicago: University of Chicago Press): 31-58.
  1962   *The Meaning and End of Religion* (New York: Macmillan).
  1981   *Towards a World Theology: Faith and the Comparative History of Reli-
          gion* (Philadelphia: Westminster Press).
  1987   'Idolatry in Comparative Perspective', in John Hick and Paul Knitter
          (eds.), *The Myth of Christian Uniqueness: Toward a Pluralistic Theology
          of Religions* (Maryknoll, NY: Orbis Books): 53-68.
  1993   *What is Scripture? A Comparative Approach* (Minneapolis: Fortress
          Press).
Snell, Jeffrey T.
  1992   'Beyond the Individual and Into the World: A Call to Participation in the
          Larger Purposes of the Spirit on the Basis of Pentecostal Theology',
          Pneuma 14: 43-58.
Snook, Juan
  1996   'Pentecostales y sus explicaciones del sufrimiento: Una busqueda de la
          justicia', *Xilotl: Revista Nicaragüense de Teologia* 16: 121-38.
Snook, Lee
  1999   *What in the World is God Doing? Re-imagining Spirit and Power* (Min-
          neapolis: Fortress Press).
Solivan, Samuel
  1998   'Interreligious Dialogue: An Hispanic American Pentecostal Perspective',
          in S. Mark Heim (ed.), *Grounds for Understanding: Ecumenical
          Responses to Religious Pluralism* (Grand Rapids: Eerdmans): 37-45.
Song, C.S.
  1994   *Jesus in the Power of the Spirit* (Minneapolis: Fortress Press).
Spittler, Russell P. (ed.)
  1976   *Perspectives on the New Pentecostalism* (Grand Rapids: Baker Book
          House).
Stackhouse, Max L.
  1988   *Apologia: Contextualization, Globalization, and Mission in Theological
          Education* (Grand Rapids: Eerdmans).
Staples, Peter
  1992   'Ecumenical Theology and Pentecostalism', in Jan A.B. Jongeneel *et al.*
          (eds.), *Pentecost, Mission and Ecumenism: Essays on Intercultural Theo-
          logy: Festschrift in Honour of Professor Walter J. Hollenweger* (Studies
          in the Intercultural History of Christianity, 75; New York: Peter Lang):
          261-72.
St Clair, David
  1971   *Drum and Candle* (Garden City, NY: Doubleday).
Sterk, Vernon J.
  1992   'Evangelism with Power: Divine Healing in the Growth of the Tzotzil
          Church', *Missiology* 20: 371-84.
Stewart-Gambino, Hannah W., and Everett Wilson
  1997   'Latin American Pentecostals: Old Stereotypes and New Challenges', in
          Edward L. Cleary and Hannah W. Stewart-Gambino (eds.), *Power, Poli-*

tics, and Pentecostals in Latin America (Boulder, CO: Westview Press): 227-46.

Stoll, David
    1990   *Is Latin America Turning Protestant? The Politics of Evangelical Growth* (Berkeley: University of California Press).

Strachan, Gordon
    1975   'Theological and Cultural Origins of the Nineteenth-Century Pentecostal Movement', *Theological Renewal* 1: 17-25.

Stransky, Thomas F.
    1985   'The Church and Other Religions', *IBMR* 9: 154-58.

Stronstad, Roger
    1984   *The Charismatic Theology of St. Luke* (Peabody, MA: Hendrickson).
    1992   'Pentecostal Experience and Hermeneutics', *Paraclete* 26.1: 14-30.
    1995   'Affirming Diversity: God's People as a Community of Prophets', *Pneuma* 17: 145-57.

Stylianopoulos, Theodore, and S. Mark Heim (eds.)
    1986   *Spirit of Truth: Ecumenical Perspectives on the Holy Spirit* (Brookline, MA: Holy Cross Orthodox Press).

Sullivan, Francis A.
    1974   ' "Baptism in the Holy Spirit": A Catholic Interpretation of the Pentecostal Experience', *Greg* 55: 49-68.
    1992   *Salvation Outside the Church? Tracing the History of the Catholic Response* (New York: Paulist Press).
    1993   'On Salvation Through a Desire of Belonging to the Church', in Oliver Rafferty, SJ (ed.), *Reconciliation: Essays in Honour of Michael Hurley* (Dublin: The Columba Press): 142-58.

Sundkler, Bengt G.M.
    1961   *Bantu Prophets in South Africa* (London: Oxford University Press/The International African Institute, 2nd edn).

Surin, Kenneth
    1983   'Revelation, Salvation, the Uniqueness of Christ and Other Religions', *RelS* 19: 323-43.

Suurmond, Jean-Jacques
    1995   *Word and Spirit at Play: Towards a Charismatic Theology* (trans. John Bowden; Grand Rapids: Eerdmans [1994]).

Swearer, Donald K.
    1995   *The Buddhist World of Southeast Asia* (Albany, NY: State University New York Press).

Swidler, Leonard
    1987   'Interreligious and Interideological Dialogue: The Matrix for All Systematic Reflection Today', in Leonard Swidler (ed.), *Toward a Universal Theology of Religion* (Maryknoll, NY: Orbis Books): 5-50.
    1990   *After the Absolute: The Dialogical Future of Religious Reflection* (Minneapolis: Fortress Press).

Swidler, Leonard, and Paul Mojzes (eds.)
    1997   *The Uniqueness of Jesus: A Dialogue with Paul F. Knitter* (Maryknoll, NY: Orbis Books).

Synan, Vinson
1971   *The Holiness-Pentecostal Movement in the United States* (Grand Rapids: Eerdmans).
1984   *In the Latter Days: The Outpouring of the Holy Spirit in the Twentieth Century* (Ann Arbor, MI: Servant Books).
1994   'The Yoido Full Gospel Church', *CPCR* 2 [http://www.pctii.org/cybertab. html].

Synan, Vinson (ed.)
1975   *Aspects of Pentecostal–Charismatic Origins* (Plainfield, NJ: Logos International).

Szemiński, Jan
1995   'From Inca Gods to Spanish Saints and Demons', in Steven Kaplan (ed.), *Indigenous Responses to Western Christianity* (New York: New York University Press): 56-74.

Tai, Hyun Chung
1988   'A Study of the Spirituality of Korean Christians: Focused on the Holy Spirit Movement and Shamanism' (DMin thesis, School of Theology, Claremont Graduate School, CA).

Talbott, Thomas
1997   'The Love of God and the Heresy of Exclusivism', *CSR* 27: 99-112.

Tang, Edmond
1991   'Shamanism and Minjung Theology in South Korea', in Jacques Van Nieuwenhove and Berma Klein Goldewijk (eds.), *Popular Religion, Liberation and Contextual Theology* (Kampen: Kok): 165-74.

Tarr, Del
1994   *Double Image: Biblical Insights from African Parables* (Mahwah, NJ: Paulist Press).

Tate, W. Randolph
1991   *Biblical Interpretation: An Integrated Approach* (Peabody, MA: Hendrickson).

Taylor, John V.
1973   *The Go-Between God: The Holy Spirit and the Christian Mission* (Philadelphia: Fortress Press).

Taylor, Malcolm
1995   'A Historical Perspective on the Doctrine of Divine Healing', *JEPTA* 14: 54-84.

ter Haar, Gerrie
1994   'Standing Up for Jesus: A Survey of New Developments in Christianity in Ghana', *Exchange* 23: 221-40.

Terrien, Samuel
1978   *The Elusive Presence: Toward a New Biblical Theology* (New York: Harper & Row).

Thangaraj, M. Thomas
1994   *The Crucified Guru: An Experiment in Cross-Cultural Christology* (Nashville: Abingdon Press).

Theron, Jacques
1996   'A Critical Overview of the Church's Ministry of Deliverance from Evil Spirits', *Pneuma* 18: 79-93.

Thielicke, Helmut
    1963   *Man in God's World* (trans. John W. Doberstein; New York: Harper & Row).

Thomas, John Christopher
    1998   *The Devil, Disease and Deliverance: Origins of Illness in New Testament Thought* (JPTSup, 13; Sheffield: Sheffield Academic Press).

Thomas, M.M.
    1985   'The Absoluteness of Jesus Christ and Christ-Centered Syncretism', *EcRev* 37: 387-97.

Thomas, Owen C. (ed.)
    1983   *God's Activity in the World: The Contemporary Problem* (Chico, CA: Scholars Press).

Thompson, Nehemiah
    1998   'The Search for a Methodist Theology of Religious Pluralism', in S. Mark Heim (ed.), *Grounds for Understanding: Ecumenical Resources for Responses to Religious Pluralism* (Grand Rapids: Eerdmans): 93-106.

Thompson, William M.
    1976   'The Risen Christ, Transcultural Consciousness, and the Encounter of the World Religions', *TS* 37: 381-409.

Thorpe, S.A.
    1991   *African Traditional Religions* (Pretoria: University of South Africa Press).
    1993   *Shamans, Medicine Men and Traditional Healers* (Pretoria: University of South Africa Press).

Tidball, Derek J.
    1994   *Who are the Evangelicals? Tracing the Roots of Today's Movement* (London: Marshall Pickering).

Tiessen, Terrance L.
    1993   *Irenaeus on the Salvation of the Unevangelized* (Metuchen, NJ; London: Scarecrow Press).

Tillich, Paul
    1951   *Systematic Theology*, I (Chicago: University of Chicago Press).
    1957   *Systematic Theology*, II (Chicago: University of Chicago Press).
    1960   'The Religious Symbol', in Rollo May (ed.), *Symbolism in Religion and Literature* (New York: George Braziller): 75-98.
    1963a   *Systematic Theology*, III (Chicago: University of Chicago Press).
    1963b   *The Eternal Now* (New York: Charles Scribner's Sons).
    1966   *The Future of Religions* (New York: Harper & Row).
    1994   *Christianity and the Encounter of World Religions* (Minneapolis: Fortress Press [1963]).

Toulmin, Stephen
    1982   *The Return to Cosmology: Postmodern Science and the Theology of Nature* (Berkeley: University of California Press).

Tracy, David
    1981   *The Analogical Imagination: Christian Theology and the Culture of Pluralism* (New York: Crossroad).

Troeltsch, Ernst
    1991   *The Christian Faith* (ed. Gertrud von le Fort; trans. Garrett E. Paul; Minneapolis: Fortress Press).

Tugwell, Simon

 1976 'The Speech-Giving Spirit', in Walter Hollenweger *et al.*, *New Heaven?
       New Earth?: An Encounter with Pentecostalism* (Springfield, IL: Temple-
       gate): 119-60.

 1977 'Is There a "Pentecostal Experience"? A Reply to Fr Francis A. Sullivan
       SJ', *Theological Renewal* 6: 8-11.

Turner, Harold W.

 1967 *History of an African Independent Church* (2 vols.; Oxford: Clarendon
       Press).

Turner, Max

 1996 *Power from on High: The Spirit in Israel's Restoration and Witness in
       Luke–Acts* (JPTSup, 9; Sheffield: Sheffield Academic Press).

Turner, Victor

 1977 *The Ritual Process: Structure and Anti-Structure* (Ithaca, NY: Cornell
       University Press [1969]).

Twelftree, Graham H.

 1993 *Jesus the Exorcist: A Contribution to the Study of the Historical Jesus*
       (Peabody, MA: Hendrickson).

Twesigye, Emmanuel K.

 1987 *Common Ground: Christianity, African Religion and Philosophy* (New
       York: Peter Lang).

 1996 *African Religion, Philosophy and Christianity in Logos-Christ: Common
       Ground Revisited* (New York: Peter Lang).

Uken, Charles

 1992 'Spiritism and the Brazilian City', *Urban Mission* 9: 20-33.

Ukpong, Justin S.

 1989 'Pluralism and the Problem of the Discernment of Spirits', *EcRev* 41:
       416-25.

Ulanov, Ann B.

 1975 'The Psychological Reality of the Demonic', in Alan M. Olson (ed.), *Dis-
       guises of the Demonic: Contemporary Perspectives on the Power of Evil*
       (New York: Association Press): 134-49.

Van Dusen, Henry P.

 1958 *Spirit, Son and Father: Christian Faith in the Light of the Holy Spirit*
       (New York: Charles Scribner's Sons).

Van Kessel, J.

 1992 'Faith Healing in the North Chilean Andes of Pilgrimage', *Exchange* 21:
       62-83.

van Rossum, Rogier

 1993 'Reincarnation in Connection with Spiritism and Umbanda', in Hermann
       Häring and Johann-Baptist Metz (eds.), *Reincarnation or Resurrection?*
       (Maryknoll, NY: Orbis Books): 54-64.

Veenhof, Jan

 1992 'The Significance of the Charismatic Renewal for Theology and Church',
       in Jan A.B. Jongeneel *et al.* (eds.), *Pentecost, Mission and Ecumenism:
       Essays on Intercultural Theology: Festschrift in Honour of Professor
       Walter J. Hollenweger* (Studies in the Intercultural History of Christian-
       ity, 75; New York: Peter Lang): 289-300.

Villafañe, Eldin
  1993   *The Liberating Spirit: Toward a Hispanic American Pentecostal Social Ethic* (Grand Rapids: Eerdmans).
Vischer, Lukas (ed.)
  1981   *Spirit of God, Spirit of Christ: Ecumenical Reflections on the* Filioque *Controversy* (Geneva: World Council of Churches).
Volf, Miroslav
  1989   'Materiality of Salvation: An Investigation in the Soteriologies of Liberation and Pentecostal Theologies', *JES* 26: 447-67.
  1991   *Work in the Spirit: Toward a Theology of Work* (New York: Oxford University Press).
  1994   'A Study in Provisional Certitude', in Bruce J. Nicholls (ed.), *The Unique Christ in Our Pluralist World* (Grand Rapids: Baker Book House; Carlisle: Paternoster Press): 96-106.
Vroom, Hendrik M.
  1990   'Do all Religious Traditions Worship the Same God?', *RelS* 26: 73-90.
Wacker, Grant
  1984   'The Functions of Faith in Primitive Pentecostalism', *HTR* 77: 353-75.
  1986   'The Pentecostal Tradition', in Ronald L. Numbers and Darrell W. Amundsen (eds.), *Caring and Curing: Health and Medicine in the Western Religious Traditions* (New York: Macmillan): 514-38.
Wafer, Jim
  1991   *The Taste of Blood: Spirit Possession in Brazilian Candomblé* (Philadelphia: University of Pennsylvania Press).
Wagner, C. Peter
  1988   *The Third Wave of the Holy Spirit* (Ann Arbor, MI: Servant Publications).
  1990   'Territorial Spirits', in Peter Wagner and F. Douglas Pennoyer (eds.), *Dark Angels: Toward a Deeper Understanding of the Supernatural Forces in Spiritual Warfare* (Ventura, CA: Regal Books): 73-91.
  1996   *Confronting the Powers* (Ventura, CA: Regal Books).
Wagner, C. Peter (ed.)
  1991   *Engaging the Enemy: How to Fight and Defeat Territorial Spirits* (Ventura, CA: Regal Books).
Wagner, C. Peter, and F. Douglas Pennoyer (eds.)
  1990   *Dark Angels: Toward a Deeper Understanding of the Supernatural Forces in Spiritual Warfare* (Ventura, CA: Regal Books).
Walker, Sheila S.
  1972   *Ceremonial Spirit Possession in Africa and Afro-America* (Leiden: E.J. Brill).
  1991   'The Saints Versus the Orishas in a Brazilian Catholic Church as an Expression of Afro-Brazilian Cultural Synthesis in the Feast of Good Death', in Kortright Davis, Elias Farajaje-Jones and Iris Eaton (eds.), *African Creative Expressions of the Divine* (Washington, DC: Howard University School of Divinity): 84-98.
Walsh, Roger N.
  1990   *The Spirit of Shamanism* (Los Angeles: Jeremy P. Tarcher).

Ward, Keith
    1994   *Religion and Revelation: A Theology of Revelation in the World's Reli-*
                gions (Oxford: Clarendon Press).
Warrington, Keith
    1997   'The Use of the Name of Jesus in Healing and Exorcism with Reference
                to the Teachings of Kenneth Hagin', *JEPTA* 17: 16-36.
Welker, Michael
    1989   'The Holy Spirit', *TTod* 46: 5-20.
    1991   'What is Creation? Rereading Genesis 1 and 2', *TTod* 48: 56-71.
    1994   *God the Spirit* (trans. John F. Hoffmeyer; Minneapolis: Fortress Press).
    1997a   'Creation and the Image of God: Their Understanding in Christian Tradi-
                tion and the Biblical Grounds', *JES* 34: 436-48.
    1997b   'Spirit Topics: Trinity, Personhood, Mystery and Tongues', *JPT* 10: 29-
                34.
Werblowsky, Zwi
    1975   'On Studying Comparative Religion: Some Naive Reflections of a Simple-
                Minded Non-Philosopher', *RelS* 11: 145-56.
Wessels, Anton
    1989   'Biblical Presuppositions for and against Syncretism', in Jerald Gort *et al.*
                (eds.), *Dialogue and Syncretism: An Interdisciplinary Approach* (Amster-
                dam: Editions Rodopi; Grand Rapids: Eerdmans): 52-65.
Westmeier, Karl-Wilhelm
    1993   'Themes of Pentecostal Expansion in Latin America', *IBMR* 17: 72-78.
Westra, Allard D. Willemier
    1991a   'Uncertainty Reduction in the Candomblé Religion of Brazil', in Jacques
                van Nieuwenhove and Berma Klein Goldewijk (eds.), *Popular Religion,
                Liberation and Contextual Theology* (Kampen: Kok): 116-25.
    1991b   'Candomblé Priests and Priestesses as Managers of Symbols in Ala-
                goinhas, Brazil', in André Droogers, Gerrit Huizer and Hans Siebers
                (eds.), *Popular Power in Latin American Religions* (Saarbrücken: Verlag
                Breitenbach): 219-36
    1998   'Market Behavior among Brazilian Consumers of the Divine: Public
                Opinion Regarding Pentecostalism and Afro-American Religiosity in the
                Provincial Town of Alagoinhas (Bahia)', in Barbara Boudewijnse, André
                Droogers and Frans Kamsteeg (eds.), *More than Opium: An Anthro-
                pological Approach to Latin American and Caribbean Pentecostal Praxis*
                (Lanham, MD: Scarecrow Press): 119-43.
White, Thomas B.
    1991   'Understanding Principalities and Powers', in C. Peter Wagner (ed.),
                Engaging the Enemy: How to Fight and Defeat Territorial Spirits (Ven-
                tura, CA: Regal Books): 59-67.
Williams, Cyril G.
    1981   *Tongues of the Spirit: A Study of Pentecostal Glossolalia and Related
                Phenomena* (Cardiff: University of Wales Press).
Williams, Daniel Day
    1990   *The Demonic and the Divine* (Minneapolis: Fortress Press).
Williams, Ernest Swing
    1953   *Systematic Theology* (3 vols.; Springfield, MO: Gospel Publishing House).

Williams, J. Rodman
    1972   *The Pentecostal Reality* (Plainfield, NJ: Logos International).
    1988   *Renewal Theology: Systematic Theology from a Charismatic Perspective*, I (Grand Rapids: Zondervan).
    1990   *Renewal Theology: Systematic Theology from a Charismatic Perspective*, II (Grand Rapids: Zondervan).
    1998   'Harvey Cox and Pentecostalism: A Review of *Fire from Heaven*', *Australasian Pentecostal Studies* 1: 23-26.
Williams, Paul V.A.
    1979   *Primitive Religion and Healing: A Study of Folk-Medicine in North-East Brazil* (Totowa, NJ: Rowman and Littlefield).
Wilson, Everett
    1988   'The Central American Evangelicals: From Protest to Pragmatism', *IRM* 77: 94-106.
    1999   'They Crossed the Red Sea, Didn't They? Critical History and Pentecostal Beginnings', in Douglas Petersen, Murray Dempster and Byron Klaus (eds.), *The Globalization of Pentecostalism: A Religion Made to Travel* (Oxford: Regnum Books International): 85-115.
Wink, Walter
    1984   *Naming the Powers: The Language of Power in the New Testament* (Philadelphia: Fortress Press).
    1986   *Unmasking the Powers: The Invisible Forces that Determine Human Existence* (Philadelphia: Fortress Press).
    1992   *Engaging the Powers: Discernment and Resistance in a World of Domination* (Minneapolis: Fortress Press).
Wong, Joseph H.
    1994   'Anonymous Christians: Karl Rahner's Pneuma-Christocentrism and an East-West Dialogue', *TS* 55: 609-37.
Wood, George O.
    1995   'The Laughing Revival' (unpublished manuscript; Springfield, MO: Central Bible College).
Wright, Nigel
    1990   *The Satan Syndrome: Putting the Powers of Darkness in Its Place* (Grand Rapids: Academie Books).
    1996   'Charismatic Interpretations of the Demonic', in Anthony N.S. Lane (ed.), *The Unseen World: Christian Reflection on Angels, Demons, and the Heavenly Realm* (Grand Rapids: Baker Book House; Carlisle: Paternoster Press): 149-63.
Yearley, Lee H.
    1990   *Mencius and Aquinas: Theories of Virtue and Conceptions of Courage* (Albany, NY: State University New York Press).
Yeow, Choo Lak
    1981   *To God be the Glory! Doctrines on God and Creation* (Singapore: Trinity Theological College).
    1997   'Christ in Cultures: with reference to Samuel P. Huntington's "The Clash of Civilizations" ', *CPCR* 3 [http://www.pctii.org/cybertab. html].
Yoder, John
    1972   *The Politics of Jesus* (Grand Rapids: Eerdmans).

Yong, Amos
    1997   'Oneness and the Trinity: The Theological and Ecumenical Implications
                of "Creation *Ex Nihilo*" for an Intra-Pentecostal Dispute', *Pneuma* 19: 81-
                107.
    1998a   'Tongues of Fire in the Pentecostal Imagination: The Truth of Glossolalia
                in Light of R.C. Neville's Theory of Religious Symbolism', *JPT* 12: 39-
                65.
    1998b   'The Turn to Pneumatology in Christian Theology of Religions: Conduit
                or Detour?', *JES* 35: 437-54.
    1998c   'What Has Jerusalem to do with Nairobi, Lagos, Accra, or Rio? Religion
                and Theology in Africa and Afro-America (A Review Essay)', *Koinonia:
                The Princeton Seminary Graduate Forum* 10: 216-27.
    1999a   ' "Not Knowing Where the Spirit Blows...": On Envisioning a Pente-
                costal–Charismatic Theology of Religions', *JPT* 14: 81-112.
    1999b   'Whither Theological Inclusivism? The Development and Critique of an
                Evangelical Theology of Religions', *EvQ* 71.4: 327-48.
    1999c   'To See or Not to See: A Review Essay of Michael Palmer's *Elements of
                a Christian Worldview*', *Pneuma* 21: 305-27.
    2000a   'On Divine Presence and Divine Agency: Toward a Foundational
                Pneumatology', *AJPS* 3: 163-84.
    2000b   'The Demise of Foundationalism and the Retention of Truth: What
                Evangelicals Can Learn from C.S. Peirce', *CSR* 29: 563-88.
    Forthcoming 'Spiritual Discernment: A Biblical–Theological Reconsideration', in
                Wonsuk Ma and Robert P. Menzies (eds.), *The Spirit and Spirituality*
                (Irvine, CA: Regnum Books).
Yoo, Boo-Woong
    1986   'Response to Korean Shamanism by the Pentecostal Church', *IRM* 75:
                70-74.
    1988   *Korean Pentecostalism: Its History and Theology* (Studies in the Inter-
                cultural History of Christianity, 52; Frankfurt: Peter Lang).

INDEXES

INDEX OF REFERENCES

OLD TESTAMENT

NEW TESTAMENT

INDEX OF AUTHORS

INDEX OF SUBJECTS